A Pioneer of Interfaith Dialogue
LOUIS MASSIGNON
(1947–1962)
THE BADALIYA PRAYER MOVEMENT

Introduced & edited by

Dorothy C. Buck

NEW JERSEY • LONDON • FRANKFURT • CAIRO

BLUE DOME
NEW JERSEY

Copyright © 2016 by Blue Dome Press

19 18 17 16   1 2 3 4

Published by Blue Dome Press
335 Clifton Avenue, Clifton
New Jersey 07011, USA

www.bluedomepress.com

Names: Massignon, Louis, 1883-1962. | Buck, Dorothy C., translator, editor. | Griffith, Sidney Harrison, writer of foreword.
Title: Louis Massignon, a pioneer of interfaith dialogue : the Badaliya prayer movement (1947-1962) / Dorothy C. Buck.
Description: Clifton, New Jersey : Blue Dome Press, 2016. | "French edition published by Les Editions du Cerf in Paris, in 2011 entitled: Louis Massignon : Badaliya : aunom de l'autre, (1947-1962)." | "Translation and annotation by Dorothy C. Buck, Marie Hâeláene Gold, Marlyse Lupis."
Identifiers: LCCN 2015046572 | ISBN 9781682060049 (alk. paper)
Subjects: LCSH: Massignon, Louis, 1883-1962--Correspondence. | Badaliya (Association) | Islam--Relations--Christianity. | Christianity and other religions--Islam.
Classification: LCC BP49.5.M3 A4 2016 | DDC 297.092--dc23
LC record available at http://lccn.loc.gov/2015046572
Translation and annotation by
Dorothy C. Buck, Marie Hélène Gold, Marlyse Lupis

ISBN: 978-1-68206-004-9

Printed by

Contents

Acknowledgements.. vii

Preface by Sidney Griffith viii

Introduction xi

The Original Statutes of the Badaliya 1947 1

Letter to Pope Pius XII in Rome Paris, September 4, 1953................................. 35

The Badaliya Today 275

Books in English by Louis Massignon... 281

Books in English about Louis Massignon.. 281

Articles about the Badaliya Prayer and a Muslim-Christian Pilgrimage.... 281

Ex-Voto of the Badaliya.. 282

The Emblem of Charles de Foucauld by Pierre Roche 282

To a great friend of Louis Massignon, Paolo Dall 'Oglio, S. J. and to all those who are inspired by the Spirit of the Badaliya, at often great cost, and who are dedicated to authentic interfaith and intercultural engagement by "crossing over" to embrace the mind and heart of the "other."

Acknowledgements

These letters by Louis Massignon to members of the Badaliya were translated into English from a copy of the original typewritten letters that were given to me by Daniel Massignon, Louis Massignon's youngest son, before his death in the year 2000. Members of L'Association des Amis de Louis Massignon in Paris later agreed that we should publish a French edition before releasing an English translation. I am indebted to Marlyse Lupis for computerizing the original French documents in order to facilitate the possibility of a French edition and to Marlyse Lupis and Marie Hélène Gold for working with me on the translation and annotation. I am also ever grateful to Maurice Borrmans and Françoise Jacquin whose dedication to this project produced the French edition published by Les Éditions du Cerf in Paris, in 2011 entitled: "Louis Massignon: Badaliya: au nom de l'autre" (1947–1962).

This work would not have been possible without the on-going encouragement and support of Nicole Massignon, daughter-in-law of Louis Massignon, and L'Association des Amis de Louis Massignon in Paris. The Preface was offered by the Reverend Sidney Griffith, Emeritus professor of Syriac and Christian Arabic in the Department of Semitic and Egyptian Languages at the Institute of Christian Oriental Research at the Catholic University of America in Washington, DC. Professor Griffith is a friend and longtime member of L'Association and a scholar of Louis Massignon and his works.

This publication has found the most appropriate publisher for Massignon's writings in the Blue Dome Press whose editors are dedicated to the philosophy of Fethullah Gülen, a Turkish Muslim advocate of Interfaith and Intercultural education and relations with a following worldwide. My many thanks for their attention and willingness to make this edition of Louis Massignon's letters to the Badaliya available to an English speaking audience.

Dorothy C. Buck

Preface

When Louis Massignon died on October 31, 1962 the Second Vatican Council had barely begun and no one at the time even remotely foresaw the course of events that would lead in due course to the promulgation of the council's 'Declaration on the Relation of the Church to Non-Christian Religions' (Nostra Aetate), promulgated by Pope Paul VI on 28 October 1965. This brief document was destined to change the church's approach to other people of faith, especially Jews and Muslims. It includes two short paragraphs that almost immediately resulted in a paradigm shift in the Roman Catholic Church's relations with the world's Muslims. One phrase in particular, in the very first sentence of the first paragraph, expresses the new line of thinking, "The church regards with esteem also the Moslems." And the text goes on to highlight points of coincidence in faith between Christians and Muslims, albeit with crucial differences on each point: the worship of the one God; God's word to humankind; submission to God's decrees on the model of Abraham; reverence for Jesus and for Mary, his virgin mother; and work for peace and justice in the world in view of the expectation of the Day of Judgment. The second paragraph similarly expresses a new attitude: "Since in the course of centuries not a few quarrels and hostilities have arisen between Christians and Moslems, this sacred synod urges all to forget the past and to work sincerely for mutual understanding and to preserve as well as to promote together for the benefit of all mankind social justice and moral welfare, as well as peace and freedom."

Looking back to those in the Catholic community whose lives and thoughts prepared the way for Nostra Aetate's expressions of esteem for Muslims and their faith, none looms larger than Louis Massignon. In fact one can readily find in his writing expressions of the specific points of coincidence mentioned in the conciliar text. It is clear that those who originally prepared the text were deeply imbued with his interreligious spirit. For from the very beginning of his conversion to his ancestral Catholic faith in 1908, and persisting to the end of his life, Massignon's religious practice was intimately intertwined not just with Islam but with Muslims. He counted Muslim intercessors among those who prayed for him at his conversion and throughout his life. He devoted his academic life to the study of Islamic and Christian mystical thought, especially in the Sufi traditions. He lived his faith in action in the public sphere, inaugurating and participating in interreligious moments of prayer as well as in civil protests against violence. And from the early 1930's onward, Louis Massignon gathered regularly with Muslim and Christian friends to study and pray for peace and mutual love and respect especially between Arabic-speaking people of faith. It was to this end that he and his close friend and associate Mary Kahil founded the Badaliya, a movement devoted to prayer and good works in mutual solidarity, a spirit that endures to this day.

Over the thirty-some years of the Badaliya's flourishing during his lifetime, Louis Massignon regularly wrote letters and conferences addressed to the movement's associates in which he spoke very concretely of the ways in which they would conduct their prayer and fasting in view of the current crises affecting the Christian and Muslim communities as well as the wider world around them. Not surprisingly the themes that constantly reappear in these personal communications echo those highlighted in Nostra Aetate's paragraphs concerning the church's relationship with Muslims. They show the interreligious way to put one's faith commitments in touch with the day-to-day rights and wrongs of life in a religiously plural world. They commend a devotional knowledge of the mysteries of faith that prompts practical action in the pursuit of justice and peace. These messages that call their Christian and Muslim recipients to solidarity in faith and action appear for the first time in English translation in the present volume. And they offer their twenty-first century readers glimpses of how people of faith might practically draw inspiration from the life and work of Louis Massignon, a western Christian pioneer in taking Islam religiously seriously, a commitment that evermore insistently demands attention as in our time suspicion and fear of Islam and Muslims increases among some Christian groups.

Louis Massignon was a twentieth-century Christian whose academic career and deep religious faith together conspired to promote interreligious empathy between peoples everywhere and especially among Jews, Christians, and Muslims, who trace their religious genealogies back to the biblical patriarch Abraham, whose obedient faith they strive to emulate. The texts published in this volume offer the reader access to the very heart of his counsel to his closest associates, and indeed to all who would learn to love God and one another.

Sidney H. Griffith
Institute of Christian Oriental Research
The Catholic University of America
Washington, DC

Introduction

1. Louis Massignon (1883–1962)

By the end of his life on October 31, 1962 at the age of 79, Louis Massignon had become a witness to the transforming effects of his own passionate relationship with God. He had become a renowned and meticulous scholar and professor of the Sociology of Islam at the Collège de France in Paris, Director of Religious Studies at the École Pratique des Hautes Études, a member of the Arab Academy in Cairo, an expert on the Arab world with an extraordinary gift for languages and linguistics, and a diplomat with experience of many parts of the world. Yet the transforming event in his life was the conversion experience that he called, "The Visitation of the Stranger."

At the age of 25 Louis Massignon was on an archeological mission for the French government outside of Baghdad, Iraq. He was also researching the life and legend of a tenth century Islamic mystic by the name of al-Hallaj for a University thesis. He thought of himself as an agnostic having long before lost interest in his Roman Catholic heritage. He had learned Arabic and Hebrew, studied Islam and made friends with a family of practicing Muslims. In the course of a few days everything changed. Unknowingly caught in the midst of the Turkish revolution he was accused of being a spy by the Turkish government and put on a steamer back to Baghdad. He began to be afraid for his life. He found himself crying out to God for help in the first words that came to him. They were in Arabic. But rather than embracing the Islam that he had been studying, he found himself drawn inexplicably back to the Roman Catholic Church and the faith of his childhood. He felt saved in part through the intercession of the tenth century mystic, saint and martyr of Islam, al-Hallaj, the subject of his research.

The first edition of "La Passion d'al-Hallaj" was published in 1922. By 1962 Massignon had completed fifty years of continuing documentation on the life and legend of the Sufi mystic of Islam, served the French government in two World Wars, become committed to the non-violent philosophy of Gandhi, and marched in the streets of Paris for an independent Algeria. He had founded the Badaliya prayer movement, established an annual shared Muslim and Christian pilgrimage in Brittany, France and written, lectured and published volumes of documents out of the spiritual depth of his soul on political and social issues, peace and reconciliation of the three Abrahamic religions, the lives and writings of saints and mystics in many religious traditions, and much more.

Massignon's vast correspondence included Paul Claudel, Blessed Charles de Foucauld, Martin Buber, Thomas Merton, popes, cardinals, politicians, artists and those seeking spiritual wisdom from traditions worldwide. In 1931 he was drawn to the spirituality of Saint Francis of Assisi and became a Third Order Franciscan. He had become both a scholar and a mystic. Later he received permission from Rome to transfer to the Greek Melkite Church in order to pray in Arabic. As the Melkite tradition allowed married priests he asked to be ordained and received permission to celebrate the daily Mass privately. He made numerous pilgrimages to the tombs of Islamic saints and to the shrines dedicated to the Virgin Mary and other Christian saints and martyrs. He was equally tortured by the pain and suffering in his own life and by that of others. In his personal life he lost his first born son who died at the age of 21, and his own father, the artist known as Pierre Roche, who died when Massignon was 39. He was tortured by the suicide of his Spanish friend Luis de Cuadra. These experiences of loss were compounded by the loss of friends and colleagues in the devastation wrought by both World Wars and the ongoing wars for freedom from colonial powers. In the monthly convocations and annual letters that he wrote to members of the Badaliya prayer movement it is clear that his spiritual life was a passion that drove him to care deeply for people everywhere, and for the world in which he lived and for which he prayed daily.

2. Setting the Scene: The Historical Context

The Badaliya prayer movement was established at a critical time in world history, and most directly in relation to what was happening in France and North Africa. In many ways it was a means of responding to the effects of the imperial political and economic period that was known as "colonial." By the eighteen hundreds European and British states were claiming territory and domination over the people and raw material resources on other continents and islands around the world. Especially after World War I when France became the second largest empire in world history, there was a prevailing attitude that the mission in expanding the French empire was to "civilize" the world. They sought to assimilate native populations into French civilization, promoting their language, culture and religious values and largely disregarding the rich cultural, religious and linguistic histories of conquered peoples as far away as Indochina and the Caribbean islands. Louis Massignon inherited the French colonial "myth" and found himself eventually at odds with it as twentieth century France was forced to confront the reality of national pride and identification in the colonies including both Zionism and Arab nationalism.

From 1830 into the 1840's when France first began to conquer Algeria, the colony included Italians and Spaniards who were granted French citizenship in 1889, along with the Jewish population. Only the Algerian Muslims were excluded from citizenship unless they were willing to give up Islam. Islam was denigrated and the predominantly Muslim population forced into subservient jobs and increasing poverty with no means to a political voice. Even so they were conscripted into the army in both world wars. After the abolition of slavery in 1848, even some native black North Africans became members of the French government in their colonies and held important positions not afforded to the Muslim population.

By 1934, when Louis Massignon and Mary Kahil established the Badaliya prayer movement and made their vow to dedicate their lives and their prayer to the Muslims, the situation in colonial Algeria was escalating and its effects were felt even in Paris. Growing numbers of Algerian workers lived in poverty while their friends and relatives in Algeria were burdened by unequal taxation, less access to education and lack of fair political representation. Colonial views, supported primarily by those French citizens living in the colonies and making a profit there, were beginning to be questioned as the indigenous Algerian Muslims both in Paris and in Algeria were claiming their equal rights. World War II and the occupation of France created an even worse situation for Algerians who were drafted into the army in large numbers. Workers were no longer able to go to Metropolitan France to work nor were those who were already there able to continue to send financial aid home.

History, being wrought with overlapping issues simultaneously, inevitably had other economic and social conditions along with changing values that contributed to world tensions. After World War I and the financial crash leading to the Great Depression, industrialized nations and their increasing technology were already dividing the world into modern developing nations and those who were technologically underdeveloped. Increasing capitalistic values led to the need for the development of more and more world markets. This created a kind of "capitalistic imperialism" which was pitted against socialist governments and ideologies. From the religious and spiritual world view, technology and materialism had the potential to become a form of idolatry that called for a contrary vision.

The Russian revolution in the early part of the twentieth century saw the rise of the Soviet Union and its domination over surrounding territories. The rise of communism influenced the policies of France toward the movements in the colonies all over the world who were struggling for independence. After World War II these movements became linked to the communist threat in the eyes of the French government. The painful wars that led to decolonization were raging throughout the years from 1947 to 1962 during which time these letters to the Badaliya members were being written.

As both a scholar and a mystic Louis Massignon was deeply engaged in the historical movements of his time and his concern is expressed repeatedly in this collection of letters. Not only did he believe in the effectiveness of prayer in relation to world events but he also realized that it is the ground of all effective social action. Thus the foundation for the creation of the Badaliya prayer movement was first and foremost a vow to God made before an altar in an ancient Franciscan Chapel in 1934. It was initially a direct response to the increasing religious and political tensions between Muslims and Christians in Egypt as the Islamic population increased there. Massignon's knowledge and love of Islam, the Arabic language, and his many Muslim and Arab colleagues and friends made him painfully aware of the need for mutual respect and understanding, especially in Egypt at the time.

After World War II, as Israel was in the process of becoming a State, Massignon recognized the dangers inherent in policies that marginalized the Palestinian Arabs, both Christian and Muslim, and his love of the Holy Land increased his concern. He was convinced that the creation of peaceful relationships among all three Abrahamic religions, Muslims, Christians and Jews, was the only solution to the rising social and political conflicts in the Middle East, especially in North Africa and the Holy Land.

The suppression of all religious freedom of expression in Soviet Russia and its satellite states, along with the advent of the cold war dividing the world into two opposing major political powers, was another issue that entered into the Badaliya prayer and Massignon's letters to its members. Massignon had a great devotion to the Virgin Mary and made many pilgrimages to Marian shrines praying for insight and direction in his life. The Russian Orthodox image and devotion to Our Lady of Pokrov (Our Lady of the Veil) inspired him to make her the patron saint of the Badaliya. It is the image of the Virgin Mother of God spreading her veil over a besieged city as a sign of protection that spiritually extends to all of humanity. She is said to have been seen on October 1st in the year 911 at an all-night vigil in the Blachernae Church of the Mother of God in Constantinople.

References to saints, such as the Palestinian Carmelite Christian, Mariam Baouardy, known as Sister Mary of Jesus Crucified, are found throughout these letters. She is the founder of the Carmelite Monasteries in the Holy Land. Massignon knew of her cause for Beatification in the Roman Catholic Church (the first step to being declared a Saint) and thought of her as the protectress of the Holy Sites especially in the Holy Lands. She was born in 1846 in Palestine and died at the age of 32 in 1878, was named "Blessed" by Pope Jean Paul II on November 13, 1983 and canonized as a Saint on May 17, 2015 by Pope Francis. Massignon's devotion to saints and mystics of all religious traditions appear throughout these letters, especially Muslims such as al-Hallaj, and those Christian saints that he understood as following in a long line of men and women through the ages who were called to take on the sufferings of humanity, to heal and absolve others through the mystical substitution for which the Badaliya movement is named in Arabic.

3. The Origins of the Badaliya Prayer Movement

The seeds of the Badaliya, (an Arabic word that means "to take the place of," "instead of," or "substitution") were planted in the heart of Louis Massignon's spirituality even before his conversion experience. Like many of the French artists and intelligentsia Louis Massignon's father, Pierre Roche, was marked by the scientific materialism and human rights movements of his time and was intent on his son's education in scientific research and art. His one Catholic friend was the painter, Charles-Marie Dulac who the young Louis Massignon greatly admired. (A street in Paris in the XVth arrondissement is named after him). Dulac had a profound understanding of the Catholic dogma of the Communion of Saints. He believed that Jesus substituted Himself out of love for us in order to take the sins of the world onto Himself and that we, like Simon of Cyrene, can participate in this act of Jesus as well. Massignon was moved by the way that Dulac simply lived his conviction.

Later, when Massignon described his own conversion experience he wrote about his impressions as a teen-ager of the painter's faith and certainty of mystical substitution. Massignon's son, Daniel, remembered his father commenting on the many paintings by Dulac in their home that caused Louis Massignon to consider the possibility of mystical substitution. Many of those paintings were later donated to the Louvre Museum in Paris. Shortly before his untimely death in 1898, Dulac arranged a meeting of Pierre Roche with the esteemed novelist and literary critic, J-K Huysmans, who was looking for an artist to create the frontispiece for the luxury edition of his book, "La Cathedrale." It was through the arts that Huysmans himself was brought back to religion. On October 27, 1900 at the age of 17 Louis Massignon visited Huysmans. Although the writer was in the process of writing a biography of the 13th century Dutch mystic, Saint Lydwine of Schiedam in which he wrote extensively of his own understanding of suffering and mystical substitution, it was not the subject of his conversation with the young Massignon.

Louis Massignon was a physics student and a professed agnostic when he met Huysmans and was still eight years away from his own conversion experience that took place in Baghdad in 1908. It was after his experience in 1908, when he was told that Huysmans had prayed for him on his deathbed in 1907 during an agonizing struggle with a painful cancer, that he took a serious interest in Huysmans writings on suffering and mystical substitution. Huysmans spoke of his belief in a kind of mystical substitutionary prayer to which some men and women were called in each generation. They prayed to take onto themselves the physical and emotional afflictions, the pain and suffering, of those who came to them for healing. These medieval mystics and saints were often martyrs for their faith and were said to unite their sufferings and death with the passion and death of Christ. Some even experienced the wounds of the crucified Christ on their own bodies that are called the "stigmata" like the 13th century Saints Christine L'Admirable and Saint Francis of Assisi. Huysmans suggested that when the evil that humans are capable of inflicting on one another escalates to the misery and destruction of life consumed with wars and conflict, looting and immorality, one of these exemplary souls would appear as a victim offered for the salvation of many. He thought that since fewer and fewer were called to the religious life in his time that God would invite more and more of us to answer this mysterious call, linking our own sufferings to the healing and salvation of suffering humanity.

Massignon was also influenced by Father Charles de Foucauld, who dedicated his life at the age of 44 to the Muslim Berber tribes called the Touareg people in the Algerian desert. Through his years of correspondence and seeking spiritual guidance from the desert priest, Massignon came to experience Foucauld as a mentor and referred to him as an "older brother." He came to understand what it is to live the Gospel by example, how to see the sacred in all other human beings. Compassion, hospitality and substitutionary prayer and penance became the foundation of his meditation. He discovered saints in Islam who were also called to this kind of substitutionary prayer such as Fatima, the daughter of the Prophet Muhammad, and the Sufi martyr al-Hallaj. As he grew in his love for Christ and his love of Islam he was drawn to the "Poverello," Saint Francis of Assisi, who was the first in the Church to approach Islam with love and compassion rather than weapons.

4. The Vow and the Statutes for the Badaliya

In 1912, when Louis Massignon first met Mary Kahil at the home of the Countess Hohenwaert, wife of the Austrian Consul in Cairo, their friend

Luis de Cuadra, who came from an aristocratic Spanish family but had converted to Islam, fell seriously ill. Massignon feared that he would die without being reconciled to the Church and invited Mary Kahil to pray with him for their friend's soul by offering themselves to God for him. Countess Hohenwaert suggested that the two young people promise to become Third Order Franciscans if Luis were to return to his Christian roots. The seeds for the Badaliya prayer movement were sown, and although Luis de Cuadra did not die and remained Muslim, his importance to the establishment of the Badaliya prayer is acknowledged over and over again by Massignon in these letters.

In 1913 Mary Kahil returned to Europe at the outset of World War I and she and Louis Massignon were not to meet again until 1934. By then, in 1921, Luis de Cuadra had tragically committed suicide. Massignon saw his unexpected encounter with Mary Kahil and the establishment of their Badaliya prayer movement in 1934 as a sign that their prayers for their friend, Luis, had been answered by God. Two years before, he had fulfilled the promise suggested by the Countess Hohenwaert in 1912 that he become a Third Order Franciscan. At his final vows in 1932 he took the name of Abraham, the great Patriarch of all three "Abrahamic" traditions, by whom he felt protected throughout his life.

Mary Kahil was an Egyptian woman from a Greek Catholic, or Melkite Christian family who was born in Damietta, Egypt in 1889. When she met Massignon in Cairo in 1912 she was already actively engaged with the feminist movement in Egypt working closely with Muslim organizations for the political and educational rights for all Arab women. In 1934 when Massignon was on one of his annual trips to Cairo he invited Mary Kahil to go with him to Damietta where they visited a Franciscan Chapel. Mary Kahil's association to Damietta would have related more to her family history and the place of her birth than to Saint Francis. She told him of the pain that she felt in this city where so many of her Syrian-Greek Christian ancestors had settled and now because of the rise of Islam, the Arab Christians were gone or increasingly marginalized. He suggested that she join him in making a vow to love the Muslims and dedicate their lives to them. When she hesitated he reminded her that she was already dedicated to the Muslim women with whom she was working so closely and that nothing is closer to hatred than love. They made the vow to dedicate their lives to working and praying for and with their Muslim brothers and sisters. Their prayer was called the Badaliya, the substitutes, and other Christian Arabs, who often felt discriminated against while living in the midst of a predominantly Islamic culture, joined them for weekly gatherings. Their inspiration was the Gospel message to love ones enemies and pray for those who persecute you, and they experienced their prayer as a sacrifice of themselves for the Muslim people.

From the monthly Convocation and Annual Letters it is clear that Massignon formed a Badaliya group in Paris that met monthly while Mary Kahil continued to meet with the group in Cairo weekly. Massignon made an annual trip to Cairo during which time they renewed their original vow together and only missed the years during World War II when Massignon was called once again into active military service. Many priests, religious and lay people joined their monthly prayer in spirit and groups formed in cities throughout the world. During the War, Mary was able to purchase an abandoned Anglican church in the center of Cairo. She named it Sainte Marie de la Paix, Saint Mary of Peace, and transformed it into the Melkite Rite. In 1941 she and a priest named Father Ayrout along with some Islamic professors created an organization dedicated to Islamic-Christian Dialogue and shared prayer called the Sincere Brothers.

After the War when Massignon was once again able to travel to Cairo they established a conference center next to the church called the Dar es-Salam, The House of Peace. There they sponsored an annual international conference on Christian, Islamic, Jewish and Arab educational, cultural or philosophical topics, and published articles. The Sincere Brothers of Christians and Muslims came to pray together there as well. Louis Massignon and Mary Kahil's vow was first acknowledged by Pope Pius XI to Massignon personally in a private audience in July of 1934. When Massignon died in 1962, Mary Kahil continued meeting with the Badaliya and the Sincere Brothers until her death at the age of 90 in 1979.

Massignon's choice of a small Franciscan chapel in Damietta for the original vows of Badaliya came from his research on Saint Francis. The saint's visit to the Muslim Sultan, Malik al-Kamil, in Damietta, Egypt during the 5th Crusade in 1219, convinced Massignon that Francis' non-violent engagement with the Sultan was an example of Badaliya, or substitutionary prayer.

Francis had offered himself for the salvation of this one Muslim soul in contrast to the violent response to Islam by the Church with its subsequent crusades. Massignon also suggests a spiritual connection of Saint Francis, who received the Stigmata after his vision of Christ in the form of an angel on Mt. Alverna, to the Night Journey of Muhammad. He saw a connection to an episode in the life of Muhammad that is recorded in the teachings and traditional history of Islam that took place in the 10th year of the Hijra (631 of the Common Era), as follows:

With the increase of Islam in Arabia there was a need for local tribal communities to establish relations with the new power in the area. A delegation from a predominantly Christian city state called Najran, came to see the Prophet. According to Islamic tradition they were impressed with the passage from the Qur'an explaining the true understanding of Christ but were unable to accept this teaching and adopt the new religion. In order to know the truth about Christ, the Prophet then suggested that they agree to undergo the "Mubahala," where both the Christians and the Muslims would gather their men, women and children to pray to Allah. Those who were lying would be cursed. Anyone with genuine faith would accept this challenge. The various recordings of this episode from very early sources all agree that the Christians preferred not to accept this challenge and agreed to pay tribute in return for protection from the State. Massignon suggested that by risking his life by visiting the Sultan with a message of peace in the midst of the 5th crusade in 1219, St. Francis was taking the place of the Bel-Harith Christians of the Najran who had refused to prove the truth of their faith by accepting Muhammad's challenge of Mubahala. By risking his life, St. Francis was an example of a true mystical substitute.

These reflections led Massignon to establish the Badaliya in the Spirit of Saint Francis, with the guidance of his mentor Charles de Foucauld, who had modeled the way to live as a Christian in the midst of Islam. Foucauld had "crossed over" to the Berber Touareg people by learning their language, documenting their poetry, understanding their culture and living as they did in the Sahara. He ministered to their physical and spiritual needs, supplied food and medicine and lived with them as a devoted Christian, witnessing to Christ's love for all of humanity. For Massignon these two spiritual giants were the true "founders" of the Badaliya and he used the writings and reflections of his friend and mentor, Blessed Charles de Foucauld, at the Badaliya gatherings.

At the end of the Second World War in 1945 when Louis Massignon and Mary Kahil founded the Dar es-Salam, the House of Peace, in Cairo, they expanded on their earlier Statutes for the Badaliya and gave them to twelve Badaliya members including Father de Bonneville S.J., the Jesuit Priest who had blessed the founders after they made their first vow together in Damietta in 1934. The Badaliya Statutes were officially recognized in the Church by Msgr. Pierre Kamel Medawar, the auxiliary to the Greek Catholic Patriarch, Maximos IV, who signed the imprimatur of the Text in Cairo, on January 6, 1947. In a private audience with Louis Massignon, the Badaliya movement was blessed by Pope Pius XII on February 5, 1949.

In these letters Massignon mentions many groups and individuals around the world who took up the non-violent prayer of Badaliya in concert with the original groups formed in Cairo and Paris. In Rome, the group was led by Msgr. Mulla, a Turkish Muslim who had converted to Catholicism, was ordained a Priest and later named professor at the Oriental Pontifical Institute by Pius XI. A member of the group in Rome was Msgr. Jean-Baptiste Montini, who later became Pope Paul VI, well known for the 1962–1965 Vatican II renewal. There were also groups that formed in Beirut, Damascus, Algeria, Casablanca and Dakar.

In his letters to Mary Kahil and many others Massignon wrote that "the Badaliya prayer movement is first and foremost a response to Christ's call to give one's life to Him out of Love. Christ is the invisible guest who asks every instant of one's life, 'Do you love me'? This love of Christ must grow to include everyone, especially the poor, the enslaved, the outcast and the despairing. It is sometimes a painful love that does not take us out of this bitter world of sin and human failings where we experience the pain of loss and death but it is also the love of one who is tortured and dies on Calvary for us, the lamb slaughtered from the beginning of time, witnessed through the tears of the Virgin." It is to this love that Massignon vowed to deliver his life. He saw the love for Christ and others as a mystical path of compassion and a means to salvation. For Massignon this love was so complete that it required the way of substitution, of Badaliya, described in these letters.

Introduction to the Annual Letters and
Convocations to the Badaliya

For fifteen years Louis Massignon sent an Annual Letter to members of the Badaliya world-wide encouraging them to meditate with him on the spiritual experience and meaning of substitutionary prayer. The original Statutes, written in 1947, is referred to by Massignon as Annual Letter # 1, therefore it begins this collection. In these letters Massignon invites Badaliya members to reflect on his own Call to this form of prayer that first took place in Cairo, Egypt, followed many years later by the Vow that he made with Mary Kahil in a Franciscan chapel in Damietta. He describes the Goal, and the spiritual and psychological means to realizing it ever more deeply over time, as he himself grew to experience it.

These letters are written in a free style as Massignon shares his own reflections on living the experience of substituting oneself daily for the salvation of others as a follower of Jesus, the first "substitute." He invites his readers to enter into his own spiritual reflections evoking powerful images and scenes from Scripture, alluding to passages from the Qur'an and interjecting words and phrases in Arabic and Latin. The meditative style in the original French text uses long paragraphs with innumerable semi-colons as he moves from one thought or image to another, often eliminating a verb or subject. Therefore the editor has added verbs, subjects and other additional words in brackets to facilitate the English reader's ability to enter into the reflective style, and to more easily understand Massignon's vision of the spiritual vocation of Badaliya members. There are fifteen Annual Letters.

In 1954, when Massignon retired from his position as a professor at the Collège de France in Paris he began sending monthly "Convocations" or invitations, to the meetings in Paris to Badaliya members farthest away from the French capital, adding an Annual Letter at the end of each year. There are 91 somewhat long and detailed Convocations. The Annual Letters and Convocations are reproduced here in chronological order, beginning with the first Annual Letter, the Original Statutes written in 1947. This work is thus presented in the form of a sort of "diary" that shows the development of the Badaliya thought from 1947 to 1962 and above all, offers to an English speaking audience Louis Massignon's "mystical reading" of the events of history, painfully lived and accepted through the spirit of a devout Christian. One can only understand that spirit by entering, as if from the inside, Louis Massignon's own spiritual journey, from his meeting with Huymans as an adolescent, to his companionship with the 10th century Sufi mystic, al-Hallaj, his admiration for Charles de Foucauld, his love for St. Francis' stigmata at Mt. Alverna, his internalization of the three prayers of Abraham and his imitation of Gandhi, the hero of non-violence. Louis Massignon's lived experience of the history of his time and his interpretations and frustrations with it are shockingly all too familiar. His predictions have often been realized in our own time, and in that sense he was a prophetic voice, and yet the spiritual ground on which he stood also led him and leads us, through God, to an ever deepening experience of compassion, hospitality and love for "the other."

Great care has been taken to offer succinct yet clarifying footnotes throughout these documents in order to help the English language reader to relate to the many historical references to events and persons. There are many references to Louis Massignon's own personal history as well that are also briefly explained in the footnotes along with references to biographical works available in English for further exploration. A bibliography of works about and by Louis Massignon in English is included to complete this work.

References

1. Andrew, C.M. and Kanya-Forstner, A.S. 1981. *The Climax of French Imperial Expansion 1880–1914.* Oxford University Press.
2. Baumgart, W. 1982. *Imperialism: The Idea and Reality of British and French Colonial Expansion1914–1924.* Stanford University Press, Stanford, CA.
3. Basetti-Sani, G. "Muhammad and St. Francis," Oct. 4, 1956, in *The Muslim World*, Hartford Seminary Foundation, Vol. XLVI.
4. Clayton, A. 1994. *The Wars of French Decolonization.* Longman, London and New York.
5. Harpigny, Guy. 1981. *Islam et Christianism selon Louis Massignon.* La Neuve, Louvain.
6. Six, Jean François. 1993. *L'Aventure de l'Amour de Dieu: 80 unpublished letters by Charles de Foucauld to Louis Massignon.* Ed. du Seuil.

The Original Statutes of
the Badaliya 1947

I n order that the vocations of the Christians in the Middle East, who are ethnically or linguistically Arabs, and who the Islamic conquest has reduced to only a "small flock," be realized and fulfilled in all its providential truth, this union of prayer linking weak and poor souls who are seeking to love God and give Him more and more praise in Islamic lands, was born in Damietta, Egypt.

Closely joined together and driven by a single impulse towards the same goal which binds us together, let us offer and pledge our lives from now on as hostages.

This goal, to make Christ manifest in the Islamic world ("Let Christ Jesus, fully God and fully human, be blessed in Islam") requires us to penetrate deeply, moved by fraternal understanding and diligent, loving concern, into the life of the families of all Islamic generations, past and present, who God has placed on the path of each of us, thus leading us to the subterranean waters of grace which the Holy Spirit wants to bring to the surface for them and whose living Source we are trying to reveal to this disinherited people who in former times were excluded from the promise of the Messiah as descendants of Hagar, and for whom the Holy Spirit preciously guards an imperfect image of the face of 'Isa ibn Maryam' (Jesus, son of Mary) in the Muslim tradition, of this same sacred face of the Christ who we worship and whom we want them to discover in His full reality, in their hearts.

In this mission of intercession on their behalf, we incessantly ask God for the reconciliation of these dear souls, for which we want to offer ourselves as substitutes, *fil badaliya* (in exchange), paying their ransom in their place, and at our own expense, it is in begging for their future "incorporation" into the Church that we are assuming their condition, following the example of the Word made flesh, we who are baptized, living in their midst each day, mixing our lives with theirs just as salt is mixed with food to give it flavor.

It is in this vocation for their salvation that we must and wish to sanctify ourselves, aspiring to become like Christ (living examples of the Gospels), in order that they recognize Him through us, and so that we might safeguard, by this silent and hidden apostolate, the sincerity of our own gift.

In their presence we must perfect and complete the Passion of Christ because our fathers, the Christians of the Middle East who transmitted the faith to us as our heritage, left it to us incomplete, having not dared to accept the challenge of Muhammad when he invited them one day at Medina to prove the truth of the Incarnation to him by subjecting themselves to the judgment of God in undergoing the trial by fire.

This trial, sought by the founder of Islam but deferred to our generation, was desired by Saint Francis who offered himself in vain at Damietta, and by so many others who offered themselves silently for Muslim souls, has been entrusted to us as a precious legacy, handed down from generation to generation, to be completed and brought to successful conclusion by us.

A task is reserved for us in this mysterious duel, in which for centuries Christianity clashed with the refusal of the reality of Christ by the Muslim world, in this struggle which has brought, through so many trials and alongside so many apostasies so much joy for all eternity, institutions of liturgical feasts, foundations of religious orders and the death of so many martyrs.

In expectation of this hour, we pray for them and with Him; each day at the moment of the three 'Angelus'[1] by affirming through the *fiat* of Mary the mystery of the divine Incarnation which the Muslims want to deny, at that same hour when the call to prayer of the muezzin[2] unites their

---

[1] Reciting the *Angelus*, recalling the mystery of the Incarnation, three times a day was a common devotion in the Catholic world at the time and continues in monasteries today. In villages everywhere the church bells were rung three times for Christians to recite words taken from the Gospel of Luke (1:26–28) followed by the Hail Mary.

[2] From the minarets in Muslim countries the Muezzin calls Muslims to prayer five times a day. This is one of the five Pillars, or requirements, of Islam for practicing Muslims throughout the world.

hearts in a single adoration of the one God of Abraham, at the taking of communion on Friday, the day of the Passion of Christ, which is also the day of their noonday gathering for prayer, the day they unconsciously choose, as we do, to give testimony to their faith.

Living in an Islamic land, under the pressure of an atmosphere which beclouds and suffocates our faith as Christians, if we would hope for this *shahada*[3] (testimony) of martyrdom, which reminds us of the vow once made by the Mercedarians[4] to take the place, in the Muslim prisons, in case of need, of the captives who they wanted to ransom, it is up to us to continue the attitude of Saint Francis and Saint Louis[5] towards those millions of souls who wait for us and look towards us; to we who are called to give testimony with our lives, and if God permits with our death, like Foucauld, who obtained martyrdom and even asked for it for his friends: to give to this Christ, who asks us to continue his passion, that shahada that we desire to offer to him, as unworthy of it as we are.

The Original Goals (1947)

1. The Badaliya is addressed to Christians in the East.
2. It comes from the awareness of a particular responsibility of these Christians towards their Muslim brothers among whom they live. They have a providential mission in relation to them and would like to fulfill it.
3. Moreover having suffered and suffering still through them, they wish to practice the highest Christian charity towards them following the precept of our Lord," To love your enemies, and pray for those who persecute you" (Mt.5:44) and according to His example

---

[3] The *Shahada* is the first of the five Pillars of Islam, "There is only One God (Allah) and Muhammad is His Messenger."

[4] The Mercedarians were members of the Order of Our Lady of Mercy established in 1218 in Barcelona. Their mission was to buy back Christians who were held captive by Muslims and if there was not sufficient money, to take their place. They became a mendicant order, or beggars, in 1690.

[5] Louis IX was King of France from 1226–1270. He was taken prisoner during the 7th Crusade and paid a large ransom, restoring Damietta, Egypt to the Sultan. He was an exemplary ruler of France and just arbiter for Christians until he died of the plague while en route to the 8th Crusade.

"When we were God's enemies, we were reconciled to Him by the death of his Son...." (Rom.5:10).

4. Thus, counting on divine grace, these Christians wish to consecrate themselves to the salvation of their brothers, and in this hope of salvation, to give faith, adoration and love to Jesus Christ in the name of their brothers, whose imperfect knowledge of the Gospels prevents them from giving it themselves.

   Salvation does not necessarily mean exterior conversion. It is already gaining a lot that a greater number belonging to the soul of the Church (members of the Badaliya) live and die in a state of grace.

5. By these traits the Badaliya distinguishes itself from the diverse associations and prayer leagues that exist in Europe and with whom the members of the Badaliya are gratefully joined.

Means:

6. There are three means: prayer, charity, and personal holiness as a witness.

7. Prayer: without any strict obligation the members of the Badaliya offer the three Angelus and their Friday Communion for their brothers.

8. Charity: Charity consists of an attitude entirely kind, affectionate, considerate, and truly fraternal, as much as prudence permits, in relation to the souls that Providence puts on the path of each one.

9. Personal Holiness does not consist of any particular means, but it must tend to make the members of the Badaliya living Gospels, in order that Jesus Christ manifests himself through them and that they give witness to Jesus Christ by their lives and, if God wills, by their death.

10. While the Badaliya does not propose exterior action, its members always look for ways to devote themselves to their Muslim brothers and they will voluntarily enter into active organizations that are able to animate the spirit of the Badaliya.

Organization:

11. The Badaliya is organized into groups including members of their choice.

12. The central group is the one in Cairo, in the spirit and directions of which the others are held to conform.

13. Members of the Badaliya are all persons who have been included in a group depending on the one in Cairo, who have accepted and signed the statutes and who regularly attend the weekly meetings of the members of the Badaliya.

14. Weekly Meetings (title of the program indicated)

It is the weekly meeting that contains the spirit of the Badaliya. They are necessary. They should be held as much as possible on a fixed day and time, but it is better to change the day, hour, and place rather than miss a meeting. All members should be notified in time of the day, hour, and place by the secretary.

It begins with 15 minutes of Adoration in the Chapel. Then we observe the following order:

1. Opening Prayer "Laudate Dominum omnes gentes..."[6] in Arabic if possible.

2. Spiritual reading preferably from the writings of Charles de Foucauld.

3. A brief and free commentary, if there is time, by the participants and the reader.

4. Reading of the notes from the last meeting.

5. An account of activities, contacts and discussion of theoretical and practical problems raised by the activities and contacts, or by the reading of documents relative to Islam.

6. Final Prayer: The "Suscipe"[7] in Arabic if possible.

The meeting must not last longer than an hour including the initial 15 minute Adoration.

Imprimatur Cairo, January 6, 1947.
Official Seal: by Pierre K. Medawar
Titular Archbishop of Péluse
Auxiliary of the Patr. Gr. Melk. Cath.

---

[6]   Taken from Psalm 117.
[7]   Traditionally attributed to St. Ignatius of Loyola (1491–1556) found at the end of his *Spiritual Exercises.*

Explanation of the Badaliya

1) The call and the place 2) The goal 3) The means which becomes the end 4) Substitution realized 5) The simplicity of attitude 6) To prove to Him that we love Him, by dying.

I) The Call and the Place

Come, let us center ourselves, slowly, where we are, in the land of Islam, in Egypt. Remembering the events in our lives, let us recollect in us this human place of election where we received a vocation. The clear and familiar landscape where the invisible Spirit of consolation and truth touched us, one time and it was forever, with the desire to heal hearts broken by the silent absence of God, having become deaf to the One that seems to them to have retreated from their lives. The lost sheep in the desert (dâllat) in the land of Islam. When the first call to this grace resounded for us it was an invitation to commit together, and to offer ourselves (it is necessary to be at least two for this grace to be granted) in order to save the life in danger of death and the soul of a renegade friend.[8] [Then, it was] by following a saint full of human tenderness, Saint Francis, who invited us to it through the voice of a tertiary from his Order. And, after many years, [it was by] holding firm [to the call] according to our promises made on becoming a tertiary [Franciscan], without knowing the secret [behind] the death of this renegade friend.[9] It is in Dami-

---

[8] Massignon is referring to the first time that he invited Mary Kahil to join him in substitutionary prayer in 1912 for their Spanish friend, Luis de Cuadra who had fallen away from his Christian roots and adopted Islam. See Introduction and Buck, 2002. "Dialogues with Saints and Mystics" p. 145.

[9] Massignon was shaken upon learning that his friend Luis de Cuadra had taken his own life on August 12, 1921 while imprisoned for an unknown reason in Valencia. Having written to him weekly and prayed constantly for him in mystical substitution, he was now more than ever concerned for the state of Luis' soul before God.

etta, the place of the heroic offering of Saint Francis for a Muslim soul, that a response to grace confirmed us in the "*Badaliya*." "Where two or three are gathered in my name, there I am in their midst" (Mt 18:20). Damietta is deserted by Arab families who were once fervent Christians and are now a discouraged and disappointed minority. It is up to us to relieve them, to bring their true mission to fruition, to perfect their sufferings by offering ourselves for Islam via the path of substitution "*Badaliya*." We have to identify ourselves through love with those Christians still tolerated in Muslim lands because they still speak and pray in Arabic, whether we are eastern or western Christians, Latin or Hellenistic. We know that at the Last Judgment God will listen to grievances against us by our neighbors, our fellow countrymen, or our Arab Muslim hosts, if after we leave we have only left among them some progress, theoretical knowledge or practical techniques. No, we can never love our guests enough. For every Arab the Guest is sacred, we who have shared the bread that he gives us in passing (*al-luqma fî sabîlillâh*). In exchange it is up to us to obtain this peace of God (*salâm Allâh*) for him by wishing it to him from the bottom of our hearts, something he so rarely wishes us. Yet this peace of God is the visitation of the Holy Spirit, *Rûh Allâh*, identical in Islam to *Isa ibn Maryam* (Jesus son of Mary), who is in fact the Good of all Goods, the essential Only One, the transubstantiated Bread on which we live in order to give it to others, so that they live before the Face of God.

II) *Zuhûr 'Isa ibn Maryam fî Islâm* (Jesus Son of Mary in Islam)

Through this Spirit of abandon, offered without reserve to our separated brothers who are also sons of Abraham, we prepare them to once again meet Jesus, who was formed through this Spirit in Mary and is inseparable from His Mother, from Maryam and through Maryam. He is able to come to life again and to take form in the depth of their hearts provided we share this attentive concern with them, this daily preparation of our lives, this experiment with destiny, that makes common cause of the confidences and advice between friends. Would that they taste this lowly and adoring acceptance with us, without convention nor reticence, full of the Will of God, *tawakkul*, *islâm*, *ikhlâs*, (abandon, submission, sincere devotion) this "*khalwa*" (solitude), this vow of chastity, renouncing gaining anything for oneself, which is the marian "fiat," the "kun," in the House of the family from *Nasâra*, to *al-Nâsira*, Nazareth, [which is] the place where every vow and every choice prepares itself and matures (Foucauld). And we taste in exchange, in simplicity, the traces of inspiration, the biblical and evangelical fragments, in Arabic, expressly preserved for them and for us in their Qur'an: condensed symbolic passages, but admirable, so admiring of the virginity of Mary, and of Jesus, and of the vows of hermits (the trilogy of the *basmala, ibtighâ mardât Allah, Mâl'da liltuma'nîna, Sâ'a, khalwatal-arba'în, In the Name of God, [Allah], the desire to satisfy God, a table in order to be secure and serene, the hour, the solitude of forty days*), that it is only a question of making it blossom. To show them again, so that they remember it, that there were discreet and humble saints among them in every era, corner stones rejected for a time, who offered themselves to suffering, to beggars and the poverty stricken, to the blind and paralytics, praying to God "*Aslih*" (Reconcile) so that the Abrahamic Community of the sons of Ishmael be one, holy, and universal. It is our comfort to recognize these friends of God among them, these saints who have only been half understood, but through whom this slow configuration to Christ will be realized; this reincorporation into the Christ who must gradually gain everyone. If the faith of Abraham still lives so strongly in our Muslim friends, it is that it adheres to this prefiguration of the Passion that is the *Hajj*[10] to Mecca where one obtains pardon for those dear ones who are absent, and the day of *Arafât*, where God "descends" in order to forgive. But the true *Hajj* is to give his heart and his life, with Him.

III) The Means which Becomes the End

The work of mercy to which we have been invited is to try to respond to their clamor for justice (*sayha bi'l-haqq*) by entering into their most painful matters of conscience, when they entrust us with them in friendship. It is that "go to the Front" that Foucauld called us to in his last letter: "One must never hesitate to ask for the *posts* where the *danger*, the sacrifice and the devotion are the most. Leave honor to those who desire it,

---

[10]   Hajj is the pilgrimage to Mecca that is one of the five pillars of Islam, to be made once during a Muslim's lifetime according to one's means.

but always ask for danger and pain."[11] There is the true Arab *"jihâd akbar,"* this "holy war" leading to suffering from the same faults in the depth of himself that we want to make up for, to atone. Such substitution, "Badaliya," goes very far. Our compassion must be complete, and universal. Let us recall the Holy Hour of the Master at Gethsemani. Substitution: for their physical, moral, intellectual and religious miseries, deficiencies and weaknesses is to deeply understand them in order that they be brought to perfection. [It is] to cry the tears of Mary for them, prefigured by those of Hagar in the desert for the first-born of the Arab race;[12] the first in the Scriptures of those who are made to find the source. [Substitution is} also to rejoice with them, and suffer with them, especially for that which they lack, in order to be worthy of carrying them. [Substitution is}total acceptance with Christ, "langueres nostros Ipse tulit," [Isaiah 53:4, "it was our sufferings that he endured"] that which *justifies* God, because it is his apparent harshness towards them that has touched us and brought us closer to them. He did not want to save them without us.

And by an exquisite intervention, the measure of our intercession becomes that of our predestination. Like Msgr. Luis Amigo of Masamagrell, Bishop of Segorbe, founder of a Franciscan Charity for Reparation, wrote to us in relation to the renegade friend for whom we offered ourselves the first time,[13] "es obra tan grata a la divina misericordia, y por que asegurarà Vd. su salvacion, porque el que salva un alma predestina la suya" (letter of July 30, 1934). Our renunciation for them makes our link with the Church, which is Mary, whose "fiat," through prayer, reveals itself as the formation of our defining personality, of our second birth. (The Role of the three theological virtues before the three powers of the soul in our meditation): through our vow of "Badaliya," our choice is consummated (memory, intellect and will).

"Badaliya" in Arabic is "replacement, or exchange with the soldier whose lot was drawn." And it is also to become one of the *"abdâl,"* one

---

[11]   During WW I Massignon wrote to Foucauld to ask if he should leave his family and the Army's Central Services in Paris and go to the Front in the Eastern Mediterranean. Foucauld's letter was written on Dec.1 1916, the day he was killed.

[12]   Genesis 21:14–20. Massignon understood this story of Hagar and Ishmael as the biblical origins of the Arab race and the Muslim religion.

[13]   Massignon is referring to his Spanish friend Luis La Cuadra who was the first for whom he and Mary Kahil offered themselves as "Badaliya."

of the rejected corner stones, humble and hidden, of the Community of true Believers in the God of Abraham, who, imitating Abraham in his intercession, share with him from age to age, according to the immemorial legend in Islam, the overwhelming (and obscure) honor of participating in the reconciliation of the sinful world with its judge. Because that is our vocation: to rediscover this primordial word of divine love to which our hearts have been predestined, to recognize it in the call of those that we go to help, and to respond to it as a witness to *Tawhîd*,[14] among them, thereby giving "a purer meaning to the words of the Arab tribe." So that the saving mission of this language, the last evoked in the story of Pentecost, is brought to completion in this Arabia through which Saint Paul began this *Bishara*[15] that gives the response to the *Sayha bi'l-haqq* of the oppressed and excluded: to their clamor for justice.

IV) Substitution Realized

Al-wafâ bi'ahd al-badaliya.[16] [Substitution is realized] by practicing the material and spiritual works of mercy in a certain way each day. "The one who considers the One for whom he works while working, ceases to consider his own works." This is our goal. We have to begin that which we cannot finish, to sow, more than to harvest the way the mercenaries do in their hurry. Certainly, we must apply ourselves to our work, cultivate the knowledge required by our occupation without becoming weary. But we don't have to act as Doctors with our separated brothers. "Teach, he said to the Christians," not with a highly theoretical science without love, but with the experimental science of behavior and consequence, [teaching] how to conceive and realize the mysteries summarized in the sign of the Cross, "*statera facta corporis*," this perfect measure of man that reveals his destiny to him. [Substitution is realized] by gradually living, starting from the House in Nazareth, the growing "fiat" of Christ and His Passion within us that started with the "fiat" of Mary. And through that, tending little by little to chastity, to the total detachment from oneself, *tawakkul, taslîm*, [abandonment, surrender], to this grace in perfect transparency that we associate with such spiritual fecundity, like the Virgin,

---

[14] *Tawhid* is the proclamation that God is One.
[15] *Bishara* means the Gospel or the Good News.
[16] Fidelity to the pact or vow of substitution.

to divine Paternity. By admiring Jesus in our brothers and sisters, loving Him in them, we love them more. To pray for all their ancestors, all past generations, because, for us, every man is the "ambassador" for all his relatives whose destiny enters into his own, and through it, enters into our prayer. And not like a dead weight but like the beginnings of a more beautiful and real future.

Would that our charity not be a tactic in service of annexation, colonialism, nor Hellenism or Latinism, nor Franciscanism, Jesuitism, or Foucauldism. And in places where the native hierarchy is Arab, that we even renounce that which would accentuate or strengthen our membership as "badaliya-ites" in the "Badaliya," living a purely ecumenical Catholicism as "Auxiliary to the Missions"[17] in indigenous diocese.

The most profound apostolate is not to try hard to "convert" from the outside, which is an attitude that makes a travesty of the Christian zeal for souls and renders it obnoxious. As our dear Father Christophe de Bonneville[18] emphasized, the question is only that a greater number of those belonging to the soul of the Church live and die "in a state of grace." We are not doing statistics. It is only God who "converts" the other when He reconciles with him "from the inside," in the solitude of the heart. And it is enough for us to thus be axially substituted for this consoled soul whose desolation at being absent from God has gone, in order that all the bitterness of transferred love in ourselves nails us to the Cross where Jesus awaits us. According to the maxim of a Muslim in agony, "*fī maqârid al-qadâq,*" "The scissors of destiny cut my flesh, but I remain faithful to praising Him."[19] Let us meditate on the example of the Christian martyrs in the Islamic world, on Arab soil, in the East, the West and all the way to our friend, Charles de Foucauld, and to the last Greek, Armenian,

---

[17] The Auxiliaire des Missions is a society of secular priests founded in 1930 by the Abbé André Boland, who agreed to put themselves in the service of the indigenous, or local, catholic hierarchy.

[18] The Jesuit, Father Christophe de Bonneville (1888–1947) was then Rector of the Collége de la Sainte Famille in Cairo, in charge of all the Missionaries to Islam in the Middle East. He was very close to Louis Massignon and Mary Kahil and became the first member of the Badaliya on their return to Cairo from making their vow in Damietta, Egypt in 1934.

[19] al-Husayn ibn Mansûr al-Hallaj, the 10th century Sufi martyr and saint whose legendary life and writings were researched by Massignon throughout his life. The first edition was published in 1922 as "La Passion d'al-Hallaj."

Georgian, Maronite, Syrian, Copts, and Chaldean, who are all witnesses to supreme Love. *Shuhadâ'l-hubb al-ajall.*

V) The Simplicity of Attitude

There is only one love, and it is God Himself, the love of the only One for the only One, of the lover for the beloved, of Jesus for the Father that he has given to us. We will only have on high, Foucauld said, that which we have given here below. The immortal life of our soul will only be "beatified" if it is totally united from here below in love. Nothing other than the Gift will remain of us, this spirit of life that we will have communicated to our neighbor, to other members of Christ, through our substitution for them, our hospitality to His Body and His Blood, to his Angels and his Saints, and our tenderness toward his Mother. Our life of naked faith will no longer be an obscure premonition but conscious of being realized. We see clearly that Islam was revealed to us in order to make us find a certain kind of holiness that its presence has provoked in the Church; a heroic response of love by us to its objections to the proposition of a trial by fire made by Muhammad to the grand children of the martyrs of Najran. [It is] our response of love that shows Islam that the Incarnation has truly taken place, since the Cross shared by us makes us live out of compassion for our brothers and makes our intercession before the Face of God pure. Foucauld is not "*qiddîs al-jâsûsiya*," the patron saint of French-Christian espionage in the Sahara, but the hermit martyred in the Hoggar, the Muslim "*dakhîl*,"[20] his guest, hostage and ransom.

VI) To Prove to Him That We Desire Him, by Dying

If it is true, my God, as You have said it Yourself, that to die proves completely to the friends for whom we die, that we love, let us premeditate together on how to die with Him in order to prove to them how much God desires them. The novitiate for our Vow is to practice tirelessly the industrious patience of love, to search with a contained and discreet fervor for the "fiat," "*fal-yakun*," of Mary; [21] to be, or not to be, a sacramen-

---

20 Literally, the one who enters, or the guest.

21 "Let it be," The Virgin Mary's response to the Angel in the Annunciation," Let it be done to me according to your word."

tal communicant "in the last rites," with the desire to pray the Holy Hour when death comes. And every minute we come nearer to it. Let us pray this Hour (He only came as one of us, for it), without conventions, without style, just as we are. Let us die to ourselves before this Eucharist of mercy and reconciliation, this morsel of grace without any face, who cast himself in us, this frail offering of an abandoned victim of torture, who leaves us completely free not to follow him to the end, to this consolation, and to this seed of immortal resurrection. As for the agony, Jesus is certainly the Muslim "Isa ibn Maryam" robbed of all divinity. He did suffer the agony, but let us report what we see today with the Muslims who dare not conceive of a "suffering God," and on the Eucharist which, without suffering, is an annihilation still more radical than the Agony. He doesn't suffer any more in Himself but rather in those of his members who have sensed his heartrending humility and who suffer more cruelly in his place from the insults and contempt that can no longer reach him, and from the nastiness of the fool who cannot tarnish the radiant Truth. Thus we are justifying our instinct of adoration for that which is holy. But we are also proving our powerlessness, our visible defeat, the apparent deception of we who are set in the "Badaliya," as substitutes for our Muslim friends who still acknowledge Him by giving witness to his Holy Abandon to Justice.

Physical death, which comes to silence every voice here below, will not have a hold over our testimony, and the expansion of its echo all around us does not preoccupy us anymore because He takes us. He has already taken us, alone with Him alone. The One who makes us die has already paid the price of blood for us, this *Diyâ* [22] of the Arabs, "that falls to the Murderer." The old outburst of compassion that originally united us together makes us thrill with hope. The painful humiliation will pass, from the Incarnation, through pure faith in transubstantiation, directly towards the peace of divine glory, to clear space. He who was made a sign for us in suffering, with his Cross, [is the One] we recognize in the Holy Sacrament where he vanished, and was resurrected, triumphant and glorious.

---

[22]   The Qur'anic Arab penal code states that one who has killed unjustly must in turn be killed which was preceded by the Hebrew Scriptures by "An eye for and eye" etc. However, the parents of the victim can agree to a financial compensation, thus, "the price of blood" or Diyâ.

Annual Letter # II

Cairo, December 17, 1948

A s I did last year at this time, I am sending you this message in order to strengthen our bond of "Badaliya." I am thinking with you of Fr. Charles de Bonneville (actually, I have just returned from Gethsemani where once again I was gripped by the memory of the holy hour spent with him in prayer), and now that I am on the edge of the other world where he preceded us, I find myself measuring the seemingly miserable results at the end of my life of my stubborn search for a new contingent of young people to entrust with the inexpressibly beautiful grace received here among you Eastern Christians. [It is] the grace of a renewal of the *Bishara*,[23] a reminder of the Annunciation to Mary and the grace of a deep compassion for the unfinished vocation of the local Christians increasingly abandoned here by their Western brothers. I am sending you this message so that your hearts give it full attention.

Never more than in this year 1948 has the Church been in such need of "Badaliya-ites," of compassionate brothers substituting themselves for their Eastern brothers who are being abandoned by the temporal powers and driven into exile as "displaced persons." (In Macedonia there are 200,000,[24] as well as 100,000 in Palestine beyond the 700,000 Arab refugees).[25] We must help them with prayers, clothing, food, and works

---

[23] *Bishara* means "Good News."

[24] In 1948 fighting in Macedonia between communist troops under Markos supported by Tito in Yugoslavia and the Greeks supported by English and Americans resulted in 200,000 refugees.

[25] On December 1, 1947 the United Nations General Assembly agreed on the establishment of two independent States in Palestine, one Arab and one Jewish, which was under a British mandate at the time. War between the surrounding Arab States and the Jewish forces resulted in the acquisition of more Palestinian territory and the declaration by David Ben Gurion establishing the State of Israel on

of spiritual mercy, the first of which is to urge them to hold on to their essential vocation as witnesses to Christ and his Mother in their native countries, especially at the Holy Sites in Nazareth, Galilee, Bethlehem, and Jerusalem. [We must urge] them, out of the depths of their present weakness and misery, to defend the honor of the Christian profession, the virginal honor of our origin on earth, before the Muslims who are scandalized by the Western Christian indifference toward the fate of the Eastern Christian communities, as well as before Israel, whose contempt for the followers of the Christian doctrine is reinforced by our mercenary cowardice. A Jewish writer, Elian Finbert,[26] recently wrote that Christianity is now withdrawing from the East after poisoning it, and rushing back to the West where it will die. "The one who wishes to save his life shall lose it" [Mt. 10–38–39, Lk. 14:27, 17:33 and Jn. 12: 25–26]. The Latin Christian charities, contemplative convents and schools, must "connect," right now more than ever, with the East in the spirit of the "Badaliya-ites," namely by substituting themselves more than ever for the souls of their Eastern Muslim brothers, in the name of the Eastern Christians. Otherwise, their native countries, France, Italy, Spain, Austria and Belgium, will lose their religious faith because they will have ceased to practice apostolic charity toward their forsaken Eastern brothers who are in no condition to fulfill their vocation alone as witnesses to Christ on Islamic soil. This is an honor-bound duty, that I am not the only one, thank God, to feel distressed about out of the depths of my impotence. One of the great voices of the Church, echoing the pontifical encyclical of October 24th repeated it to me for your sake: "Let us die, when honor dies" (Chesterton) (and this is one word from this "Badaliya" that pierced me as Nazareth was being abandoned this summer).[27]

May 14, 1948. The West Bank was annexed to Transjordan and the Gaza strip declared an Egyptian mandate. The UNWRA, United Nations Relief and Works Administration, was established creating the still existing refugee camps for the millions of Palestinian refugees who fled to neighboring countries, including the West Bank that had become a part of Jordan.

[26] Elian J. Finbert (1899–1877) Jewish, Egyptian essayist.

[27] Territories including Nazareth and other parts of the territory originally designated by the United Nations as part of a Paletinian State were taken by the Israeli army on July 17, 1948. At that time Massignon cried out at the scandal in a brief article written on August 23rd in "Christian Witness," further developed in an article for "Franciscan Life" written in October 1948. (These can be found in French in

Let us reread together the first paragraph of our mission statement: "In order to realize and fulfill, in all its providential truth, the vocation of the Arab or Arabic speaking Christians in the East, who the Muslim conquest reduced to not more than a small flock..." We must more than ever live each day among our Muslim brothers at this time when disagreements and growing hatreds risk cutting us off from them, which would cause distress for Eastern Christian communities who would cease to be able to show the Muslims that Christ loves them, through us, [we Christians] who want to love them at any cost, and "mingle with them like salt."

How can we prove this to them?

[We prove this to them] by going back to our origin, to the principle of our adoption (as adoptive children of the Blessed Virgin at Calvary), by going back "into the womb of our Mother" as Our Lord told Nicodemus, through a second birth, and by recovering in the depth of our heart the virgin point of our election to Christianity and the axis of the will of God in us. Just as Mary herself found [this axis of the will of God] for all the chosen by saying "yes" to the Annunciation by the Angel in Nazareth, by accepting to abandon herself completely to God. "Fiat mihi secundum verbum tuum" ["Let it be done according to Your Word"] ("kun," "so be it," as one says in Arabic when defining this true Islam, this total surrender to the sovereignty of Providence that Mary realized in her heart so that the Savior could come to dwell among us).

As we wait for Christmas in this time of Advent, let us listen to the advice of divine grace, as did Charles de Foucauld, when he left The Trappists (1/23/1897) in order to go to Nazareth to pray in the very same place as the Annunciation; to meditate on how to abandon himself, in union with Mary, to the saving compassion for souls. May the birth of Jesus, as it is told in the liturgy on Christmas night, not find us like those who search the graves looking for past memories and only stir up dust that is dead, but rather like this young Mother expecting her First-Born, attentive and full of respect for the sacred as she prepares herself to welcome and protect this living Presence of divine Love among us; attuning our reflective souls to the suggestions of grace that turn us towards our neighbor. She understands that the movements of this blessed Child in

Opera Minora vol. III, pp. 490–493 and the 2008 publication called Ecrits Memorable p. 760–763) "Nazareth et nous, Nazorians, Nazara."

Her womb must persuade our hearts to console the afflicted and to transfigure the despair in this Muslim country, by centering ourselves on the Holy Virgin Mary in a vital and ever growing communion with the divine Guest that She bears within Her since the day of the Annunciation.

How close to our heart the call to the Angelus has become these days. [It is] a call to which, following St. Francis, Charles de Foucauld invites us to respond three times a day, thereby coinciding with three of the muezzins five daily calls to prayer. At those times let us remember to say the "Fiat" of our vocation, as She Herself did in Nazareth for all the Chosen, in union with the promise made to her ancestors, David, and above all, Abraham. "Ecce ancilla Domini" [Here is the servant of the Lord] is the prayer of all beginnings, a "renaissance," a novitiate that love does not grow weary of renewing because the Desire for God never reduces its gift of engagement and self-offering to a dead formula. In our persistent unworthiness that guarantees our humility, let us meditate on the incredible honor of this "association" with Our Lady, and with the Church in her humble and daily sufferings over the smallest of her children and the most forsaken of men. These sufferings should not be deemed trivial, because the maternal intention of Mary in which we foresee the coming of Jesus Savior, illuminates them with compassionate and serene Holiness. This year it is true that many of our Christian brothers in the Middle East are abandoning the defense of the faith in this country, but we want to stay here in their place. It is true that very few of their brothers in the West come to support them through this age-old ordeal that has so humiliated them, but we will honor their vocation as confessors of our faith right to the end, in its country of origin, around the Holy Sites that we cowardly Westerners abandoned. (If I forget thee, O Jerusalem, let my hand wither).[28] It is also true that the few Muslim friends who have tried to understand the nature of the friendship felt for them by the "Badaliya-ites," declare that we do not love them enough to deserve their complete trust. But we keep meditating, with Mary, on her "Fiat," for them, [because] her humble beginnings make us sense and desire the whole sacrifice that her compassion brought to completion, with Jesus, for the salvation of these beloved souls.

---

[28]   From Psalm 137, the psalmist, returned from the Babylonian exile in the sixth century BCE, recalls how the Jews refused to sing for their captors and remembered Jerusalem.

Annual Letter # III

December 27, 1949

On this feast of St. John, the Virgin Apostle, let us rest our head against the Master's heart, as we stand next to his Cross on which He is always nailed, with such utter abandonment!

And, let us go over this desolate year of 1949 in His forsaken presence. Several of us were given the chance to see, but without giving enough of ourselves in response, the kind of Compassion He asks us to have as members of the Badaliya, for the Arab refugees, Muslims and Christians, who have been crammed into internment camps for Displaced Persons. The disparaging materialism of the UN provides them with minimal food and supplies without the slightest emotional comfort or reason to hope for the future, and treats them as incurably lazy cowards. Thus 90,000 of them are dragging their wretched lives around Hebron, the same place where God found a host in Abraham (at Mamre).[29] Our racist and contemptuous colonial practices have denied these unfortunate Arabs, who have been sacrificed, victimized and sent into exile, this sacred respect for the guest, this divine hospitality, of which Arab tribal honor is now the last guardian, and that the bourgeois of Bethlehem, nearly 2000 years ago, already denied to the Holy Family. Our ineffectual visits have at least helped us to offer better prayers for them, "beseeching" prayers that thirst for justice, and we were able to rekindle a new wave of almsgiving and compassion in the French Church.

A mission of the French Episcopate to Bethlehem, where two members of the Badaliya happened to be staying, received a fraternally warm welcome from the Muslim elite of Hebron, that provoked a great move-

---

[29] Gen. 18:1–15 the visit by three angels of the Lord to Abraham, a demonstration of hospitality, and the promise that Sarah, who was barren, will give birth to a child.

ment of veneration in Algerian Islam for our common ancestor, Abraham, around whom the prayers of the exiled Muslims rally each day.

These two members [of the Badaliya] also prayed at Taibe,[30] the place of Christ's last retreat before His Passion. And in Jerusalem, as well as in Bethlehem and Beit Sahour, the Badaliya-ites more clearly realized the extent to which they must assist Christians of the Eastern Rite whom European and American benefactors tend to neglect in order to first help the two that Latinization and Anglicization are uprooting from the Holy Land. Moreover, one of the Badaliya-ites understood that the consummation of our vocation to our work lies in giving himself to the Eastern Rite, which is a privilege directly granted to him by the Pope, along with a special blessing.[31] We are thus re-entering into the foundation of our adoption, centered in the bosom of our Mother, the virgin point of our election.

With scheduled meetings that vary, the central group (Cairo) and the groups in Beirut, Casablanca and Paris have carried on with their activities.

A dispatch from Reuter the evening of November 24th (*Le Monde*, Paris, 11/26) gave a summary of a "Memorandum" from the Sacred Congregation for the Propagation of the Faith, the authority concerned with all the issues relative to mission countries, declaring that Muslims and Christians could join forces "for God and against atheist communism;" taking note of "a very vivid religious sensibility among Muslims, an ardent desire for grace and a sincere wish to be united with God." This memorandum is a great comfort to the Badaliya.

This year we came to a better understanding of the word *l'ightirab*, the displacement we experience in our "substitution" for Muslim souls, this grace from God that justifies them before Him as it sanctifies us. Our prayer of desire, to which the world is blind and deaf, frees us from the perverse despair that disconnects our suffering from this profound Divine Attraction of which it is a mere shadow. And our suffering delivers us to it through the Marian "fiat." Our prayer for our neighbor becomes

---

[30] John 11:54 describes Jesus retiring to a place called Ephraim, today the Christian village in the West Bank 25 kilometers North East of Jerusalem called Taybeh.

[31] Massignon is referring to himself. On February 5, 1949 he received the permission of Pope Pius XII to change his affiliation from the Latin Rite Church to the Greek Catholic Melkite Church that celebrates the liturgy in Arabic. See Buck, "Dialogues with Saints and Mystics" p. 152.

the very source of our immortality, our access to this inner miracle of never-ending resurrection, which is the divine life in Three persons. Because God, who is well above the Law of laws, is the miracle of miracles who lifts our admiring love above his most magnificent Works and makes us sense that the universe is not co-eternal with Him. In our heart of hearts our forgiven souls, along with the whole Church, become "this unique Virgin, "where God alone penetrates in order to be conceived there-in," in the way that "Thought descends into the mind." "*Asrârunâ Bikrun... lâ yakhtiru fîhâ illâ shuhûd al-Rabb.*"[32] And without planning it, the two members [of the Badaliya], who long ago founded the association in Damietta in memory of a friend who had despaired of Islam after abandoning Christianity, found themselves together in the unity of Golgotha on August 12th, the anniversary of his death in 1921.[33]

Among those who died in 1949, our beloved Msgr. Arthur Hughes[34] should especially be remembered before God. He was the first Internuncio on Islamic soil and wished to be one of our members. During the seven years he spent in Cairo we were invited to join him often, and he had us choose the emerald for his ring at his consecration in St. Joseph Church on May 20, 1945. He gave himself entirely, in total substitution, to this Egypt where our Association was born. He used his last strength consoling the broken hearts of prisoners of all races and of Arab Displaced Persons driven from their homes in the Holy Land. "Semper interpellandum pro nobis, [Always quick to intercede in our favor] we could say, since we want, as he did, to substitute ourselves for them, as we count more than ever on his paternal blessing.

---

[32] "Our mysterious secrets consist in a Virgin.... only seen as testimony to the Lord"

[33] Massignon is referring to Mary Kahil and their friend Luis de Cuadra. "The unity of Golgotha" calls us back to this feast day of St. John the Apostle, who in the Gospel according to John is interpreted as representing all of us who are given to Mary, the mother of the Church, by Jesus from the Cross. (John 19:26–27).

[34] Msgr. Arthur Hughes (1902–1949) was a White Father, French missionaries to Africa, from the Westminster diocese in Great Britain. He became the Apostolic Delegate to Egypt and Palestine on February 12, 1945 and titular of Hieropolis in May. He was named Internuncio of Cairo August 23, 1947 and was a loyal friend of the Badaliya.

Annual Letter # IV

Hebron and Bethlehem Christmas 1950

T he Christian liturgy, when lived in the spirit of "Badaliya," has no need of a *physical* journey to unite us with the mystery of the Nativity and the prophetic joy it gave in advance to the patriarch Abraham, Jesus tells us. ("Abraham rejoiced to see my day; and he saw it and was glad" [John 8:56]. This probably took place on the day of the Promise of the Three Angels at Mamre). However, it is very sweet to be in Bethlehem and Hebron on Christmas Eve and, in the spirit of our Algerian Muslim friends, Cheikh Tayeb el-Okbi[35] (and the Qadi Mohamed Benhoura), to make the consoling visit that they made there to the Muslim refugee camps in February 1950 while they were united in prayer with us. We gave a few toys to the children in the camp, *d'el 'Arrûb* and we received a little water at Mamre drawn from the well of Abraham by an old widow named Fatima.

The Badaliya is neither a rule of prayer nor a systematic method of propagating the faith. The Badaliya is a way of putting ourselves at the spiritual disposal of Jesus in His desire for souls, so that we can answer His call in their place. This is a spiritual displacement through which we offer Him hospitality in those other souls, with complete humility, modesty and faith. The deepening of this spirit does not preclude our going to pray in the blessed places where our patron saints offered themselves to souls in the spirit of "Badaliya," whether we transport ourselves there

---

[35] Massignon's note: "Let us pray for a new desire for rapprochement with the Catholic Church which is taking shape at this moment in Arab managed areas in Muslim Egypt."

Massignon was very close to Cheikh Tayeb el-Okbi, president of the Ulemas of Algeria, who, before the Algerian war of 1934 to 1945, created the Circle of Progress there advocating a purified and modern Islam.

mentally or whether we make the actual journey, (provided it is occasioned by grace and not by curiosity). Thus, those of us who were able, went to pray in Tamanrasset, in the "bordj" where Father de Foucauld died without anything to show for his apostolic work, and there we gained a better understanding of why he is one of the two sources for our vocation of substitution with our Muslim brothers.[36] Happy are the fraternal souls among us, who were able to go to Damietta this year, in the name of us all, to thank St. Francis of Assisi for offering himself with Jesus for the conversion and salvation of a single soul.[37] At least as much as Foucauld, St. Francis is our master in "Badaliya," as he bore the visible signs of it in receiving the stigmata of Compassion. Indeed it was just and right that the first female member of the Badaliya who was allowed to make her solemn vows in a religious congregation, should have gone this year to pray with St. Francis at Mt. Alverna before taking up her new commitment among the Sisters of Foucauld in Rome.[38]

It is with great fraternal joy that we see the spirit of Badaliya being brought to particular congregations who seek to understand and practice it. We are just a group of beginners who, like the friend of the Bridegroom, sow the kind of desire that moves souls to give themselves to God, and leave it up to Him, and them, to clarify the way of responding to this gift. Depending on our circumstances, we strive, each one according to our ability, to develop our adaptation to the Arabic language (a)[39] and our knowledge of the various forms of Islamic prayer and beliefs. We look lovingly at these for evidence of the One Truth, and venerate the fragments of grace found there and the calls from the Holy Spirit, without Whom piety would no longer exist. We combine them with the all-pow-

---

[36] In November of that year Massignon and his wife were able to complete the pilgrimage to Tamanrasset that they had tried to do on their honeymoon in 1914 but were stopped by the authorities due to World War I.

[37] An allusion by Louis Massignon to his ordination to the Melkite priesthood on January 28, 1950 and his vow of substitution for his friend Luis de Cuadra made at that time.

[38] Iva Kemeid, a cousin of Mary Kahil entered the Little Sisters of Jesus in 1946. Despite ill health she was able to serve as the assistant for the entire Middle East to the foundress, Little Sr. Magdeleine, until her death in 1962, a few months before that of Louis Massignon.

[39] (a) Extended to the liturgy in Arabic.

erful plea of the suffering Christ in His agony and of his Sorrowful Mother. Let us imitate Blessed Robert d'Arbrissel, a preacher of the first Crusade on Islamic soil who dedicated his Order (Fontevrault, whose missal included a special office for the feast of St. Abraham) to these words that Christ said to St. John from the Cross, while showing him the Virgin of Sorrows and Intercession standing on Calvary, "Here is your Mother." Let us keep in mind that the unique source of our substitution for the souls of our separated brothers, *our spiritual direction*, springs from this maternal, and at the same time Virginal heart that teaches us that our vow of abandonment must be as intense as it is modest. The Marian desire for souls is not a literary fantasy like that in the works of earlier novelists who called themselves "Lovers of Souls."[40] Rather Our Lady, Mary assumes all the flaws of sinners in her pierced Heart, and She assumes them not through her own spirit but through the infinite and unrecognized purity of Jesus. With a humility we cannot possibly imagine, she brings her own offering as a "Spouseless Virgin" to the divine Transcendence, bringing about this reconciliation for which Jesus as Priest dies in order to rise from the dead with us in the Church, which is "identical" to Our Lady.

Once again, the Badaliya is not a joint research project on the statistical results of evangelization. Nevertheless, the question was raised at least three times this year, as to whether badaliya-ites should play a part in the [eventual] baptisms of those for whom we "substitute" ourselves. We neither have to request it nor refuse it, but we should insist that a discernible maturity be present in the desires expressed by neophytes. But if their desire for a sacramental consecration of their attraction to God is truly and purely this same desire for God that we are called to seek for all those souls, and in all of them, we have no choice but to answer their call, with due consideration for the ad hoc regulations of the church hierarchy in the place where we happen to be. For we desire to "become One" with Christ, forever, and at any price.

---

[40] At the beginning of his literary career Maurice Barrès (1862–1923) defined himself in this way in his *Du sang, de la volupté, de la mort: un amateur d'âmes (souvenirs de voyages)* 1894.

Annual Letter # V

Paris, Cairo Dec. 7–8, 1951

I n the course of this year, amid the considerable anxieties and difficulties that were not small for most of us,[41] we strived to reflect
more deeply on our inner vocation of "substitution" for the afflicted
and the oppressed, as well as on our duty to bear witness as believers who
pray, and declare that we pray, when divine Justice is publicly violated.

The Paris Badaliya prayed at the time of the grossly unjust execution of the Vietnamese hostages in Dalat[42] because one of the distinctive
features of our vocation among our compatriots was at stake, the sacred
respect for the right of asylum.

During a flurry of anti-Muslim attacks in the French and Belgian press,
the Paris Badaliya prayed for one of their members who went the next
day with a few friends to meditate in front of the *musalla*[43] of the Paris
Mosque on October 19th at 2 pm, during the solemn Friday prayer. Our
purpose was to show our respect for the faith that was insulted, [that of]
our friends, fellow citizens and Muslims in Africa and the rest of the world,
with whom we intend to "substitute" ourselves more and more before the
God of Abraham, especially at trying times. [We will do this] in Morocco
as well as in Egypt.

During the Catholic Conference on Refugees held at St. Odile in Alsace,
we were able to campaign for the continued activity in times of peace of

---

[41] Suffering due to the conflicts engaged in by France in Indochina, Morocco and Egypt
that reeked of broken promises as well as Massignon's temporary rupture of relationship with Mary Kahil, imposed by her spiritual director at the time, Fr. Maurice
Zundel.

[42] Dalat is in South Vietnam where efforts to resolve conflicts with the freedom movement failed.

[43] *Musalla* is an open space outside of a town or in front of a mosque.

an international organization to protect Refugees and Displaced or State-less Persons, who are our divine guests. We also campaigned for the creation of neutral security zones for Refugees in times of conflict. (Much like we envisioned for the preservation of the world's artistic treasures, and as the Geneva Convention of August 12, 1949 envisioned for wounded persons cared for by the Red Cross). Our goal is to prevent Refugees from being mobilized as mercenaries after being interned as "political hostages:" a double sin, which risks fomenting disaster for the UN.

The Cairo Badaliya was pleased to see one of its members restore a parish of the Eastern Rite in Jordan where another member will settle next year.[44] The Badaliya continues its works of mercy as well as its work in the intellectual sphere by engaging in a series of lectures on the theological perspectives that offer possibilities of a rapprochement between Muslims and Christians.

The Badaliya groups in Beirut and in Casablanca are in the process of being reorganized. Last but not least, the anniversaries of the Marian liturgy on Aug. 14–15th, September 8th, and September 19th, allowed us to deepen our reflections on the rule of life demanded of members of the Badaliya by a Marian spiritual orientation, as presented in our letter # III: "All the intensity and the modesty of our vow of abandonment" was taught to St. John by the pierced, virginal Heart of MARY at the unique moment, in the inner life of the nascent Church, when the words of Christ on the Cross, "Woman, behold your son—behold your mother," prepares them both for the thrust of the spear. "The adoptive Son took Her into his home."

This is the central mystery of our Badaliya about which we went to Ephesus for further reflection on September 19th (feast of our Lady of La Salette). According to St. Grégoire of Tours and St. Willibald of Eichstatt (in 723–726), it is in this mountainous area "near Ephesus," that St. John loved to pray for long hours for the Christian people. How could he have prayed in any other way than by uniting himself to the sorrowful compassion of his adoptive Mother and to her interior outcry, about which St. Ignatius speaks in his epistle addressed to Ephesus (XIX). [St. John was thereby] "substituting" himself for Her who had survived [Jesus' death]

---

44   Fr. Georges Dumont, a Belgian Priest from the Société Auxiliaire des Missions (SAM) friend of Massignon and Kahil's study center the Dar es Salam in Cairo.

for the sole purpose of forming this new son in the suffering image of her Only One. It is to this harrowing yet hope filled meditation that the members of the Badaliya are invited according to our vocation. [Praying] before an image of Our Lady of Seven Sorrows such as Our Lady of Absam (near Innsbrück), they are led into this mystery of Ephesus, which is not only what the Spaniards call *la Soledad*, the dark night of Good Friday, but also a vivifying compassion with the Cross where St. John has us participate in his filial tenderness for the sorrowful Mother, and for all endangered souls that this maternal and torn heart was offering, along with her inner desolation, to divine mercy.

Ephesus is certainly the place where St. John lived, meditating on his Gospel (so full of the intimate knowledge of Christ)—and his Apocalypse (written nearby, on the island of Patmos) until He comes for him in an ever more poignant union with Our Lady's Compassion. It is also almost certain that Ephesus is the place to which St. John took the Blessed Virgin to live, away from Palestine [where she was subjected] to growing threats and suspicions. And this little house on the mountain, mentioned earlier, where St. John would go by himself to pray "for the people," is perhaps the place where the Dormition of the Blessed Virgin took place.

We shall not enter the debate over the two opinions on the place of the Dormition—Jerusalem (Gethsemani) or Ephesus (Panaya Kapouli)—but let us note that it was in Ephesus that the Mystery of the Marian Compassion, first experienced by St. John, was made manifest through the definition of Mary as "Theotokos" (Mother of God) by the Council of Ephesus in 431, "Holy Mary, Mother of God, pray for us... in the hour of our death" (as the Latin Christians say).When founding the imperial church of Blachernae 17 years later, Empress Pulcheria (who protected the Council of Ephesus), gave it the new ecclesial title of "Mother of God" and in order to protect Constantinople, the City of Christianity's triumph, she placed relics of the Blessed Virgin in the church, notably her great Veil (*Maphorion*), the "Pokrov" of the Russians, already prefigured in the feasts of July 2nd (transfer of the small veil to Blachernae) and October 1st that celebrates the vision of St. Andre Salus c. 909. In this same consecrated chapel, after weeping for a long time, the saint saw the Blessed Virgin, supported by the Precursor and by St. John, spread her *Maphorion* over the people as a sign of her tutelary protection. (See Ménées, May 28).

In its letter of October 6th the Melkite Patriarcate kindly let us hope for the liturgical restoration of the Marian feast of October 1st.[45] We are praying that it may then be instituted as the "patron feast"[46] of the Badaliya because it is the Feast of the interceding Compassion of the Blessed Virgin, substituting herself through her Immaculate Tears for us sinners that we may be reconciled with God.

For our calling, Ephesus is not only the City of the Theotokos and of St. John. Two of our members who were there also visited the tomb where the Magdalen remained buried until the 10th century (she was then transferred to Constantinople, and perhaps moved again to St. Baume in 1279). [Her tomb] lies at the entrance to the catacomb of the Seven Sleepers, these confessors of the Christian faith, who were "buried alive," and for the last thirteen centuries have been invoked every Friday in all the mosques as the Holy Intercessors of the Last Days (according to chapter XVIII of the Qur'an). Members of the Badaliya will take invoking them to heart, for these Seven Sleepers (whose catacomb is surrounded by more than 700 tombs of pilgrims and contains numerous graffiti by visitors) have their feast on July 27th in the Roman martyrology and on August 4th and October 22nd in the Eastern synaxarion.[47] Muslims celebrate them on the 13th of *Rajab* and the 4th of *dhû'l-qa'da*.

In the course of these liturgical days, may all these dry details not make us lose sight of the effect of grace in our unworthy hearts which are more and more "engaged" in the daily reality of giving our lives to the Lord.

Let us pray with our Patriarch, who went to Jerusalem last month to pray for the Arab nations and for their reconciliation with Europe. Let us also pray for all the Turkish Muslims, who for the last two years have been going to Panaya Kapuli near Ephesus to pray to the Blessed Virgin, "Hazreti Meryem Ana."

---

[45] Massignon's note: This Marian feast was restored by the Orthodox Church of Athens but moved to October 28th.

[46] On October 1, 1952 Massignon designated Our Lady of Pokrov (the veil) as the patron saint of the Badaliya.

[47] Synaxarion is the book of biographies of the Saints with short descriptions of their feast days in the Eastern Churches.

Annual letter # VI

New York, Dec. 16–17, 1952

This last year was particularly solemn and "trying" for our little Arab community of prayers and sacrifices. Due to the social unrest in January and the revolution on July 23rd,[48] which brought about such important social justice reforms, the Cairo "Badaliya" found itself praying more than ever, and offering all its hopes to God, for the separated brothers to whom we gave ourselves from the depth of our souls with St. Francis and St. Louis in Damietta, and with Foucauld in Nazareth.

The pursuit, until death, of our goal, [which is to pray for] the glorious manifestation of *Isa ibn Maryam* [Jesus son of Mary] in the hearts of our Muslim friends, who so profoundly honor the purity of the Blessed Virgin, and await with so much faith the triumphant return of her Son "to fill the world with justice that until now has been filled with iniquities,"[49] led us to pray beside them in Hebron near the tomb of Abraham. And there, in January 1952, they told us that they were praying for the quick return of Jesus and His reign of justice. (This was in Beni Naïm on January 13th, which is traditionally identified with Kafr Barucha, the place where Abraham came to watch the divine Fire raining over Sodom). We also visited Refugees held in their camps nearby.

We know that the Al-Aqsa Mosque, south of the Jerusalem Temple, is the place to which the founder of Islam was transported (in a vision)[50]

---

[48] After the Israeli defeat of the Arab armies in Palestine, the Anglo-Egyptian treaty of 1936 was denounced leading to uprising in the streets and governmental instability. On July 23rd 1952, led by Nasser, the democratic and socialist Republic was established and entrusted to General Muhammad Naguib.

[49] The Qur'anic verse 43:61 and numerous *hadith* (sayings of the Prophet) validate this eschatological interpretation but others dispute it. See Maurice Borrmans, *Jésus et les Musulmans d'aujourd'hui*, Paris, Desclée, 2005, p. 315.

[50] The first Mosque is the Ka'ba in Mecca and the second, constructed by the Umayyads in Jerusalem, has been known since then as the Al-Aqsa. Massignon

by the desire to ensure that the benefit of Abraham's sacrifice be extended to the Arabs, Abraham's children through Ishmael, the son of Hagar. We also know that 20 years later the Muslims entering Jerusalem identified the Al-Aqsa with the church of the Mother of God "Theotokos," that was in that place—a place precisely named in the Qur'an as the place of the *Marian vocation*, the *Mihrab Zakariya, the place of the Presentation of the Virgin at the Temple.* It is the place where She consecrated herself to God, preparing her entire destiny for our salvation under the protection of *Zachariah.*[51] The Qur'anic verse on the Temple *"Mihrab of Zachariah,"* is written on the *qibla* of many mosques, especially in Constantinople, and particularly when they were once churches. In that way they conserve a Marian character and testify to the respect that Muslims have for the contemplative vocation of the Virgin Mary.

For Muslims the Al-Aqsa Mosque is also evidence of the authenticity of their Prophet's vocation, and as Christians, we should take Muhammad's testimony into serious consideration when he reproves the Jews for denigrating the honor of the mother of Jesus. We therefore had the duty to defend the charitable trust founded in the XIVth century at the very door of the Al-Aqsa Mosque (Door of the Maghrebines), by the Andalusians who had taken refuge in Tlemcen (Algeria, now a French colony). This trust, known as the *Waqf of Abu Madyan Choaib,*[52] depends on income generated by the cultivation of lands in Aïn Karem, (St. John in Montana, the probable place of the Visitation), that are lands currently sequestered by the State of Israel. Thanks to the sorely missed Consul General, René Neuville, to the Christian Committee on Franco-Islamic friendship (Jean Scelles), and to the Grand Vicar of Algiers, Msgr. Poggi, who was born in Tlemcen, we were able to create an Algerian supporting committee in Tlemcen, that obtained two annual subsidies (2 million

---

adopts the prevalent Muslim interpretation of the Qur'anic verse 17:1. Others interpret that it refers to a mosque found in heaven.

[51] The chapel on the left remains dedicated to the Presentation.

[52] Abu Madyan Shu'ayb (1126–1197) is a celebrated mystic in Andalusia, Spain, who lived and died in Tlemcen, Algeria where he became the patron saint. The *waqf* which was established to provide hospitality to Muslim pilgrims in Jerusalem was dedicated to the saint. After the six day war in 1967, Israel occupied this Muslim neighborhood in Jerusalem that had been protected by Jordan and leveled much of it to establish an esplanade providing access to the western wall.

francs) from His Majesty, the Sultan of Morocco and from His Highness, the Bey of Tunis. The committee also obtained a solemn and unanimous vote from the Algerian Assembly (including the French settlers) in favor of a proposition from its vice-president, Mr. Mesbah, asking the French government to ensure respect for the Waqf Abu Madyan.

In the same spirit we took part in [supporting] the films and lectures presented in Muslim countries instigated by Reverend Father Abdeljalil, OFM,[53] on the Virgin Mary in the Muslim tradition. Several facts in this tradition such as the Presentation of the Virgin at the Temple, are not mentioned in the Four Gospels, but they are sanctioned in the Church by the Roman and the Byzantine liturgies on November 21st. (See the feast of St. Zechariah, on September 5th in the Byzantine Rite).

Several of us visited the old Byzantine church in Damietta, *Keniset el-Arwam* (a feast celebrated on September 8th), which is so important for the Badaliya. In memory of St. Francis in Damietta, a Mass was celebrated in San Francisco, [U.S.A.] (in addition to being the largest city dedicated to this Saint, San Francisco is also the place where the "Mission Dolores" for poor Indians was founded. The large convent of Franciscans of the Holy Land in Washington took great pains to replicate the Mission's chapel, which is part of an ensemble of reproductions of the main Christian pilgrimage sites, and of the Roman catacombs, all made of fragments of stones from the Holy Sites in Nazareth, Bethlehem, and Calvary. [We were able] to venerate them there). One of us was given the chance to identify the Muslim counselor to Melik Kamel, who met with St. Francis in Damietta. His name was Fakhr Fârisî, who was a disciple of Hallaj and his tomb still exists in the Qarâfa of Cairo (S.E. of the tomb of Imam Shafi'i).[54]

The intensifying of the sacrifice of Abraham, so very Christian, as it is "symbolized" by the Muslim Hajj to Mecca, and as it was achieved by

---

[53] Father Jean Abd al-Jalil OFM was a Muslim convert to Catholic Christianity and became a Franciscan Priest. His correspondence with Louis Massignon was published in a French edition by Les Éditions du Cerf, *Massignon-Abd al-Jalil Parrain et filleul 1926–1962*, presented by Françoise Jacquin, Paris. 2007.

[54] Massignon did an extensive study of this Cemetery in Cairo. His article *"La cité des morts au Caire"* appeared initially in the *Bulletin de l'Institut Français d'Archéologie Orientale*, LVII, 1938, pp. 25–79 and can be found in *Opéra. Minora*, vol. III, pp. 233–285 and in *Ecrits Mémorables*, vol. II, pp. 441–452 Éditions Robert Laffont, 2009).

the Muslim mystic and martyr, Hallaj, who died as an "anathema" for his Muslim brothers in Baghdad in 922,[55] led us to interest some Muslim souls in his doctrine during two visits to Baghdad (Dec. 1951, March 1952).

The Farsi edition published in Kabul of a summary of his life created quite a stir in Afghanistan. During three months (Sept.-Dec. 1952) of lectures given in the United States at several universities (in response to an official invitation motivated by the gratitude of a Muslim man who was led to Christ by studying the death of Hallaj), the English speaking audiences, mostly composed of reformed Christians, were asked to turn their attention to the importance, for the spread of Christ's influence in the world, of the Muslim's annual meditation on the Hajj, on the prophetic Sacrifice of Abraham, and on its realization in Islam by the "abdâl," the humble, compassionate, hidden intercessors sacrificing themselves each year for the entire population.

A Mass was said on July 27th in honor of the Seven Sleepers of Ephesus, those Christian Martyrs who are also the Intercessors at the Muslim prayer on Fridays. The Mass took place in churches [dedicated to them] in Vieux Marché, in Plouaret (France), and in Ruhstorf near Passau (Bavaria), for the intentions of the Badaliya.

In Montreal we prayed in very close union with the Sisters of Foucauld (205 Murray Street), and with Fr. George Briand, a worker priest from Croydon on the East bank of the Saint Laurence river, and with Fr. Matéo-Crawley for Reverend Mother Mary Agnes, born Violet Susman, who died February 20, 1950.[56] A Muslim academic from Bengal, Professor Muhyieddin from the University of Dacca, told us how, in Chittagong and Faridpur, it is precisely the meditation on Hallaj's martyrdom which

---

[55]   The life, witness and influence of the 10th century Sufi martyr and mystic of Islam, al-Hallaj lies at the heart of Massignon's 50 years of research and his own spirituality. His definitive thesis, *La Passion de al-Hallâj, martyr mystique de l'Islam*, Paris, Gallimard, in 4 volumes in 1975 was translated in 1983 by Herbert Mason. Princeton, NJ: Princeton University Press as *The Passion of al-Hallaj: Mystic and Martyr*. A one volume summary was published in 1994.

[56]   Violet Susman was an English Jewish woman who was baptized in 1922, was an admirer of Charles de Foucauld, entered religious life and became a spiritual "substitute" for the most abandoned in the Sakuramachi hospital in Tokyo. She died in 1950 as Mother Mary Agnes of the Sisters of the Annunciation in Dover.

is now saving the cult of the God of Abraham from the reaction of the Hindu Shaytaniya.

Thanks to his trip to the US, one of us was able to check the traces left in Franco-Canadian and Franco-American souls by the sacrifice of a twenty-year-old child who died in the spirit of the sacrifice of "Badaliya," of substitution, for the souls of French settlers in Madawaska, New Brunswick, on October 20, 1935.[57] He died in Paris without being able to go to Madawaska (but his sister went there eleven years later). After seventeen years, the fragrance [of his sacrifice] persists and Masses were said, notably at St. Basil of Madawaska, a parish founded in 1792, and at St. Anne of Madawaska in New Brunswick. The whole Franco-American issue of the possibility of complementary relations between the French and English languages within an international bilingualism [which is a] promoter of worldwide Christianization, is already contained in the problem raised by this humble prayer for the survival of the Franco-American working class in the Northeast of the United States, (Maine, Massachusetts, Connecticut, N.Y. State, Rhode Island) and in Louisiana. Dechristianization due to industrialization and to the disappearance of their French heritage, is proving to be a looming and serious threat to the workers in Montreal (the second French city in the world to be dominated by Brother André's St. Joseph's Oratory, as Paris is dominated by the Sacré-Cœur). Prayers and Masses were said there, as well as in Nova Scotia and Louisiana for a Christian reconciliation on social grounds, a Franco-English reconciliation in the spirit of the sacrifice of St. Joan of Arc whose statue overlooks the plains of the battle of Abraham in Quebec, and whose other very timeworn effigy still stands in front of the church in Napoleonville, south of New Orleans (the daughter of the Maiden's city).

---

[57] Massignon's visit to this area was due to an invitation to give a series of talks in American Universities. His first stop was to the Canadian border where his son Yves, who died of Tuberculosis in 1935, had begun a study for his Graduate School diploma on the nonviolent resistance of a small catholic colony to the Anglo-Protestant conquest in Madawaska, Canada. Massignon had written a preface for his son's incomplete study that appears in *Parole donnée*, Éditions du Seuil. Paris 1983. pp. 250–253 as *La Haute-Vallée du Saint Jean acadien*. At the end of World War II Massignon's daughter, Yves sister, Geneviève, an ethnologist, went there to collect popular stories in the dialect of the region in relation to her thesis on Acadia.

We visited the main communities of Arab Christian expatriates in North America: Our Lady of the Assumption in Brooklyn (Msgr. Skaff), St. John the Baptist in Chicago (Rev. Fr. R. Briand), Our Lady of the Redemption in Detroit (Rev. Fr. Agapios Riashi), and Notre Dame in Montreal (Msgr. Chatawi, Rev. Fr. Greg. Abboud) are all Greek Catholic Melkite churches. There are also numerous Maronites in these communities. They were told about our little prayer association.

Among Jewish circles, which are so powerful in North America, we met some noble souls who venerate the memory of Judah Magnes, the founder of Hebrew University in Jerusalem, who wanted the new State of Israel to be a bi-national, Judeo-Arab state in which the sons of Abraham would have all been *equal*. Our first visit was to his grave in Cypress Hill, Brooklyn.

We also prayed in the place where Abraham Lincoln, "Father Abraham," as the Negroes call him, was assassinated in Washington (1865) for bringing about the emancipation of the Negro slaves after ordering a day of solemn fast ("day of humiliation, fasting and prayer," April 30, 1863). [He ordered the fast] so that justice might be brought to the oppressed, the "*mustad'afin*," as they are called in the Qur'an, which is a gesture worthy of Gandhi that no other US president appears to have dared to repeat.

Even the Masonic lodges, which are very influential (and officially recognized) in the US, are willing to consider the question of "equality," for Muslims that His Excellency Msgr. Fulton Sheen courageously raised on the radio in New York. In Alexandria (near Washington, on the road to Mt. Vernon, where George Washington is buried), an enormous "Masonic National Monument" shaped like a lighthouse was erected by a Masonic sect founded in 1870, whose members wear the fez, the *keffie* and the *iqal*, [rope holding the traditional head veil, or *keffie* in place] and have Muslim names (although they do not know Arabic), and call themselves the "Ancient Arabic Order of Nobles of the Mystic Shrine." These Shriners, who have over 200 lodges in the US, do not venerate the Temple of Jerusalem, but the Taj Mahal in Agra.

We prayed to God in St. Louis, the largest city ever dedicated to our St. Louis of Damietta. In 1927, one of the sons of that city, Lindbergh, the aviator, came to pay his respects to Notre Dame in Paris aboard the "Spirit of St. Louis," which he thought would have struck a chord in the hearts of the Parisians.

Living our inner "cloistered" life, under the great Veil, the "Pokrov" of the *Panhagia*, we reflected on Mary's feast (Oct. 1ˢᵗ for the Russians and the Ruthenians) while trying to participate in Saint John's reflections, the "son of Mary," in his house in Ephesus that symbolizes the consummation of the Christian life, just as the house in Nazareth is the symbol of its origin. Meetings were able to take place in Cairo, Paris and Casablanca. A project for a book in the spirit of the Badaliya, initiating readers into the Arabic language and the institutions of Muslim countries, is under way. After founding the Oseïran-Mallouk-Sawwaf, Fr. Azouz, supported by His Excellency, Cardinal Tisserant, is founding another charity in Islamic countries.

Letter to Pope Pius XII in Rome

Paris, September 4, 1953.

My Dear Holy Father,

The little sodality of the Badaliya, born in 1934[58] in Damietta, prostrates itself in praising God,—under the apostolic blessing that You sent to it August 19th (S.S. # 305.732); to the France-Islam Committee;[59]—as promoters of the fast on August 14th,—that the Badaliya had expressly asked to advertise—among prayerful souls of compassion.

In our foundational charter it is written that "Islam expressly holds in its imperfect Muslim tradition, as an imprint of the sacred face of Christ, who we worship, as ISA IBN MARYAM, that we want to make Islam rediscover in its heart."

And now God wished that within the Islam found in Morocco we make it rediscover, "rediscover in itself" this adorable Face, of the ravaged Christ; ridiculed, bloodied; since August 20th, for nine months, a regime of terror has trampled an unarmed people in French Morocco, where their celebration of the Sacrifice of Abraham was desecrated.[60]

Several thousands of these oppressed Muslims joined us in our fast for the Vigil of the Assumption, in Fes, with Moulay Benlarbi Alaoui, the

---

[58] Louis Massignon was encouraged in his mission of Badaliya in a private audience with Pope Pius XI on July 24, 1934.

[59] Massignon created "le Comité Chrétien d'Entente France-Islam" with André de Peretti and Jean Scelles in 1947.Peretti remained the President of L'Association des Amis de Louis Massignon in Paris until 2009.

[60] Massignon worked diligently to re-instate the Sultan and resolve the crisis in Morocco. Massignon's note: Deported August 20, 1953 to Corsica then to Madagascar, Sultan Sidi Mohammed V was returned to his people in November 1955. He greeted our representative August 20, 1956 on his arrival in Rabat, receiving him on the 22nd and made our private fast known through Radio-Tanger at noon on the 23rd.

great preacher, at their head. Their fasting makes us hunger and thirst for Justice.

Also we come to ask You, not because of we unworthy Christians who are aligned by double relations to their tormentors,—but in consideration for all these Muslim souls associated with this fast on the Vigil of the Assumption of the Blessed Holy Virgin Mary, of the "Victorious in the battles for God," as You have called her: to bless our vow: to fast from now on, without fail, *every first Friday of the month*; as long as God has not liberated the captives and cured the brokenhearted.

"The measure of our imitation of Him is that of Love" said Father Charles de Foucauld. It is thus their fast, that of the Muslims, and the sacred fast of Israel, the fast of the first Christians, [fasting] without letting up [according to] our profession of "Badaliya," of Substitution, that we ask You to continue to bless as you did on August 14th. It is the offering of our impotent poverty, substituted for these "broken and humiliated hearts." genuflexos et genuflexas benedic, Pater Sanctissime.

p.c.c. Louis Massignon (21 signatures)

Annual letter # VII

Jerusalem 9–13, December 1953

T he beginning of the Marian year, decreed by Pope Pius XII, was celebrated yesterday on the feast of the Immaculate Conception at St. Anne of Jerusalem. It is from St. Anne that we are reviewing this year, so full of promises for our little sodality.

[Our sodality] was in fact called upon by His Excellency Msgr. Descuffi, the Latin Archbishop of Smyrna, to observe the fast on August 14th, the last day of *Siyam al-'Adhra* for the Eastern Christians, and the day when we Christians were joined by 300 Muslims in order to go up to the sanctuary of Panaya Kapulu near Ephesus. The Archbishop read a message to the pilgrims from the Pope opening this sanctuary "to any person professing a special devotion to Mary, without any racial or religious distinction." About twenty monasteries—Trappists, Carmels and especially Poor Clares—members of the Hierarchy, poor or sick people and prisoners answered our call to fast. Our Holy Father, the Pope, blessed this fast (See letter from Msgr. Montini) and the Msgr. from Smyrna thanked us. We know that the Turkish government sent representatives to the celebrations in Ephesus and issued new stamps depicting the sanctuaries of Mary, John and the Seven Sleepers. Two organizations were founded in Paris and Basel.

During the time of the call to fast,[61] from Smyrna, a plaque for the Badaliya was cast, several copies of which were placed as ex-votos [votive offerings] in Damietta, in Cairo, in the church of the Seven Sleepers in Plouaret (Vieux-Marché, Brittany), in Panaya Kapulu and in the

---

[61] Fast of the Virgin.

crypt of St. Anne in Jerusalem.[62] This plaque is similar to Foucauld's but the heart is pierced, and the Arab text replacing the Latin text, adds "ibn Maryam" to "Yasu" and replaces "Caritas" with "Huwa'l-hub:" It is He who is Love. The Poor Clares of Rabat placed this plaque in their meditation room (then had it transferred to Mt. Alverna).[63]

Our first private *fast* took place on Friday, June 12th (the feast of the Sacred Heart which coincided with the last day of Ramadan in the Maghreb) after a Mass celebrated by Rev. Fr. Voillaume[64] for the return of a serene peace in North Africa. A prayer was said in the cell in Dover where Sr. Violet Susman (Reverend Mother Marie-Agnès) died, after a life of self-immolation for Japan and of prayers for the Foucauld fraternity and the Badaliya. Many Muslims from Istanbul to Fez joined in our fasts on June 12th and August 14th. On September 19th, *Quatre Temps de Septembre*, the feast of Our Lady of La Salette, which coincided with the Jewish Kippur and the Muslim Ashura, Jews fasted with us from the Ihud group under Martin Buber's direction, which wants equality between Jews and Arabs in the Holy Land (in memory of Judah Magnes).

This fast, which is to be observed with the discipline of silence following the first Christians, and the tradition in Islam, made a profound impression and gave the participants a deep sense of inner peace. The act of fasting is the virginal basin into which flows the word of divine Justice, the word of Resurrection. Fasting makes us hunger and thirst for

---

[62] Ex-Voto of the Badaliya Described by Louis Massignon
"A plaque was designed and created in September 1953, thirty-three years after our vow to fast monthly, (during the exile of the Sultan of Morocco), the inscription in Latin, "Jesus-Caritas" was translated into Arabic, "Yasu' ibn Maryam huwa l'hubbu," (It is He who is Love), and the heart was pierced.
At the top of the Cross, the sword of compassion burns and seals the Heart of Mary; the angelic reverberation of the Thrust of the Lance of the soldier, felt through the wounds of mystical substitution. It was offered as an ex-voto as often in its Latin form as in its Arabic form in several chapels in the Middle East: Tehran, Baghdad, Damascus, Jerusalem, Beirut, and Ephesus; In Africa: Cairo, Damietta, Namugongo, Tamanrasset, Beni-Abbes, Rabat; and in Europe: Vieux-Marché, Aix-en-Provence."

[63] The Superior, Mother Véronique (Clotilde Vacheron) and her small Greek Melkite community were devoted to the essence of the Badaliya.

[64] The prior General of the Little Brothers of Jesus who were establishing foundations throughout the Muslim world following the spiritual legacy of Blessed Charles de Foucauld.

Justice, which is the consummation of Love. Fasting is an action, an active prayer of Badaliya. We have asked the Pope to bless it every first Friday of the month for the return of a serene peace between Christianity and Islam. The prayer for the dead is also an act of "Badaliya" since it is from our substitution for them, and from it alone, that they can receive the consummation of their love of God.

We were fortunate to have Reverend Fr. Blondel[65] celebrate a Mass at Beni Naïm (formerly Kafar Barik, the exact place of Abraham's great prayer of "Badaliya" over Sodom) with the approval of the Superior Generals of the White Fathers (recruited as early as 1920 by His Excellency, Msgr. Livinhac).[66] As early as 1908 (in Baghdad) and later in 1913 we meditated on Abraham's prayer in its literal and symbolic sense: in relation to a renegade [Luis de Cuadra].

Substitution is the source of the works of mercy, as is hospitality, and two members of the Badaliya have been organizing regular visits to the Muslim prisoners in the Paris jails. Other members, supported by the Church Hierarchy have conducted an investigation into regulated prostitution, still active in North Africa, despite the French law of 1946 and the international convention of 1949 against the enslavement of Human Beings, that France is the only country not to have signed under the pretext that the Muslims want to maintain the regulation. Now, the Qur'anic verse 24:33, prohibits regulated prostitution and denies all validity to the procurer's testimony. We have known of atrocious cases and we are asking everyone to pray for the little Moroccan girl, Fatima Bt. Lahcène, who is still a slave against her own will, and for the Bishop of Fréjus. Pity for the prostitutes and concern for their rehabilitation are essential desires of Our Lady Immaculate, and the Paris Badaliya has decided to pursue the struggle against those in power who live off procuring women (a).[67]

---

[65] Fr. Maurice Blondel (1906–1981) Superior at the time of the Missionaries of Africa (the White Fathers) consecrated his entire life to the formation of Greek Melkite clergy in the Seminary of St. Ann in Jerusalem that was altered due to the restriction of movement in 1967 into a center for international spiritual and biblical retreats.

[66] Mgr. Léon Livinhac (1846–1922) of the White Fathers was one of the first evangelizers in equatorial Africa. It was he who blessed Louis Massignon and his wife in 1914 when they were unable to visit Brother Charles de Foucauld in the Sahara due to the danger at the time.

[67] (a) The Moroccan "bousbire' [brothels] were closed, one after the other, from 1954 to 1956 except in the colonies where prostitution was authorized and regulated.

In the course of this year we understood Mary's compassion, through the feast of the Pokrov (the veil of her intercession, that the Melkite Synod of 1953 examined. She is the patron of our Badaliya), or through contemplating Our Lady in the solitude of Ephesus, before her Assumption, as she reflected on the thrust of the Spear into the Heart of Christ. Our Lady [is] the Queen of the Stigmatized.

A series of lectures (b)[68] on the place of Mary in Islam based on Fr. Jean Mohammad Abd al-Jalil's book, focused as much on Our Lady of Ephesus, whose spiritual influence is becoming worldwide, in Paraguay, Acadia etc., as on the Mihrab of Zachariah at the Al-Aqsa in Jerusalem. An impressively large pilgrimage to Ephesus scheduled for the 1954 Marian year is in the process of being organized, and as Daniel Rops[69] writes, Ephesus is going to have the same importance as Lourdes and Fatima.

Blessed by its protective Archbishop in 1947[70] on the feast of the Epiphany, the day when the Mother of God is inseparable from her Son *Isa ibn Maryam*, as the Muslims say, the Badaliya is abandoning itself to Mary's Compassion at the beginning of this Marian year, and is covering its poverty, its agonizing feelings of powerlessness for all the afflicted and oppressed, under the Veil of the Holy One, whose luminous Tears render Her Victorious in the most supreme of battles.

1. Convocation - February 5, 1954
21 rue Monsieur, Paris 7

The meeting will take place on Friday, February 5, 1954, at 7 pm at the Dames de Nazareth, 20 rue de Montparnasse, (with Adoration in the Chapel at 6:45 pm). It will end with Benediction at 7:45 pm at the close of our monthly day of *Private Fasting*. Accounts will be given from our mission in the East (groups from Cairo and Alexandria, the Damietta visit, Father Basetti-Sani's[71] Franciscan brochure regarding the Franciscan importance of Damietta for Islam); to the Holy Land (conference on the

---

[68] (b) By Madame Charles Barzel (the 99th to the Ferté-sous-Jouarre).

[69] Henri Petiot, known as Henri-Daniel-Rops (1901–1965) was a Catholic historian and popularizer and the author of a monumental History of the Church.

[70] The Greek Melkite, Bishop Medawar in Cairo.

[71] Father Giulio-Francesco Basetti-Sani (1912–2001) an Italian Franciscan who was one of the disciples of Louis Massignon. His books include works on St. Francis and Islam and A Christian reading of the Qur'an as well as one translated into English.

Mihrab of Zachariah[72], Mass in Arabic on December 11, 1953 at Beni-Naïm, with special intention for the Badaliya); to Rome (group started in Rome).

Reports also on the situation of the North African workers and their wives in Paris;

Christian-Islamic relations in North Africa and the prolongation of the incarceration or deportation of the "suspects."

2. Convocation - March 5, 1954
21 rue Monsieur, Paris 7

At the close of our XIth day of *Private Fasting* for a return to *serene Peace* between Islam and Christianity (and Israel), especially in North Africa, set for the first Friday of the month since September 4, 1953, therefore Friday March 5, 1954, meeting at 7 pm at 20 rue de Montparnasse at the Dames de Nazareth. Beginning at 6:45 pm, recollection in the Chapel for 45 minutes then Adoration of the Blessed Sacrament (in the Chapel) at 7:45 pm. We will examine signs of improvement, the level of awareness among Christians overseas since the start of our efforts, and how to reassuringly ask for pardon and amnesty.

3. Convocation - May 7, 1954
21 rue Monsieur, Paris 7

Our monthly day of *Private Fasting* on Friday, May 7 will coincide with the first Friday of the Muslim Ramadan. The day will close in the evening at 7:30 with a Mass at the [Sisters] Soeurs de Nazareth, 20 rue de Montparnasse, Paris VI. During the meeting following the Mass accounts will be given of the Islamic-Christian situation in Tehran and at the convention at Bahamdoun.[73]

See: Basetti-Sani, Giulio O.F.M. 1974. Trans. A.H. Cutler *Louis Massignon: Christian Ecumenist*. Chicago, IL: Franciscan Herald Press.

[72] The Al-Aqsa Mosque in Jerusalem on the Temple Mount, known as the Haram al Sharif in Islam. A Mihrab (niche), found in every mosque points the worshippers in the direction of Mecca. In the Al-Aqsa it is called the Mihrab of Zechariah, the father of St. John the Baptist.

[73] A conference initiated by the American Friends of the Middle East and Pastor Garland Evans Hoplins in the city of Bhamdoun, Lebanon in order to study the

N.B. We are asking our Badaliya members, in memory of that last Friday of Ramadan 1372 (June 12, 1953) when we fasted with our Muslim brothers, to also fast on the last Friday of Ramadan 1373, that is, on Friday, May 28th.

4. Convocation - July 2, 1954
21 rue Monsieur, Paris 7

July 2, 1954 at the close of the monthly day of *Private Fasting*, Mass at 6:30 pm, meeting at 7 pm, 20 rue de Montparnasse, at the Dames de Nazareth. A report will be given on the Vigil at Notre Dame and our efforts towards amnesty overseas.

5. Convocation - October 1, 1954
21 rue Monsieur, Paris 7

Our private fast for the restoration of a serene peace in justice between Christians and Muslims, especially in North Africa, falls on Friday, October 1st.

According to the Byzantine calendar, October 1st is the date of the apparition of Our Lady of the Pokrov in the imperial chapel of Blachernae in Constantinople at the beginning of the Xth century. Supported by the Precursor [John the Baptist] and by St. John the Evangelist, She wept over her people, then spread her veil of intercession (Pokrov in Russian) over them. Our Lady of the Pokrov is the patroness of the Badaliya, and we have requested that the Greek Catholic Rite revive this solemn feast, that the United Ukrainians (who form 5/7th of the Uniate Church) never gave up, and that the autonomous patriarchate of Athens reinstated two years ago. In Marseille, the Latin Archbishop blessed the foundation of an association for the reconciliation between the Greek and Latin Churches that bears the name of *Hagia Skepi*, or "Holy Veil." ("Pokrov" in Russian).

At the request of several people, His Eminence Cardinal Feltin, authorized the solemn celebration in the Eastern Rite of the Office of Our Lady of the Pokrov for the United Ukrainians on Sunday, October 3rd, in the Church of St. Roch (Paris I).

---

spiritual values in the two religions, Islam and Christianity. 74 representatives from 22 countries participated.

We shall pray for all these intentions during our fast on October 1st.

We shall also pray for the Holy Land, too forgotten during this Marian year, and especially for Nazareth, the town of the Annunciation, recently stained by the murder of unarmed Arabs whom the Israeli police gunned down under the pretense that they were communist sympathizers. The blood that was shed there is the very sacrilege against the Virgin of Israel that Dr. Judah Magnes had feared as early as July 1948 (See his letter addressed to us appearing in TEM; Chr. 8.II.48). Let us pray that the Marian year may not end without there being some noble souls among Jewish believers who share in our sadness over Nazareth during their Yom-Kippur (on October 7th). At the request of Dr. Martin Buber—the successor to Dr. Magnes as the head of *Ihud*[74]—several of us will join in this most solemn of feasts this year, as we did on September 19, 1953 (when it coincided with the Muslim *Ashura*[75] and with the feast of Our Lady of La Salette).

We shall also pray that the Franciscan order in Nazareth may not simply let the humble crypt of the Annunciation [Church] be crushed under the enormous heap of stones that international capitalism is erecting there to the glory of Mary, but may also keep in mind that St. Francis would have thrown it all down and gone first to help the poor and the desperate of Nazareth who are being driven by this kind of capitalism toward class war.

At the close of the day of private fasting on October 1st, there will be a meeting of the Badaliya, 20 rue du Montparnasse at the Dames of Nazareth's (after the 6:30 pm Mass).

6. Convocation - December 3, 1954
21 rue Monsieur, Paris 7

Our monthly meeting will be held next Friday, December 3, 1954 at the Dames de Nazareth, 20 rue de Montparnasse. Mass at 6:30 pm followed by the meeting.

---

[74] Ihud (union), a movement aimed at the establishment of an Arab-Jewish, bi-national state in Palestine.

[75] The tenth of the Muslim month of Muharram when Shii Muslims commemorate, through dramatic street processions and passion plays, the martyrdom of the Prophet's grandson, Imam Husayn at Karbala in 680 CE. This event led to the division of the Muslim community into Sunni and Shii, the Sunni caliphate and Shii Imamate.

We will have fasted and prayed especially that peace be re-established in North Africa without massive repression and innocent bloodshed. There will be a report on the Pilgrimage to Our Lady of Fatima[76] [in Portugal] and on the visit to the prisons of Valencia[77] [in Spain] at the end of this Marian year.

---

[76] Accompanied by his wife Louis Massignon made a tour of the Spanish peninsula ending at the pilgrimage site of Santiago de Compostela.

[77] Massignon's Spanish friend Luis de Cuadra committed suicide while imprisoned at Mislata, Valencia in 1921.

Annual letter # VIII

Cairo, December 29, 1954.

H ere in Egypt, which is the epicenter of the Muslim countries, we come together to reflect on the events through which we have followed our vocation of substitution for the "sheep of Abraham" lost in the Arabian desert. (See our original Statutes written at the end of 1947.) We lived through these events from day to day, according to the unpredictable ways of God's grace. After starting the Marian year with Masses for the Badaliya at St. Anne of Jerusalem (the probable place of Mary's conception by her Mother) and in Beni-Naïm (where Abraham prayed for the Cities condemned to being eternally denied hospitality), [we]were able to bring it to conclusion with Masses at Our Lady of Fatima (Portugal), Santiago de Compostela (witness of the Lord on Mt. Tabor and in Gethsemani, with St. John and St. Peter), in Valencia, at the feet of a friend's Patron, Mater Desertorum, Nuestra Seño-ra de los Desamparados, and in a prison, Mislata (a name derived from the Arabic *Manzil 'Ata*), where, 33 years ago, this desperate friend committed suicide. Through the voice of a tertiary female member of his Order, "St. Francis, a saint full of human tenderness," invited the first two members of the Badaliya to offer themselves [to God] for him.

If it is true, above all for Christians, and especially for us, that, as Ibn Arabi[78] thought, the fervent practice of a rule of perfection brings Jesus to life in us, and prepares his Second Coming as Judge, the Marian year did put us in close touch with this truth by frequently answering our miserable supplications.

---

[78] Muhyiddin ibn Arabi (born in Murcia in 1165 and died in Damascus in 1240) is one of the greatest mystics in Islam and the most quoted in Islamic literature.

First, *The Release of Prisoners*. From Cairo, the statutory center of our sodality, it is difficult to understand, let alone imitate the spirit, thanks to the private (and unostentatious) fast we keep on the first Friday of the month, which was able to sustain the campaign for amnesty of political prisoners incarcerated in Paris, throughout France and overseas. Our members and associates, (whose numbers have tripled in Paris with massive memberships from 53 public school teachers, students of teacher training, and strong support from more than 20 convents, especially contemplative ones) all participated in the campaign, especially through *prayer vigils* authorized on June 12th in Notre Dame de Paris by His Excellency Cardinal Feltin with the presider, His Excellency Msgr. Mercier from the White Fathers, Bishop of the Sahara. One vigil, authorized by His Excellency Msgr. Duval, Archbishop of Algiers, and directed by Fr. Jean Scotto, took place in the Husseindey Church in Algiers, and another, authorized by His Excellency Archbishop Martin took place on December 17th in Rouen. In Paris, the silent vigil before the Blessed Sacrament was interspersed with recitations of the mysteries of the Rosary. The joyful mysteries were said in Malagasy by the people of Madagascar, the sorrowful mysteries by Vietnamese men and women (in a deep and poignant lament), and the glorious mysteries in Berber and Arabic. Before his Excellency Msgr. Mercier gave the blessing, a choir started singing the "*Ayyuhâ'Imalik al-samâwi'Imu'azzî*"[79] from the Byzantine liturgy in Arabic.

Shortly after this vigil in Notre Dame de Paris, we heard of the release of a very dear friend, Dr. Sadighi, a Persian historian and philosopher, whom we had been able to visit in the Qâdjâr prison in Tehran in April. Then, of those prisoners whose pardon we had requested at a large meeting of over 2,000 people at the Mutualité[80] on June 24, 1954, a few were released little by little, such as our friend Lyazidi, the brother-in-law of our dear Rev. Fr. Jean Mohammad Abd al-Jalil, and his comrades from the Moroccan Istiqlâl, as well as the Moroccan Qadi Moulay Benlardi Alaoui, a former Justice minister who had fasted with us on August 14, 1953 and was released only recently, after three successive assaults with pleas [for his release].

---

[79] O, celestial King and consoler.
[80] The French Mutual Benefit Insurance System.

Remaining are the Malagasy members of parliament, Christians whose pardon, promised for July 14th, then postponed to August 25th, then to next January 1st, was granted only to one out of seven prisoners, Mr. Rabiala. The Tunisian fellaghas[81] having amnesty, after a smart political transaction, will no doubt obtain an extension of the amnesty to other political prisoners held in Tunisia. We are fervently praying that in the wake of the repression of the Algerian insurgents from the Aurès, wide measures be put in place to free the Algerian political detainees who have been in jail since 1945 and 1952, in often inhumane and definitely discriminatory conditions in spite of our official promises to respect our Muslim fellow citizens and their wives. (The Paris Badaliya offered special prayers for Nedroma in Oran [Algeria], where Muslim women were subjected to harsh treatments from the police that no Christian conscience can possibly tolerate). Economic poverty and the impossibility of voicing any complaint on behalf of their scorned religion and their systematically abused Arabic language, (this is the view of a member of the Badaliya who for the 10th time has just been made president of the jury d'agrégation d'arabe[82]), as well as the openly cynical and pre-arranged elections, may well leave no choice to the Algerian Muslim voters but to join a general uprising.

The admirable little group of Algerian Badaliya-ites, supported by priests from the Mission of France in Souk Ahras, vowed to persevere in our method of "substitution" for our persecuted friends in order to defend, appease and console them, even at the price of death threats and beatings.

Here in Cairo, where roles are in danger of being reversed, and where French capitalists declare "that there is no obligation to be generous when one has possessions to defend" (sic), a statement that Egyptian capitalists could easily throw back at us—we must unwaveringly hold on to our discipline of prayers, fasting, and non-violence. Their brothers and sisters from Paris who come to visit the Badaliya-ites in Alexandria and Cairo know that it is to their silent suffering and disappointments that our groups in Paris, Rome and Lyon owe the grace of the release of the prisoners mentioned above.

---

[81] A French name given to Algerians fighting for independence.

[82] Massignon was for the 10th time President of this jury evaluating students of a competitive examination for University teachers of Arabic.

We are receiving encouragements from all sides. A group of about fifteen French Protestant ministers asked to take part in our monthly fasts for a serene peace between Christians and Muslims, especially in North Africa. Thanks to them, a message from the Badaliya (in Arabic) was read at the "Muslim-Christian Convocation of Bhamdoun (Lebanon) in April, and the "Continuing Committee on Muslim-Christian Cooperation" from Herndon (Virginia, Box 396, USA) is intent on maintaining contact with some of our members.

Increased practice of devotions common to Christians and Muslims:
The Badaliya participated through various activities in the pilgrimages to *Our Lady of Ephesus* (Basilica of the Theotokos—the chapel in Panaya Kapulu where our dear Brothers of Foucauld made their home in March 1955). They have reported on this in detail in letters #4 (3/21/1954), #5 (7/2/1954) and #6 (11/21–26/1954) of the Society of the Friends of Ephesus and of Anne Catherine Emmerick.[83] Let us single out as being of special interest to the Badaliya, the Breton Pardon [pilgrimage] to the *Seven Sleepers of Ephesus* (July 24–25, 1954 in Vieux-Marché, Côtes du Nord, France) where, with the authorization of NNSS of Ephesus, St. Brieuc and Tréguier, Muslims were invited side by side with the Christians; and blessings were obtained. The preacher, Father Pierre Bourdellès, strongly emphasized the importance of the early resurrection of these saints who were buried alive, which deeply affected the Middle East into the Vth and VIth centuries, and they are the main proof in the Qur'an of the general Resurrection.[84] In Brazzaville, Sumatra and also in Turkey the echo of this "pardon" moved Muslim men, and Muslim women even more. In Algeria a Muslim professor who is also a friend, discovered in Guidjel (Ikjan), south of Setif, the seven pillars in honor of the Seven Sleepers (*saba' ruqud*) that the nascent Fatimid dynasty, that later was to found Cairo, erected there while in exile. The [seven saints] were greatly revered because

---

[83] Massignon founded this small organization in 1952 in order to encourage awareness of the spirituality of the visionary German mystic, Anne Catherine Emmerick (1774–1824). The House of Mary in Ephesus, Turkey, attracting both Muslim and Christian pilgrims, was discovered as a result of her visions.

[84] The 18th Sura of the Qur'an is called *Ahl al-Kahf*, the People of the Cave, and tells of the persecution and ultimate resurrection of 7 young Christian men in the 2nd century. The story remains prominent in the Eastern Orthodox Church traditions as well.

they proved that God does not indefinitely let pagan tyrants bury the protests of those who endure martyrdom for the sake of justice. This is a motive for veneration that the Badaliya shares, and not without results.[85]

The Badaliya received reserved but encouraging responses from several Muslim authorities consulted on the possibility of making joint visits with Christians to all the Seven Sleepers' crypts scattered throughout the Muslim world, and even to the Christian crypt of Vieux-Marché, in Brittany. Responses were reserved [not unexpected] from countries hardly liberated from their colonial regimes, such as Indonesia where the devotion moved women but where the religious lawyers point out that Christian missionary works have been so compromised by the Dutch administrators that they fear any Muslim and Christian religious observance of this kind.

A theologian who is playing a part in the renaissance of religious education in Istanbul[86] writes to us that he does not stop thinking about the problem of the Seven Sleepers, that the official restriction of pilgrimages to three holy sites (Mecca, Medina and Jerusalem) should not put aside, since Ephesus is a place of resurrection.[87] He considers it permissible for Muslims to come there to recite the *Fatiha* before beginning their meditation, just as Fr. de Bonneville considered it permissible for Christians as well.[88]

With regard to the pilgrimage to Our Lady of Fatima, which we visited from October 31–November 1, 1954, we are more and more convinced that we stand on the threshold of the mystery of the Marian reconciliation with Islam so intensely desired by the Badaliya.[89] This is why we

---

[85] The Muslim and Christian pilgrimage that Massignon grafted onto the annual pilgrimage in this village in 1954 continues to this day every year on the week-end closest to the Feast of Mary Magdalen on July 22nd in the tiny hamlet of Vieux Marché in Brittany, France.

[86] An Indian Professor, Muhammad Hamidullah, who pursued his doctorate at the Sorbonne under the direction of Louis Massignon.

[87] Massignon's note: and perhaps also of an Assumption [of the Virgin Mary].

[88] *Al-Fatiha*, the Opening, is the first verse found in the Qur'an and is recited by Muslims at the beginning of their prayer at minimum five times daily. Fr. de Bonneville felt that it was also "legal" for Christians to pray it, as did Massignon.

[89] Fatima was one of four daughters of the Prophet Muhammad and his wife Khadija. Favored by the Prophet she married his cousin Ali and bore two sons, Hasan and Husayn. Conflict over succession to the caliphate after the death of the Prophet led

are urgently asking the Badaliya-ites in Cairo to pray before her image at St Joseph of Ismaïlieh (near the Misr Bank), and at her church in Heliopolis. We are working for the erection of a church by the Carmelites in Baghdad dedicated to our Lady of Fatima. While on a mission to Tehran in April, we collected documents on the devotion of Muslim women to Fatima (the daughter of the Prophet), that justify what His Excellency Msgr. Fulton Sheen was writing this year about Esther and Fatima: in the same way that Esther is a figure of the First Coming of Jesus for Israel, (her tomb in Hamadan was visited again by one of us), Fatima may be a "figure of Mary" for the Second Coming. Details on this can be found in vol. 3 (currently being printed) of the "Mardi de Dar es-Salam" ["Tuesdays at Dar es-Salam."]

We all remember the allusion on October 31, 1942, made by His Holiness Pius XII in his act of consecration to the "hidden icon" of Our Lady of Fatima in Russia, which is reserved for the hour of conversion of [that country]. By far the most well-known of all the Marian icons in Russia is Our Lady of the Pokrov (Hagia Skèpi), in the basilica at the palace of Blachernae in Constantinople, revisited this summer in the name of the Badaliya, for whom she is the Patron Saint. Last October 3rd, a solemn Mass [dedicated to her] in the Byzantine rite, with His Excellency Msgr. Feltin as presider, and celebrated in St. Roch Church in Paris, unexpectedly inaugurated a series of radio broadcasts on the Eastern Churches. And thanks to a steadfast invocation to the Blessed Virgin under the Veil of her tears (tears of light), a Russian sacerdotal ordination desired by His Holiness Pius XI, was able to be authorized for the Church of Nazareth during the very last days of the Marian year.

In 1949, an inaugural Mass was celebrated at the request of the Badaliya for the French Bishops' Mission on behalf of the Palestinian Arab refugees. It took place in the church of Gif-sur-Yvette, a parish which includes a very poor hamlet that at one time was named "Damietta" by a lord and companion in captivity with Saint Louis. In 1954, following the celebration of a Mass of thanksgiving in Gif, the Badaliya heard that the bishop of Versailles was creating a new parish for the housing developments in

---

to the establishment of the Shi'ite tradition in Islam. Fatima died shortly after her father and is revered as a holy woman in this tradition. Massignon envisioned a correspondence with her to the appearance of the Virgin Mary at Fatima, Portugal.

this hamlet and had accepted that its church (whose site we visited) be dedicated to *St. Louis de Damiette.*

7. Convocation - February 4, 1955
21 rue Monsieur, Paris 7

As the February circular will be sent out later, this notice is a reminder for our monthly Mass and meeting at the close of our day of private fasting. Mass will be held as usual at the Dames de Nazareth, 20 rue de Montparnasse, on Friday, February 4, at 6:30 pm. Reverend Father Dom Albéric, from Bricquebec monastery and friend of the Badaliya will celebrate Mass. Professor Massignon, back from the Orient and Rome, will join us. The meeting will follow Mass.

February 4, 1955

We will have our next monthly meeting of the Badaliya on the first Friday of the month, February 4, 1955. Mass at 6:30 pm followed by the meeting at the Dames de Nazareth, 20 rue de Montparnasse.

Added to the regular and always current intentions of the Badaliya, we will extend a special thought for the condemned overseas, those in Madagascar.

8. Convocation - March 4, 1955
21 rue Monsieur, Paris 7

Monthly meeting, Friday, March 4, 1955, at the close of our monthly day of private fasting for the renewal of peace in justice between Christians and Muslims (especially in North Africa), at the usual location (20 rue de Montparnasse, Dames de Nazareth).We will begin with Mass at 6:30 pm.

There will be reports on the enquiry into the deported families from Madagascar to Tananarive, as well as the pilgrimage to Namugongo (Uganda) and the Islamic-Christian conference in Alexandria, February 9–14, where, similar to Bhamdoun, our separated Protestant brothers demonstrated their sympathy for our initiative of private fasting.[90]

---

[90] In order to prepare a second meeting in Bhamdoun, 28 delegates met from the 9th to 15th of February 1955 in Alexandria, Egypt and adopted a common Muslim and Christian Declaration

In view of the worsening North African situation and the beginning of Lent, numerous members of the Badaliya have asked us, each in our own way, to be conscious of the serious nature of this canonic fasting period, and to observe a day of fasting weekly, preferably on Fridays from Ash Wednesday to Good Friday as prescribed by the Church. We are to do what we can in a spirit of humility, petition and compassion towards all those who are the recipients of our acts of mercy, acts upon which we will be judged.

9. Convocation - April 1, 1955
21 rue Monsieur, Paris 7

Monthly meeting on Friday, April 1, 1955, at the close of our private fasting day (usually monthly but weekly during Lent), for the renewal of peace in justice between Christians and Muslims (especially in North Africa), at the usual address (20 rue de Montparnasse, Dames de Nazareth) beginning with Mass at 6:30 pm.

Items on the agenda will include:

1. A broadening of our substitutionary prayer to include our Muslim brothers worldwide by using documented data (especially the IV Index (sacred) to the 4th Edition of the Annuaire du Monde Musulman [Annual Report on the Muslim World], released on March 25).

2. A reminder of their *Mi'râj* feast[91] (linked to the Presentation of Our Lady at the Al-Aqsa Mosque). Project to dedicate prayers to our Lady of Fatima for Muslims, during the Marian month of May.

3. A renewal of the Badaliya in Beyrouth; thanks be to God.

4. Prayer to avert declaration of a state of emergency in Algeria prior to the renewal of our country's unfulfilled promises regarding religious freedom for the Muslims and the teaching of Arabic, contained in the Algerian Statute of 1947.

---

[91] The Muslim feast called Isra al-Mi'raj and falls on the 27th day of the Islamic lunar calendar month of *Rajab*. It refers to the Muslim tradition of the Prophet Muhammad's Ascension to heaven from the Temple Mt. in Jerusalem, the Arab *Haram al-Sharif*, that is now the site of the Dome of the Rock. It was then that he received the revelation for Muslims to pray five times a day.

10. Convocation - May 6, 1955
21 rue Monsieur, Paris 7

Monthly meeting on Friday, May 6, 1955, at the close of our monthly private day of fasting for the renewal of peace in justice between Christians and Muslims, at 20 rue de Montparnasse at the Dames de Nazareth. Mass will begin at 6:30 pm.

Yesterday, on April 29th, the first Friday of their Ramadan (Lent), Muslims in Guinea,[92] faced with the assassination attempts against men and women killed without the authorities intervening against the aggressors, have been fasting as a sign of their grieving, and they have asked us to join them in this fast. We ask all members of the Badaliya who were not contacted in time, as well as all others, to make this participation in compassion their main intention for the private fast on May 6th.

11. Convocation - June 3, 1955
21 rue Monsieur, Paris 7

Monthly meeting on Friday, June 3, 1955 at the close of our monthly private day of fast for the renewal of peace in justice between Christians and Muslims (especially in North Africa), at the usual address (20 rue de Montparnasse, Dames de Nazareth. Mass will begin at 6:30 pm).

All of France is presently anxious about its future in North Africa. For 7 years now, we have not adhered to the Algerian Statute solemnly proclaimed in 1947. For 4 years there has not been a harvest in the Aures and the bees have died in their hives of starvation. We now see the bitter fruit of our lack of material care for these Muslims. Let us try to pray even more humbly and passionately, to fast and suffer, so that our leaders regain their awareness of France's duty towards Islam on time. It is because of the promise made to the French king in Damietta in 1249 that Eastern Christians had forty years of respite at the end of the Crusades. It was through a promise by Islam to the king of France at the battle of Pavia in 1535 that our nation has been able to remain independent in Europe. Let us not be afraid in our turn to keep our promise to the Muslims that we made as we landed in Algeria in 1830 and renewed when

---

[92] The assassination of the well-known Mlle. Balla Camara, later proclaimed a heroine by Sékou-Touré, marked the beginning of this conflict that lasted until 1958. The conflict in Guinea escalated before Sekou-Touré took power in 1956.

entering Tunis and Rabat.[93] At this solemn moment in the vocation of our small endeavor of substitution, we renew our offer. We pray God that we do not let ourselves be tempted by premature gestures that may provoke martyrdom. As that is the ultimate grace and we must be made worthy. We do not hesitate to intervene each time a Muslim is mistreated, that we should endure, in his place, the indignation of our people.

12. Convocation - July 1, 1955
21 rue Monsieur, Paris 7

Meeting Friday July 1, 1955 at 7 pm at 20 rue du Montparnasse at Dames de Nazareth. Mass will be celebrated at 6:30 pm in the chapel at the close of the monthly day of private fast.

Now more than ever we need to pray, fast and suffer, and offer [ourselves] for the renewal of peace between Islam and Christianity on the mainland and overseas especially in North Africa, Tunisia, Algeria and Morocco. Let us beg God to inspire our secular leaders to keep their word, especially in Algeria, where it still remains just a promise.

For the anniversary of our vigil for amnesty at Notre Dame on June 12, 1954, the parish priest at St. Séverin offered a parish Mass on the 17th at 1 pm for our intention of amnesty and made a public announcement. The National Petition with 15, 838 signatures, of which 8, 759 came from Madagascar, was personally handed over to the President of the National Assembly the 21st but the Parliament decided not to discuss the bill and innocent victims have been waiting 8 years in the penal colony. Moreover, the deferment of capital punishment, implored since our June 12, 1954 vigil, is precarious, especially in Algeria.

We ask our members to get permission for Father Peter to visit the slums in Algiers (Fontaine Bleue) as this visit may diffuse present hatred from turning to violence, in Algiers itself.

---

[93] The theme of parole donnée, a promise or sworn statement, was central in Louis Massignon's personal and international relations. Historical broken promises by governments in French history in relation to respecting Islam were a painful reality. Here he is referring to the treaties by the French government with Tunis in 1881 and 1883 and with the Sultan of Morocco in Rabat in 1912. For this reason the first collection of 31 of Massignon's articles published in 1962 by Vincent Monteil was called *Parole donée*. Paris. Juilliard Press.

One of our dearest Muslim friends[94] has paid wonderful homage to the Blessed Virgin, Our Lady of Fatima, in the presence of more than 6,000 people on May 30 in Gaumont, in the name of that same Islam whose many pure young girls fast between the 12th and 14th in the month of Rajab, to imitate the Blessed Virgin at the Temple, awaiting the visitation of the Word of God in silence. This surpasses all apologetics and is the goal of the Badaliya "to find in the depth of the heart" of our friends, the Sacred Face of 'Isa ibn Maryam' [Jesus, son of Mary].

13. Convocation - August 5, 1955
21 rue Monsieur, Paris 7

For our meeting next Friday, August 5, 1955, our day of monthly private fast for peace in Justice between Christians and Muslims, especially in North Africa, we have asked that Mass at the Dames de Nazareth, 20 rue Montparnasse be celebrated as usual at 6:30 pm by Father Cyrille Haddad, one of our senior members. Born in Nazareth, he is the Melkite Rector in Montreal and has just returned from offering Mass on July 27 in the Chapel of the Seven Sleepers of Ephesus at Vieux Marché (North Coast) where three days earlier the traditional Pardon [pilgrimage] was celebrated in the Eastern rite by Monsignor Nasrallah, Rector of St. Julien le Pauvre,[95] in the presence of more than a thousand pilgrims, including more than a dozen of our Muslim friends.

Let us thank God for the release of Dr Raseta, deported to Calvi, and pray God that the French army in Morocco cease firing on young girls who are rebelling against the perjury and false witness that their beloved country is experiencing through our fault. That is the Sign of Women's Indignation that will shatter everything on the Last Day. "Deposuit potentes de sede" [He has put down the mighty from their thrones. From the Magnificat].

P.S. As the 29 rue Montparnasse Chapel is closed in August, Mass will be celebrated at St. Julien le Pauvre (Father Haddad's address: 52 rue René Boulanger).

---

[94] 'Uthmân Yahyâ (1919–1997), an Egyptian, was a well-known specialist on the Islamic scholar and Sufi, Ibn Arabi.

[95] The Melkite Church, St. Julien le Pauvre is located in Paris. Louis Massignon was given permission to celebrate Mass privately there as a Melkite Priest.

14. Convocation - October 7, 1955
21 rue Monsieur, Paris 7

Our members will have their hearts set on attending the Mass at Notre Dame, organized by Pax Christi for peace in North Africa, next Friday October 7, 1955, at the close of our monthly day of private fasting for that peace.

Our meeting is postponed to the following day, Saturday October 8 at 7 pm, 20 rue du Montparnasse (Dames de Nazareth). Mass will be celebrated in the chapel at 6:30 pm.

Let us thank God for the release of the prisoners for whom we have prayed; Dr. Raseta, a member of the Madagascar Parliament, released on August 7; the Justice Minister has authorized us to visit his five companions still retained in Calvi after 8 years; then the eleven F.F.I[96] released last Saturday who were held for eleven years in Valencia, Spain (at the San Miguel de Los Reyes prison that we visited on November 9, 1954. A mass was celebrated at Compostella at the Apostle's tomb on November 16, 1954).

Let us thank God for the successful Franco-Muslim Pardon of the Seven Sleepers of Ephesus at Vieux Marché (North Coast) on July 23, 24 1955 where, despite the present crisis, Muslims joined us even from afar, from Algeria and Mecca. The Bishopric of Saint Brieux and Tréguier has authorized a local committee of *"Friends of Ephesus,"* whose first meeting took place on September 28, 1955 (President: the priest from Cleuziou).

More than ever Badaliya members need to remember that one of their founders was once saved from execution as a spy, in a Muslim country, due to the right of Asylum[97] and that a promise given to a guest, even an enemy, is sacred. The Badaliya is founded on substitution for the Guest, even if he is the enemy, since the Guest is the guest of God. We need, through prayer, fasting and self-sacrifice, to overcome the racial fanaticism that confronts violence with violence in North Africa. Let us serve God first. [Words made famous by Joan of Arc.]

---

[96] Forces françaises de l'Intérieur ("French Forces of the Interior"), the organization of the fighting movements of the French Resistance within occupied France during the Second World War. (Wikipedia)

[97] Massignon is speaking about his own conversion experience in Baghdad in 1908.

15. Convocation - November 4, 1955
21 rue Monsieur, Paris 7

Meeting on Friday November 4, 1955, at 7 pm, 20 rue du Montparnasse (Dames de Nazareth). Mass will be celebrated at 6:30 pm, at the close of our monthly day of private fasting.

The fast offered for suffering Morocco and blest by Pope Pius XII on August 19, 1953 (the day before the catastrophe) was accepted in a mysterious way: unity has been achieved, after two cruel years, around the name of the deposed sultan.[98] Fully abandoning ourselves to non-violence, let us continue to pray, fast and suffer for a serene peace in justice.

Algeria is far from this peace, drawn into an ever more bloody fratricidal struggle in which the desperate on both sides are hounding the innocent. Seeing that in India, in Mahrauli near Delhi, the authorities have revived the old pilgrimage of Saint Qutbuddin Bakhtiyar, where Gandhi had prayed for justice with the Muslims who had fasted with him (this revival took place on October 29, 30 and 31, 1955), let us join in spirit with these Muslim and Hindu pilgrims of Delhi. Let us share in the same hope so that the bloodshed may cease.

16. Convocation - December 2, 1955
21 rue Monsieur, Paris 7

Meeting at the close of our day of private fasting on Friday, December 2 1955 at 20 rue du Montparnasse (Dames de Nazareth) at 7 pm following Mass at 6:30 pm.

There will be a report on contacts made in Algeria, at Tlemcen, Béni-Abbès, Oran and Algiers. We must pray more than ever for an end to the bloodshed.

---

[98] Various parties within France and Morocco agreed to call back the deposed sultan, Mohammed V, who voluntarily abdicated on August 20, 1953 so as to make it possible for Morocco to free itself from French domination. He was reinstated two years later.

Annual letter # IX

Cairo, December 22, 1955

Throughout this year contacts and social exchanges between Christians and Muslims have clearly become more difficult both in the West and in the East.

In the West, in North Africa, the political emancipation of Tunisia, followed by that of Morocco, triggered a crisis in Algeria, that calls the very future of metropolitan France into question. If France does not want to give equal rights to the 400,000 North African Muslim workers who are marrying French women in increasing numbers, Muslim Algeria, owing to an implacable rule of reciprocity, will not want to treat the one million French settlers who live privileged lives there as brothers.

The protest from Muslims who are presently smashing the equipment of co-religionist wine sellers in Paris, should encourage us to get rid of the dealers who are poisoning the French race with alcohol. Conversely, the exalted inviolability of Christian marriage should encourage Muslims to recognize this monogamy in the Qur'an, where it is recommended, and that the Prophet not only observed with Khadija, but also imposed on his son-in-law Ali when he had him marry Fatima.[99] Finally Islam could help Christianity recover two essential notions: the elimination of the procurer's role as a witness in court, and the sacred character of the right to hospitality.

It is not only in Algeria that there is a genuine "war" opposing Muslims and Christians, but also in the Turkish and Arab East. In Turkey, the Greeks were exposed to a brief flare of hatred, deliberately incited. For-

---

[99] Massignon is referring to Sura 4 verses 2 and 129 in the Qur'an about monogamy in marriage.

tunately it did not reach the Turkish pilgrims who continue to go to the chapel of Panaya (in Ephesus).

In the Arab East, where new nations in the process of becoming independent want to achieve their unity, not only with Arabic as their national language but with Islam as their State religion, Christian minorities run the risk of having to return to a regressive Ottoman regime without protective capitulations. Civil courts (*madanî*) would render justice according to some kind of "canonical" laicism, a form of justice penetrated by an Islamic legalism that tends to have as little regard for the morals of Christian families as it does for that of the most backward class of fellahs.[100] As the true Badaliya dictates, it is only by taking into serious account the desires for moral reform of the most enlightened and noble spirits among their Muslim friends that the leaders of Christian minorities will secure total protection for the high, and challenging, moral precepts that Jesus left to them, in order that they may endure in the midst of their fellow Muslim citizens "as salt impregnates, with all of its flavor."

The Arabic version of the Badaliya ex-voto was placed in three new chapels:

- In the Carmel of Antananarivo in Madagascar, in memory of the Masses and prayers said in that city for the release of those held captive; Sultan Sidi Mohammed ben Youssef (visited by one of us in Antsirabé in January, released and reinstated on his throne last month) and the Malagasy parliament members, (deported eight years ago and visited by one of us in the prison in Calvi, Corsica, in August. We know that the French Justice Minister announced that Dr. Raseta is to be released on July 25th, and the others on November 10th).

- At the Martyrium of Namugongo (Uganda) where catechumens of Msgr. Livinhac, Blessed Karoli Lwanga and his companions, were burned. The 70th anniversary of these first martyrs of the White Fathers, who died for the sake of male chastity, is to be celebrated next year.[101]

- On the door of the chapel of the first hermitage of Charles de Foucauld in the Sahara, at Beni Abbès, (where several of us, who had been invited by the Bishop of the Sahara to participate in the establishment

---

[100] French term for peasant, agricultural laborer.

[101] These Catholics and Anglicans were killed on June 3, 1886, declared martyrs and beatified in 1922 and canonized in 1964.

of a Federation of the disciples of Foucauld, testified to their attachment to his original *Directoire*, which has been the main text used for meditation by the Badaliya in Cairo since 1939).

At the session in Alexandria (February 1955) of the American Continuing Committee founded in Bhamdoun in 1954, a delegate from the Badaliya explained our method of "fraternal substitution" (in a text duplicated in English and published in a French translation in the June 1955 issue, Paris, # 321, of "L'Âme Populaire;" it should be published in the USA as well).

On May 30, 1955 (Pentecost Monday), at the closing of the first month of Mary, based on the definition, "Mary, Queen of the World," two associates from the Badaliya, one a Christian, the other an Azharian Muslim,[102] spoke in front of 7,000 people at the Gaumont Cinema in Paris, in order to celebrate Mary, Queen of the World, under the name of "Our Lady of Fatima" in relation to Christianity and Islam (the text appears in the June 12th issue of "l'Homme Nouveau.") The Archbishop of Paris ordered the Muslim text to be printed in "Semaine Religieuse" at the worst moment of the Algerian crisis. In the same spirit we gave the text of the prayers which the Nusayris of Syria[103] have been saying for over a thousand years on Christmas Eve, to the next issue of the Canadian review "Marie," which is coming out in three days.

In relation to this theme, "In Islam, Fatima may be considered as a pre-figuring of Mary for the second coming of Jesus, as Esther was for Israel before the first coming" (Msgr. Fulton Sheen). Three brochures have been published in Paris, Cambridge, and Rome; the first is going to be translated [into Arabic] in Nejef.[104]

During this year 1954–1955 we continued to bring our fraternal support to our Muslim brothers in the five major areas of their religious life:

1) Private fast for Peace between us (especially in North Africa, Turkey and Egypt) on the first Friday of the month.

---

[102] Uthmân Yahyâ (1919–1997) Egyptian specialist on Ibn Arabi.
[103] Members of an extreme Islamic Shi'ite sect from Kufa, founded by Ibn Nusayr, this small community plays an important role in current Syrian politics.
[104] A village in Iraq, 10 kilometers south of ancient Kufa where the tomb of Ali, the martyred son-in-law of the Prophet is a place of pilgrimage for Shi'ite Muslims.

2) Joining the request for help expressed by the Islamic *Fatiha*, on which Fr. Christophe de Bonneville loved to have us meditate with our Muslim friends. We did precisely that in Ephesus (VII Sleepers) and Vieux Marché (Brittany, Seven Sleepers) in July; in front of the Paris Mosque on October 12th for the victims of the Algerian war, especially the women and children fallen on both sides, and at Sidi Bou Medine in Tlemcen on November 13th for those who are preserving access to the Oratory of Zacharia. In the Al-Aqsa Mosque it is the place of the Presentation of Mary, where she devoted her life to God.

In relation to the Fatiha, a critic wrote: "No Christian could remain indifferent to the nobility of thought emanating from it;" but "were the Muslims themselves asking of the Catholics anything more than to turn to God in the faith which is theirs, and with the prayers of their own church?" (sic). The Badaliya demands more; it wants to "have Islam discover within itself, within its heart, the sacred face of ISSA IBN MARYAM already traced imperfectly in its Muslim tradition." This critic is a Latin Christian; if he was from the Eastern Rite, he would understand that the recitation of the *Fatiha* in Arabic does not constitute any sacramental "communicatio in divinis," but only a poignant recourse to the universal witness that any human language gives to God whenever it formulates a fervent prayer to the Judge of Judgment, the God of Abraham.

3) Participation in pious visits and common pilgrimages: this year, on July 23rd, ten or so Muslims at the Breton pilgrimage of the VII Sleepers of Ephesus in Vieux-Marché (Côtes-du-Nord) came out of the crypt carrying candles, joining the Christian procession coming out of the upper chapel in order to participate together in the lighting of the Fire of Joy[105] (see the article by Mme Chauffin[106] in "Die Furche," Vienna, October 22nd, and by André Rousseaux in "Dépêche Tunisian," November 13th). The next day, July 24th, a High Mass in the Byzantine Rite was celebrated in Arabic by the Rector of St. Julien le Pauvre, Msgr. Joseph Masrallah, who had the Breton participants recite the "Creed" and the "Our Father" in

---

[105] After the Saturday evening Mass in the small Chapel of the Seven Sleepers the community processes carrying banners and a statue of the Virgin Mary chanting the Magnificat to the village square where a large bonfire is lit.

[106] Mrs. Yvonne Chauffin (1905–1995) a Breton catholic novelist and Niece of Father de Bonneville. She became a faithful follower of Louis Massignon after meeting him in 1951.

Celtic, their native language. They were very moved to be able to pray in their mother tongue for the first time in this chapel. In this way the Greek-Catholic Rite affirmed its ecumenical vocation in its highest form by uniting Greek and Arabic, Celtic and French, before Christians and Muslims. In relation to the Byzantine Rite, one of us went to visit the only French Greek-Catholic parish in Cargèse (Corsica), whose Algerian affiliate, Sidi Mérouane, near Constantine, must have a pastor who celebrates in Arabic. It seems increasingly clear to people in high places that utilizing an Arabic liturgy in the Church in North Africa, that uses one and the same language for prayer, is the only way to reconcile the Muslims with the Christian settlers.

While we were praying at Vieux-Marché in the chapel of the Seven Sleepers, two Muslim friends went to pray for us at the mosalla of the "*Ahl al-Kahf*"[107] (Muslim name of the VII Sleepers) in Guidjel (*Ikjân*) near Sétif (Algeria). See the "SEVEN SLEEPERS" brochure (with iconography, Paris, Geuthner).

4) Participation in almsgiving to poor Muslims; individual packages were sent to Muslims illegally deported from France, and incarcerated, without trial, in so-called "housing" camps.

An Algerian member of the Badaliya asked in a letter to Rev. Father Michalon[108] that we not forget the Muslims, who venerate Mary, Virgin and Mother, during the Week for Unity (when prayers are said for the union of Churches).

The releases this year obtained for prisoners for whom we fasted and prayed, plus various other answers from divine grace and reflection on their approaching death, led the co-founders of the Badaliya to submit a number of questions to their advisers in the Hierarchy and to their friends:

    a) The Badaliya is a simple Eastern Rite sodality; in order to remain a group of "universal brothers," it should not request a canoni-

---

[107] This Sura 18 in the Qur'an tells the story of the Seven Christian "Sleepers", a resurrection story still honored in Christian Eastern Orthodox churches. Many Icons depicting them can be seen in these traditions.

[108] Founder of an ecumenical center in Lyon, France called "Unité Chrétien" with a revue of the same name published triannually.

cal recognition that would result in reducing the range of its members.

b) It seems that nothing should prevent members of the Hierarchy in charge of Rites from permitting the Badaliya, in a more official manner than it has done so far, to have as its patron The Most Blessed Virgin, known as Our Lady of the Veil (Hagia Skepi, Pokrov); it is the name under which the Most Blessed Virgin answered our plea this spring in Nazareth, for the ordination of one of our most fervent members; it is the icon to which His Holiness Pius XII seems to have pointed as the one Russia "venerates in secret," (while awaiting the fulfillment of the Marian promise of Fâtima).

c) The following question was raised at the Foucauld Conference in Beni Abbès, and also before the Archbishop of Paris (who, with SB [His Beatitude] the Patriarch Maximos V, became one of the two Presidents of the federalized Association of the disciples of brother Charles de Jesus, Père de Foucauld): Should the Badaliya be united with the group of Foucauld's disciples who remained attached to Father Foucauld's original *Directoire*, that their Excellencies Msgrs. de Provenchères, Duperray and Mercier entrusted to M. Massignon at the Conference?

It is important that the Badaliya of Cairo along with those of Alexandria, Beirut, Rome, Algiers and, above all, Paris, reflect, pray, seek advice and give their opinion on this question. Then the members of the small group of Foucauld disciples, who remained attached to the original Directory, should be individually questioned. The link between them is pretty loose as they are all of the Latin Rite, but the specialization of the Badaliya, and the consequences effected by our "substitution" during this Islamo-Christian crisis, individual as they may be (each one bearing witness according to his social situation), may cause them to hesitate in taking the step forward that this question represents.

The fact remains that the question has been raised, and that very dear friends, such as Reverend Father René Voillaume would like "the Latin section of the Badaliya" (Paris and Rome groups) to incorporate itself into the federated Association of Brother Charles de Jesus, founded in Beni Abbès a month ago by means of the "original Directoire."

17. Convocation - February 3, 1956
21 rue Monsieur, Paris 7

Monthly meeting on February 3, 1956, at the close of our day of private fasting for a renewal of peace in justice between Christians and Muslims (especially in Algeria) and for fruitful negotiations in Morocco. Meeting at 7 pm as usual at 21 rue du Montparnasse at les Dames de Nazareth, preceded by Mass at 6:30 pm.

18. Convocation - March 2, 1956
21 rue Monsieur, Paris 7

Monthly meeting on Friday March 2, 1956 at the usual address and time (20 rue de Montparnasse, VI, with Mass at 6:30 pm followed by the meeting), at the close of our day of private fasting for the renewal of peace in justice between Christians and Muslims especially in Algeria (and in Egypt), a preliminary condition for a serious, peaceful settlement in Tunis and Rabat.

Our small endeavor now enters, with Lent, a period of "elective retreat." Let us pray, fast, suffer and offer ourselves so that a little Christian heroism may lift France above retribution by revenge, or renunciation by fear, and towards its true vocation that has set its historical fate in Africa since St. Louis and the Crusades.

Let us plead with our people to treat the 500,000 Algerian Muslim immigrant workers in France seriously and definitively as brothers, that God may then inspire the Muslim majority in Algeria to once again be hospitable to the minority Christian settlers who have imposed a purely materialistic technical progress on them for 125 years without any common hope in the divine promise made to our common Father, Abraham. There will be no salvation for our country or our Church without this.

P.S. Members are invited to join a larger community of prayer for an hour of reflection and adoration of the Blessed Sacrament for the salvation of Algeria. This vigil of adoration will take place on Passion Friday, the feast of Our Lady of the Seven Sorrows, on March 16, 1956 at 7 pm at St. Séverin church (St. Michel or Odéon Metro).

19. Convocation - April 13, 1956
21 rue Monsieur, Paris 7
Good Friday

The church's solemn Fast today unites our small Badaliya to the offerings of our many fellow-countrymen for all victims of the Algerian tragedy.

At the request of Father de Foucauld's disciples, numerous bishoprics in France held a prayer vigil for a serene peace in Algeria last March 23 at the same time as we did at St. Séverin; at St Pothin of Lyon (Cardinal Gelier); at St. Brieuc Cathedral (Monsignor Armand Coupel, on the 25th, for all parishes in the St. Brieux and Tréguier dioceses). And Cardinal Feltin confirmed on March 24 the importance of the appeal that he made known through "La Croix"[109] the previous day.

The North African situation is becoming increasingly disturbing because we cannot reasonably hope to regain the confidence and friendship of the Algerian Muslims other than by the same means used with their neighbors in Tunisia and Morocco; and through a heroic effort in understanding, founded in our common adoration of the same God, the God of Abraham, and in sacred hospitality, as Monsignor Lefèvre, archbishop of Rabat, and Monsignor Armand Coupel, bishop of St. Brieux and Tréguier, have pointed out.

Our next meeting at the close of our day of private fasting will be postponed from the first Friday in April to the second, on April 13 (the meeting will begin at 7 pm at the Dames de Nazareth, 20 rue de Montparnasse, following the 6:30 pm Mass).

On Holy Monday, March 27, we received a remarkable blessing: The six parliamentarians from Madagascar imprisoned since 1947 were released by the President of the Republic on March 22, in time for these Christian brothers to join in the Pascal Alleluia.

Similar to our efforts for Morocco in 1953, we continue to depend on the Christians in Ephesus as the well as the prayers and sacrifices of the Brothers of Foucauld who minister in the Sanctuary of the Assumption, near the Crypt of the Seven Sleepers, cited by both Islam and the Eastern Church. Let us also pray for the Muslim and Christian pilgrimage to the Church of the Seven Sleepers at Vieux Marché, (near Plouaret,

---

[109] *La Croix* is a French Catholic daily newspaper.

North Coast) that our young people in Paris are currently organizing for the end of July.

The Muslim students in Paris showed their solidarity in spiritual friendship with us on the occasion of Mrs. Popovitch's death on March 12; she was one of our original members, one of the 21 signatories to the monthly days of fast that began on September 4, 1953 and blessed by Pius XII.[110] They joined us at the church and the cemetery and they had prayers said for her at the mosque in Paris as well as numerous other mosques in Morocco and Tunisia, in thanksgiving for her great hospitality to them, before the God of Abraham.

We also ask you to pray for the repose of the soul of Reverend Father Soueid, a member of the Badaliya, who died in Mexico where he served as the priest of the Greek Catholic parish.

20. Convocation - May 4, 1956 (Letter written April 14, 1956)
21 rue Monsieur, Paris 7 Ramadan,
April 13, 1956—1375 of the Hegira

This year, Ramadan, the Muslim annual month of fasting, began yesterday. Hundreds of thousands of Muslims, faithful to the Commandment of the Ancient Law, and following Jesus' example in the desert, will fast for 29 days during the daylight hours, that God may forgive sins committed by the Community of believers during the year.

In this solemn year when Islam is caught between two adversaries, it will be a fast with vigorous hope in the triumphal renewal of Islam's power, from the liberated Arab Orient where oil gushed, to the Maghreb where the independence of Morocco and Tunisia exposes the Algerian problem.

Three years ago, on the last Friday of Ramadan, through prayer and fasting in substitution for our separated brothers, believers in the same God of Abraham, we began our monthly private fast for peace in Morocco. Two years later, we were blessed to see this peace, through an unexpected grace, renewed with the legitimate Sultan.

---

[110] Mrs. Popovitch was a Ukranian Catholic who was connected to the Massignon family for many years. She worked with great devotion as a social worker with students from the Maghreb.

Today, when our nation wants to remain in Algeria, feeling that its Christian destiny of life or death is focused on North Africa, it is the "Badaliya's" duty to understand the value, before God, of the great fast begun by all of Islam, first of all for Algeria. The fast is for forgiveness, with almsgiving, meals shared in hospitality and reconciliation. Let us be part of this Ramadan through prayer, that it may remain "open" towards Christians, and not closed by retaliation in hatred and xenophobia. Let us understand it, through daily prayer, and let us unite in Islam's supplication that will culminate with its mysterious Night of Fulfillment, Laylat al-Qadr (literally "Night of Destiny" that Foucauld spoke about), whose undecided date (between the 21 and 29) is popularly set on the 27th day of Ramadan (May 8, this year). This Muslim Night corresponds to what Israel expects from God at the end of Yom Kippur, with Naïla's prayer: the coming liberation that we Christians know to be peaceful, "virginal" and "Marian."

At the initiative of our friends from Tunis, we request every Badaliya to celebrate a Communion Mass in the evening, without homily, fervently and in interior silence, every Friday, April 13, 20, 27, and May 4, during this Ramadan. A Mass primarily to honor the precious Blood of Christ, poured out from his Heart, pierced with a spear when his soul descended into Hell, the Blood that was shed for all mankind without exception, Christians and Muslims. A Mass to redeem the blood of innocent men and sinners, indiscriminately and uselessly shed through all kinds of excesses on both sides. A Mass, finally, to obtain God's Mercy, because there is great suffering everywhere, here on earth.

We are requesting spiritual support from the North African Bishops, the Archbishop of Smyrna (for Our Lady of Panaya), the Cardinal-Patriarch of Lisbon (for our Our Lady of Fatima),[111] the Bishop of St. Brieuc and Tréguier (for the Seven Sleepers of Vieux-Marché) and of our Patron Archbishop, Monsignor P.K. Medawar (requesting him to advise the Archbishop of Aix, leader of the Charles de Foucauld disciples). We will ask the Holy Father for his paternal blessing as we did in September, 1953.

Members in Paris are invited to the Friday Mass at St. Séverin, at 7 pm. They will receive confirmation for the May 8 vigil.

---

[111] Cardinal Manuel Gonzalves Cerejeira, Patriarch of Lisbon from 1929–1971 revealed the third secret of Fatima to the Holy Father that John Paul II published in 2000.

21. Convocation - June 1, 1956
21 rue Monsieur. Paris 7

Let us note that the day after the May 8 vigil in the St. Sulpice Crypt, under the direction of Father Le Sourd,[112] with 300 people united in prayer for our separated brothers in Islam, on their Laylat al-Qadr, the same vigil was celebrated at the same hour with a similar number at Saint-Pothin in Lyon, by the pastor of the Basilica; the abbey of Galard, united in prayer with His Eminence Cardinal Gerlier; in Aix-en-Provence, at Our Lady of Sède, with His Excellency, Monsignor Archbishop of Provenchères presiding; in the basilica of Our Lady of Hope at Saint-Brieuc under the direction of M. the Canon Prudhomme and the authorization of His Excellency, Monsignor Coupel, bishop of Saint-Brieuc and Tréguier. We have not received confirmation of the vigil we requested in Algiers. However, we are told that it was also held in Reims. In all these places, we are indebted to our friends at the Foucauld Fraternity for the majority of participants.

Meditation on the mysteries of the Rosary at the St. Sulpice vigil allowed us to emphasize a number of devotions common to Muslims and Christians, both the Ascension of our Lord as well as the Crowning of Our Lady. We are reminded that in Islam, she is *"sayyidat al-nisâ"* (Queen of women), in the sense that we greet her in the Hail Mary, and also in the invocation "queen of the world" proclaimed by Pius XII on November 1, 1954, in relation to Our Lady of Fatima, assigning her the liturgical closing of the month of Mary.

Next Badaliya meeting on Friday, June 1, 1956, at 7 pm, 20 rue du Montparnasse, Dames de Nazareth, preceded by Mass at 6:30 pm.

We are recommending, as of now, the Seven Sleepers pilgrimage in Vieux-Marché in Brittany,[113] on July 21 and 22 1956. The Muslim feast

---

[112] The Sulpician Father Henri Le Sourd (1907–2002) was Curé of Saint Sulpice Church in Paris and then Superior of the Mission de France in 1961. He was a member of the Badaliya from 1938, welcoming the gatherings in the crypt of Saint Sulpice, especially for the Islamic celebration of the *Night of Destiny* near the end of Ramadan.

[113] In the Qur'an the story of the Seven Sleepers is known as Ahl al-Kahf: The People of the Cave (or grotto). Their story is reported in the 18th Sura of the Qur'an: a number of young men fleeing religious persecution, seek refuge in a cave. They fall asleep and wake after a considerable period of time has elapsed. The story has parallels in the Christian tradition known as the Seven Sleepers of Ephesus:

of Sacrifices[114] (9 Dhu al-Hijjah 1375) will have taken place the night before in Mecca. It is our duty to pray for this collective pardon that Muslims implore for their community.

22. Convocation - July 6, 1956.
21 rue Monsieur, Paris 7

Monthly meeting on Friday, July 6 1956 at 7 pm at the close of our monthly day of private fasting for a serene peace in justice between Christians and Muslims, particularly in Algeria. Mass will be celebrated at 6:30 pm. (20 rue du Montparnasse, Dames de Nazareth).

As we did three years ago, we will lay our hope at the sacred heart of the Most Pure, where Christians and Muslims together invoke Our Lady in the mystery of her Assumption, at Ephesus, and in her earthly Reign, at Fatima.

Together, we will also invoke the Seven Sleepers, the martyrs who were immured alive, in the mystery of their anticipated resurrection for Justice, these *Ahl al-Kahf* of Ephesus, whose Breton pilgrimage in Vieux-

---

around 250 A.D. seven brothers, not wanting to renounce their Christian faith, were immured alive on the orders of the Emperor, Decius. They woke up after a *dormition* of 309 years, thus able to bear witness to the miraculous nature of their experience. Their cult rapidly spread throughout the East and the West. The story is not merely that of a miracle, it also prefigures the resurrection promised by the Prophets, which probably explains why it was integrated into the Muslim religion—this Sura is read in mosques every Friday. The story of seven resurrected martyrs, common to Christianity and Islam, was considered by Louis Massignon as "Islam's Apocalypse." Attending a pardon at Vieux-Marché during the early 1950s, Massignon was struck by the similarity between certain verses of an old *gwerz* (Breton word for song, lament) sung by the pilgrims and certain verses of the 18th Sura. This inspired him in 1954, to instigate an annual gathering of Christians and Muslims in Vieux-Marché that would take place the night before the traditional village Pardon, and during which they would join in prayer for peace. This Islamo-Christian pilgrimage continues to this day.

[114] Massignon is referring to the Qurban known as the Eid al-Adha which commemorates the willingness of Abraham to sacrifice his son (Ishmail in the Islamic tradition), as an act of obedience to God. It falls approximately 70 days after the end of Ramadan and the day after the end of the pilgrim's annual Hajj (pilgrimage) to Mecca, on the 10th 11th and 12th day of the lunar month of Dhu al-Hijjah. The ritual sacrificial animal is slaughtered and given as charity to the poor.

Marché (near Plouaret, (Côtes-du-Nord) will take place on July 21 and 22. Remember the pilgrimage at Guidjel, in Algeria.[115]

Our Lady of the Deported, Our Lady of the Condemned to death, Our Lady of the Abandoned, Nuestra Senora de los Desamparados will know how to rekindle the fount of Mercy in hardened hearts, deafening them to the senseless calls to the "crusade" and to "holy war," as the three Bishops, protectors of the Sons and Daughters of Charles de Foucauld, lift up their voices to solemnly call young people to act according to their true Christian nature and their vocation to be heroes and not to act against nature, or life or love.

Let us listen to the call of two East African Bishops, Monsignor Knox, Apostolic Delegate in Mombasa, and Monsignor MacCarthy, Archbishop of Nairobi (Kenya), from deep in the darkness of forests and manhunts. They have asked us to promote on June 12, throughout the world, a solemn plea to the youth whose tarnished and perverted hearts aspire to crime, calling on a pure hero from there to save them, the Blessed Charles Louanga, leader of the young black martyrs of Uganda, burnt alive on June 3, 1886, in Namugongo: "Do pray for us, you martyrs burnt alive, like Joan of Arc, to set the world ablaze with love divine."

23. Convocation - August 3, 1956
21 rue Monsieur, Paris 7

As it did last year, August vacation is depriving us of Mass in the chapel of the Dames de Nazareth on Friday, August 3, 1956—at the close of our monthly day of private fasting for a serene peace between Christians and Muslims, particularly in Algeria.

Several of us had the consolation of participating in the prayer vigil for peace in Algeria that took place during the Breton Pardon[116] of the Seven Sleepers of Ephesus at Vieux-Marché (Côtes-du-Nord) on July 21/22, *on the actual feast day of St. Mary Magdalen.* Several hundred very fervent

---

[115] There is also a shrine honoring the Seven Sleepers story in Guidjel, Algeria with a pilgrimage that L. Massignon associated with the one in Brittany.

[116] Pardon: (from the Latin *perdonare* and modern French *pardonner*, to forgive) signifies in Brittany the feast of the patron saint of a church or chapel. In 1954 Louis Massignon encouraged Muslims to join the traditional pardon due to the story of the Seven Sleepers found in both religious traditions.

believers were present. The solemn Mass was celebrated according to the Eastern Rite by Msgr. Nasrallah, rector of Saint-Julien-le-Pauvre in Paris, and the presider was Msgr. T. G. Raymundos, Bishop of Chariopolis and ecclesiastical advisor to the France-Orient Committee; Archbishop Bourgès represented the Bishop of Saint-Brieuc and Tréguier; the Archbishop of Rabat, Msgr. Lefèvre, had told us that he would join us in prayer; the Bishop of Oran cabled a message of "fervent prayers from the Oran province" (signed: Msgr. Lacaste); the Bishop of the Sahara, Msgr. Mercier, wrote to us on July 22nd from Rome that he would be "in very close prayerful union, particularly for Algeria," with "the Vieux-Marché pilgrimage."

On the Muslim side, in Vieux-Marché itself we had about thirty friends, Algerians who had come from Paris, Lannion and Paimpol, along with two Moroccans and one Tunisian who said the *Fatiha*[117] in front of the crypt. Meanwhile at the Maqâm of the Ahl al-Kahf in Guidjel-Ras el Mâ (southeast of Setif),[118] the Mufti of Setif, Khebaba Mohamed Tahar, let us know that he would pray to God in union with us on the 22nd.

24. Convocation - September 7, 1956
21 rue Monsieur, Paris 7

Friday September 7, 1956 we will resume our monthly Mass at Saint Severin Church at 7 pm at the close of our day of private fast for a serene peace between Muslims and Christians—particularly in Algeria.

Several of our Israeli friends are asking us to associate ourselves with their Yom Kippur (Yom Hakipourim) fast, the night of September 14th

---

[117] The Fatiha is the opening Sura in the Qur'an, the first prayer learned by every Muslim child.

[118] Near the chapel of the Seven Sleepers in Vieux-Marché, there is a spring also dedicated to the Seven Sleepers. It consists of seven stones and its water runs forth from a horizontal stone pierced with seven holes, or veins. A similar spring can be found near Guidjel in Algeria. Aside from France and Algeria, sanctuaries dedicated to the Seven Sleepers can be found in Scandinavia, Germany, Turkey, Syria and Yemen. In English, See Buck. "Dialogues with Saints and Mystics: In the Spirit of Louis Massignon" Chapter 8. 2002 KNP London/New York. Photos related to the chapters in the book, including the 50th anniversary of the Breton shared Muslim and Christian pilgrimage in 2004 can be seen at www.dcbuck.com.
Also under Articles at this web site "A Shared Muslim-Christian Pilgrimage" SUFI Spring 2005.

and 15th "for a calmer future and the re-establishment of peace in the Middle East, in Cyprus and in Algeria."

Several of our members participated in the International Congress organized by the Benedictine Fathers of Toumiline,[119] which was an important event in the spirit that animates our small union. They were able to identify the Cave of the Seven Sleepers at Séfrou, which is also dedicated to the Prophet Daniel where both Muslim and Jewish women come to offer prayers.

They have noticed the echo which our Muslim/Christian pilgrimage on July 22nd (Vieux Marché) has had in parts of Morocco.

They have also observed that people still remember that three years ago at al-Sunna de Rabat mosque (Soueïka district) the preacher Ben Abdallah (Abelouahed-ibn'Ali) invoked the name of Joan of Arc as an intercessor of God, the Almighty, on behalf of all the oppressed, not only French Catholics. And they noted that it was there that an effective spiritual solidarity started between Christians and Muslims in keeping with their common veneration of the Virgin Mary. May those of us who can go to Domrémy [Shrine dedicated to Joan of Arc], "in spirit and truth," think of this from now on, especially for Algeria.

We must intensify our supplication to God, through the mediation of Our Lady, in order to hasten peace in Algeria. For that, we have the obligation to multiply our works of mercy, both spiritual and material, uniting us with our Muslim friends. This is not a disputable "communicatio in divinis," this is an irrefutable "commercium in spiritualibus;"[120] in the end it is precisely on this sacred Hospitality, that all of us will be judged.

25. Convocation - October 5, 1956
21 rue Monsieur, Paris 7

Friday, October 5, 1956, monthly Mass (Chapelle des Dames de Nazareth-20, rue Montparnasse) at 6:30 pm, and meeting at 7 pm at the close

---

[119] Toumliline is a small village in the Atlas Mountains of Morocco where the Benedictines founded a monastery in 1952. To meet the intellectual needs of young independent Moroccans they organized summer seminars inviting well known speakers on politics, current affairs and religion.

[120] A "communion of divine things" risks confusion and the possibility of syncretism whereas "communion of spiritual things" envisions interreligious dialogue in which Muslims and Christians have much to offer one another.

of our monthly day of private fasting for a serene Peace between Christians and Muslims, particularly in Algeria.

We will look at contacts made between those that prayed at Toumliline (Morocco) in August, as well as the "revelation" without our authorization (and not without substantial mistakes) made by Radio-Tanger, on August 23, concerning our "private fast" on the occasion of the 3rd anniversary of the deportation of the Sultan (which motivated the scheduling of it, set at our meeting September 4, 1953).

While regretting this publicity, we cannot deny, in a world devoid of the sacred, such an independent declaration of the effectiveness of the "arma Christi," the spiritual weapons through which we substitute ourselves for the oppressed, exposing ourselves in their place, witnessing to the Truth.

With the Muslims, in particular: they believe, like us, that for a final manifestation of the Truth, Christ will return to this world. And, due to the events in Palestine, where they believe this return will take place, Christ's Return is even more imminent for them than it is for us.

For them as for us, most believers interpret this Return as the external Righting of wrongs committed against one's own, one's nearest kin, first of all. However, for many spiritual Muslims, especially those from the Maghreb and Sahara, this Return is an "interior" event that begins gradually in all souls who "judging themselves in order not to be judged," submit themselves to a Rule of religious life that is strict for them, but kind and compassionate for others. The exception are those who want us to believe that their violence is Justice and who want to corrupt us by offering us charity acquired through wrongdoings. As long as the common sinner remains unrepentant, he is unable to cooperate in Christ's Return in souls, and the great mistake of many Christians is to have forgotten the discipline of the early Church that forbade even the destitute from accepting charity from unrepentant public sinners, who flourish with cynicism today in our colonial endeavors, for the satisfaction of communist propaganda.

Conversely, we should more courageously discern Christ's return among us in the anguish and spiritual poverty of the worst public sinners, prisoners and the deported, the excluded; it is their desperate prayer, "slandered" and scorned by men, that will save the world from global death in the Hatred between classes. Let us hope that we can make them understand the immense dignity of the work of Grace within them; inclining us towards them rather than scorning them.

It is impossible for serene Peace to be established between Christians and Muslims through mutual awareness of Christ's return in compassionate and prayerful souls, particularly in Algeria, as long as we continue to subordinate them to a humiliating acceptance of our technological superiority, the end to vendettas, food distribution to the hungry, payment of overdue family allowances, bilingual education to the illiterate and consolation through posthumous reparations to the broken hearted.

26. Convocation - November 2, 1956
21 rue Monsieur, Paris 7

Friday, November 2, 1956, monthly Mass at 20, rue Montparnasse (Chapelle des Dames de Nazareth), followed by meeting at the close of our day of private fasting for a serene peace between Christians and Muslims, particularly in Algeria.

Since the *Qurban*[121] of August 20, 1953, our monthly private fast has "substituted" us, in Morocco only, for the anguish of a prostrated Muslim people, deprived of its legitimate religious leader. His freedom unexpectedly regained, this leader, matured by his exile, accepted from our leaders, a little earlier than expected, a road to peace with neighboring Algeria in order to stop the bloodshed, especially that of Muslims. However, we have also shed blood in the agonizing ordeal of October 22, 1956, that struck Sultan Mohammed V in the heart.[122] We who have fasted and

---

[121] Qurban: "offering or oblation" a term used here for the commemoration of the "failed sacrifice" of the son of Abraham, during the pilgrimage honoring the "Feast of Sacrifices." Mohammed V, the Sultan of Morocco, was deposed during this Feast on August 20, 1953, which for L. Massignon had the character of a sacrilegious act of political usurpation.

[122] Mohammed V and Bourguiba had invited leaders from the Algerian Liberation Front (FLN) to Tunis; La Marsa, Minister Ben Bella, Bou Diaf, Aït Ahmed and Khider, but the Moroccan airplane that transported them (as "guests" of the King of Morocco) was captured October 22 by the French aviation under the order of the Secretary of State, Max Lejeune: These leaders remained prisoners in France until 1962. That failure of every effort at mediation with the goal of a solution to the conflict in Algeria painfully affected L. Massignon, even more so as the attacks and fighting in Algeria multiplied in 1957.

prayed for him for the last three years, pray and fast that God may make him persevere in this mission that is, and remains, holy and without blemish.

North African reconciliation between Christians and Muslims is inevitable, now that he has told Tunis not to "despair of France's African calling," at the same time that France opposes his involvement in the liberation of all his Muslim brothers, including the Algerian "rebels." God will make him overcome, in this struggle of his conscience, violent and deceitful ways; he will make him understand that, for the scales of justice to be equal, his compassion for Muslim victims of the Algerian drama must also embrace our victims, as was the case for Abdelkader in Damascus.[123]

At the beginning of the Muslim State, his ancestor Fatima, the Prophet's daughter, died unknown and insulted for defending foreign preachers, the Mawâlî, against the colonial racism of the Arab nobility in Mecca. Let us pray that Sultan Mohammed V, may now also know how to "universalize his compassion" and direct his thoughts towards the Jerusalem qibla, towards the Al-Aqsa, towards this Marian chapel of Zachariah where Muslim women's prayers unite with Our Lady of the Presentation to the Temple.

Let us pray that the Holy Sites, and especially this one, remain international as requested by Pius XII of everyone. Now when, in a curious contrary maneuver, England sees itself holding equal balance between Israel and Arab Jordan, and when France retaliates by offering to help Israel move as far as Jordan in case of an attack from Iraq, let us pray, despite the unworthiness of our prayers to be heard, that France does not abandon its secular mission to protect the Holy Sites, and does not abandon the Savior's Tomb in 1956, as it abandoned the Crypt of the Annunciation and the defense of Mary's purity in 1948 at the siege of Nazareth.[124]

---

[123] Here L. Massignon is referring to the magnanimity of the Algerian leader 'Abd al-Qâdir al-Jazâ'irî who, having chosen to live in Damascus after his exile in Pau, then Amboise, was generous enough to protect, with his personal guards, the Arab Christians threatened with death by the Druze in the uprising of 1860.

[124] The decision of the UN in 1948 in favor of effecting the creation of two States, Israel and Palestine, expected a "corpus separatum" for Jerusalem with an international statute. Count Folke Bernadotte who was to implement it was assassinated September 17, 1948 and the States in conflict would forget little by little to

In its pagan hatred of the Arabs, these "Semites," the national press leaves its columns open, only in France, alas (not in Spain), to a barrage of slander and racist threats, similar to the ones they previously spread against other "Semites," the Jews hunted down by the Gestapo.

If Algerian communists have been strengthened, by atheistic materialism, to find a common homeland here on earth with Muslims by fraternally confronting similar torture and fire at the electric stake in Oran, let us Christians suffer humbly with Mohammed V for the insult inflicted on his conscience for his belief in the God of sacred hospitality, in the King of the Last Judgment "Malik Yawm al-Dîn" of the "Fatiha," this King of the Oppressed, of all the Oppressed, the one whose name we Catholics believe we know, and that on the 29th, "Christ the King," we should not celebrate for ourselves alone, but rather for all mankind.

27. Convocation - December 7, 1956
21 rue Monsieur, Paris 7

Friday December 7, 1956, vigil of the Immaculate Conception (Latin Church): Monthly Mass in the chapel of the Dames de Nazareth, 20 rue du Montparnasse at 6:30 pm followed by a meeting at the close of our day of private fasting for a serene peace between Christians and Muslims—particularly in Algeria and in Egypt where the Badaliya was born in 1934.

On the next day, December 8, 1956, vigil of the Vow of St. Anne (the Immaculate Conception in the Greek Church), Mass in the Eastern Rite (Slavic) dedicated to *Our Lady of the Veil* (Pokrov in Russian), *patron saint of the Badaliya* in the Church of St. Joseph, 161 rue St. Maur (Paris XIe), sung by the Ukrainian choirs: at 7 pm.

In order to confront the world threat now blazing in the East,[125] nearly a thousand of us prayed for Hungary in Paris on November 4th during

---

realize this goal, while L. Massignon unrelentingly attempted to intervene in order to get them to respect this statute, expressing himself several times in the press. (See *Témoignage chrétien, L'Aube, EcritsMémorable,* vol. I, pp. 763–770).

[125] In the heart of Europe, Hungary saw the liberal Imre Nagy regain power October 25 and a national insurrection arose against the Soviet occupation; J. Kadar replaced him immediately and called on the USSR which led to the intervention by the military from Moscow, fighting in the streets of Budapest and the taking of the city by Soviet troops (November 4–13). Imre Nagy was condemned to death and executed in June 1958.

the evening Angelus, under the sign of Our Lady of Mariazell, an Austro-Hungarian pilgrimage founded by Louis d'Anjou, a French king of Hungary; the betrothed Marie-Antoinette went to pray there before becoming the queen of France. There were even more of us praying for Hungary and Poland at the feet of Our Lady of Czestochowa on the 6th during the evening Mass in the Church of St. Severin. Tomorrow we shall have to pray for Romania, a country as sorely afflicted as her two Christian sisters. But these three nations mark the boundary between the Latin Church, bearing witness, and the silent Russian Church. Our prayer must go beyond this boundary.

For us, invoking Our Lady of the Veil of Pokrov is a means of joining with the silent Russian Church from here by entering into her heart, sharing in the "fiat"[126] of enduring the persecutions that have tortured her for the last forty years. It is this icon of Pokrov, this image of Marian devotion, hidden in the depths of every Russian home, that, as early as October 31, 1942, Pius XII wanted us to rediscover one day. We think that this day has arrived.

Under the great Veil of Silence that the advance of Russia is spreading throughout the East, Greek as well as Arab—because we have failed to appeal to the East for the restoration of peace between Christians and Muslims in North Africa—let us join our friends in the Badaliya in Beirut, Cairo and Alexandria, who are crying out to us to hold fast to our offering.

And since "salvation is from the Jews,"[127] we should listen to the cry "let us fast together for justice" that is coming to us from a Zionist who fasted with us on Yom Kippur last September 14–15th. It is not by tossing dice and resorting to expedient measures verging on the sacrilegious that the world will be saved, but by praying and fasting. The French minutes of Joan of Arc's trial edited by Fr. Doncoeur indicate that it was "*on a day of fasting*, at noon, on a summer day, while she was in her father's garden, that the Angel's voice called her to save her country." Let us, more than ever, call upon Joan of Arc on our day of fasting December 7th,

---

[126] Massignon is referring to Mary's "fiat," her total acceptance of God's will for her when she is approached by the angel and told she would bear a son. Massignon saw Mary's "fiat" as the witness of how all Christians are called to respond to God. Here he calls for members of the Badaliya (in substitutionary prayer) to offer themselves for the silenced church in the Eastern Bloc countries.

[127] Jesus to the Samaritan woman (Jn.4:22).

so that she may save Algeria along with Christian France, which is in danger of losing her soul through racist arrogance.

This is a solemn moment; our prayer must ask of God that He tear apart the blinding veil that prevents our beloved homeland from seeing in itself the flaws that it stigmatizes in others. As Bernanos once said, "scandal is not in telling the truth but in telling only part of the truth." Lastly, let us judge ourselves so that we may not be judged or condemned for having scandalized not only other nations but these little Algerian Muslim children towards whom we turned an armed campaign in our solicitous need for "pacification." With all of its administrative powers our army should observe the 1949 Geneva Convention on the respect due to wounded persons, prisoners and civilians in "troubled" times, ratified by France in 1952.

Several Masses were celebrated in France, Morocco and the Near East for our dear friend Antoine de Chaponay[128] who died in Rabat on September 9th; he was a personal friend of the Sultan, and since 1953, one of the guarantors to him of our national honor. Let us pray that God may protect the Muphti of Sétif, Mr. Khebaba Taher, a misunderstood man who received threats and insults for having so nobly joined us in thought on July 22nd during our pilgrimage to the Seven Sleepers.

---

[128] The Chaponay were one of the great families of France. Antoine de Champonay settled in Morocco at the beginning of World War II and worked with intelligence and devotion for Moroccan independence.

Annual letter # X

Paris, Christmas Eve 1956

Summary

1. Cases of transference.
2. The extension of "substitution" in time and space: the two Cities.
3. How the "Badaliya" is born in the soul; the Sorrowful Virgin, patron of the Badaliya: Our Lady of the Veil.
4. The humble and central role of "substitution" in preparing for world unity.
5. Truth and violence
6. Statistics: the small number and the majority.
7. At the Limit.
8. Moral report on the year 1956.

It will soon be the tenth anniversary of the episcopal approval of our little sodality, founded in Damietta on February 9, 1934, and approved in Cairo on January 6, 1947, by Msgr. Pierre K. Medawar at the chapel in Gezirat Badrân.

Let us meditate together on the meaning and importance of our commitment. If "substitution" is first and foremost a thought, a wish of our soul, it can only be accomplished in our lives if we take into our hearts of flesh the sorrows of others, their bleeding wounds, as we practice non-violence, show compassion, shed inner tears and offer advice to others.

We feel deeply that non-violent compassion is the corner stone of any reconstruction of human society, provided that we persuade others of it by showing them that this notion of compassion makes it possible to solve the harrowing psycho-social problem of the contagious influence of evil.

1. There Are Cases of Transference of Other People's Pain and Suffering

The *psychoanalytic process* has shown how such transferences take place involuntarily in patients who are unconscious, innocent or not responsible for their actions. These patients suffer from various kinds of phobias, obsessions and neuroses whose cause, detected in the analysis of dreams, lies in a trauma inflicted many years before (a disturbing word or a scandalous gesture from another person). The conscious mind believes it has forgotten the trauma, but in the silent receptivity of the soul, the subconscious mind remains obsessed with it, as with an unsuccessful "conception" of an idea.

The Freudian psychoanalytic school looks upon these mental traumas as traces of a faulty recording mechanism, as sensory perceptions wrongly "intentionalized" and "personalized" by the subject. Thus it is necessary to cure the patient, through acknowledging, and thereby aborting the inner dream that torments the patient unnecessarily. There is nothing good to be had from the pain of others (sic).

Sociologists have studied the reasons why some men offer to have the debts and penalties incurred by others transferred onto themselves, requesting to become hostages and ransoms in their place. These gestures, which are frequent in primitive societies (they can still be observed, especially among Arabs in Iraq near Ur and in Yemen), tend to disappear among us, in favor of the legal irresponsibility of "anonymous corporations." Inspired by a social tribal structure and by the compelling demands of honor, [these gestures] are an exteriorizing, potent affirmation, of the public upholding of one's word of honor.

Durckheim's school of sociology considers these "immoderate and obsolete" gestures of hospitality to be the residue of "pre-logical" judgments, of totemic beliefs and manifestations of ruinous generosity (Potlatch). What reasonable judge could accept the transference of personal responsibility, let alone a fault, or a sin, before a just God, who in the end must judge everyone according to his works (Qur'an 6:164, 72:22[129]).

---

[129] The first verse declares, "Every soul draws the need of its acts on none but itself: no bearer of burdens can bear the burden of another." The second states, "No one can deliver me from God," a verse that was dear to al-Hallâj, the 10th century mystic researched by Massignon whose words became a spiritual guide for him.

Doesn't this gesture amount to giving Providence a lesson in insolent generosity?

Thus, psychologists and sociologists would concur in reducing the problem to two pejorative categories in order to eliminate the two types of transference from social life considered above: the transference of pain unconsciously endured and the transference of pain willingly claimed. Disregarding all evidence, they end up teaching that in society men should share only profits and satisfactions, and as for painful difficulties and debts, they could liquidate their own by running away from them, and dismiss those of others. Is this possible, or even desirable? What soul could escape the intimate wound of the body it inhabits without mutilating its very being? (the soul will only be saved in the body assigned to it). "It is not good for man to be alone;"[130] and even if the visitation by an "unknown" other in a dream (in Paradise) wounds us at first,[131] this unexpected act of hospitality is the wholesome foundation of any open human society, from the exogamic[132] married couple to the pedagogic community requiring segregation of the sexes (it is especially in monasteries that "substitution" finds the fulfillment of its purpose and prepares future society: there is only spiritual fecundity in the vocation of perpetual chastity).

In fact, religious history mentions numerous cases of life casualties making a virtue of necessity thanks to a chronic and incurable disease, who were initiated by the pain of others and discovered the experimental science of compassion. Thus they found themselves introduced to a mysterious world unknown to the profane: "the eschatological world of the sacralizing stigmatisation" where they join, little by little, all the labor pains of humanity. No longer self-centered, they are able to understand, and this understanding liberates them by sublimating their own pains. The oldest archetypes from human folklore become real to them through heartrending intersigns, their destinies shattering even their most secret wishes. The providential convergence of their own ordeals with those endured by loved ones sublimates the bitter fellowship of their forced labors into constellations of loving tenderness. All the wounded descen-

---

[130] Genesis 2:18

[131] Massignon described his own conversion back to his Christian faith in his twenties in Baghdad as an experience he named, "the Visitation of the Stranger."

[132] Exogamic: marriage outside of a specific group especially as required by law or custom.

dants of Adam and Eve exiled in the "bosom of Abraham" are assumed into them by a virginal, transhistoric hospitality—in Israel, from Elijah and Myriam, the sister of Moses, source of purifying Water (and Esther)—in Islam, with all the orphans adopted by Fâtima, Salmân[133] and Hallâj—in Christianity, with all the contemplative witnesses to the thrust of the Spear, Mary, John and the Magdalen.

2. Extension of "Substitution" within Time and Space: The Two Cities

The last cases mentioned above are those of an explicitly universal compassion. But even the most humble case of a most ignorant, yet compassionate and "stigmatized," peasant woman is implicitly destined for this universality.[134] Huysmans, (died May 12, 1907), who was brought back to the Catholic faith by a bad priest, thanks to this unfortunate priest's research on cases of mystical transference, had foreseen this fundamental doctrine of "apotropaic[135] sanctification," of solidarity in original sin, reversible in Our Lord.[136] His last confessor, Fr. Daniel Fontaine (died November 10, 1920), who breathed new life into the society of the Priests of the Heart of Jesus founded by Fr. de Clorivière, during the Terror, confirmed Huysmans in his perceptions by assisting him in his holy agony, which he suffered in full union with such compassionate souls as Lydwine of Schiedam and Anne Catherine Emmerick. It is through them that we inherited this mode of personal union with Jesus, Mary, the Magdalen and John. The "Badaliya" commends itself to the prayers of the successors to Fr. Daniel Fontaine, Msgr. de la Celle, Canon Bouvet, and now, Msgr. L. Igonin, rector of the Basilica of Fourvière.

---

[133] Salman Pâk, the first Iranian to become Muslim, a Companion to the Prophet Muhammad, for whom Massignon had a particular interest.

[134] Reference to Anne Catherine Emmerick.

[135] Apotropaic: designed to avert evil, such as an "apotropaic" ritual.

[136] A discredited Priest, Fr. Boulan introduced the well-known French author, J. K. Huysmans to the concept of mystical substitution. At age 17 Massignon met the author who was researching the life of a 13th century Dutch mystic, St. Lydwine of Schiedam. See Huysmans, *Ste Lydwine*, p. 80 and Buck: "Dialogues with Saints and Mystics" p. 33.

Our mission statement specifies that the "Badaliya requires a deep engagement, grounded in fraternal understanding and thoughtful attention, with the lives of generations of Muslim families both past and present." Every immortal soul can thus take on a legacy of graces to be cultivated, or of betrayals to be expiated.

Through "substitution," without usurping any genealogy, we enter into the place of those who failed to answer the Lord's invitation in the Nuptial Parable, into uninterrupted chains of fortuitous witnesses solicited by Divine Grace at the crossroads, in the midst of the "*abnâ al sabîl*" (passers-by), and suddenly promoted to the rank of "apotropaic witnesses" (*abdâl*) of Divine Mercy. Through this, we have been torn away from our blood relatives, thus causing them pain, and through this "virginal" deprivation, we become affiliated with the angelic privilege of the guardian angels, even surpassing the limits of their immateriality, in order to humanly complete that which is lacking in our sinful, deported, excluded and outlawed brothers so that they may be pardoned and offered amnesty. *They ask this of each and every one of us,* "from the depths of your soul, from your most turbulent blood, from your most luminous dreams, from your most stormy desires, from your most intense incantations; Ah, may the power of your faith burst forth with the cry of their deliverance" (Th. R. Tana, January 28, 1955).

After Columbus and Magellan, the cycle of the discovery of the globe ended, and in a symmetrical fashion, the three Abrahamic expansions also ended, including the dispersion of the Jewish Diaspora, the conquests of the Muslim Holy War and colonization by the Christian nations.

It seems that, through an Einsteinian curve of Time, these expansions are making us return to the time of Abraham, Father of all believers, and that the commandment "Lèsh Lèsha" ("Leave your City") is once again hurling the last faithful pilgrims of the Apostolate of universal Compassion out of their national boundaries into the seasonal, roaming life of transhuman flocks, like the desperate movements of unskilled laborers.

The Two Cities of This World and
Their Attitude toward "Substitution"

The two world wars catapulted humanity towards unification, but today they have ended up reducing us into two Cities. *The City of the Godless* has not yet explicitly become the City of the Damned of the Earth, but it no longer extends the right of asylum to the pariahs who do not want to join the [Communist] Party! *The City of the Western Nations* can hardly call itself the City of God's Chosen anymore (which Chosen, which God, considering its pluralistic skepticism?), but its exclusivism (empty of any positive orthodoxy) no longer thinks that there is anyone outside of the City walls who could remove their guilt out of compassion for their pain and misery.

In the first, the City of the Godless, there is no longer any means of maintaining a word of honor because Communist self-criticism consists in accepting the necessity of Nothingness without hope. The criterion for truth is in the conformity of our word to the Party line and in the refusal to mentally "substitute" oneself to the thoughts of the opponent, for this too would only be the purely demoralizing tactic of a liar, or a spy. Inside the iron curtain, these orders are meant to be absolute. Outside of it, "substitution" is practiced for limited periods of time, in the same way that maintaining one's word of honor is only temporary. The case of midshipman Maillot[137] proves it: he reneges on his word to France, but then keeps the second promise given to Algeria by going so far as to have himself killed in a state of "substitution" without hope, and godless heroism. This is what attracts the whole world's proletariat to the City of the Damned, the Suicide Bombers who annihilate themselves in a demonstration of utter terrorism (it is a temptation).

In the second, the City of the Western Nations, a majority of formerly Christian States, now secularized, profess a policy of unofficial alliance with the Churches and the Synagogue, in which fidelity to one's word is nothing more than a guarantee of economic advantages whose main purpose is to increase material wealth. In a paternalistic fashion, [this policy] neglects the works of mercy toward the mentally disabled, the careless who count badly, the unlucky and the maladjusted, making simple pawnshops into profits for the wealthy. This paternalism, hardened into contempt, pushes the proletariat to join the communist City and to its

---

[137] A provocative reference to a militant communist become traitor by delivering arms to the Algerian FLN in April 1956 who was later killed in an ambush.

egalitarian nihilism, rather than remaining subjected to the oligarchic plutocracy[138] of the other City.

It is clear to any sincerely faithful member of the Churches and the Synagogue that they must remain spiritually free from any enslavement to government or financial institutions especially when these are [run by] public sinners who try to corrupt them and cut them off from the mentally disabled, the poor and the outcasts. The faithful spiritual believer knows that we shall only be forgiven if we ourselves have forgiven, that the key to power is not one-sided, that the leader on the rope must not cut the rope, and that the one who wants to save his soul, will lose it. They are aware of this as long as the spirit of greed does not come to obscure their faith and destroy the impetus of their compassion. They know, however, that the first sign in the soul of her reconciliation with God is the desire to reconcile others with Him, and that ultimately, when the soul discovers that God loved her first, predestined her, she suffers in all the souls who have not been found like she has, or who have not yet discovered Him.

Instead of this compassion, do we see anything, especially in countries colonized by supposedly Christian states, other than a morbid eagerness, on the part of lay and religious servants of the public Order (who actually see themselves as its owners) to exile and excommunicate all those who, due to their weaknesses, errors and wrongdoings, have difficulty reaching our gates? Far from "substituting" themselves for them in their pain in order to fraternally "complete" what [their suffering] is lacking, some servants of the public Order [go so far as] to manage a strange and sinister transference. Such is the case of the Vice Squad officer who pressures a submissive prostitute into presenting false evidence to the Judge in order to "complete" the accused man's indictment. Protecting the accused at the expense of this woman, this officer is unloading his own forgery onto a poor outcast, as if he could dupe the true Judge (God).[139] The Jewish industrialist who employs a Sabbath-goy, operates in the same way, as does the Muslim ship broker who buys himself a

---

[138] Oligarchy is a government in which a small group exercises control for corrupt and selfish purposes. Plutocracy is government by the wealthy.

[139] Refers to "False Henry" in the Dreyfus Affair and the Kahoul Affair (Algiers 1937) who was directly known by various members of the "Badaliya."

Christian associate who will carry the sin of his usury. All of these cases make it clear that eliminating the "Badaliya," the principle of compassion through "substitution," destroys the ecumenism presupposed for the true City of the Elect.[140]

For that reason we cannot remain silent. Our commitment to bearing witness to the truth demands that we protest at our own risk, in the very heart of our City, against the hypocrisy of its Pharisaism. The salvation of our City and the authenticity of our vocation as "Badaliya" are at stake. Two phenomena will thus occur, one of which was already mentioned by Gandhi. Faced with our protest, "the servant of the public order" drops his favorite victim and turns his hatred on us; we who dared to insert ourselves. He picks up stones (or a grenade) in order to throw them at us, and puts his fingers in his ears or, even better, goes in quest of witnesses from the press who will mutilate our words, turning our prayer into blasphemy. This may allow the victim to save himself. As for us, we must not panic over the blows we have to endure on the victim's behalf, for we have faith that when we are hit by those who hate His Name, God would sooner come down from Heaven than let us lose strength; it is Another One who comes and suffers in our place, through "substitution."

3. How the "Badaliya" Is Born in the Soul

"Even pain, in the soul, as well as in the body, becomes noble, in Him." (Sr. Violet Susman, letter from Tokyo, May 23, 1928 [in English]).

"*Falâ budda min shakwä ilâ dhî muruwwatin/yuwâsika, aw yuslîka, aw yatawjja'u;*" "you need to confide your pain to a good-hearted man who will console you, help you forget or begin to suffer with you" (Hamâsa by Abu Tammâm).[141]

The one who finds a sense of emptiness in the depths of his own pain, who finds, in the depths of his fault, a liberating alibi, the desire for

---

[140] Massignon's Note: "With respect to the relations between our Muslim and Christian fellow citizens, we find it bitter to see the watchdog of our City label himself as a "vicious dog," in order to track down and bite the wild she-wolf, who is outlawed and smoked out when she lies down in order to give birth or die. It is forbidden to systematically train dogs to become "vicious" to persecute the Stranger or the Poor Man, for he may be an Angel or a Guest sent by God."

[141] Celebrated Syrian Arab poet (804–845) whose *qasîda,*, or verses, were gathered in numerous *Hamâsa*, or collections.

something other than that, for a "heartrending purity," is tasting the death from divine love, which in its very excess pierces the heart in a sudden upheaval out of himself, his "I." This breaking through a strait toward the open sea, this coming out of evil, surpassing the legal order and its punishment, [now causes him to feel that] he must help the most forsaken to taste this on their desperate lips, as he clings to them like St. Julien the Hospitaller[142] to his last traveler or St. Catherine to the victims of torture in Siena, by placing his wounds over those of the Crucified stretched naked on the Stone by his friends for the last anointing, on the threshold of the Holy Tomb.

Our desire for substitution, His desire for "badaliya" for the most unfortunate, the most forsaken and for our "enemies," leads us little by little to discover the secret of history, which, according to Léon Bloy,[143] belongs to suffering and compassionate souls; and it is through "substitution," by achieving it, that they decipher [this secret].

The Sorrowful Virgin, patron of the "Badaliya:" Our Lady of the Veil.

The face that Mary turns toward us, in our vocation as "substitutes," is "coperto d'umiltà." It is not the majestic face of a protecting Matron equal to her son in divinity, such as the Nabatean goddess Kaabou, mother of Dusares, who the pre-Islamic Arabs confused with the Marian icon of the Epiphany (Qur'an 5:116[144]). [She is not] the mother goddess characterized by too many Protestants and Jewish Ebionites, who saw in Maryam "animal mother," who forgets her vow to the point of having litters of children with a human spouse.

For us, the face of Mary is the face of the Servant of the Lord who bows down and implores, who judges herself unworthy and useless, the face

---

[142] The Church recognizes the Feast of St. Julien on February 12th who founded a hospital to care for the very poor in expiation of the assassination—by mistake—of his parents.

[143] Leon Bloy (1846–1917) was a vigorous and acerbic polemicist and intransigent Christian, an adversary of any compromise of the demands of the Gospel. He had a particular influence on Louis Massignon and his godson, Jacques Maritain.

[144] Massignon is alluding to the first part of the Sura 5, verse 116 in the Qur'an, "And Behold! Allah will say, 'O Jesus the son of Mary! Did you say to men, worship me and my mother as gods in derogation of Allah? He 'Glory to You! Never could I say what I had no right (to say.)' (trans. 2002. Abdullah Yusuf Ali, Asır Media, Turkey).

of the Virgin of Transcendence, of the Presentation in the Temple, veiled forever with the Veil of Humility and of Soledad.

Her vocation as a virgin, that substituted her for the humiliation of all wives who are sterile (before becoming their joy at the miracle of the Visitation), will expose her to all kinds of suspicions and bitter ordeals, making her an outcast, crossed off the Megilloth,[145] and in her final exile, "leave your kinsfolk," (dying as a foreigner in Ephesus). Furthermore, she will not have "spared" (like Abraham) this Son who, in spite of everything, God gave her because of her exemplary submission to the Torah (she will be faithful until her death to the Jewish date for Paques [Passover]), and she will have prefigured the face of this King of Israel, torn by the hedges of thorns by the Law,[146] substituting herself, even to the fruit of her womb, for all outcasts.

Most especially, we call her Our Lady of the Veil, a name which the Eastern liturgy likes to give her, especially since that apparition on October 1st one thousand years ago, when, after shedding tears of light, She spread this great veil over her city, Constantinople, the city of the Christian Triumph, in order to protect it from the pagan Russians. [Her] tears [were shed] over the Greek Church, [as they were] over the Latin Church in La Salette, on September 19th. With all the Eastern churches and the Russian Church of Silence, let us invoke Our Lady of the Veil (Our Lady of Pokrov in Russian) against the new paganism oppressing Russia, and also threatening Turkish, Iranian and Arab countries, where it is infiltrating into the Muslim proletariat.

In order to achieve the prophetic intuition of Pius XII when speaking in 1942 of a salvific Marian icon, that devotion to Our Lady of Fatima (Portugal) would help rediscover in the heart of Russia, there is cause to think that it is the Icon of the Pokrov that will tie together the return of Communist Russia to Christ and that of Islam to Mary, "Queen of the World" (Our Lady of Fatima; *Sayyidat al-Nisâ*).

---

[145] An allusion to five books of the Bible, here specifically to the Book of Esther, the model Jewish woman.

[146] A Talmudic expression commonly employed to indicate that following the episode of Moses and the burning Bush, the Torah and the Jewish people are forever separated from the *goyim* (non-Jews).

4. The Humble and Central Role of "Substitution" in Preparing for World Unity

The growing interdependence of economic and pedagogic systems is steering mankind toward an inescapable international world unity.

It is consequently surprising to see violent, nationalistic reactions erupt here and there within the three blocks visible on the map: Western capitalism of the "Christians," Soviet communism of the "atheists," and the block of the "backward," more or less "decolonizable" by the other two blocks (the Hinduized and Islamized nations of the Bandoeng pact[147]).

The tactical exploitation of these nationalistic reactions by a financial synarchy[148] of the capitalistic block or by the unionization of workers at the service of the USSR, in the name of Blood (racisms) or Gold (plutocratisms), shows that among these three blocks, the only one where the desire for world unity is still pure, is that of the "backward," of the proletariat on its way to national liberation. The professional honor it wants to recover is the honor of one's word among comrades, the sacred pact of the right of asylum, that, despite the efforts of the International Red Cross, the two blocks, Western and Soviet, continue to ignore.

But this effort of Hinduized and Islamized workers toward an original regulation of Labor requires a practiced consecration, that of religious Faith, which is as absent from the UN as it is from UNESCO.

Can the Churches give this [consecration] to the workers? We have to pray, suffer, substitute ourselves, so that our Church may become aware of the dignity of this effort and consecrate it; faced with the expulsion of the French Muslim workers from the CGT[149] (7/14/53), who the FO did not deign to take in, the CFTC should have shown fraternal compassion,

---

[147] Bandoeng, a city west of Java (Indonesia) where leaders of the *third-world* met in April 1955 (Nasser, Nehru and Tito as well as Heads of State from thirty Asian and African countries) declaring solidarity in development and the struggle against racism and colonialism in the name of a "positive neutrality" between the Soviet East and Western capitalists.

[148] *Synarchy*: control by a small group of the wealthy.

[149] CGT: [Confédération Générale du Travail] Major association of French trade unions associated with the Communist party. FO: [Force Ouvrière] Moderate worker's union formed out of a split with Communist CGT in 1948. CFTC: [Confédération Française des Travailleurs Chrétiens] French Trade Union.

instead of letting Rihani[150] and his religious friends from the MNA be suspected and executed by the laicized unionists from the FLN.[151]

As for us, we prayed and fasted with Muslim workers from Paris and the suburbs, and said the *Fatiha* with them.

The French national reaction may well accuse us of helping the Algerian national reaction, [which is] a strictly regional Algerian reaction of those workers. On this point, I wish French nationalists would understand that the current multiplication of small nations—a definite obstacle to a desirable world unity—comes from the treacherous technique of certain unifications, such as the one against which Joan of Arc roused the French people: English annexationism. [I wish] French nationalists would understand that we cannot hope to retain Franco-Algerian unification, as long as we persist in founding it on blood, violence and scorn, as did the XVth century English, and as long as we do not substitute ourselves with the Algerian Muslim believers from whom a fading Christianity could draw a more active Faith [that would] cure alcoholism, hate usury and refuse alms from public sinners, objected to by the Church of the Catacombs. On all these points, Algerian Islam is the creditor and our French ideal of unification, the debtor.

Just as the plurality of nations counters the hypocrisy of so-called "international" finance, the provisional plurality of churches testifies against certain conferences on world unification; orthodox truth is not the systematization of compromise.

Beneath these apparent pluralities, there are signs of eventual spiritual unification. Under the framework of the incessant weaving and unweaving of political and economic interests and the strategic geography of the 22 products necessary for economic life monopolized by politics, a more biological look at today's world reveals a dynamic geography showing spiritual frontiers and zones of pain inflicted and endured, confined to areas of friction between different national cultures, all of them more or less colonizing. From where do authentic cries come, rather than imposed slogans? Wild cries punctuated with brief invocations to half-remembered Names of legendary heroes of compassion and "substitution," Names miraculously helpful to those dying of pain, such as

---

[150] Sadek Rihani was the leader of the MNA (Algerian National Movement) in Algiers.

[151] FLN: [Front de Libération Nationale] National Liberation Front in Algeria.

the names eulogized in the litany commending the soul, which the Essene communities bequeathed to the Church of the Catacombs.

These frontier lines of painful scars between mutually hurtful communities form, under an ephemeral web of murders, famines, epidemics and wars—a fibrous tissue, which, with all the wrenching prayers of the masses, provides the structure for a liturgy of shared pain shaping the final unity of mankind in simple, clear and intelligible "lines of force."

"Lex orandi, lex credendi," "vox populi, vox Dei.[152]" In order to participate in this desire for world unity in its true sense, in order to grasp and express its growth, in justice and in truth, one must go to the most humble workers, become their guests, "back of the yards" (Saul Alinsky, Chicago),[153] "in the heart of the masses" (Fr. R. Voillaume[154]), in a spirit of non-violent substitution.

In [the spirit of] "Badaliya," with the other disciples of Charles de Foucauld, let us envision, in all its symbolic strength and final significance, the precursory gesture Foucauld makes by leaving the Trappists on January 23, 1997 and dedicating himself to living off the work of his hands from now on, like the poorest of workers, which he first realizes in Nazareth as a farmhand for the Poor Clares. Following his example, we think that what we must do is to renounce the supersubsidized technology of the Zionist racist type used in the kibbutzim, and in a spirit of poverty, share the trades used by the "under-developed" (Gandhi's spinning wheel) in order to fully "substitute ourselves" for the hardly decolonized laborers from the "Bandung third force," especially the Muslims, the most harshly treated by God, among the children of Abraham. This is what the Little Brothers of Foucauld (Father Voillaume) in their fraternities, and the Little Sisters of Foucauld (Little Sister Magdeleine) do everywhere, mixing with their neighbors, as their guests, and sharing the same humble tools, the same standard of living, the same bread.

---

[152] "The principles of prayer are the principles of faith," "The voice of the people is the voice of God."

[153] Saul Alinsky, an agnostic American Jew totally given to fighting for economic and social justice in the USA. A friend of Jacques Maritain and an inspiration.

[154] Founder of the congregation of Little Brothers of Jesus, René Voillaume's book, *Au coeur des masses, la vie des Petits Frères de Père Foucauld*, received great success in its message of a modern apostolate in service of the poor.

But man does not live by bread alone, he also lives by hope in a better life. It is in vain that the propaganda by the two blocks of Muslim laborers offers them a share in false hopes, which are all material and based on an industrialization of robots devoid of any real future.

We want to share in the humble hope of the poor Muslim workers themselves, the hope in a Day of Justice, the gateway to eternal life. Hope [is] by preparing for that Day through the total abandonment of our faith to divine will and patience in an unassailable non-violence, day-by-day (this means renouncing the idol of progress, but not the reforms).

5. Truth and Violence

Pascal wrote: "It is a strange and long war in which violence tries to oppress truth. All the efforts of violence cannot weaken truth, and only serve to raise it up all the more. All the lights of truth can do nothing to stop violence and only manage to irritate it even more" (Provinciales XII).

On the other hand, defenders of the truth cannot minimize it, out of neutralistic pacifism, or they shall betray it. Bernanos said: "Scandal is not in telling the truth, only in telling part of the truth."

From the above we can deduce the prohibition ("it is forbidden to..."), to which we respond here to several objections that are often made to our "non-violent substitution" and its "public witness to the truth," Gandhi's *satyagraha*.[155]

1. It is forbidden to forcefully impose the revealed truths that we have been privileged to receive on those who are deprived of them, while neglecting the basic truths of natural religion, despising human dignity in the weak and the prisoners, and exhibiting a paternalistic contempt for the seeds of a superior religious life that both Islam and Israel contain. At a time when so many Christians are joining the Israelis in their scorn for Islam's Abrahamic monotheism, let us reread the Qur'anic verse (5: 21) denouncing the complacency of "the Jews and the Christians who claim to be God's favorites." The colonial pharisaism of so many arrogant practices by Western missionaries will not only end up having us expelled from those countries, but also in arousing God's indignation

---

[155] Through his political non-violent witness in the 1920's, Mahatma Gandhi was a model for Louis Massignon. *Satya* (truth), *agraha* (firmness), and *ahimsa* (non-violence) admirably coincide with the values Massignon always worked to promote.

against us; God will judge the Privileged on the way they will have used their privileges toward those who were deprived of them; a providential deprivation precisely intended to awaken the compassion of the privileged and save them from greed, by suggesting "the work of mercy par excellence, hospitality." It is amazing that the Western States should discard the "declarations of human rights," these noble components of yesterday's masonic laicism, by denying freedom to backward illiterates, to the coolies of forced labor, and by organizing, to their detriment, the rational exploitation of the world by the "superior civilized races." [It is amazing] that without bothering to notice it, this racist form of financial nationalisms, finding so-called Christian partisans of this oligarchy, accelerates the adoption by Islam and the entire Bandung "Third Force," of the anti-capitalist, anti-bourgeois Soviet doctrine of class struggle.

2. It is forbidden to "civilize" the "under-developed" by mechanically imposing our ideas upon them, like so many mechanical movements onto robots unworthy of understanding them. This is a demoralizing parody of the civilizing mission of European culture. It is odd to hear our exhortations to the silent heroism of non-violence[156] being labeled as "demoralizing," as "emasculating" the nation by causing those who listen to us to become deserters or enter hermitages.[157] As if non-violence could be inoculated by command, dictatorially, all at once, like an anesthetic, to the bulk of the population, while it in fact requires an inner effort towards ascetic conversion by each person. It takes time to arrive at abstaining from rendering evil for evil, as does turning the other cheek.

---

[156] Massignon's Note: They question the spirit of non-violence of Joan of Arc; of this symbolic Judith who affirmed that she had "killed no one." They refused to see that the crusade that she proposed in order to reconcile the English invaders with the invaded French was a free reconciliation, a testimony to mutual understanding, the kind offered to the Sarrasins that is not the kind of submission to violence that she had fought against in France. When Péguy affirmed that it is the soldier who gives value to the cradle, who gives his life for the sake of our country's philosophy and Faith, I will not do him an injustice by thinking that he wishes to thus justify the legions of Caesar, the "dragonnades" [raids by Louis XIV on the Protestants], les Bleus in Vendée [soldiers of the King's Republic during the French Revolution], and M. Thiers in May 1871.

[157] Massignon's Note: In January 1947, in Sirondi, the fast from which Miss Amat as-Salam almost died, shamed only two proponents of violence, who gave up their weapons; however, this was enough to save the honor of Gandhian non-violence.

Non-violence is a personal matter, a gradual vocation, not an instant contagion of cowardice or a collective abdication of responsibility. The best of the non-violent are noble, all of their pride and their honor is internal and no insult or blow can violate it.

3. It is forbidden to propagate non-violent pacifism as a simple thought of neutrality bogged down by the lack of skeptical distinctions, in interchangeable subjective assertions and unverifiable demonstrations of sincerity; inside amorphous, supremely mistaken consciences, lies the hidden perfidy of the "fallen angels," who mock the truth rather than violently opposing it, disconnecting desire from pain and privation from quest, renouncing experience and imagining a false peace, which is negative, inactive, and numb with doubt.

It is this quietism that our "badaliya" is committed to fighting, through bearing witness to the truth.

6. Statistic: The Small Number and the Mass

"Misereor super turbam."[158] Our compassion wants to bear witness "to the heart of the masses," especially to the mass of 370 million Muslims, whose *Fatiha*[159] for thirteen centuries, so tragically calls out in the name of the God of Abraham to the King of the Last Judgment: "*ihdinâ*," give us a leader, a "*mahdî*," clearly guided by You.

This King, "in the name of the Invisible God" is His Word, the Expression of His Face, the human Face of the Foreign Guest, who we should not expel after having him beaten and tortured,—He who will judge us all on the ways we have granted Him the sacred hospitality of Abraham.

We Christians claim that he is called "Jesus, Son of Mary," for he must carry the predestined name of the only perfect Hostess, a Virgin "mother of God." An entire Muslim tradition going back through Shafi'i[160]

---

[158] Quoting Jesus who is often described as having pity for the people: See Mt. 14:13–21, Mk 6:32–44.

[159] The *Fatiha*, the Opening, is the first verse in the Qur'an recited at the beginning of prayers five times daily and often throughout the day.

[160] Muhammad al-Shafi'i (767–820) constructed his "theory of Islamic Law" founding the Shafi'ite canonical school of Sunni Islam.

to Hasan Basrî,[161] thinks that there is no mahdî but Jesus, whose Spirit continues to inspire mystic saints from age to age, who live in Jesus through their Rule... But an immense majority of Muslims (especially women) await the mahdî as a son of Fâtima. For many Muslim women, Fâtima,[162] this unrecognized, ever prayerful humiliated woman, prefigures the intercession of Mary beside her Son, the Judge at the Day of Judgment. It is therefore with the greatest respect that our prayer, going back through generations of Muslims to the very first, recapitulates through them the desires, originating in the masses, for a Fatimid mahdî who would fraternally bring back the son of Mary to Jerusalem for the Judgment. There are so many traditions which express this desire: let us therefore substitute ourselves with this desire for a mahdî "who will fill the world with justice, as it was filled with iniquity" (yamlä; ldunyâ; adlan kamâ mulyat jawran;" for, according to Fr. Monchanin's[163] thinking, to "convert" Islam implies the conversion of all its dead; converting them "retroactively" means nothing if we do not eschatologically live the convergence of their desire for social Justice with ours.

It is precisely because of this that, far from getting discouraged, our small number finds comfort in praying on the spiritual "lines of force," that converge throughout the history of Islam, toward the most profound liturgy of the Christian prayer, the Marian liturgy, that envisions the entire life of Jesus, from the Manger to the Cross. [Among these "lines of force" are] the traditional fast of the Shi'ite virgins from the 12–14 Rajab "in imitation of Mary's fast in the Temple," the prayers in the Oratory of Zachariah in Jerusalem and in front of all the mihrâbs inscribed with this verse from the Marian oratory (Qur'an)—the invocation to the linked names of Mary and Fatima, "Lady of Sorrows" in the pains of childbirth, and the linked names of Salman the Christian and Fatima who both shared bread with their fellow laborers—the prostration in prayer taught to

---

[161] Hasan al-Basrî (642–728) celebrated preacher who contributed to the foundation of Sufism, the mystical tradition of Islam.

[162] Fâtima was the daughter of the Prophet Muhammad who married his nephew, Ali ultimately leading to the dispute over the successor to the Prophet after his death and the split of Sunni and Shi'a forms of Islam.

[163] Fr. Monchanin (1895–1957) from the diocese of Lyon, knew Massignon in the 1930's. He became a hermit in India from 1939, incarnating a vocation of substitution in the midst of the Hindu community.

Fatima by her father, [Prophet Muhammad] every Friday from *asr* to *maghrib* (3 pm–6 pm)[164] in order to meditate on the creation of Adam (Ibn al-Hâjj, *Mudkhal*, I, 284;[165] we [Christians] would say, his redemption), and the invocation to Mary in Ephesus, who supplants Fatima in the final assumption of humanity into justice. "When the sun will be folded up like a coat" (Qur'an 81:1), according to the apocalyptic sign of the Marian apparition at Fatima (Portugal).

When will Islam answer en masse the call of Christian substitution, and Fâtima bint al Rasûl [daughter of the Prophet] to Our Lady Mary of Fatima? God knows the moment that is unknown to us, but we find the reproach, that is not very apostolic, strange that qualifies our prayer for the Church's accessibility to immense masses who have no leader or pastor, like those of today's Islam, as a prayer for the violent dispossession of the old Western Christian nations, exclusive hereditary owners of the Church's sources of grace.

We cannot turn a deaf ear to the cries, as wild as authentic, that so many ex-colonized Muslim and pagan people raise against our refusal to let them benefit from our Christian morals, share in our social life as equals or in this ecumenical Catholic ideal from which we have excluded them.

From Montreal, on November 26, 1956, the voice of a Cardinal from the Holy Roman Church[166] responded to one of our female members, and through her to the Badaliya: "... it is with all my heart that I shall pray for the intentions you have entrusted to me. It is obvious—to any mind willing to pause and give it thought—that the events now taking place in the world predict profound structural changes. Tomorrow the people of Asia and Africa will stand before the entrance to the Church of Christ Jesus. Shall we open the door to them? They will enter, in spite of us, because they will be pushed by the Spirit. The Church will welcome them and with them She will inaugurate a new chapter in Universal History..."

---

[164] The time of the five daily prayers of pious Muslims are determined by the place of the Sun, at sunrise (*fajr*), noon (*zuhr*), late afternoon (*'asr*), sunset (*maghrib*), and beginning of night (*'isha'*).

[165] A fourteenth century celebrated Egyptian jurist, a disciple of Ghazali, whose Madkhal al-shar' al-sharîf (Introduction to the Noble Islamic Law) is an ethical reference book.

[166] Cardinal Paul Émile Léger (1904–1991), who played an important role in the Second Vatican Council.

'I am with you always till the end of time...' (Mt. 28:20). Let us, through humility and strength of soul, be judged worthy of taking part in this sublime and urgent endeavor."

7. At the Limit

At the limit, where our effort as imploring intercessors between two terrorisms brings us down to our knees, overwhelmed, like Gandhi at Noakhali in 1947,[167] let us lift up our eyes toward eternal life, toward "the cloud of witnesses who preceded us." They too have been branded, abandoned as hostages and ransoms of Justice before their time and they are waiting for us in the participation in the Chalice of the Passion, in shared Solitude with the Lord, in the seclusion of Essential Desire:

"Sharibnâ'alä dhikri'l Habîbi mudâmatan..." "In memory of the Beloved we have drunk the intoxicating wine..." (Ibn al Fârid).[168]

It was necessary to pass, like them, like him, through "frisking by police" and torture, through the penitentiary stripping of slaves, to be betrayed by Hope, abandoned by the Father, with nothing left in our hearts but the mark of our original nature, the *fitra*, an unfissionable atom of Faith, *dharra min al-'iman*, meant to burn our condemned debris to ashes; the Faith of a disowned son, of an expelled orphan who can no longer weep, and gives way beneath the pressure of the mysterious Guest who nevertheless cradled him a long time ago in his mother's womb, in the dreams of his wandering nights, and who now buries him in the womb of the earth from which He drew him.

Buried alive, we still have this ultimate spark of faith in our hearts, revived in us by the look of convicted criminals far more than by the look of the conformist bon vivant, by the look of hunted Muslims far more than by the look of the "Christians" and "Jews" who hunt them down as scapegoats. [This spark is revived] even when noteworthy theologians in the service of the secular arm have doubts as to whether this Muslim Faith is theological; this heroic Faith of our Father Abraham [who was] ordered to sacrifice his son; this Faith of the poor, the backward, the

---

[167] Gandhi walked from village to village in his bare feet preaching reconciliation and non-violence in response to the struggle between Muslims and Hindus in Bengal, India, the future Bangladesh.

[168] 'Umar ibn al-Fârid (1191–1235) a celebrated Egyptian Sufi.

ignorant detested by our skeptical Christianity; this Faith in which there is only one mystery in God: that of his unity: the pure Act in which He unifies Himself: "*Tawhîduhu' iyyâhu Tawhîduhu.*"[169]

We want to enter this pure Act, through the non-violence of the Marian "fiat;" through our Muslim friends, our brothers, so that we, as substitutes for them, may be "One" together with them, as God is One.

For these forsaken ones there is only one work of mercy—hospitality—and it is through hospitality alone, not through legal observances, that one can go beyond the threshold of the Sacred. Abraham showed it to us.

Let us therefore search with Abraham for this ultimate spark of faith among the Muslims who we drive into the most atrocious despair and shove into the Cursed City, the City of the quintessential Refusal, the City of the Denial of the Hospitality that was demanded of Lot. It is there, in Egypt (Apoc. XI:8) that the first two members of the "Badaliya" founded it based on the suicide of a desperate man, a renegade from Christianity, then from Islam, who died in Mislata (Valencia), at the feet of Nuestra Señora de los Desamparados.[170]

We want to embrace the criminal in his outrage at those who point the finger at him, slander and beat him, embracing him in the hyperextension of his whole being as it bristles under the executioner's revolting precautions. Even though our imperfect substitution loathes doing it, it is the Truth of our wretchedness that calls us to kiss him, it is the Justice of our sentence which will chain us to his arms with Jesus the Savior.

"Tell the Truth, even should it burn you with the Fire of the dammed" (Harîrî).[171]

The transfiguring light of the Universe will not come from our skeptical and tepid Establishment, which excuses and normalizes the worst aberrations because they are "natural," that legitimates the simultaneous extermination of the guilty and the innocent because it is "scientific" and "atomic."

---

[169] His unity, He who is his unity.

[170] Massignon is referring to the laying of the foundation for the Badaliya in Egypt with Mary Kahil when they agreed to pray for the "salvation" of their friend Luis de Cuadra who later committed suicide in prison in Valencia.

[171] Abu Muhammad al-Harîrî (1054–1122) celebrated Arab philologist from Basra, Iraq.

Long ago, Abraham, the friend of God, questioned Him in order to save ten sparks of Faith still burning, ten believing Jordanian guests living in Sodom, from the Fire. Without doubt this is the foundation of the spirituality of Sodom, the Hell of "Il Primo Amore" [Satan], where Jesus descended to re-ignite the extinguished fire of hospitality that aroused the saving Indignation of the Judge.

8. Moral report on the year 1956

During the year 1956 our spiritual and material assistance to our Muslim friends through the works of humble mercy "commercium in spiritualibus" rather than lofty "communicatio in divinis,"[172] despite the current events, has worked to strengthen the following of the five pillars of their social and religious life:

A. Testimony (*Shahada*)

We must bear witness, but in serene non-violence. It is in this sense, in a lecture given at the Academia dei Lincei in Rome (on St. Francis in Damietta), that we clarified the sentence on the Islamo-Christian ordeal of the Mubahala in our founding text: "the Christians not daring to take up the challenge" should be interpreted according to Luke (9:53–56). They were not to resort to violence, and according to common theology, one should not tempt God into entering a judicial duel.

B. Prayer

Since November 2nd, at each of our monthly meetings, we have been saying the "*Fatiha*" in Arabic, the Muslim prayer to the King of the Day of Judgment, "Mâliki Yawm al-Dîn," in front of a crucifix in order to clearly identify this Judge for whom they are waiting like us, with his words: "I was hungry and you gave me food..." During Ramadan (April-May) we had a Mass for them every Friday, and on the 27th of Ramadan, we made our own their hope in "the descent of divine mercy," during the vigil of their Night of Destiny (*Laylat al-Qadr*), prayed by Foucauld. [This was] on May 8th

---

172 Massignon suggests that a "communion of divine things" risks confusion whereas "communion of spiritual things" envisions interreligious dialogue in which Muslims and Christians have much to offer one another.

at Notre Dame de La Sède, in Aix-en-Provence, thanks to the Archbishop; at St. Pothin in Lyon, thanks to the Cardinal; at St. Sulpice in Paris; and at the cathedral of St. Brieuc, thanks to the Bishop. Several of us prayed for our dead this year: Father Paul Soueïd (Mexico), Mrs. Popovitch (Paris), and Marquis Antoine de Chaponay (Rabat). Upon the organizers' request, by cable we joined the seventh centenary in Persia of Nasîr Tûsî, the great Shiite theologian, author of the prayer to Fatima, "Lady of Sorrows." Ch. Niazi Qutbi, custodian of the sanctuary of Mehrauli, (near Delhi where Gandhi went to pray), prayed twice with us for Algeria and had others do the same.

C. Fast

In addition to our private monthly fast, several of us fasted during the critical days of Algiers and Suez.[173] Sultan Mohammed V to whom we were able to pay our respects in Rabat, on the 3rd anniversary of his deportation, had Radio-Tangiers disclose on August 23rd that we had fasted for his return from exile. Taking up Messali's[174] example (1937), several MNA detainees managed to obtain the status of political prisoners by 12 consecutive days of fasting (29. XI.XII); they had asked us to testify in court and appeal to ministers on their behalf in order to justify the religious character of this hunger strike. We fasted on Yom Kippur with the Ihud.

D. Alms

We visited some Muslims in jail and at the hospital. On March 22nd, through the Elysée we received joyful news of the so long desired liberation, just in time for Easter, of the five Malagasy parliamentarians, as well as the trip to Algeria of a mission of the International Red Cross from Geneva to examine the issue of mutual respect for the 1949 Convention. Those of us who are fighting proxenetism[175] in North Africa have succeeded in getting more bousbirs [brothels] closed. We were represented at the Islamo-Christian Conference in Bhamdoum.

---

[173] Refers to the French-English military intervention in Suez from October 30th to November 5th, 1956.

[174] Messali Hadj (1898–1974) fasted in 1937 to obtain the status of a political prisoner.

[175] Proxenetism refers to procurers making money off prostitution.

E. Pilgrimage

Conscious of how important the example of the Seven Sleepers of Ephesus is for our fasts as "badaliya," (these martyrs who fasted to death for Justice), we all met in Vieux Marché (Côtes du Nord) on July 22nd with a thousand pilgrims, including over twenty Muslim workers and the support of four African Archbishops and Bishops. On the same day, the Muphti of Setif, Mr. Khebaba Taher, prayed for a serene peace in union with us, at the Seven Sleepers of Setif. At Ra'a el-Mâ, there is a spring with seven veins like the one at Vieux Marché, and the *mawsim* [seasonal pilgrimage] is observed twice a year on the dates of the Byzantine calendar: in memory of the Byzantine occupation (6th to 7th century).

An essay was published on the oratory dedicated to the Seven Sleepers in Rome (Via Appia). It was restored in 1710 during the papacy of Clement XI. The pilgrimages to Ephesus continued. An essay came out on the Islamo-Christian pilgrimages at St. Elie (Khadir-Eliyas; appeared in *Et. Carmelite*).

Two archbishops from Kenya (Mombasa, Nairobi) and the Superior General of the Fathers of St. Joseph of Mill-Hill (Reverend Father TH. MacLaughlin) have taken up the organization of the pilgrimage in Namugongo (Uganda) where Blessed Charles Lwanga and his companions were burned alive, martyrs of male chastity (6/3/86). They intend to institute an "international rescue for perverted young men"

N.B. We know how severely the European armies were contaminated by uranism[176] in Muslim countries, and how much, as a result, the recruits from Christian minorities fear barrack life in Egypt and elsewhere. We also know the extent of this contagion among young European students, especially in England. The heroic example of Charles Lwanga has the stark beauty of the Indian widow's *suttee*: "potius mori quam foedari."[177]

"Do pray for us, you, martyrs burnt alive, like Joan of Arc, to set the world ablaze with Love divine."

Note: Arabic ex-votos of the Badaliya were placed this year in Toumiline (Benedictine), in Rabat (Poor Clares: in order to replace the one that was transferred to Mt. Alverna), in St. Anne de Madawaska (New Brunswick, Canada), and in Damascus (Sisters of Charity).

---

[176] Uranism is male homosexuality.

[177] Rather die than sin.

28. Convocation - January 4, 1957
21 rue Monsieur, Paris 7

On Friday January 4, 1957, two days before the feast of the 1957 Epiphany (10th anniversary of the approval of our little sodality by the Auxiliary Archbishop of the Greek Catholic Melkite Patriarch of Antioch, Jerusalem and Alexandria)—Monthly Mass in the chapel of the Dames de Nazareth, 20 rue du Montparnasse at 6:30 pm, then meeting at the close of our day of private fasting for a serene peace between Christians and Muslims—particularly in North Africa and in the Near East.

The Mass in the Eastern Rite celebrated on December 8th in St. Joseph's Church (Paris XI) before a large and fervent gathering under the sign of Our Lady of the Veil ("*pokrov*" in Russian), the patron saint of our sodality, brought out the importance of solidarity in times of hardship, and of the redemptive suffering through which all the Eastern churches with their Slavic and Greek populations find themselves gathered together with the Muslim, Turkish, Iranian and Arab populations.

With regard to the Latin Church, it is necessary to insist on the posthumous as well as supranational missions of such predestined and compassionate souls as: the little Arab Carmelite of Bethlehem, Maryam Baouardy (Sr. Mary of Jesus Crucified, 1846–1878),[178] whose beatification is being requested by the Latin Patriarchate of Jerusalem as a means of ensuring the safety of the Holy Sites—the stigmatic Augustinian nun from Dulmen in Germany, Anne Catherine Emmerich (died in 1824), who is at the origin of the pilgrimage of Our Lady of the Assumption in Ephesus (Chapel of Panaghia Kapulu much venerated by Turkish Islam)—and finally St. Joan of Arc, whose intercession we must tirelessly invoke on behalf of those peoples overseas whom France had been mandated to emancipate and not to abandon: for example, those in Canada where a young congregation has been dedicated to St. Joan since 1917 in Bergerville near Sillery (Quebec, where a monumental statue of the saint, erect-

---

[178] See www.dcbuck.com article: "Louis Massignon and Mariam Baouardy: A Palestinian Saint for Our Time." Summer 2004. SUFI. Founder of the Carmelite Monasteries in Bethlehem and Nazareth, (extended to Haifa and Jerusalem after her death), Maryam of Jesus Crucified was beatified in 1983 by Pope John Paul II. She is the patron Saint of the Badaliya USA prayer movement re-created in the spirit of Louis Massignon's vision on December 8. 2002.

ed in 1938, overlooks the plain of Abraham); this congregation of the Sisters of St. Joan of Arc was founded by an Assumptionist (Rev. Fr. Clement; died in 1936); they have a branch in Beaulieu (Oise, [France]).

Neither should we forget the North African Muslims who are French citizens and who, through St. Joan of Arc, are appealing to the true France that brings consolation and liberation to the afflicted. Several of us are thinking of going on a pilgrimage to Domrémy so that "God, the first served" may help our homeland recover its true face in the eyes of the French Muslim citizens of Algeria, especially Algerian [infantrymen], *tirailleurs* and *spahis* [names of regiments], as well as the 150 Muslim officers who were enrolled in the regular army; fidelity to our word commands us to allow this true Army of Africa, which has been part of the French national army for 100 years, to return with heads held high to their native land at the time of Algerian reconciliation, that must not be long in coming,.

In the press several of us called for a Christmas truce in Algeria between Christian and Muslim believers—from the 22nd to the 26th of December; a truce preceded by "a common preparatory prayer," from the 17th to the 22nd of December in order that a "cease-fire" be obtained and that "an Algerian peace be established in justice and mutual respect." A few Muslim workers in Paris joined us in memory of our union with them last May 8th for their "Night of Destiny" (27th day of Ramadan): isn't "Christmas Night" a true *"Laylat al-Qadr,"*[179] when, with the permission of the Lord for everything, the Angels and the Spirit descend; that night is Peace until the rising of the sun. (Qur'an 97: 3–5).

Our perseverance in observing private fasts over the last three years for "a serene peace in justice" is swaying our Muslim friends at this moment as it did our Christian brothers; several of them, reduced by the scorn of the powers that be to the status of common law prisoners, fasted in a spirit of faith (they were members of the MNA),[180] and following insistent appeals to the Prime Minister and the Minister of Justice,[181] eventually got the status of political prisoners. Gandhi showed us with what

---

[179] Laylat al-Qadr: Night of Destiny, the 27th day of the Ramadan fast. This feast marks the night in which the Qur'an was first revealed by God to the Prophet.

[180] MNA: Acronym of the Mouvement Nationaliste Algérien founded by Messali Hadj in 1954.

[181] Edgar Faure and Robert Schuman respectively.

prudence we should resort to these fasts, and we exhort our associates to suggest them only to humble and fervent believers who dislike spectacular shows of faith and who are attentive to "God alone, the first served."

29. Convocation - February 1, 1957
21 rue Monsieur, Paris 7

Friday, February 1, 1957, monthly Mass, Chapelle des Dames de Nazareth, 20 rue Montparnasse, at 6:30 pm followed by our meeting at the close of our day of private fasting for a serene peace between Christians and Muslims, particularly in North Africa and the Near East. Through a letter from the Secretariat, on January 19, Pope Pius XII has informed us that he "is aware with paternal interest" of our Christmas appeal, through the Christian committee for France-Islamic relations.

Through the same channel, he had written to the Archbishop of Aix, the day before, sending his apostolic benediction to the disciples of Charles de Foucauld and Monsignor de Provenchères insisted on including us in his letter.

The Archbishops of Aix and of Rabat are happy to support us against inaccurate statements, fringing upon false witness, that some have used to denounce our "Islamomania." Various incidents have shown, moreover, the bias of our opponents, for whom we must pray rather than enter into discussion. In these times of extreme tension when our country is shaken under the dual temptation of gold and blood at the service of racist revenge, we must remain inflexible in the area of non-violence, applying the "arma Christi" of penance, prayer, and compassionate suffering for the poor. We must, as Gandhi said, incur the worst by our refusal of all demoralizing violence.

Let us pray for those who, through their fasting and silent mourning, hold firm, in this solemn moment in our national history, that it is impossible for us to accept further bloodshed in Algeria. The obligation of the members of the "Badaliya" is to pray that, should we become materially impoverished, the peoples of Asia and Africa, caught now in the noose of the economic battle between the USSR and the United States, may access material possessions, taken from their soil, even to the detriment of our privileges as superior technicians.

Likewise, on the spiritual level, we must not selfishly keep the superiority of our Christian morale for ourselves, but rather give equal access to the peoples of Asia and Africa, who sense the significance for the well-being of the world of a truly Christian spirit, practicing the universal fraternity dear to Charles de Foucauld.

From Montreal, from this Canada, once abandoned by a selfish and de-Christianized France, the voice of a Cardinal from the Holy Roman Church,[182] on November 26, 1956, wished to encourage members of the humble Badaliya to remain faithful to their vocation in these terms: "It is from the bottom of my heart that I will pray for the intentions with which you have entrusted me. It is obvious, to all who will stop and reflect, that events now unfolding in the world predict profound modifications of structure. Tomorrow, the people of Asia and Africa will be at the gates of the Church of Jesus Christ. Will we open the door to them? They will enter, despite us, since they will be ushered in by the Spirit. The Church will welcome them and she will initiate, with them, a new period in World History... 'I will be with you until the end of time'...May we, through humility and strength of spirit, be able to be judged worthy to participate in such a sublime and urgent task. Amen."

30. Convocation - March 1, 1957
21 rue Monsieur, Paris 7

Friday, March 1, 1957, monthly Mass at 6:30 pm in the Chapelle des Dames de Nazareth, 20 rue Montparnasse, prior to our meeting at the close of our day of private fasting for a serene Peace between Christians and Muslims, particularly in North Africa and the Near East.

The growing appeal of the example of Joan of Arc, dying for an unrecognized homeland, scorned, mistreated and persecuted among peoples said to be "backward," proves that through Joan of Arc, they can regain confidence in that *France, ideal Christian nation*, that we must strive to create, the consoler and liberator of nations; with noble English, American, and German friends, France can save these Muslim lands, Syria, Egypt and Morocco, where humble women, and even men, increasingly depend on the prayers of this French virgin, from economic slavery, whether Soviet or Atlantic.

---

[182] Cardinal P. Emile Léger.

More and more often we must go to pray at Our Lady of Bermont (3 km from Domrémy), that France regains awareness of its moral obligation towards Muslim Algeria and towards our African Army, infantry and spahi,[183] so often sacrificed for us in the frontlines.

Last February 15, following a prayer vigil in the room of Maréchal Lyautey (the one who kept his word to the Muslims) where he had prepared his final reconciliation with the Church through the Jesuits in Nancy, we had the opportunity to go to *Our Lady of Bermont*, where Father Pierre Frison celebrated Mass for our "badaliya" intentions, before coming back down to meet us at Domrémy in the parish church and Joan's home.

We must also pray at Beaulieu-les-Fontaines (Oise), in Joan's prison, where the Canadian "Sisters of Joan of Arc," founded in 1917 in Bergerville, near Quebec, have their French mission, so that we can entrust to them all Muslim souls faithful to Joan.

One of our members from the "Friends of Gandhi,"[184] writing from India, has begun a calendar of joint prayers for Islamic-Christian reconciliation with the Sajjada-Nishin[185] from the Mehrauli Mosque (near Delhi) where Gandhi offered himself, praying with Muslims for reconciliation, 4 days before he was killed (1/31/48). Two of his spiritual daughters, a Muslim, Miss Amat al-Salam, and a Hindu, Miss Asha Devi, support our prayers and fasts.

The United Nations, has given France and England a few weeks respite to revise, in a somewhat more humane way, their policies of common technological exploitation of Muslim Arab countries. May our two countries become aware once again of their Christian dignity.

Let us pray for *Muslim Egypt*, the homeland of the Badaliya. The agreement reached between the Vatican and Egypt concerning Christian schools, at the same time that our press, as much Christian as Jewish, was provoking their closures through insults, should encourage us to better understand Egypt. This people of humble *fellahs*, childlike and cheerful, long resigned to the worst, are who we strive to infuriate, asphyxiating

---

[183] Spahi: native Algerian troops.

[184] Madame Camille Drevet, secretary of the lay association "Friends of Gandhi" of which Massignon was the President.

[185] The *Sajjada Nashin* is the descendant of a *Sufi Pir* (Saint) or descendant of a disciple of a *Pir*, who tends to the tomb or grave, known as a *Dargah* or *Mazar*.

them "for their own good" (and ours?), in the case of the Aswan Dam as well as that of the Suez Canal. It is the Land of Refuge for the banished, from Joseph, son of Jacob to Memphis, to Joseph and the Holy Family to Old Cairo, and at Matarie, Land of the heroes of the Ascent of the Desert Fathers, from Anthony and Pacôme to Dhû l-Nûn Misrî and Fakhr Fârisi. It is the country of the Exiled that weep in the Desert, from Agar, Mother of the Arabs, to Mary the Egyptian,[186] from the Arûsat al-Sahrâ to the most chaste Nabîla al-Wafâ'iya (died 1934), all of them buried at the foot of the Moqattam.

Prolonging Egypt's suffocation in order to avenge Israel from an Arab blockade that our supplies have made illusory, and where Egypt's participation was only to defend the rights of Arab Refugees expelled from their homes for more than ten years following the horrid Oradour of Deir Yassin,[187] can only bring all kinds of misery to Israel. It is not fitting for the disciples of Moses or those of Christ, to collaborate with arrogant technicians in the "genocidal" scorn towards people that are backward and underfed and thus judged unworthy of understanding what liberty and honor represent for those who want to survive.

Let us pray for *Muslim Algeria* to which we, Christians, have a fraternal responsibility even more disturbing to our conscience. Our persistence in being the spurred and booted policeman towards vagabond tramps and strikers, for the sake of an Order that is no longer God's but Mammon's, puts us in a critical position with the "Malik Yawm al-Dîn" of the Fatiha (Master of Judgment Day), that Judge with pierced hands, who will at the end show himself, and to Whom we will then have to admit that it is our secular greed, our hardness of heart as the "privileged" from France, that is at the root of the worst excesses of the desperate armed militants. Our "clear conscience" towards the Arabs is as good as the Amer-

---

[186] Mary of Egypt (ca. 344–ca. 421) is revered as the patron saint of penitents, most particularly in the Eastern Orthodox, Oriental Orthodox, and Eastern Catholic churches, as well as in the Roman Catholic and Anglican churches

[187] The Deir Yassin massacre of hundreds of Palestinians took place on April 9, 1948, when around 120 fighters from the Irgun and Lehi Zionist paramilitary groups advanced on Deir Yassin near Jerusalem, a Palestinian-Arab village of roughly 600 people. The invasion occurred as Jewish forces sought to relieve the blockade of Jerusalem during the period of civil war that preceded the end of British rule in Palestine.

ican's "clear conscience" towards the Negroes and the Puerto Ricans. It is time for us to judge ourselves so as not to be judged.

31. Convocation - April 5, 1957
21 rue Monsieur, Paris 7

Friday April 5, 1957, monthly Mass in the chapel of the Dames de Nazareth, 20 rue du Montparnasse at 6:30 pm, then a meeting at the close of our day of private fasting for a serene Peace between Christians and Muslims, particularly in North Africa and in the East.

During this 1957 Lent, which coincides in a crucial way with the 1376 Muslim Ramadan (April 1st–May 1st), let us ponder over the French Bishops' warning as we face the Algerian drama; may we become aware before God and before men of the duties we have neglected; may we not claim our rights before having purified ourselves.

Our "vocation" as "substitutes" for our Muslim brothers places us, wretches that we are, at the very heart of the problem.

For the last 127 years God has wanted France to go into North Africa (and *stay there*) in order to bring life rather than death to poor and needy believers, by loving them and sharing a hope of communal immortality with them. The only way that will move them to fraternize with us is in the way that we welcome them, in the mystery of the Crucified's love, that puts its indelible mark upon us, despite ourselves and our unworthiness.

This is being written on the eve of the Annunciation, on the day, dear to me, two days before the martyrdom of the mystic Hallaj in Baghdad in the year 922, when he offered himself as a "paschal victim" for his Muslim brothers.

On *Good Friday*, April 19th, from 3 pm to 6 pm let us remember to kneel down *alone* in spirit, keeping silent if possible, with our hearts and minds turned toward our *Qibla*,[188] Jerusalem, thereby imitating Fâtima, the Prophet's daughter who was taught by her father to do the same every Friday from *Asr* (15h. [3 pm]) to *Maghrib*[189] (18h. [6 pm]), in memory of

---

[188] *Qibla*: The direction in which the Muslim believer orients himself or herself to pray. The *qibla* is always directed towards the Ka'ba in Mecca, but for some time in early Islam (from 622 to 624), the direction was toward Jerusalem.

[189] *Asr* and *Maghrib* are two of the five prescribed Muslim Daily Prayers.

the Hour of the Creation of Man (Ibn al-Hâjj, *madkhal*, I, 284); for our part, we shall say, "in memory of his Redemption."

Besides our three days of fasting on April 5th, 12th and 19th, we shall renew our vigil, their "Night of Destiny" (*Laylat al-Qadr*) on April 27th, if possible in the same churches as last year (Aix, Lyon, Paris, St. Brieuc; we shall also ask churches in Nancy[190] and in Algeria to join us). Let us pray that in His kindness the Merciful One may bless the Ramadan of our brothers and sisters in Islam.

On that day let us pray in union with the dead of the Army of Africa,[191] with the French officers bonded by friendship with their Muslim comrades, such as colonels Henry de Vialar, Henri de Castries[192] (through whom we met Foucauld and Lyautey) or Maréchal Lyautey, who requested to be buried in the Muslim cemetery of Chella in order to appear with his brothers-in-arms before the same Judge, Mâlik Yawm al-Dîn[193] of the "*Fatiha*," which we shall say together for them.

Several Christian women are presently asking us to respond, in order to avenge it, to the call of the French blood spilled in Africa by Moroccan terrorists. As if we could avenge this blood while turning a deaf ear to that other call of French blood that was shed in Algeria and is indissolubly mixed with that of the Muslims "outside the French law" who we made our fellow citizens through the Statute of 1947. The blood of Christ is in both of these bloods. It is high time that we stopped shedding it; may Joan of Arc intercede on our behalf; she who shuddered with horror at the sight of the French blood shed by the invader.

There is a French-Muslim community: our duty, as a "Badaliya," is to save its life and its honor; the life and honor of its young women and men. Under the sign of the Virgin Mary.

First the women: I am talking about those humble workers, those French women, now in the thousands, who have married Muslims, thus setting up monogamous households about which J. H. Louwyck wrote a

---

[190] Nancy: Massignon is referring here to the capital of Lorraine.

[191] Army of Africa: Armée d'Afrique—a special French army corps which conquered Algeria in 1830 and fought in all the French colonial ventures thereafter.

[192] Commander Henri de Castries ((1850–1927), a close friend of Charles de Foucauld who was one of the pioneers of South Algerian exploration.

[193] *Mâlik Yawm al-Dîn*: The King, or the Lord of the Day of Judgment—one of the several names of God invoked in the *Fatiha*.

penetrating psychological study, ("*Tayeb*"). They did not give themselves to their husbands in order to evangelize them; nor were they moved by vile indecency like those unfortunate women who were shaved and whipped in 1945. No, they were seized by a deeper instinct, that of the poor woman who gives herself in an act of royal generosity to someone whom she guesses to be even poorer than herself, to a helpless exile whom her favor fills with rapture; a reflection of the Foreign Guest whom the angel announced to Our Lady. A reflection of the sweet face of Mary hovers in the minds of the Muslim husbands,[194] of Mrs. Messali Hajj, Mrs. Bourguiba, Mrs. Faraj, Mrs. Doualibi, Mrs. Taha Hussein.

Let us pray that the new "security" measures which some wish to be taken around Paris and elsewhere against the "bad" North African workers (possibly 1/3 of the entire North African population according to an expert, just as with the *bad Angels*) may not destroy these humble Franco-Muslim households, already decimated last January 18–24th: fathers were taken away, interned in Algeria without being brought to trial, and family allowances suspended. We are asking God that they may be reallocated to these mothers.

Now the young men: Let us pray for the 30,000 young Algerian Muslims whom we have just mobilized, transferring them to metropolitan France, far from the "bloody pacification" of their villages; may their French comrades give them a fraternal welcome since, for the time being, supervision by officers of their race and faith is not being provided. Our young men here in France can help them escape the dangers, familiar to doctors and military chaplains, of male promiscuity found in African camps. For the men, far more numerous, who are kept there for the sake of "pacification," let us offer one last prayer. It is not true that these dangers cannot be averted, that this ill, caused by sexual segregation, cannot be cured; General Gouraud once told me, in his position as commander, that he did not punish certain friendships; that [he thought] a heroic confrontation with mortal danger would undoubtedly redeem, purify and turn them into a spotless friendship that would shine beyond

---

[194] The Algerian political activist and founder of the MNA Messali Hajj, the Tunisian President Habib Bourguiba, and the Egyptian writer Taha Hussein were married to Christian French women, hence the reference to "le doux visage de Marie" the sweet face of Mary, who is also revered in Islam.

death. It is to this kind of friendship that the dying Maréchal Lyautey[195] testified when he requested to be buried in the Muslim cemetery of Chella in
order to appear with his Muslim brothers-in-arms before the same Judge,
Mâlik Yawm al-Dîn of the *"Fatiha,"* that we will say for them, together.

To surmise, on the contrary, that this promiscuous behavior is incurable, as if Jesus were not the Master of the Impossible, leads in the end
to the unleashing, on behalf of Order, of the wild animal trainer's bestiality advocated by certain sociologists who base their pedagogy on the
Bat. d'Af. of Biribi;[196] this amounts to condemning these sinners to the
absolute denial of hospitality that caused the cursed City to be burned
in spite of Abraham's prayer [Sodom].

The "Badaliya," which, from the very beginning, found itself face to
face with these unfortunates in Islam, is asking all of its contemplative
members to intercede so that the bestial temptations to which both terrorists and anti-terrorists are prey, may not hurl the two enemy camps
into the abyss from which these very temptations came.

32. Convocation - May 3, 1957
21 rue Monsieur, Paris 7

Friday, May 3, 1957, monthly Mass at 6:30 pm in the Chapelle des Dames
de Nazareth, 20 rue Montparnasse followed by meeting at the close of
our day of private fasting for a serene Peace between Christians and
Muslims, particularly in North Africa, in the East, and in India.

Our Lent and Holy Week have helped us better understand the theocentric character and real meaning of our separated Muslim brothers'
Ramadan: to recover, between brothers who are divided, respect for the
right of Asylum, the Sacred Hospitality of Abraham. One of ours, who
prayed for the Badaliya in Mecca at the Hajj in 1955, has just visited us
concerning the "kidnapping" of the president of the Reformist Ulemas

---

[195] By mentioning Lyautey whose homosexuality was known to all of his colleagues,
Massignon is tactfully providing an example of the transformation through heroic
death of *certaines camaraderies* (certain friendships) into *amitié sans tache* (spotless friendship).

[196] Bat. d'Af. stands for Bataillons d'Afrique, the name given to disciplinary regiments
located throughout North Africa, notably in Biribi (Tunisia) during the colonial period.

(Cheikh Tebessi)[197] and of a harmful trend to outlaw all French Muslims in Algeria (and even in France), even those that ask to be treated like humans beings and not like mad dogs. Our visitor would like the Badaliya to concretely intervene, so that our spiritual attitude of non-violence is not complicit with the "merciless repression" that makes some think it acceptable "by tempering it with words of charity and love" (sic).

Our non-violence position is a basic principal for us. Prayer, fasting and sacrifice are not capitulations but rather spiritual weapons, not to "temper" but to overcome the excesses of the two opposing terrorisms. If our position substitutes us *firstly* for all the Algerian Muslims, it is because we have made them "incarcerated" everywhere, in the intolerable prison of our scorn, hatred and private revenge, so much so that their worst acts of cruelty, in torturing our brothers for their race and their faith, are the "hateful reflexes" of *"captives"* who have no other recourse against a biased State, forgetful of its word most solemnly given, naming some of us as guarantors (21/8/47). It is never permissible for the State to lower itself in service of private revenge, stirred up by capitalists who push their hypocrisy to the extent of calling convicts, who are without arms or homes, "feudal," because their clever abuses have driven them to rebellion.

Before God and man, we are not permitted to equate "atrocities" committed by outlaws and "atrocities" tolerated (accepted under the seal of a word of honor...) by Agents of Order, who renounce their very reason to exist, before God and man. Let us pray that they understand, and that they find a way to reintegrate the Algerian Muslims, within the Human Law of the Guest, with a view to another means of contact, other than "physical contact" (sic: torture). *Only then* will the exasperated outlaws understand that they will only achieve political and social Liberty by ceasing these "atrocities" associated with convicts.

People will object that Islam is becoming communist and that the Atlantic nations feel that we cannot have any "spoken" contact with those whose doctrine it is to obey the Party when it demands bearing false witness. What we are aware of, that is in fact very common, is that the order to bear false witness is also contaminating more and more the Party of National Interest, and our principal calling is to prevent Islam from adopt-

---

[197] The Algerian Association of "Ulama" Reformists was established in 1925 to encourage the renewal of Algerian Islam.

ing this order. Let us pray, in this regard, for India, where the conjunction of extremes there, as in all the countries of the Bandung Declaration,[198] makes more and more Muslims suspect, even in the eyes of those who witnessed Gandhi's sacrifice for a serene peace with Islam. Let us pray, fast, and humble ourselves to prevent a general outlawing of Islam by the oil industry in the two blocs.

Let us thank God, in this regard, for the magnificent 20 day fast by Lanza de Vasto,[199] Gaschard (Bernard Gaschard—peasant) and Parodi (Pierre Parodi—doctor), for Algeria (14 rue du Landy, Clichy, in the St. Vincent de Paul parish). May it awaken the United States whom we have asked to revive Lincoln Day, on April 30 (the anniversary of the April 30, 1863 "day of fasting, humiliation and prayer") that Abraham Lincoln decreed so that his country may cease dishonoring itself by mistreating the Negroes. *We will fast* so that the real America will once again liberate us, this time, from our hundred year sin against Algeria, a nation where God needs France despite everything.

33. Convocation - June 7, 1957
21 rue Monsieur, Paris 7

Friday June 7, 1957, monthly Mass in the chapel of the Dames de Nazareth, 20 rue du Montparnasse at 6:30 pm, then a meeting at the close of our

---

[198] The first large-scale *Asian-African* or *Afro-Asian Conference*—also known as the *Bandung Conference*—was a meeting of Asian and African states, most of which were newly independent, which took place between April 18 and April 24, 1955 in Bandung, Indonesia. The conference was organized by Indonesia, Burma, Pakistan, Ceylon (Sri Lanka), and India and was coordinated by Ruslan Abdulgani, secretary general of the Indonesian Ministry of Foreign Affairs. The conference's stated aims were to promote Afro-Asian economic and cultural cooperation and to oppose colonialism or neocolonialism by the United States, the Soviet Union, or any other imperialistic nation.

[199] Lanza del Vasto (Giuseppe Giovanni Luigi Enrico Lanza di Trabia), (1901–1981), was a philosopher, poet, artist, and nonviolent activist. He was born in San Vito dei Normanni, Italy and died in Elche de la Sierra, Spain. A western disciple of Mohandas K. Gandhi, in 1948 he founded L'Arche communities modeled on Gandhi's ashrams. Along with Denise and Robert Barrat he denounced the use of torture in Algeria. He was an advocate of inter-religious dialogue, spiritual renewal, ecological activism and nonviolence.

day of private fasting for a serene Peace between Christians and Muslims, particularly in North Africa and in the East.

This is the day before the eve of Pentecost, the coming down of the Holy Spirit, the Spirit of Life, Wisdom and Truth, "dulcis Hospes animae." ["Sweet soul's Guest"]. May He come into our hearts.

While a whirlwind of lies and atrocities are raging over Algeria, like the dry, violent Sahara winds—where it appears that, in spite of everything, a new, albeit ambiguous nation is soon going to be born, and where the two races presently killing each other are already beginning to cohabit post mortem, their bloody dead buried pell-mell in the same common soil—let us stay firm in our faith in the God of Abraham, the God of us all; [firm in our faith] to the One and only God to whom we, Christians, entrusted the future of our French brothers in Africa on April 27th, the eve of the Night of Destiny, *Laylat al-Qadr*, thereby joining the desire for the future, through prayer and fasting, held by our Muslim brothers in Africa and in the East, as they were ending their Ramadan.

Let us remain especially fraternal and more affectionate than ever toward the North African Muslims working in metropolitan France where an atmosphere of suspicion and hatred may well engulf these exiles and harden them into the despair of Spartacus, the escaped slave—driving them into a primitive rebellious anarchy, in a horrible search for freedom in death, through a cosmic suicide that will hurl them, forever bound to their more or less paternalistic "persecutors," into hell.

We can no longer forsake Algeria because we cannot send these workers back there at this moment; let us remain hospitable and just toward them; several thousands of them have married French women; we have brought 8/10th of our Muslim Algerian soldiers into metropolitan France and Germany as well as 30,000 Muslim draftees enrolled last fall. Are we going to put them in cages like wild beasts under the pretense that their race and their religion are inciting them against our race and our religion, as some of those who preach about a Savior, tortured and crucified for the salvation of sinners and criminals, have the audacity to say and write publically?

Only if we in France behave like brothers, practicing the works of mercy, especially hospitality—a crucial virtue at a time when some of our administrators encourage hotel keepers and charitable organizations to deny lodging to the *"bicot"*[200] because he is a suspect character—that the murderous folly of the hunted *fellaghas*[201] abate in Algeria and that they regain a glimmer of hope in a shared future for our two races in their country.

Let us pray with all our strength for our Franco-Muslim pilgrimage on July 27–28th to the chapel of the VII Sleepers of Ephesus in Vieux-Marché (Côtes du Nord), on the feast of the Octave of St. Mary Magdalen.

A third booklet about this pilgrimage is going to be published by P. Gauthier, 12 rue Vavin (Paris VI) with plates showing a detailed plan of the dolmen crypt[202] and of the chapel in Vieux-Marché, of the oldest Mongol miniature of the VII Sleepers (1307), the icon of the Sleepers (in the Monastery of St. Catherine on Mt. Sinaï; photo J. Leroy), five block prints of incunabula[203] and the sketch of the seven holes (laid in a triangle) from which water gushes forth at *Ra's El Mâ* near Guidjel[204] (Setif where our Algerian Muslim friends will come and pray in union with us on July 27th and 28th).

The Portuguese bishop of Leiria (the diocese in which Our Lady of Fatima is found) favorably accepted the suggestion that the crypt of the Byzantine church which is being built in Fatima, be dedicated to Our Lady of the Veil (Pokrov), the Patron of our little sodality.

The case for the beatification of the Arab Carmelite Maryam Baouardy (Sr. Mary of Jesus Crucified) who was born in Abellin and died in Bethlehem in 1878, may be reopened in Rome.[205] She is prayed to by Arab Christians in the Holy Land and by several of us. She is venerated in France at the Carmel of Pau (Basses Pyrénées) where a Mass is going to be celebrated for us.

---

[200] Bicot: an offensive slang word designating a North African Arab.

[201] Name given by the French to Algerian Fighters for Independence from colonial France.

[202] The crypt was built at the site of an ancient standing stone called a dolmen.

[203] Incunabulum, a Latin term, is a wood block printing of a book before 1500.

[204] The shrine honoring the Seven Sleepers story in Guidjel, Algeria.

[205] Sr. Mary of Jesus Christ Crucified, a Palestinian Carmelite, founder of the Carmelite Monasteries in the Holy Land, was beatified in Rome on November 13, 1983. Patron Saint of the Badaliya USA established on December 8, 2002.

34. Convocation - July 5, 1957
21 rue Monsieur, Paris 7

Friday July 5, 1957, monthly Mass in the chapel of the Dames de Nazareth, 20 rue du Montparnasse at 6:30 pm, then a meeting at the close of our day of *Private Fasting For a Serene Peace* between Christians and Muslims, particularly in North Africa and in the East.

It is for this precise intention that we began our fasts four years ago, after a Mass in the Church of St. Severin celebrated by the Prior General of the Little Brothers of Foucauld.

On the Saturday following Easter last year the Little Brothers received a heartrending answer from God when Br. Maurice Tourvieille was killed in Aïn Ouarka near Aïn Sefra. They offered this death for the serene peace they constantly ask of God.

Now comes our turn, after keeping vigil on the eve of the Night of Destiny (*Laylat al-Qadr*) over the last two years for the restoration of this serene peace, to receive the same heartrending answer from God.

One of our dearest Muslim friends, an Algerian man born in Djidjelli, Professor Hajj Lounis (Mahfoud ibn Messaoud) from the Lycée Albertini in Sétif was mortally wounded by a mechanic, Beloud Mohamed Tahar, and died the next day, leaving a widow and two children.

Hajj Lounis was not only the friend who had openly prayed in Mecca at the Multazam of the Ka'ba,[206] during the Hajj of 1955 for our little association of "substitution," or Spiritual Hospitality, but it was he who, at our entreaties, had accepted to go on a yearly mission to Jerusalem to inspect the Tlemcen Abu Madyan Waqf at the Al-Aqsa Mosque[207] and protect the moral obligation of France toward the management of this trust

---

[206] Multazam: the short length of wall between the door of the Ka>ba and the corner containing the Black Stone. At the completion of their pilgrimage Muslim pilgrims embrace this part of the wall, thus expressing their love and reverence for the house of Allah.

[207] Waqf: a religious endowment in Islam, usually a property (building or plot of land) whose revenues are used for religious purposes. The waqf in question here—a part of the Al-Aqsa Mosque in Jerusalem—was named after Abu Madyan, a Sufi saint (died 1198), who was born in Seville, and spent time in the Algerian city of Tlemcen. The revenues of this waqf were used to provide for the needs of poor Muslims coming from Tlemcen (and possibly other places in North Africa) on a pilgrimage to the holy places in Jerusalem, such as the Al-Aqsa Mosque.

set up for the needs of poor pilgrims.[208] It was he who discovered the documents proving the authenticity of the pilgrimage of the Seven Sleepers of Ephesus at Guidjel near Sétif, and who had prayed, in fraternal union with us on the dates when we were praying to the Seven Sleepers in Vieux Marché (in Brittany) for a serene peace in justice.

Moreover, having learned this year that we would keep vigil for our distressed Muslim brothers during the Night of Destiny in five churches in France, he wrote us the following on April 25th: "On the eve of Laylat al-Qadr, that is to say on the evening of Friday the 26th I intend to go—but alone—and pray before the Seven Sleepers of Guidjel for a serene peace—I prefer to commune alone with Allah and not cause harm to anyone."

It had indeed been insinuated by some that through our union of prayer we were leading him to embrace passive non-violence and resign himself to a collective repression that we, as well as he and the Muphti of Sétif, have always condemned.

What Hajj Lounis believed is that there are sacred places that provide sanctuary for Muslims and Christians who are determined to extract serene Peace from the one God of Abraham, Father of all believers, through prayer, fasting and sacrifice, salâm Allâh.

Neither in the case of Little Brother Maurice nor in that of Hajj Lounis did the murderer know what he was doing; and we have implored the family of our Muslim friend, a victim of unleashed hatred, to intercede so that his murderer will not be executed. Like Hallaj, the martyr of Baghdad, Hajj Lounis died for the greatest love there is. The intimate letters from this noble soul, enjoins us to commit ourselves to reciting every day, in his place, "fîl Badaliya" [in Badaliya], the Fatiha of Islam, which is an appeal to the King of the Day of the Last Judgment, this crucified King whom we recognize in every man killed for a serene Peace.

The Fatiha will be said for Hajj Lounis in Vieux—Marché in front of the dolmen-crypt, next July 27–28th.

One of our colleagues from the University of France, Professor René Louis, a scholar of Romance languages, has just identified a previously

---

[208] For Massignon, France, as the governing authority in Algeria, had a moral obligation to make sure that money from the waqf in Jerusalem was properly allocated to the poor Algerian Muslims in need of it for their pilgrimage: this was the object of Hajj Lounis' yearly mission.

unexplained allusion in the "Chanson de Roland" [Song of Roland] to an earthquake that, according to the Chanson, took place "at the VII Sleepers in Brittany," when the hero, mortally wounded, tried in vain to break his sword, Durendal, against the "perron" of Roncevaux (see Bédier edition, verses 1427–1429, and W. Foerster edition, verses 1278–1281). This passage, according to Ferdinand Lot, dates from the beginning of the Xth century, and therefore cannot possibly allude to the "seven Holy Bishops of Brittany," venerated in seven separate places after Dol ceased to be a metropolis (1199), since what we have here is a single place, a "perron" (the dolmen), thus at Vieux-Marché.[209] The text of the "chanson" also connects these two "perrons" to the Pilgrimage of Santiago de Compostela, which started in the IXth century, at a time when people in Brittany still remembered that Roland was Count of the Breton March when he went to die at the front in the Crusade in Spain.

We are asking the members of the "Badaliya" to be mindful this summer of two pilgrimages, that of Vieux-Marché and that of Domrémy (or Beaulieu) in memory of Joan of Arc, liberator of oppressed nations.

35. Convocation - August 2, 1957
21 rue Monsieur, Paris 7

Monthly mass for Badaliya intention (for a serene peace between Christians and Muslims, especially in Algeria) will be celebrated next Friday, first Friday, August 2, 1957, at 7 pm at Saint-Severin. We will add two intentions in thanksgiving (for the pilgrimage of the Seven Sleepers in Britta-

---

[209] Roland, a historical figure whom the *Chanson de Roland* turns into an epic hero, knowing that he is going to die, does not want his trusty sword, Durendal, to be used by the enemy, and strikes it with all his might against the stone "perron" of Roncevaux, near a pass in the Spanish Pyrénées. The stone breaks, but not the sword, and Roland's mighty strokes reverberate all the way from Spain to Brittany where they create an earthquake at the site of the dolmen-crypt of the Seven Sleepers, which Massignon, to make the point of the story more striking, calls a "perron" even though a "perron" and a dolmen do not resemble each other. A dolmen is a prehistoric stone table while a "perron" is a set of steps usually man-made (the Webster's dictionary, defines it as "an out-of-door flight of steps—usually applied to medieval or later structures of some architectural pretensions") but sometimes formed by nature as seems to have been the case in the *Chanson*.

ny and for an acquittal) and we will be particularly united, through prayer, to the sessions at Toumliline.[210]

36. Convocation - September 6, 1957
21 rue Monsieur, Paris 7

Friday September 6, 1957, monthly Mass in the Church of St. Severin at 7 pm, at the close of our day of *private Fasting for a serene Peace* between Christians and Muslims, particularly in North Africa and in the East.

Due to the death of our dear friend Hajj Lounis, the pilgrimage of July 27–28th to the Seven Sleepers of Ephesus at Vieux-Marché was particularly meaningful. On August 14th, sixteen sprays of flowers were placed in the dolmen-crypt in his memory by one of our Canadian friends, along with cards from: Msgr., Bishop of St. Brieuc and Tréguier, Canon Prudhomme, (director of Our Lady of Hope), the Director of the Seminary of St. Brieuc, the Superior of the Marist Fathers, the Director of the St. Charles School, the Superiors of the Nuns of Montbareil, Divine Mercy, St. Thomas of Villeneuve, the superiors of the Daughters of the Holy Spirit (Mother House: St. Louis Clinic), the Daughters of Divine Providence, the Sisters of the Cross, of Good Help, of the Presentation (former Carmel, Godet clinic) of St. Brieuc; and from the Superior of the Good Savior (Bégard).

---

[210] In 1952, 20 Benedictine monks left the Abbey of En-Calcat in southwestern France and sailed to Casablanca, Morocco. They built a monastery originally called the Priory of Christ the King which became known as Toumliline, after a nearby natural spring. In the spirit of the now Blessed Charles de Foucauld they became the only Christian monks in Muslim North Africa at the time. They served their Muslim Berber neighbors, establishing an orphanage and supplying medical needs to the local population. Under the patronage of the sultan, King Mohammed V they hosted an annual interfaith seminar inviting Muslims, Christians and Jews. Massignon is referring to those seminars held at the monastery called Toumliline. This second annual "International Summer Seminar" held from August 10 to the 25th, 1957, had "Education" as its central theme. The Sultan received the participants in his palace in Rabat at the end of the session. It was on the occasion of this trip that Louis Massignon had the honor of being decorated with the Grand Cordon du Ouissam Alaoui (the equivalent of the French Legion of Honor), for rendering eminent service to the State of Morocco. See: Beach, P. and Dunphy, W. "The Benedictine and the Moor: A Christian Adventure in Moslem Morocco," Copyright 1960 by Holt, Rinehart and Winston, Inc.

A Mass will be said at the Seven Sleepers on September 9th, the first anniversary of the death of our friend Antoine de Chaponay in Rabat.

A year of prayers offered by the Sons and Daughters of Charles de Foucauld in memory of the centenary of his birth in Strasbourg in 1858, will begin on September 15, 1957; we will take heart in uniting in spirit with the ceremonies over which Msgr. De Provenchères will preside at Sainte Baume on that day. He had let us know by cable of his prayerful union with us during our pilgrimage to the Seven Sleepers on July 27–28th. Also we will have a Mass said on that day in the chapel of the dolmen-crypt with the Brothers of Foucauld from St. Gildas (near Penvénan).

Terrorism keeps raging on both sides in Algeria; let us join our ever more insistent prayer to the Mass that will be said at Our Lady of Bermont (Domrémy).

Our friend, Dr. Martin Buber wrote us that the Jewish Kippur falls on October 5th this year. Several of us will fast on that day so that Israel (as well as our own country) may at last recover the awareness of its holy vocation, and also pray for a serene peace.

37. Convocation - October 4, 1957
21 rue Monsieur, Paris 7

Friday October 4, 1957, monthly Mass at 6:30 pm in the Chapel of the Dames de Nazareth, 20 rue du Montparnasse at the close of our day of *Private Fasting for a Serene Peace* between Christians and Muslims, particularly in North Africa and in the East.

Saturday October 5th, *Yom Kippur*, Israel's fast of atonement. Upon the request of our noble friends from the *Ihud*, Dr. Judah Magnes (died in 1948) and Dr. Martin Buber, several of us will fast this year for a truly fraternal reconciliation between Isaac and Ishmael, especially this year, when the Israelis and the French have so much to atone for, beginning with the operation "Kadesh" (sic: against the Sinaï), all the way to the Suez coup: we shall move our day of private fasting from the 4th to the 5th and say the prayer *Naila*.

The Muslim pilgrimage to Mehrauli (India) will take place from October 7th to October 9th; we shall join with it in prayer, as did Gandhi before he was killed, by reciting the *Fatiha*; October 2nd is the 100th anniversary of Gandhi's birth. Let us pray for our beloved and revered Fr. Jules

Monchanin who was brought back from his ashram to the St. Antoine hospital via Pondichéry. He gave himself entirely as an offering for India.

The widow of our friend Hâjj Lounis (Mahfoud) told us of her close spiritual union with us as we were commemorating the violent death of her husband, killed by his blinded brothers: for the Greatest Love.

Let us pray that the best among the Zionists, conscious of being doomed to "encirclement" by an aggressively colonialist Asian policy, may seek God's peace in order to live in peace with others. And that their Algerian Jewish friends may open the eyes of our other settlers in Algeria to the inanity of their scornful hatred toward the Muslim majority that will surely go on "encircling" their little enclave and its electrified barbed wire fence in this immense Black Africa, which has been gradually gaining freedom over the past year (as in Ghana, Togo, Nigeria, Cameroun).

Let us pray that the eyes of so many French people who are blinded by money may come to see the absurdity of practicing torture and secret executions on a massive scale, as has been the case since July 20th, thus adding thousands of mostly innocent victims to the monthly toll of those killed in the open countryside, not by troops operating on an official assignment, but by us alone, whose cowardly indifference has not yet dared say, in the face of evil: "enough."

Yet the French bishops did warn us. They did tell us the Truth: "It is not permitted to seek the Good of our Country *through intrinsically wrong means.*" It is our duty to say it again. Every Mass at which no blood was spilled[211] weeps at the torture inflicted upon the pure and sacred body of Jesus in the name of our beloved Country and of her Honor. As we did for Morocco in 1953 and for Algeria in 1957, let us confess—before the Great Day of Justice—that we recognize the Crucified of our vocation in all those hounded and tortured Muslim men and women: the very same people whom the Algerian Statute of 1947 had established as our fellow citizens and whom we are now, in violation of the law, cornering into having nothing to oppose the overwhelming bestiality of our technology

---

[211] A declaration by the Assembly of Cardinals and Bishops March 17, 1957. Massignon is referring to Masses celebrated in Algeria that were not subjected to terrorist attacks.

but their torn "virgin point,"[212] the utter destitution of the *muçabbelîne*,[213] of those "vowed to the death;" like that which long ago brought victory to the great Christians of France, such as Joan of Arc.

Recently, the head of the repression in Algiers, said of Si Mhidi[214] whom he ordered to be tortured to death for having blasphemed against France, that this "fanatic" had died, knowing *how to suffer*. What a horrendous phrase; we made him into a *Man of Sorrows*, as did the Roman legionnaires with the Other One. Let us offer our prayer, from afar, for the repose of Si Mhidi's soul and ask that his executioner, "who does not know what he is doing," may be forgiven, let us sing the *Prayer at Dawn*[215] that not long ago some incarcerated Christians sang to help their Muslim fellow prisoners on their way to the guillotine.

Let us pray that God may save the French homeland and the Roman Church from the dual temptation of Blood and Gold. It is not by getting our draftees to learn how to mistreat and kill the Poor that we shall teach them courage. The honor of the police is in discovering crimes, not in committing them in secret. The honor of the army is not in guarding the secret about certain powerful criminals by lying to cover for them; after obeying their orders. So much for Blood.

---

[212] "Le point vierge:" a theme borrowed from the 10th century Sufi mystic and martyr, al Hallaj, the subject of Massignon's magnum opus. After his correspondence with Louis Massignon, Thomas Merton refers to the "point vierge" several times in his *Conjectures of a Guilty Bystander*: As the "center of our nothingness where one meets God—and is found completely in His mercy" (p. 151). "This little point of nothingness and of absolute poverty is the pure glory of God in us" (p. 158). For *le point vierge* in the writings of Louis Massignon and Hallaj see Buck, D. "Dialogues with Saints and Mystics: In the Spirit of Louis Massignon" Chapter Seven. 2002 KNP London, New York.

[213] "Muçabbelîne," an Islamic term referring to those who, on the path to God, accompany the *mujâhîdun*, combatants for God.

[214] Massignon is probably referring to the French General Paul Aussaresses who in 2001 published a memoir, *Services Spéciaux, Algérie 1955–1957*, in which he admitted participating (with the French government's authorization) in the torture and murder of dozens of Algerians, among whom was the FLN leader of the Algiers province, Larbi Ben Mhidi, referred to here as Si Mhidi.

[215] "La Prière de l'Aube," or Prayer at Dawn, in Arabic "*Salât al-Fajr:*" The first of the five daily prayers that Muslims recite every day. As its name indicates, it should be said before sunrise.

And now about Gold. Let us obey Foucauld who said to his disciples: "They never will refuse to pay a single tax, no matter how abusive it may be (Directoire, art. XXI. Ed. 1928, p. 57). Let us pray that the Church may follow this discipline, at a time when so many plutocrats, all of them unrepentant sinners of the worst kind, offer perverse alms to the Church; their offerings "for her charitable organizations," including Marian ones, constitute a cynical percentage of their tax evasions, which they want the Church to absolve so that they can continue to practice them. This complicity, tolerated by the bourgeois State, between the plutocrats and the black market of the "right-thinking people" will not ensure victory over Communism whose followers are more straightforward with the Party; instead, it will hand them over to Fascism, which has no sympathy whatsoever toward men of the Church, especially when they protest their loyalty toward the State while helping rob it at the same time. Let us pray with the psalmist: "Don't gather my soul with sinners, O Lord, nor my life with bloodthirsty men; in whose hands is wickedness, their right hand is full of bribes."[216]

In its August 9th issue, the New York Catholic weekly, *Commonweal*, published the last part of an article in which the Badaliya is being urged to hold on to its program of non-violent action: "[the Badaliya] does not forget that it is better to suffer injustice than to commit injustice, and that it is the test for a *Muslim* ('one who has surrendered to God') that proves that he is a *Muslim*. And for us, as St. Augustine pointed out, it is the *test* of a Christian. Amen."[217]

38. Convocation - October 31, 1957
21 rue Monsieur, Paris 7

It is at the first vespers of All Saints' Day, on *Thursday October 31, 1957*, that our monthly Mass will be celebrated at 6:30 pm in the Chapel of the Dames de Nazareth, 20 rue Montparnasse, followed by a meeting at the close of our day of *private Fasting for a serene Peace* between Christians and Muslims, particularly in North Africa and in the East.

Let us stay calm and firm in our commitment to non-violent "substitution" in the midst of the tumultuous Algerian tragedy into which our

---

[216] Psalm 26.
[217] Massignon is quoting the excerpt from *Commonweal* in English.

compatriots are plunged day after day. No longer is it only in Algeria that a majority of poor and backward people are clashing with the privileged minority of the wealthy and the educated—this is also happening in France, where the majority of the said privileged remain tranquilly inactive in order to "*Denounce*" a minority of poor immigrant North African workers, likening them to "an army of occupation" (as in 1940–44) that "poses a threat" to the mothers and wives of the young draftees, who are being "deported" to "huge labor camps" away from home (Algeria thus being equated with the Germany of WWII). And this is being published in Paris in order to "form" Catholic consciences in the practice of denying the right of asylum to the victims of our colonial system.

Let us contain our indignation in front of these brothers, whether truly blinded or not; let us secretly deepen our prayers, our fasts and our sacrifices without altering their rhythm or their discipline. We had to fight for three years with "Christ's spiritual weapons" in order to rescue Muslim Morocco and its Chief from certain shameful methods.[218] It is also three years since the Algerian Muslim insurrection started (on November 1st, 1954) in response to the government's systematic failure to apply the provisions of the 1947 Statute regarding civic, religious and electoral equality (the same went for Catholics in England, who until 1829 were deprived of the right to vote).

We do not believe that God will tolerate an attitude of such racist hatred and contempt any longer as it is so perfectly contrary to the vocation of loyalty and honor that the entire world recognizes in France.

As for the scorn of certain Catholics and Jews for the efficacy of the prayers that the Muslims, in accordance with the Qur'an, address to Abraham, to Moses and to the Prophets, to Jesus and His mother, "God first served,"—members of the "Badaliya" are substituting themselves for them in order to suffer in their place, praying that God forgive these Christians and Jews the weight of their mercenary and "Proprietary spirit" in matters of divine grace and in participation in the sufferings of the oppressed, whether guilty or not—and to bring about Justice.

Whether we are talking about Islam, Israel or the Eastern Churches, that may or may not be united with Rome, let us keep in mind that *Mem-*

---

[218] Refers to the tortures practiced by the French police during the period when Morocco was fighting for its emancipation (1953–56).

ory must be transformed into Hope, as St. John of the Cross tells us; that it is absurd to pit the West against this ancient East that we all came from; that we shall not be wholly reconciled with it unless we go back to our origins and recover our ultimate Unity; let us enter into the eternal liturgical cycle, beyond our divisions, predestined from time immemorial to all the filial and genealogical descendants of Abraham, following an Einsteinian curve of Time through contemplative worship.

39. Convocation - December 6, 1957
21 rue Monsieur, Paris 7

Friday, December 6, 1957, monthly Mass at 6:30 pm in the chapel of the Dames de Nazareth, 20 rue du Montparnasse at the close of our day of *private Fasting for a serene Peace* between Christians and Muslims, particularly in North Africa and in the East.

Despite our misery and seeming uselessness before this national and international tragedy, let us stay firmly rooted in our commitment to the exclusive use of Christ's non-violent weapons, namely, prayer, fasting and the sacrifice of substitution. As we keep bearing public witness to the truth, let us avoid even the slightest suggestion of aggressiveness or hatred toward those who are blind but will not always remain so. Here are a few consoling signs:

The sacrifice of our dear friend Hâjj Lounis (Mahfoud ibn Mas'ûd) is beginning to bear fruit. The inspection of the Waqf Abu Madyan, which he was not able to conduct this spring, was taken over this summer by the Qadi[219] Ben Houra. May God reward him for this.

In the wake of the death of Hâjj Lounis, (to whom we continue to "respond" by reciting the *Fatiha*, as he had said it for the Badaliya in Mecca), comes another death sentence, this time on the other side: that of Djamila Bouhired,[220] the heroine of the defense of the Kasba; fortunately, her sentence, which was pronounced in the most scandalous and revolting circumstances, has not yet been carried out. We allow ourselves to see in this an answer to the prayer we offered on our pilgrimage to Joan of Arc at Notre Dame de Bermont. In fact, it was the Secretary General of a

---

[219] Qadi: a judge ruling in accordance with Islamic law.

[220] A heroine of the Algerian revolution, her condemnation provoked general indignation, even by the army. She married her Lawyer in 1963.

well thought of, and strongly anti-Muslim "Joan of Arc Association," who unexpectedly wrote an article in which he vented his indignation by crying "no, no, no" at the illegality of the trial of Djamila Bouhired who was framed by military "psychologists." Let us pray to Our Lady of Bermont for André Frossard.[221]

Let us admit, as he does, that the French justice system is rapidly deteriorating. Let us pray that the French Court of Cassation[222] from which Algerian cases were unduly removed in favor of a phony military Court of Cassation in Algiers, may see its rights restored as soon as possible; may it recover its sense of duty instead of turning a blind eye to the lack of implementation of its past decisions, especially with regard to a torturer who came to public attention in 1945 and 1951 and who, by being illegally kept out of jail and under the protection of "special powers," contributed to the unofficial diffusion of scientific methods of desecration of the human body designed by specialists.

Let us acknowledge our pain at the moral weakness of those chaplains in responsible positions who let themselves be hired to "appease" the consciences of officers and soldiers "troubled" by the above mentioned methods, which they went so far as to justify. They have not yet been punished even though they quoted the words of Caiaphas on the "expediency" of putting an innocent man to death; what a disinterested and vicariously masochistic attitude. Our prayer cries out to them, "enough."

On the international plain, let us pray for our country, brought to such ruin by the fratricidal Algerian war that it is tempted to pocket the money that it has to beg for abroad in order to escape bankruptcy. It is *Unwilling to Listen* to the wise advice of its neighbors or finally find a way of COHABITATION with the Muslim Maghreb, made inevitable by the presence of oil in the Sahara—Islam, faithful to the *Hospitality of Abraham*, had offered this cohabitation to us early on in Algeria, but since we have violated it so many times we have disgusted Islam from ever

---

[221] André Frossard: Noted French author (1915–1995). A Marxist at first, he converted to Roman Catholicism and wrote among other things a biography of John-Paul II and a book on Maximilian Kolbe. He was a strong critic of the French government's policies during the Algerian conflict.

[222] The "Cour de Cassation" and the "Conseil d'Etat" are the two French Supreme Courts. The Cour de Cassation has jurisdiction over judgments issued by all judiciary Courts.

believing in its possibility; yet Islam's hospitality is its main claim to the right to exist next to Israel and the Christian community, both oblivious to Abraham's legacy.

As the Cardinal of Montreal wrote to us a year ago, on November 26, 1956: "To anyone willing to stop and give some thought to what is happening in the world, it is obvious that current events are heralding deep structural changes..." In Asia, as in Africa, the only way to stop the fatal duel between the Two Powers, their H-bomb threats and their rocket launchings, is to organize the imploring intercession of a Third Force, that of the "sacrificed," and "backward" peoples who do not have any H-bombs or rockets at their disposal. Held hostage between the two powers, Europe should ally itself to the Pact of Bandung with the Asian and African nations who are equally helpless. This is what Charles de Foucauld, whom we knew and understood very well, is truly calling us to in this centenary year of his birth.

Let us pray that people may understand what this *Absolute Weapon* is that the Two Powers are researching and fighting over. They are wrong to look for it in an explosive, destructive, material Force since it was born of an immaterial thought from pure mathematics. Handicapped by its fundamental materialism, the USSR devised the planetary satellite, the "sputnik," in order to conquer outer space thereby expanding this Force indefinitely, dooming her to be destroyed by it. Handicapped by its capitalistic formula, the US believes that spiritual force is obtainable by purchase. They try to buy the Absolute weapon, from the piety of women, to the humility of the Orantes,[223] to the Rosary of their joys, sorrows and intimate glories, in egotistical defense of "their prosperity." They think that Our Lady of Fatima will sell herself through simony,[224] along with all those whose lives are being bruised and sacrificed in the jails of this world, so that the God-fearing rich may triumph thanks to the extermination of the Damned on the other side of the iron curtain, there, where the Church of Silence is weeping under the veil [pokrov] of Marian tears, a divine hostage who should not be included in the same catastrophe.

---

[223] Massignon is referring to the "Orantes de l'Assomption," an Assumptionist congregation of women religious founded in 1896.

[224] The act of buying or selling places of honor in the church.

Let us recognize that the Absolute weapon exists, that it is spiritual, [but] non-violent, feminine, silent, *Marian*; that its origins and its scope are universal, an idea that the "militarism" and naiveté of the Blue Army[225] cannot even conceive of fearing. Fortunately, it is present even in the Blue Army's ranks, but also, and above all, in the "backward" countries that the Two Powers are fighting over. Notably in Algeria where we have repeatedly desecrated the bodies of our adversaries (as if the dissection of corpses could reveal the secret of life), and where by committing rape (electric or not) on women and even virgins, we have struck at the Sacred Source of Life, the virgin point of humanity. Thus, losing all shame, we have laid bare the Absolute Weapon in its absolute truth. This was done, we are told, in order to avenge the French women tortured to death at El Aliya (our most ardent prayers are for them). As if the heinous atrocities committed by desperate and illiterate men had given our technicians permission to present their method of desecrating women as a penal measure meant to repress the misogynous, homicidal instinct of an Islam that will never convert. While in fact there always have been noble souls in Islam, who, at the risk of their lives, did not wait for our "punishments" to redress the wrongs done to women, beginning with Fatima Zahrâ, the Prophet's beloved daughter, whose pride was insulted and whose nobility was not recognized. And there remains in Christianity, and particularly in France, an intolerable "tolerance" on the part of religious and civil authorities toward the "Fresh Girls" (white slave) trade, lawyers who shield it, and specialists in charge of the physical training and placement of the victims. It is not these filthy contributors to parish or town funds who will obtain for France the intercession of the "Woman clothed with the sun,"[226] the "Queen of France," and "Queen of the Universe" on the last day.

Questioned by the press, the head of the repression in Algiers[227] tried to defend torture on the grounds of "efficiency," where Caiaphas had advantageously preceded him. But when asked about the question of "rape," he confessed that he couldn't do anything. Indeed women, especially virgins, are infinitely more courageous and more resistant to force than men. All of human folklore cautions dictators against the mortal danger of committing rape. The trial of Joan of Arc lets us know that she

---

[225] An American branch of the Army.

[226] A description found in the Christian Scripture's book of Revelations (12:1)

[227] General Massau.

could not be executed since she was a virgin, at least not until she ceased being one, (which an English "milord" tried to bring about), or unless she admitted to being possessed by the devil, which a bishop zealously tried to have her do. The British state knew that it would be lost if it burned a saint, but it believed that holiness was just a matter of physical integrity and that a written renouncement obtained by coercion could cancel out the truth. This absurd idea is the very one that informs the repression in Algeria.

Let us pray that the French state may not execute Djamila Bouhired: France would bear a mark of infamy. Not that the heroism of this young girl (she *Sang* the news of her death sentence to her fellow prisoners listening in their cells upon her return to the Barberousse Prison at 3 in the morning) guarantees her holiness, which remains God's secret. But she is holy, because through her and her sisters, other young Muslim women who have been insulted through their sex like her, we are assaulting the infinitely precious integrity of the immaculate body of the Virgin Mary from whom we must beg forgiveness.

Where is She, the Assuntà?[228] I would like to bring our meditation back to this mysterious sign of our times, the Russian "sputnik," which shows us the utter futility of our desire to annex the undefined stellar spaces by violating their hospitality. Such a promethean attempt cannot free us from gravity or from the magnetic attraction that keeps us bound to the interstellar cells in which we are closeted. But it does help us understand how to "enter into heaven," into the divine Hospitality once granted to Abraham. We are allowed to enter into this heaven, toward which the sputnik has made us raise our eyes anew, by regressing, through contemplation of our finality, back to invigorating its [heavenly] origins. As we follow an Einsteinian space-time curve in the liturgical cycle of our predestination to Love, we are attracted by the radiant beauty of long extinguished nebulae which, in our eyes, are *still* shining. And, according to Lemaître's theory, the cosmic rays that escaped from the first moment of the creation of the universe, long before Life was to appear, continue to assail our present existence from all sides, *Coeli enarrant gloriam Dei,*[229] invisibly, like the host of Witnesses who preceded us, like Marian grace.

---

[228] "The one who was raised to heaven" refers to the Assumption of the Virgin Mary.
[229] "The Heavens announce the glory of God."

Annual letter # XI

begun in Lahore (Pakistan) December 29, 1957
completed in Paris May, 18, 1958

It is here in Paris, on All Saints Day in 1932, at the International Islamic Conference, that one of us, invited by the University as a non-Muslim expert, brought an official message from the Collège de France: recalling the visit that the philosopher and poet, Muhammad Iqbal (born in Sialkot in 1876, died April 4, 1938 in Lahor) made to the philosopher, Henry Bergson, [Iqbal] came afterwards to speak to his colleague, the professor of Muslim Sociology, about his theory of personalism in the civic claim to the truth, then on the physical appearance of the mystic of Baghdad, Husayn Mansûr Hallâj, who he came to describe in his "Jâvid Nâmé" as a promethean soul, "ravisher of the Fire of heaven," supplicant of Divine Love.

Since then, Iqbal has become the Eponym of Pakistan, having foreseen this foundation of autonomy in the heart of maternal India (Iqbal was the grandson of a converted Brahman, Sapru). Would that this foundation, that was violently established under the vice-royalty of Lord Mountbatton in 1947, falls apart, since it provoked the sacrificial death of Gandhi, whose life, thus instantly lost, was offered for the Unity of India.

Today, Pakistan is the largest Muslim State—and Iqbal is precious to it because he is the first modern Muslim thinker, the precursor of a "reconstruction" of the religious thought of Islam, founded on authors such as Rûmî and Ibn Taymiya, Ghazâlî and Walîullâh and capable of putting pressure on the great European critics like Schopenhauer, Nietzsche, and Bergson.

Nevertheless, the Colloquium is not able to be inspired by the "modernism" of Iqbal because its Muslim representatives, charged with harmonizing the perspectives on Ijtihâd (legal effort at social reconstruction) proposed by expert orientalists, mostly Americans, clash with the conservative Muslim ulamas, attacked on two fronts by a "methodist" minimizing of the Creed and by a Marxist minimizing of human personalism.

Now more than ever, our obligation is to "understand from the inside" the renewal of the collective conscience that is increasingly regrouping Muslim believers in the world, and to think fraternally with them in order to prepare for the reconciliation among all the children of Abraham.

We will not repeat its basic themes, but as in letter # 10, via the five pillars of Muslim social and religious life, we will approach the moral report for the past year and review the prospects for material and spiritual assistance that we have reflected upon, and begun to implement, through the works of mercy offered humbly "commercium in spiritualibus," and not by lofty "communication in divinis."

A. Testimony

It is necessary to witness to, and peacefully claim, truth and justice in serene non-violence. We must not tempt God through trials by fire, judicial duels that, in our atomic age, will result in suicidal wars.

It is necessary, and this is more difficult, not "to limit" our "compassionate substitution" only to oppressed Muslims, to whom the "Badaliya" is consecrated. Father René Voillaume profoundly understood this, extending the "Foucauld fraternities," that were originally only intended for the Muslim world in the Maghreb, to the entire world. To defend the oppressed without working to touch the hearts of the powerful sometimes results, (alas!) in nourishing a "vengeful class struggle" turned against the "powerful" who have become the oppressed in their turn.

In former times we saw this in the countries of the Alawites where the abrupt emancipation of the serfs, given uncultivated plots of land and unjustly exploited, resulted in their refusal to pay taxes.

This year in France we have experienced the hardening of the hearts of many French people against the North African workers. For example, the assistance that we were able to lend them became less each day to the degree that their despair, as the "under-developed ones," led to criminal behavior that surpassed the patience of the average French person. Thus we have to "transform" little by little the "good" conscience of "respectable people" into authentic Christian compassion, waiting to reproach them until they are in a state to be able to understand. We wanted to move quickly, as it is difficult not to be able to immediately help acute suffering other than by silent prayer, fasting and the sacrifice of oneself. However, it is the example of the Master throughout his Passion. Let us ask Him to join us in forgiving those of us who have not yet understood that it is necessary to speak and apply the truth to all the sanctions in the military Code of Justice, for example, above all, to those that condemn violent abuse committed in cold-blood that lack serenity and raise indignation.

The low percentage of sanctions acted on vis-à-vis the number of abuses committed in the domain of missionary "indifference," corresponds to the low percentage of opposing refusals in relation to the "perverse alms [offered by] impenitent public sinners."

Here again it is a question of slowly and patiently correcting the errors of conscience to make them succeed at this heroic spiritual resistance spoken of by the dying Saint Louis, "potius mori quam foedari." Do not use the gifts of God to make war on Him. The "arma Christi" must first be used by us against ourselves.

A reunion of the Badaliya in Cairo took place December 27, 1957 in the presence of one of the members of the Badaliya in Paris who unexpectedly arrived Christmas Night for the morning Mass. During this short stop, as in Beirut in January, he was able to recognize the tragic position of Christians in the East, a paralyzed minority in the midst of the Muslim majority of their own race, for whom emancipation from certain economic constraints takes on a violent allure when confronted with ideas coming from North Eastern Russia. There is still time to persuade our Muslim brothers in Egypt and Syria that Christianity is "native" in Arab countries, and that in the Arab language the Christian (and even the Jew) can and must support the cultural renaissance, la Nadha,[230] by infusing it with [the Arabic] "science of compassion." This is the essential function of the Badaliya since it was founded in Damietta in 1934, nineteen years after the benediction at Maison-Carrée of a household[231] blessed by Father Foucauld in the heart of his prayer association in 1913.

---

[230] The Christian Arabs, especially the Syrians and Lebanese, some of whom emigrated to Egypt, closely participated in the Renaissance of arab culture, la Nadha, at the end of the XIX century.

[231] Massignon is referring to the blessing of his decision to marry and start a family given to him by Foucauld in a letter written from Tamanrasset in 1913. At the

B. Prayer

World events for the year, such as the launching of the first "sputnik," has enlightened us on the ephemeral nature of a powerful material will exploding into interstellar space in order to seize a universe in flight. And again we have been given the whole sense of the Assumption "entering into the skies." We had already understood (see letter # X) that in the liturgical cycle of our predestination to love, contemplation of our finality restores us more and more to our archetypal origin, following an Einsteinian curve throughout. Similarly, the cyclic gathering of our destinies and our vocations finds a symbol in the skies of modern astronomy. There we see the dispersion of nebulae in flight shining in vain to attract us while it is already extinguished. Also, contemplation of their radiation (that no sputnik would know how to recapture in their expansiveness) must return us to its sacred origin, toward this primordial point of the creation of the world (according to Lemaître) where cosmic rays have escaped that still bombard our existence: towards the marial, immaculate "Fiat Lux" of the Genesis,[232] source of all prayer.

C. Fasting

Our 1957 Lent coincided with Ramadan. Its Night of Destiny (Laylat al-Qadr, April 26–27) celebrated by us in the church in France (in Aix, Lyon, Paris, St. Brieuc, Bermont) was celebrated by our friend, professor Hâjj Lounis Mahfoud ibn Mas'ûd, from the Albertini High School in Sétif, at the cemetery of the VII Sleepers in Guidjel (described in the Revue des Etudes Islamique, 1954, p. 80, followed by plate XIV). He wrote to us that he went there alone, not to compromise anyone else, in order to pray "for a serene peace," "united with Allah." Soon after, on June 5th in Sétif, he was killed, having offered his life for love in order to conquer hate. Like Father Maurice did, from the Brothers of Foucauld on our side.

---

same time Massignon also asked that he be able to remain one of the first members of Foucauld's newly forming Prayer Association. He and his new wife tried to visit Foucauld at Tamanrassett in 1914 but were not permitted to pass due to the danger, and returned via Maison Carrée where the Superior of the White Fathers, Monsignor Léon Livinhac, blessed their marriage in place of Foucauld.

[232] Gn. 1:3 "Let there be Light."

At the Breton pardon [pilgrimage] to the VII Sleepers in Vieux-Marché July 27–28 the Fatiha was said for Hajj Lounis Mahfoud and red roses were placed for him on the stone altar in the crypt-dolmen.

Several of us fasted on Yom Kippur, October 5th.

D. Alms

We prayed that attenuating circumstances be granted to the young Algerian Muslim terrorists, Ben Sadok and Djemila Bouhired, in order that French honor and justice be maintained. We prayed for the generous Christian men and women who voluntarily exposed themselves to suffer the same ill treatment (contrary to the Law) as their Muslim sisters and brothers in Algiers, in the name of Sacred Hospitality.

E. Pilgrimage

We meditated at two pilgrimage sites invoking the intercession of Joan of Arc, the one near to God, the patron, not only of the oppressed in France but of all people who are oppressed; especially when it is Christians not treating Muslims with justice, as we saw in the case of Sheik Abdelouahid ibn Abdallah who called on Joan openly in the mosque in Rabat (Soueïka), and in the case of the Muslim officers in the African Army devoted to Joan. The first pilgrimage was to her first prison in Beaulieu les Fontaines in Oise which has become the monastery of the Canadian Sisters of Joan of Arc. The Sisters of Joan of Arc were founded on Christmas in 1914 in Worcester, MA, in the USA by an Alsatian Assomptionist, Father Clément, who died in 1936. The current Archbishop is Msgr. Wright and their Mother House is in Bergerville near Sillary in Quebec. The second pilgrimage was to the Chapel of Notre Dame in the woods in Bermont to the northwest of Greux-Domremy where several of us have gone to pray since the Mass on February 2, 1957.

In India, one of our members went to pray in Mehrauli, the place of the last pilgrimage made by Gandhi, at the tomb of Qutbuddin Bakhtiyar. The *mawsim* took place from October 7th to the 9th.[233]

---

[233] Mehrauli is where Gandhi had come to pray with a group of Muslim women at the tomb of this well-known mystic when he was killed. The member of the Badaliya

In Germany, we visited the Chapel of the VII Sleepers in Rotthof on August 31, 1957, in front of Notre Dame of Altötting, where there is the celebrated ex-voto designed by Ysabeau de Bavière [Bavaria] for the cure of Charles VI. It took the silversmiths 24 years to create it.

In France, the pilgrimage to the VII Sleepers in Vieux-Marché took place July 27–28, 1957 where a thousand people gathered including about thirty Muslims. The *Fatiha* was said before the crypt-dolmen (See the article by Msgr. J. Nasrallah, Rector of St. Julien le Pauvre, in the White Fathers of Rayak (Lebanon) "Courrier de Ste Anne de Jerusalem" 3rd year, # 18 pp. 12–13). Professor R. Louis believes he is able to identify this pilgrimage site with the "VII Saints in Brittany" found in the Song of Roland (manuscript in Paris, published by Foerster, verses 1278–1281. Also the manuscript in Oxford, published by Bédier, verses 1427–1429).

During the year, some members of our charitable work followed one another to Jerusalem, to the last place, the tomb of Lazarus.

P.S. Included in letter # XI is a photo of the plaque of the Badaliya, (Foucauld's Sacred Heart).[234]

40. Convocation - January 3, 1958
21 rue Monsieur, Paris 7

Friday, January 3, 1958, Mass at 7: 00 pm (this time in the Church of St. Severin) at the close of our day of *private Fasting for a Serene Peace* between Christians and Muslims, particularly in North Africa and in the East.

The sacrifice of our friend Hajj Lounis Mahfoud ibn Mas'ûd is beginning to bear fruit. First, because one of the two projects for peace between Christians and Muslims that he started with members of the Badaliya, namely the upkeep of the Waqf Abu Madyan[235] in Jerusalem (in front of

---

was Camille Drevet, who came to pray at the sight of Gandhi's assassination. (See Convocation November 4, 1955.)

[234] *The emblem of Charles de Foucauld*
A Plaque in metal made of Copper on a brass foundation was designed in 1920–1921 at the request of Louis Massignon by the sculptor, Pierre Roche, (Ferdinand Massignon, Louis Massignon's father). It was based on the monogram from the letters of Charles de Foucauld with the words "Jesus Caritas," (Jesus is Love) on his drawing of the Sacred Heart mounted on a Cross. (Massignon's ex-voto for the Badaliya is taken from this design.)

[235] Waqf Abu Madyan: Waqf: a religious endowment in Islam, usually a property (building or plot of land) whose revenues are used for religious purposes. The waqf

the Al-Aqsa gate that leads to the Chapel of Zachariah, where Muslim women regularly invoke the intercession of the Blessed Virgin in the mystery of her Presentation in the Temple)—has just been granted 7 million francs for its madrasa.[236] Let us pray that this Franco-Muslim charity may be able to prosper in peace.

Secondly, because the violent death of our friend got us to explore thoroughly, from the point of view of the Badaliya, the problem of the political assassin's responsibility, and also his "exemplarité" [237] in inflicting the death penalty.

The two opposing terrorisms confronting each other in Algeria have a common doctrine that sees no other solution to their fratricidal duel than a hellish cycle of reprisals. Murder is inexorably followed by capital punishment.

Like Our Lord Jesus, Gandhi declares that Cain should not be killed for murdering Abel, and he affirms that the only way to bring an end to the fratricidal war between the sons of Abel and the sons of Cain is to intercept, at our own risk, the one who avenges a death by killing, by diverting his fury onto ourselves. Without this there is no true "Badaliya." *Lex talionis* (an eye for an eye) is abolished through voluntary substitution.

Hâjj Lounis was threatened with death in September 1956 by FLN[238] terrorists in Setif for two reasons; the government had ordered that all FLN structures be destroyed by every possible means, and, as a reprisal for the non-violent attitude of our friend, who through the Seven Sleepers' pilgrimage and the Abu Madyan Waqf in Jerusalem had helped us keep France's promise to Algerian Islam, he was viewed by the FLN as a

---

in question here—a part of the Al-Aqsa Mosque in Jerusalem—was named after Abu Madyan, a Sufi saint (died 1198), who was born in Seville, and spent time in the Algerian city of Tlemcen. The revenues of this waqf were used to provide for the needs of poor Muslims coming from Tlemcen (and possibly other places in North Africa) on a pilgrimage to the holy places in Jerusalem, such as the Al-Aqsa Mosque.

[236] The word *madrasa*, also spelled madrassa in English, originally designated a residential college for Qur'anic study attached to a mosque.

[237] *Exemplarité* means "worthy of imitating" or a model for right behavior.

[238] FLN: Front de Libération National, an organization of Muslim Algerian nationalists who fought for independence from France from 1954 through the cease-fire (Accords d'Evian) of March 1962. It later became the sole Algerian party and is now one among many Algerian parties.

"concession" to Christian France's spiritual force, and had to be punished as such. Twenty-two years ago an Algerian nationalist student, M. B. S. de B., wrote us "I cannot forgive myself for having loved you, because you disarmed me," referring to the doctrine of violence. (About which, they say, he is somewhat disappointed today).

We have requested that the mechanic who killed Hâjj Lounis not be subjected to the talion law; let us fervently pray for this. We have also requested that the plumber who killed Ali Chekkal[239] not be executed. Some dared reproach us for acting as witnesses for the defense, as if friendship beyond death should inevitably serve the cause of hatred. Chekkal's friends, especially the Christian ones, should understand that they did not love him well, that they used their sacred guest to partisan ends, pushing him forward and making him the head of a Franco-Muslim party tolerant of the State's continuing disregard for its own commitments toward Islam, such as they were formulated in the Statute of 1947. They exploited Chekkal's known sympathy for Christian colonists (the father of a baptized child did not have to make a policy of breaking the State's promises to Islam). It is because of the selfish paternalism of his friends that Chekkal became the target of the FLN. Wrongfully viewed as a manifestation of the same paternalism, our friendship with Hajj Lounis, although free of "social" calculations, led to his becoming the target of the FLN as well. We should have exposed ourselves in his place, as we in fact said in our letter "to whom it may concern" in Setif in September 1956: in vain, alas. "For the one who loves, it is painful not to be able to do all that love demands."

As the year begins, let us pray, in the words of our rule, that we may be allowed to bear witness through our Life, and if God permits it, through our death, "offering the gift of ourselves" (Ozan'am).[240] Therein lies the crucial "exemplarité" of "penal" death.

---

[239] Ali Chekkal, a one-time vice-president of the Algerian National Assembly and one of France's most vocal supporters. He was assassinated in May 1957 while attending a soccer game in the French town of Angers.

[240] Fréderic Ozanam (1813–1853), a professor at the Sorbonne who dedicated himself to the poor and organized the Saint-Vincent-de Paul Society that spread throughout the world. Its work is still supported by the Roman Catholic Church. He was beatified in 1997 by Pope John Paul II.

41. Convocation - February 7, 1958
21 rue Monsieur, Paris 7

Friday, February 7, 1958, monthly Mass at 6: 30 pm in the chapel of the Dames de Nazareth, 20 rue du Montparnasse, at the close of our day of *private Fasting for a serene Peace* between Christians and Muslims, particularly in North Africa and in the East, and also in the Middle East and the Far East.

A mission to an international Islamic colloquium in Lahore dedicated to the memory of our philosopher and poet friend, Dr. Muhammad Iqbal, included non-Muslim orientalists and allowed us to turn our "Badaliya" prayer for these Muslims in two directions: linguistically, by going deeper into the cultural value of the Arabic language (1), which is the sign of unity, through the prayer of all Muslims to the God of Abraham, from Siam to the Philippines; and socially, by exploring in depth the intense "identification" (according to the word of V. Grünebaum[241] (from the University of Chicago), who insisted a little too much on the unconscious and irrational aspect of this "wish to live together," that each humble believer wants to attain with the Islamic Community in the "ecumenical," "catholic" sense of the "Badaliya" (the word "kathlaka" was actually used in Lahore), instead of fostering a modernist "*ijthihâd*,"[242] a free examination [of the texts], which would only split up social unity. We must also pray for a more equitable (and more Islamic) distribution of the lands, which our paternalism is very careful not to encourage.

(1) Same tendency in Morocco. The UNESCO of Arab Nations is opening in Fez on January 27.

On the way there—on Christmas eve ("stille Nacht, heiligste Nacht") and a comforting meeting of the Badaliya in Cairo—on the way back, a presentation of the Badaliya plaque (for the foundation of a Chaldean Carmel) in Baghdad (fiftieth anniversary of a return to God;[243] the church of Our Lady of Fatima is rising from the ground), renovation of the "Badali-

---

[241] Gustave Edmund Von Grünebaum (1909–1972): German orientalist who taught at the University of Chicago and UCLA.

[242] *Ijtihad* literally means hard striving or strenuousness but technically it means exercising independent legal reasoning to give answers when the *Qur'an* and *Sunnah* are silent. We would say independent critical thinking today.

[243] Massignon is referring to his own conversion in Baghdad in 1908, when he was 25, that led him back to his Roman Catholic roots.

ya" from Beyrouth to Jerusalem; recitation of the Fatiha for Hajj Lounis Mahfoud ibn Mas'oud at the Waqf Abu Madyan and at Beni-Naim[244] and for Fatima, the daughter of Hussein (the martyr of Karbala) in front of her grave at Nabi Yaqîn[245] (See: "La Cité des Morts au Caire," ap. BIFAO, LVII, 77 and pl. 16) and for the Refugees (Ism. Obed is now in Saîr).

Let us pray with Joan of Arc to Our Lady of Bermont (See: the Mass celebrated a year ago) that the highest military authorities give all their attention to the unquestionably troubling issue of the status of the Muslim officers of the Army of Africa. This is an essential prerequisite to any kind of peace in Algeria.

Meanwhile the daily bloodletting that has been going on with administrative zeal for the last three years in Algeria is filling Christian hearts with revulsion and ruining French honor.

Let us make sure that two centenary dates happening in 1958 will be celebrated in a spirit of friendship, devoid of any stupid paternalism, "with the Muslims." That of Our Lady of Lourdes where many Muslims will be coming[246] (According to a medieval legend, Lourdes is the place where a Saracen émir would have made an offering to the Virgin), and the centenary of the birth of Charles de Foucauld in Strasburg. Those of us who knew him personally, are aware of his love for the Muslims. It is distressing to realize that he is being falsely celebrated as a "French spy on Islamic soil" thus turning Muslim souls away from invoking this defender of the oppressed people in the Sahara. As in Joan of Arc's case, they judged that he was "an intercessor strictly reserved for French Catholics" (sic). We must publicly and tirelessly denounce the absurdity of this kind of spiritual racism.

42. Convocation - March 7, 1958
21 rue Monsieur, Paris 7

Friday, March 7, 1958, Mass at 6:30 pm at the usual address.

We shall move forward our day of fasting for a serene peace between Christians and Muslims in North Africa and in the East to *Friday, Febru-*

---

[244] Beni Naim: a village east of Hebron.

[245] *Nabi Yaqin*: an ancient cemetery on the border of the Hebron desert.

[246] Louis Rouani was the faithful organizer of these annual pilgrimages held on December 8th.

ary 28 1958, so that it will coincide with the national day of fasting proposed by the French organizations of spiritual resistance through nonviolence.

Our personal experience of the violence being taught to French youth, under the impassive watch of those in charge of public order, moves us to put our humble trust in God and turn to the solemn means of reparation and reconciliation that Christ taught us when he fasted for forty days before his Passion.

We are also fasting that day so that France's homage to Our Lady of Lourdes on her centenary may be washed free of all blood spilled in our beloved country. May our Lady enlighten France about her destiny among the nations.

43. Convocation - March 1958
21 rue Monsieur, Paris 7

Our Christian Lent is getting nearer to Holy Week and the Feast of the Resurrection. Let us remember our Good Friday of 1957, when at 3 pm, we renewed, in accordance with our statutes, the express offering of ourselves "in the place" of our Muslim brothers—as much for those who made us suffer as for those who suffer because of us. This year, the vigil of Good Friday on March 26–27th coincides with the death on the Cross of a great Lover of the divine will, Husayn Mansûr Hallâj, condemned in 922 CE for teaching that we should offer ourselves up for our brothers, as victims of the Abrahamic sacrifice of *Qurban*[247] (this coincidence is quite rare, one has to go as far back as 1891 and 1812 to find it again). Every year, members of the Badaliya go and visit Hallâj's cenotaph[248] in Baghdad; let us join them in prayer on this coming Good Friday.

---

[247] *Qurban*: the obligatory yearly sacrifice of an animal to Allah for any Muslim who can afford it. The Feast is called *Eid al-Adha* ending the *Hajj* (pilgrimage to Mecca) commemorating Abraham's readiness to make the ultimate sacrifice of his son to God. The Qur'an names this son of Abraham, Ishmael. The animal sacrifice symbolizes that, like Abraham, Muslim pilgrims are willing to sacrifice that which is most important to them in obedience to Allah.

[248] A monument to Hallaj in Baghdad where he was crucified and dismembered, then burned. His ashes were thrown into the Tigris River without any respect for the Sufi saint.

In a great meditation on the history of Christianity, Dostoevsky was the first to show how much Christianity depends on the degree to which we imitate Christ in his *Response to the Tempter's three questions* at the end of his forty day *Fast* in the desert, as well as the degree to which our compassion resembles His Passion:

1. "If you are the Son of God, Command that this stone to turn into bread." Instead of performing a technical miracle of lulling mankind with the mirage of a luxurious and idle life, Christ, through the humility of manual work, "the holy work of one's hands," draws us into desiring the offering of his last fraternal supper, this poor relic of his Passion in which he hands himself over to us, torn apart, dying, in order that we rise from the dead, we, his murderers whom he takes as his Guests into the humble Paradise of his Heart.

2. "Throw yourself down from the Temple so that, as it is written, the Angels of God may preserve you from all harm." Instead of delivering men from their self-inflicted pains and tortures by sparing them the use of their own free will, Christ permits that those of humble and virgin heart be stripped and nailed on the Cross of infamy and glory, thereby revealing the radiant, dazzling beauty of Truth unveiled.

3. "Behold, all these kingdoms and their glory. Prostrate yourself in homage before me, and it shall all be yours" Instead of letting us adore the idol of Science, (the artificial work of his hands), as if Science could give us eternal life here below, Christ invites us to die from compassion for the Outlaws and the Convicts, to renounce all authority and prestige, to surrender to Grace, to the Spirit of Consolation, and, burned by its Fire, set ablaze by prayer, to let ourselves be scattered to the four winds of the Spirit.

We are united more closely than ever this year, through brotherly compassion, to the Muslim Ramadan (March 11–April 10) in Mecca—this immense "enclosed garden" in which the Muslim world, in order to escape the technological assaults of a godless colonialism, fasts and shuts itself away, jealously eager to humble itself, bowing to the insignificance of creatures before God Alone, "*Allah akbar;*" and also "*Allah akram.*" He Alone is Great, He Alone is Merciful. Whether Islam realizes the ultimate value, the perfect "via negativa" of this somewhat haughty gesture of renunciation by an entire penitent Community (like ancient Israel on Yom Kippur) depends entirely upon us and our fraternal union. The ill treatment that the (blinded) police have inflicted upon these believers during this sacred time is perceived as *Sacrilegious* acts committed against the God of Abraham (public display of corpses, people arrested for having bandaged or hospitalized "suspects.")

May we suffer with them.

Like last year, or perhaps with even more intent, let us celebrate the *Night of Destiny*, the *Laylat al-Qadr*, on the 27th night of Ramadan, the evening of April 7th, in union with our fallen Muslim friends, such as Hajj Lounis Mahfoud. And after celebrating let us join in our prayer vigil for a Serene Peace. Our local groups will make a point of meeting that night in chapels that Church authorities have given us permission to use; in Paris at 8:30 pm in the same crypt as last year; in Aix; and in some other cities as well. We shall be especially close in spirit that night to His Majesty Mohammed V, who will go up to Fez, Fez Jdîd, (the new Fez) (Moulay Abdullah Mosque) to pray and give alms, near the grave of his mother, Lella Amina, who died from grief eight days after he went into exile.

Let us start thinking right now about organizing a pilgrimage to Our Lady of Bermont (near Donremy) on May 8th, St. Joan of Arc's feast day; in the very place where, with the maid of Lorraine as our mediator, we entrusted Our Lady with the honor and rehabilitation of Algerian Muslim officers, especially Lieutenant Abdelkader Rahmani,[249] who was finally liberated, then relieved from active duty. Our prayers for him remain faithful and those among us who are French officers give him "full membership" in our passion for the honor of the Army.

Let us pray for our friend Msgr. Paul Mulla,[250] the leader of our group in Rome, who died on March 3rd and was buried near San Lorenzo (Campo Verano).

---

[249] A French officer in the Legion of Honor (1956) who was ousted from the Army, along with 57 other officers from the Maghreb, who was seen blocking a mission of mediation with the FLN.

[250] Born a Turk on the island of Crete, Ali Mehmet Mulla Zade (1881–1959) received his education in France where he studied under the aegis of the French Catholic philosopher Maurice Blondel and eventually converted to Christianity. In 1924, thanks to Blondel's intervention, the now Christian Paul Mulla began teaching Islamic religion at the Pontifical Oriental Institute, and continued to do so for 35 years until his death. He is among those who in the first half of the twentieth century did the most to promote the dialogue between the Catholic Church and Islam.

Like last year, we are hoping that the Jewish community of Sefrou (Morocco) will favor us spiritually with a pilgrimage to the Seven Sleepers (West edge of the oasis).[251] on the day of the Lag-de-Omer,[252] 18 Ayyâr,[253] *For a Serene Peace* whose coming depends more and more on a new awareness of Israel's true destiny among the nations.

Convocation

Since this year Good Friday coincides with the Crucifixion of Hallaj, we shall offer our fasting on that day for the same intention as the one for which we pray on our first Friday private fasts—a serene peace between Christians and Muslims, especially in North Africa and the Middle East. In the spirit of the liturgy, our regular day of prayer, silence and fasting will be therefore moved up this time. It will not take place on the first Friday of April, which is Easter Friday, but on the last Friday in March, Good Friday, as is required from us by the Church. Furthermore, our *Monthly Mass* will be celebrated on Tuesday, April 7th, at 8:30 pm in the *Crypt of the church of St. Sulpice*, within the context of the prayer vigil that we now hold regularly on the "Night of Destiny" (therefore there will be no meeting or Mass on Friday, April 2nd).

44. Convocation - March 28, 1958
21 rue Monsieur, Paris 7

Our monthly day of fasting coinciding with Good Friday this April, let us set our hearts on sanctifying this holy day through prayer and sacrifices for a serene peace between Christians and Muslims in North Africa and the Near East.

---

[251] Sefrou, a walled city at least 1000 years old, is surrounded by an oasis, in the foothills of the Atlas Mountains. Close by are numerous caves, once venerated as tombs of holy men by both Jews and Muslims. One of them is said to be that of the Seven Sleepers.

[252] Minor Jewish holiday taking place on the 33rd day of the *Omer*—the seven weeks between the second night of Passover and Shavu'ot. The first thirty-two days constitute a period of partial mourning during which religious Jews refrain from marrying, cutting their hair or dancing. The 33rd day of the Omer, which is what *Lag-de-Omer* literally means, marks the end of this period of mourning. Families gather and light bonfires and young people often choose to marry on that day.

[253] *Ayyâr*: 2nd month of the Jewish year occurring in April/May.

Our monthly meeting that should take place on the first Friday in April, will be moved, along *With the Mass*, to Friday, March 28th, and will take place at 3 rue des Prêtres, St. Séverin (parish lecture hall) at 6:30 pm: it will include a lecture (by Mr. Massignon) on Fr. Charles de Foucauld, followed by a prayer vigil. Mass will be celebrated at 8 pm.

We remind our members of the solemn day of prayer for Peace in Algeria designated by the Council of French Cardinals and Archbishops; it is scheduled for May 18th, under the sign of Our Lady of Lourdes.

During this time of Lent, as we prepare ourselves to participate in the Passion of our Master, let us not respond to the criticisms or the threats of those evangelizing Pharisees and patriotic Sadducees who are causing us much grief, in Israel as well as in France, for not wanting to apply the *Lex Talionis* [an eye for an eye] to "our Muslim and Arab enemies." Our founding charter forbids it. It is written in Paragraphs I-4 of our rule about our "particular responsibility toward our Muslim brothers among whom we live," that: "*Having suffered in the past and still suffering now because of them, we wish to practice the highest kind of Christian charity toward them, according to our lord's precept 'love your enemies and pray for those who persecute you'*" (Mt. 5:44).

We ask all of our members and sympathizers to reread this text solemnly on Good Friday, April 4, 1958, preferably at 3 pm, in front of a crucifix or a plaque of the Badaliya. The only reason for our sodality's existence in the Church is to be faithful to this precept through our life "and, if God permits it, through our death."

Let us do it, as Charles de Foucauld wrote us, "...without asking ourselves whether pride plays a part in this behavior; this is our duty."

Do what you must do, come what may.

In view of this, we must, in this crucial year for Algerian Muslims, renew our participation in their Laylat al-Qadr, their "Night of Destiny" on the 27th day of Ramadan 1377, which falls on April 15/16th 1958. We will have a prayer vigil in the same French churches as last year so that the reconciliation promised to those fasting with a pure heart, may take place. Since our dear friend, Professor Hâjj Lounis Mahfoud (died June 5, 1957 in Setif) risked his life for us by praying "with us" in the cemetery of the Seven Sleepers of Guidjel on the Night of Destiny in 1957, this vigil is a sacred duty of friendship for us.

45. Convocation - May 2, 1958
21 rue Monsieur, Paris 7

Friday, May 2, 1958, monthly Mass at 6:30 pm in the chapel of the Dames de Nazareth, 20 rue du Montparnasse, followed by a meeting at the close of our day of *Private fasting for a Serene Peace* between Christians and Muslims, particularly in North Africa and in the Near East.

This date is of exceptional importance for our little sodality:

It is the fiftieth anniversary[254] of the imprisonment and release of our oldest member (May 1–5 1908), which took place on the banks of the Tigris in front of the palace of Chosroes,[255] where the True Cross was kept hidden, and where so many martyrs were killed under the Sassanid Empire; this is also where Salman, Muhammad's Christian confident and faithful friend, was buried. After Muhammad died, Salman became the close adviser of the Prophet's family, his daughter, Fatima, her husband, Ali, and of their children; two other Companions of the Prophet, Hudhaïfah and Jâbir Ansâri, are also buried there.

It is [also] the 25th anniversary of the founding (May 4, 1933) of the Poor Clare convent in Rabat who, with their Father Superior, Fr. Monchanin, have been supporting us in our monthly private fasts for a serene Peace from the very beginning in September 1953.

Two weeks before this very important date, we shall set our hearts on joining all Muslims as they present their humble and confident Ramadan plea for an end to the Algerian drama. We shall keep vigil with them in a church, as we did on May 8, 1956 and on April 27, 1957 (as in years past, the vigil will take place in Paris in the crypt of the Church of St. Sulpice, followed by The Rosary and Holy Mass at 8:30 pm): this is our Night of Destiny vigil, this *Laylat al-Qadr* on the 27th day of Ramadan, for which King Mohammed V of Morocco, in the same desire for a serene Peace in

---

[254] Massignon is referring to himself and to the events leading to his own conversion experience.

[255] The palace of Chosroes, named for Chosroes II Parviz, the Sassanid King who reigned from 590 to 628 and conquered Jerusalem in 614 for the Persians. He carried the Holy Cross away and was afterwards vanquished by the Byzantine Emperor Heraclius II, who reigned from 610 to 641 and conquered the Persians near Nineva in 627, returning the Holy Cross to Jerusalem, which established the liturgical celebration of the Holy Cross on September 14th. Chosroes was assassinated by his own son Siroes, who restored the Cross to Heraclius.

Justice, made a solemn appeal during the prayer of the Faithful on the Moroccan National Radio March 31st.

It is in a spirit of non-violence, of universal brotherhood, in full Christian acceptance of all the bitterness and pain that we shall experience that day, May 2nd; in the spirit of hospitality, of "*diyafa*," with which Arab and non-Arab Muslims welcomed so many of our Christian brothers into their homes in Africa and in the Near East; the same spirit that moved them to intercede in the name of the hospitality of Abraham on behalf of our oldest member, freeing him from captivity fifty years ago, not far from Ur in Chaldea, Abraham's homeland.

Let us pray that the right of asylum, this sacred foundation of all civilizations, may no longer be denied by our beloved country, once so welcoming to all refugees, immigrants and poor "crouillats."[256] This is how the Arabic word "akhouya," my brother, is being currently distorted in our land.

46. Convocation - June 6, 1958
21 rue Monsieur, Paris 7

Friday, June 6 1958, monthly Mass at 6:30 pm in the chapel of the Dames de Nazareth, 20 rue Montparnasse, followed by a meeting at the close of our day of private *Fasting for a serene Peace* between Christians and Muslims, particularly in North Africa and in the Near East.

Let us fervently pray to St. Joan of Arc for the intention mentioned in our convocation last February 7th: may "the highest military authorities pay more attention to the unquestionably tragic issue of the status of the Muslim officers in the Army in Africa; this is an essential prerequisite to any kind of *serene* peace in Algeria."

There are two pilgrimages to Joan that we particularly recommend: to her first prison in Beaulieu-les-Fontaines (Oise) that is now a convent of the Canadian sisters of St. Joan of Arc, a community founded in Worcester (Mass. U.S.A.) on Christmas Day in 1914 by an Alsatian Assumptionist, Fr. Clement (died in 1936). Our friend, Miss Regine Pernoud,[257] just returned from a visit to the Archbishop of Worcester, Msgr. Wright, who,

---

[256] "Crouillats," a pejorative and racist term used to describe North Africans in French.

[257] Régine Pernoud (1919–1998) a medievalist who studied the Middle Ages and the role of women in society. She paid particular attention to Joan of Arc, causing Massignon to contact her as he felt that the truth about the French Saint was being exploited by the French in service of rousing hatred against the Arabs.

in his fervent devotion to Joan of Arc, would like to found a truly ecumenical community through which the oppressed could invoke this pure image of France's Immortal Vocation.

The second pilgrimage is to Our Lady of Bermont, in the middle of the woods, north-west of Domrémy-Greux, that several of us visited last year following Mass on February 15, 1957. Very recently, for the anniversary, two of us made a particularly moving and fervent pilgrimage there. It is impossible for Joan not to have heard our anguished plea.

Let us also think about our next pilgrimage to the Seven Sleepers at Vieux-Marché on the first Sunday following the feast of the Magdalen (July 22nd); the pilgrimage begins on Saturday afternoon.

After Mass on June 6th, we hope to be able to give you news of the Eastern Christians for whom the Badaliya exists first and foremost, and whose situation in Lebanon is suddenly taking a tragic turn. More than ever, we must invoke our Lady of the Pokrov on their behalf—the Marian intercession that the Church of Silence favors the most. Let us hope that God will save our Eastern Arab brothers, both the Muslim majority and the Christian minority, from the fate endured by the faithful of the Church of Silence.

God is the Master of the impossible, the Miracle of miracles. Let us pray in an indestructible spirit of nonviolence.

47. Convocation - July 4, 1958
21 rue Monsieur, Paris 7

Friday, July 4, 1958, monthly Mass at 6:30 pm in the chapel of the Dames de Nazareth, 20 rue Montparnasse, followed by a meeting at the close of our day of *private Fasting for a serene Peace* between Christians and Muslims, particularly in North Africa (Algeria) and in the Near East (Lebanon).

For the last five years, our humble and obstinate call to Fast has been making its way into compassionate and prayerful souls. Following the surge of fasts provoked by Sakiet,[258] we now have a suggested *Day of Fast-*

---

[258] *Sakiet* was an incident resulting from the increasing tensions between France and Algeria's neighbors, Tunisia and Morocco, over their alleged support of Algerian rebel forces. In retaliation for an Algerian rebel ambush against French forces, in February 1958, the French army bombed Sakiet, a small town in Tunisia, where a number of Algerian civilians had fled to escape the violence at home. The bombings left a significant number of unarmed Algerians dead or wounded.

ing with the formal approval of the Cardinal Archbishop of Paris for the feast of the Sacred Heart during the Novena of Pax Christi. Let us pray that other dioceses follow suit, and that August 15th may not pass without a Marian Truce, in the name of Our Lady of Lourdes.

On June 27th, several Masses made us mindful of the anguish of the Algerian Muslims during their feast on that day of the Sacrifice of Abraham, the *Id al-Qurban* or *Id al-Kabir*. Many, feeling under threat, did not dare sacrifice the symbolic lamb in union with the Muslim Paschal Sacrifice celebrated on the same day at the Hajj in Mecca, in Arafat and in Mina. We cannot possibly forget how God, in times past, granted the mystic Hallaj (died in Bagdad, 922) his wish to die as a rightful sacrificial victim for the Muslim community. Nor can we forget the day of *Qurban* in 1953, when the Sultan of Morocco was deported, and we decided to make a *Monthly* practice of our day of private fasting in union with the convent of the Poor Clares of Rabat. Several people noted that June 27th was the day of the Latin feast of Jesus the Sovereign Priest.

Next July 2nd, let us make a point of invoking Our Lady through the mystery of her Visitation in her Byzantine Church in Blachernae, where the faithful would venerate her Robe and her Belt on that day, as they would, on October 2nd, the apparition of the Pokrov (the protective veil of her Tears), which defended the Greeks against the paganism of the Russians a thousand years ago (and still does today): she is the Patroness of the Badaliya.

On that day we shall especially pray to Our Lady for the Badaliya in Cairo, in our beloved church of *Dar es-Salam*,[259] as well as for the Beirut Badaliya so threatened by the Lebanese civil war.

Since May 13th, the situation in Algeria has been moving toward a solution; our prayer solemnly acknowledges the change of attitude toward the Muslims that seems to be emerging in Algiers. Let us pray that the idea of "fraternization" descends from people's lips to their hearts, and that the anti-Marxist struggle stop imitating Marxist tactics by declaring all kinds of myths and slogans to be "true;" something that free men of conscience reject.

---

[259] The Greek Melkite Church in Cairo, Notre Dame de la Paix, where Massignon and Mary Kahil established the *Dar es-Salâm* conference center for encounters of Christians and Muslims.

July 26–27th is the Breton pilgrimage of the Seven Sleepers of Ephesus at Vieux-Marché (near Plouaret, Côtes du Nord) where the *Fatiha* will be said for our friend Hâjj Lounis Mahfoud, in front of the dolmen-crypt. A brochure on the pilgrimage, printed in St. Brieuc by the Emulation Society, will be distributed. We know that this year the Bulletin of St. Anne of Jerusalem (White Fathers' Melkite Seminary) published an essay on the pilgrimage, written by Msgr. J. Nasrallah.

48. Convocation - September 5, 1958
21 rue Monsieur, Paris 7

Friday, September 5, 1958, monthly Mass at 6:30 pm in the chapel of the Dames de Nazareth, 20 rue Montparnasse, followed by a meeting at the close of our day of *private Fasting for a serene Peace* between Christians and Muslims, particularly in North Africa and in the Middle East.

The August vacation made it impossible for us to report earlier on the great fervor of the gathering of pilgrims, as many Christians as Muslims (at least 27), who took part in the Pardon of the *Ahl al Kahf* (Seven Sleepers of Ephesus) in Vieux Marché on July 26–27th. The Secretary of Veterans Affairs, Edmond Michelet, was present in a private capacity, praying as he formerly had with the disciples of Charles de Foucauld, with the Little Sisters who had come from Paris and the Little Brothers who had come from St. Gildas Island. Fr. Kador from the Carmelites of the Mission of Baghdad (Avon) had joined Msgr. J. Nasrallah, who was representing Cardinal Feltin. The Fatiha was said in front of the crypt, in memory of our dear friend Hâjj Lounis Mahfoud, and before the ashes of the Fire of Joy[260] for all of us.

The Conference on the History of Religions, which begins on August 27th in Tokyo, invited one of us (as did the Gandhian Seminar in Delhi in 1953) to talk about certain "cases of transmissible compassion as stated among Muslims,"[261] a subject that makes it possible to introduce an audience from the Far East to the experiential basis for an apostolic extension of the notion of "badaliya," or "substitution," which is not only

---

[260] Part of the Breton traditional pilgrimage is to light a great bonfire in the village square after a long procession circles the fields carrying several church banners and a statue of the Virgin, singing in her honor. The procession of pilgrims gather in the square for the blessings by the Priest and the lighting of the Fire of Joy.

[261] This quote is in English in the original text.

compassionate in its words and in its deeds, but also shares in the sufferings of the body and the soul. In those countries this form of heroic
tenderness is all too often misunderstood and presented as a proof of
"the transmigration of souls" and of "metempsychosis."[262] Here is a brief
summary of this lecture, through which we attempted to answer the call
of a close associate of ours, Sr. Violet Susman (died Feb. 20, 1950), who
for 17 years ran an organization providing social relief to the very poor
in a Tokyo slum, and had asked us to come to Japan with a few of Foucauld's disciples in order to help her (as early as 1928 she had had Fr. V.
Totsuka[263] translate the writings of "our model" into Japanese).

This paper is based on our letter # X (Christmas vigil 1956) and on
"cases of transference of the suffering and moral pain endured by others."
We showed that the Badaliya had no other goal but to have the most humble among us become aware of the barely visible sufferings and hidden
experiences of "transmissible" compassion, found in abundance in the intimate history of souls, and yet often unsuspected by them.

How do we know whether the ordeal of "painfully overstretching
oneself out of love," is real, whether the co-sufferer is truly identifying
with the other person's "need" in the desire to fulfill it? By hidden tears,
if we cannot give our blood, by a scorching thirst for justice, if our breast
cannot offer the milk of human kindness. Water and blood, milk and fire,
these humble resources found in any home can be accepted by the Guest,
the mysterious stranger to whom we offer refuge through the sacred practice of hospitality (for the lack of which one of the pilgrims at the Breton
Pardon has to suffer at this very moment—let us pray for him). All of this
is verifiable to the degree that we have returned to "our Mother's womb,"[264]

---

[262] Metempsychosis: to enter into the soul of another at death.

[263] Due to the influence of Charles de Foucauld this Japanese Doctor converted to
Christianity, became a priest and founded a hospital at Sakaramuchi for this poor
neighborhood in Tokyo with S. Violet Sussman. He was the first translator of
Foucauld's *Directoire*.

[264] Allusion to the encounter between Jesus and Nicodemus during which Jesus speaks
of the necessity of being (re)born of the spirit, and to which Nicodemus replies,
"How can a man be born when he is old? He cannot enter his mother's womb and
be born a second time, can he?" Massignon's interpretation of this passage ema-
nates directly from his immense devotion to the Virgin Mary whose adoptive sons
and daughters we are. In his letter to the Badaliya written from Cairo on December
17, 1948, Massignon wrote: "By going back to our origins, to the principle of our

that we have pledged our word to those with whom we work, eating the same pure Bread with them that we have lawfully earned together, and by following the same path that alone will lead us to find the Truth of our common vocation.

This is the Ford, the *Tirtha* of the Hindus, through which one passes from the sphere of obscure premonitions and cryptic intersigns, (over which one should not split hairs), to the Kingdom of Heaven in one's heart. Leaving the material order of the universe through an Einsteinian "distortion" of Space and Time and rising toward a "sky" full of constellations of painful (and how glorious) psychic events, grouping, as in the liturgical cycle, so many souls with ours, according to their names, following their chronograms and their chosen affinities; this does not happen through principles of cause and effect but through "apotropaic,"[265] therefore "transmitted" synchronization; nor does this happen genealogically, but through a kind of virginal sacralization of the vestals of the Sacred Fire, of love.[266]

Thus it seems that it is in this apotropaic sacralization by means of taking on another person's suffering that one can begin to see the metaphysical realization of our personal immortality. Our immortality is not this "evaporation" of individual Karma, this obliteration of the weight of our actions, bringing back the living as well as the dead, moved by the implacable Wheel of Predestination. Immortality would come, from within, in the process of our giving birth to our personal vocation, in our hearts, it would be an Escape forward that would lift us up like a harpoon, an anchor thrown to catch our wounded hearts and save them—a twinkling star snatching us up, from above.

---

adoption we become the adoptive sons of the Blessed Virgin at Calvary by entering "our Mother's womb," as our Lord was saying to Nicodemus, by being born a second time, by finding at the bottom of our heart the *virgin point* of our election to Christianity, and the axis of God's will in us: as She herself found it, on behalf of all the chosen, by saying "yes" to the Angel's annunciation in Nazareth, by accepting to abandon herself totally to God: "Fiat mihi secundum verbum tuum."

[265] Apotropaic: designed to avert evil, like an "apotropaic ritual."

[266] From his other writings it seems here that Massignon is referring to the examples of those saints like St. Lydwine, St. Catherine and others whose vocation of self-offering and of "substitutionary" love served to cleanse and heal others thereby joining them to the liturgically celebrated "communion of saints" in heaven.

Annual Letter # XII

Started in Ise[267] (Japan) On the night of September
5–6, 1958 (completed in Paris June 24, 1959).

Here we have a milestone—at a first class sanctuary in Japan for the IXth International Congress of the History of Religions in Tokyo, one of us was unexpectedly allowed to participate. As his contribution to the experimental research of this Congress, he brought documentation relating to the deepest personal roots of our vocation of "substitution" through the compassion of the Badaliya, (here, not only to Muslim souls, but to Japanese souls as well).

Japan was completely wounded by the American occupation and still suffering from the "inferiority complex" carved in its flesh by the atomic bombs of Hiroshima and Nagasaki (on August 6–9, 1945), and by MacArthur's decree advocating abortion as the most effective means of birth control. Not fully recovered from the imperial decision renouncing the immemorial legend of the divine genealogy of the Mikados (1947), Japan was trying to get hold of itself and reclaim the injured dignity of its religious men by showing the world the authenticity (at least subjective and social), of its various spiritual families. The touching but very clumsy USA "protectorate" recommended [these spiritual families] to the members of the congress, starting with the Christian sects, then the Buddhists (Zen), ending with Shintoism, (that was so compromised by dictatorships during the war.)

---

[267] Massignon was invited to participate in this International gathering in Tokyo and while there he visited the VIIth century Shinto Shrine at Isé. Profoundly moved by this experience he wrote his reflections. (For an English translation see: "Meditation of a Passerby on His Visit to the Sacred Woods of Isé" in *Testimonies and Reflections, Essays of Louis Massignon*. Introd. and trans. Herbert Mason. Notre Dame Press 1989. P. 165–172.)

The extremely minute percentage of Japanese Christians (1%) is not given credit for the quality of the compassionate writers and founders of Christian Japanese social welfare projects. We prayed at the tomb in Koganei (Tokyo) for one of them, our friend Dr. V. B. Totsuka who died August 17, 1939. The Gandhian group led by Mr. Kagawa was not represented at the Congress. We mainly visited Zen Buddhist convents (at Kamakura, Hashiman, Engukoji, Sojiji; in Nara) or Tenri (in Nara, which was founded by a woman, Nakayama Miki who died on January 26, 1887.) We noticed their discipline in mental concentration and their Satori,[268] but, except for Tenri, their mystical vocabulary remains "imported" (Sanskrit or Chinese). The primitive core of the religious soul in Japan remains Shinto, and more than three million pilgrims, belonging to the masses of people, come every year to fulfill their personal vows at its historic center in Ise. It is here in Ise that the people begged for and obtained the defeat of the invading Mongolian armies on August 15, 1281, and asked (in vain) for the defeat of the Americans in 1855 and 1945.

Lost in the masses of Japanese pilgrims, I noticed the curious progression of grace in myself that had led me all the way to Ise. Notations written on the press release in Japanese about the Activities of the Congress, and in the notebook in 1959 from the "Mardis de Dar-es-Salam," had established the mode of communication for enunciating the fundamental notions of the "Badaliya" in the Japanese context of the Tokyo Congress. Just as they had been established in Alexandria, Egypt, on June 9, 1955 for the session of the "Continuing Committee for Muslim Christian Cooperation" (the translation in French appeared as "L'Ame Populaire" ["The Soul of the People"] in the "Sillon Catholique" ["Catholic Path"], Paris, June 1955).

[Through grace I arrived at establishing this mode of communication] here in the Far East, by examining how to recapture the significance of the divine personal presence (Christ) as it imprints itself in Christians through the *Psychosomatic shock of compassion*, suddenly inclining them towards the distress of a stranger. In this Far Eastern culture human solidarity with every being is imposed as a Necessity by the Wheel of the Karma of reincarnation. Here the penalty of suffering this solidarity only disappears through the intercession of a feminine Being, (in Shintô, in

---

[268] *Satori*: "Spiritual awakening" of the Buddha and his devoted followers.

Ise, The Solar Virgin Amaterasu Omikami, coming out of the Cavern with the Mirror and the Sword that her Vestal virgins wave while they dance to ward off the evil spirits), or in Northern Buddhism with the feminine "bodhisattva of compassion," Lokeçvara, to whom Jayavarman VII, the great sovereign of Angkor who died around 1215, dedicated the "Bayon" and the basin of the healing water of Neak Pean that were feminized in the Chinese devotion to Kwanyin and the Japanese devotion to Kwannon.

The idea, so ancient and so "seductive," of the reincarnation of souls, metemsomata[269] (and not metempsychosis)[270] comes from an error confusing Compassion and sexual desire. One must state quite clearly that the love in Compassion is not at all an avid commiseration with an inferior being, but rather the love of admiration for the divine wound whose disarming beauty causes us to feel it as well, by witnessing via the virile word what the woman conceives in silence. *Compassion is itself the "fiat" of the Holy Spirit*, making us see in the disarmed and pierced heart of Mary, and with a virginal chastity, the eternal Filial word, the crucified testimony by the Son of the Father. The poor ex-voto of the "Badaliya" tries to express this, with the pierced Heart representing the aftereffect in Mary's Heart of the thrust of the Lance into the Heart of Jesus. [This represents] *the exchange of heart*, that transfers the inborn unity of their breathing, moving at once beyond number and time, *"Cor Jesu, Cor Mariae"*

To reduce Compassion to sexual desire is to reduce Inspiration to metemsomata, where souls reappear as "seeds" planted in the illusory body of the Woman (solely masculine souls in the *Alouites*, Shiites in Syria, and fractions of the soul, 1/7 or 1/9 male or female, in the Far East). With the Alouites, the woman not having a soul, only glides over the immortal spiritual reality during pregnancy, thanks to a prenuptial ablution in the Water blessed by the Immaculate Virgin ("Mary" or "Fatima," depending on the cycle) which is the "fiat," the "kuni," a kind of immaculate conception which applies to all predestined souls. In the Far East, souls are as illusory as earthly bodies and dissolve in the illumination of Nirvana, which seems to suppress, together with any sexual desire, all Compassion and therefore every personal Resurrection.

---

[269] Transcending the body.

[270] The passing of the soul at death into another body either human or animal.

The primacy of spiritual Compassion over sexual desire is beautifully expressed and illustrated in the "Cukâdêva dialogue," [belonging to] the first and largest number of *bramacharis* ascetics, and seen in the "Aspara Rambha" (the icon of the Marianmane pagoda in Saigon painted according to the poem in Marathi by Uddhava Chighan).[271]

In the Proceedings (being printed in Japanese) of the IXth International Congress of the History of Religions, and in the 1959 book from the "Mardis de Dar es-Salam" (being printed in English and French in Paris, by Vrin), one can find two reports on these "revivals" of compassion, which are not "sequences" of penalizing reincarnations linked to the wheel of Karma, but are free "constellations" of "apotropaic" vocations of mystical substitution. [They are] outlines of anticipated Resurrections—converging testimonies (but sensually independent ones)—the proclaimers and martyrs of the Justice that is persecuted in them, in vain.

Moral Report for the Year 1958

Our monthly letters have expressed every solemn anguish of that year. After having withstood the aggression on February 17th at the Diocesan Center of Catholic Intellectuals as a guest there during a tribute to Foucauld,[272] and after his name was taken off the list of the Conference of St Vincent de Paul, (The reason: having been authorized to visit prisoners, he requested a legal statute in France for Conscientious Objectors—as it is done in Anglo-Saxon countries), our oldest member was able to celebrate in "perfect joy" the fiftieth anniversary of his captivity from May 1–3, 1908 where he found Faith again on the Tigre in front of Salman Pak (in Ctesiphon, Iraq).[273] At the same time we were also celebrating

---

[271] This story of an ascetic who resists the temptation of the most beautiful of goddesses led Massignon to research the origins of the legend in ancient Sanskrit and Marathi, the main Indo-Aryan language of the state of Maharashtra in India. See: "The Temptation of the Ascetic Çuka by the Apsara Rambha (1961)" in *Testimonies and Reflections, Essays of Louis Massignon*. Introd. and trans. Herbert Mason. Notre Dame Press 1989. P. 173–178).

[272] Massignon was brutally attacked at this well-known conference by a French Algerian extremist. He later wrote that he was slapped in the face below his right eye and called a traitor to which he responded by "thanking his attacker."

[273] Massignon is referring to the anniversary of his conversion experience in 1908 in Iraq.

the 25th anniversary of their foundation with the Clarisses of Rabat, our Associates in Fasting.

In 1958, the Algerian explosion on May 13th, that coincided with the feast of Our Lady of Fatima, and the strange glimpse of a possibility of fraternal Franco-Muslim relations through an "operation" of emancipation for Muslim women, plus the trial of our liberal male and female friends tortured in Algiers, left us with no other recourse than to turn with renewed energy to our only weapons, prayer, (vigil on the Night of Destiny, April 15, 1958), fasting, (on Kippur, October 5th), and pilgrimages (to Beaulieu-les-Fontaines, Joan of Arc's first jail, to Worcester, Massachusets, where the Canadian Sisters of Joan of Arc were founded, to Our Lady of Bermont, and to the cave of Dianelet, the VII Sleepers of Sefrou, where Jewish friends went to pray the Lag-be-Omer in unison with us).

Our pilgrimage on July 26–27 to the dolmen crypt of the VII Sleepers in Vieux-Marché was privately attended by our friend, Minister Edmond Michelet, to whom General de Gaulle had wished "good luck" in a cable to the President of the Barristers in Algiers. Thanks to Mrs. Charles-Barzel, Abbot Onfroy, Abbot Cyprian and Mr. J. Arthur, we were able to insist, in unpredictable circumstances, on organizing a Muslim pilgrimage to Our Lady of Lourdes on the feast of the Immaculate Conception on December 8th, the very same year of the centenary of the Apparitions. Pope John XXIII congratulated the pilgrims who were guided by our friend Louis Rouani[274] and a group of pilgrims from Vieux-Marché. Many of our friends came for the centenary of Foucauld's birth on September 15th, some to Rome and others to Tamanrasset. A Foucauld exhibition took place in November 1958 at the National Archives. In Koganei (Tokyo, Japan) one of us was able to visit the grave of the first Japanese translator of Foucauld's "Directory," so dear to the Badaliya. He recounted in the "Proceedings" of the IXth Congress on the History of Religions in Tokyo (July 28, 1958) how he had been led, by a grace characteristic of "Badaliya" to come and pray at the cemetery of Aoyama Boshi in Tokyo at the grave of his friend, admiral Yamamoto Shinjiro who died February 20, 1941, fulfill-

---

[274] Louis Rouani (1892–1979), a Kabyle (Berber) Christian, who worked closely for years with Massignon teaching courses in Math and French to North African workers. In 1940 he established the Association of North African Residents in France. (ANARF)

ing his vow after 37 years to display a Japanese Marian icon (for it's dead) in the church of St Anthony, from the XV-XX, where Abbot Daniel Fontaine had promised him that it would be welcomed. That is what Abbot Ronco accomplished in 1958.

A study by professor Louis Massignon on "*La Cité des Morts au Caire*" (The City of the Dead in Cairo) was published in 1958 (Volume LVII of the Bulletin of the French Institute of Oriental Archeology in Cairo) showing the paramount importance in Muslim religious history of the visit of the women in Islam to the cemeteries on Friday night, in the hope of resurrection (See Hebrews 11:25); [like the] visits to the Qarâfa cemetery in Cairo planned by many members of the Badaliya for so many years. This custom is inherited from Fatima, praying at the Baqî in Medina, under her "tent of suffering," at the death of the Prophet.

In Lebanon, the outburst of the civil war has revived the prayer of our members whose meetings, that were suspended then, were restarted in 1959. The hardening of police agents in both the Western and Soviet blocs in all the under developed countries where the right to remain neutral is denied, has naturally aggravated the relations, not only between Christians and Muslims, but also between Muslims themselves, where the two blocs try to "harness" powerful men, (to the distress of noble and free souls, such as Kamel Chadirchi, head of the Iraqi P.N.D.,[275] who we were able to visit in prison in Baghdad on January 11, 1958. [He was] freed 15 days before the revolution on July 14th, which continues to tear apart the two blocs because of oil).

It is still oil that prolongs the war in Algeria due to the struggle between rival foreign companies. One can catch a glimpse of hope since the Mediterranean Talks in Florence, October 4, 1958, organized by our friend the Franciscan tertiary Giorgio La Pira,[276] in an agreement between Morocco, representing the Arab States, and Israel. Three of us went up to Mt. Alverna at the conclusion of this Congress which had been preceded by a *Fast for serene Peace*.

Let us now go back to the order followed in our letter #XI, to the contacts with the Muslim "works of mercy" that the Badaliya pursued in 1958:

---

[275] National Democratic Party.

[276] Giorgio La Pira (1904–1977), Mayor of Florence, Italy from 1951, devoted his life to the poor and to peace.

Profession of Faith or Testimony[277]

The authoritarian regime that France has accepted since May 13, 1958 has substantially limited the non-violent claim to truth and justice by, in fact, suppressing the public meetings where we requested the cessation of the judiciary extortion of confessions (written out in advance) through physical or psychological force, the silent demonstrations, and the maintaining of the decree of November 4, 1955 eliminating the right to asylum (this fundamental law, engraved in all hearts that are free). Concentration camps have conquered France with methods of administrative inquisition, to "protect civilization against the F.L.N. and communism." All of this unfortunately only accelerated the physical and psychological uprooting of the "regrouped" Muslim populations; and "psycho-analyzed" even the humble act of Faith from the heart, which is considered as expressing an "exorbitant feeling" of their human dignity (sic). Too many faithful among us resign themselves to these practices that are as debatable from the point of view of social morality as from their political efficacy. The Head of State has clearly declared that in life in common where Muslims have been "integrated" by France, *freedom to equality* must be granted to them. Since November 1954, too many hundreds of thousands have been killed for that. We, who pray equally for the dead on both sides, think of the rights of the living to social equality, on both sides. The humiliating platitudes that our technocratic paternalism imposes on the poor North African workers to earn their daily bread, breaks our hearts, and our civic claim to truth must share in the "bread of suffering" that these outcasts endure in order to give them back their pride and the respect due to workers. It is only by sharing the lawful bread (*halâl*) of these fellow workers that we will find the *Truth* of the African vocation in France, the one that Foucauld had glimpsed, not a vocation of oligarchical and racist exploitation, but a brotherly vocation of believers in the God of Abraham, Isaac and Jacob.

We do not dispute that the often violent action performed by the army in Algeria for the emancipation of the Muslim women in an effort to make them into "conscious and organized citizens" since May 13, 1958, did not have the great merit of putting an end to the atrocious masculine

---

[277] The first Pillar of Islam: A Muslim is one who proclaims "There is no deity but Allah and Muhammad is the Messenger of Allah."

restrictions, tolerated for centuries by the Malekite law.[278] But the character of the utilitarian methods of this action, achieved through outside constraint, and not (as it is starting to happen in Indonesia) through an internal evolution planned by Muslim jurisprudence, is preparing us for serious surprises. To break apart the Muslim home by freeing women from their males (fathers, husbands, sons) is going to make Algeria the center of the worst human crisis, the rupture between the two sexes as stated in a prophecy by Alfred de Vigny, inspired by Saint Paul, on the end of paganism and of procreation. Here in Algeria, divided into two sterile cities because of the feud between the two sexes, the man already had Sodom, the woman will have Gomorrah. Two sterile fraternities, against the law of nature, where the Fire of divine Compassion becomes ashes. Current communist China is not asking for as much in its segregation of the sexes through and for industrialization.

At the present moment it would seem that, for fear of communism, our Western technocracy is intent in persisting in the same race against the clock towards cosmic suicide as it was against Nazism in 1942. Then, America had quickly solved the problem of atomic fission, the division of the atom, allowing it to use nuclear weapons against Hiroshima. In the same way, in 1959, we are trying to defeat Communism swiftly by the "division of the believer's soul," thus violating the consciences of Muslims in Algeria. But nuclear explosions, even though they may be of tremendous force, will look like nothing when compared to the explosion of Faith in the God of Abraham, in the virgin point, violated in the soul of the outcasts.

49. Convocation - October 3, 1958
21 rue Monsieur, Paris 7

Friday, October 3, 1958 will be our day of *private Fasting for a serene Peace* between Christians and Muslims, particularly in North Africa and in the Middle East. Contrary to general practice, our monthly Mass has been moved to Friday, October 10th at 6:30 pm in the chapel of the Dames de Nazareth, 20 rue du Montparnasse.

---

[278] The founder of the Malekite school of a restrictive conservative jurisprudence in the 8th century, was an Arab judge from Medina named Imam Malik ibn Anas.

The rapidly changing situation in Algeria compels us to do our Christian duty and stop responding to the cruel terrorism with *lex talionis* since such tough practices are not able to disarm it. Prayer, fasting, sacrifice, the full gift of oneself, Christian love of our enemies, and nothing outside of these *arma Christi*, can save France and make it fulfill its African vocation.

[Let us use Christ's weapons] under the sign of Charles de Foucauld, whose vow of mercy and love that was personally known to us, caused him to be killed in Tamanrasset. We see a sign of hope in the ceremony that took place on September 15th in this blessed spot [Tamanrasset] where the Bishop of the Sahara welcomed the Secretary of Veterans Affairs sent there by the French Prime Minister for the centenary of the birth of our venerated friend,[279] in union with the visit "ad limina" to Castelgandolfo by 600 disciples of Charles de Foucauld (who joined us in spirit by cable with messages of fraternal affection).

Let us pray that the "Mediterranean Conference" that will be gathering Christians, Muslims and Jews in Florence from the 3rd to the 6th of October 1958 under the auspices of Giorgio La Pira and the crown prince of Morocco, and under the sign of St. Francis of Assisi, completes, through its international plan, the call for a Christian Peace for which our Secretary of Veterans Affairs invoked Foucauld in Tamanrasset, after joining our pilgrimage of the Seven Sleepers of Ephesus in Vieux Marché (Muslim *Ahl al-Kahf*) [Qur'an, Sura 18].

Beyond Foucauld and St. Francis, our recourse is in the humble and powerful Virgin Mary, Our Lady of Ephesus, Our Lady of the Pokrov, Our Lady of La Salette, Our Lady of Fatima, Our Lady of Bermont. Several persons have asked if they could organize a Franco-Muslim pilgrimage to Our Lady of Lourdes on December 8th. As we know, Islam believes that Jesus and his Mother are the only two Beings whose births were immaculate. Thus it seems that this idea for a pilgrimage on the feast of the Immaculate Conception should be given a try.

One of us was able to go to Tokyo to the 9th international conference on the history of religions: he reminded those in attendance that the secret of human history belongs to the compassionate and sorrowful souls who take on and make explicit the blind suffering of myriads of human beings.

---

[279] Charles de Foucauld was born in Strasbourg September 15, 1858.

To what we have already said about this (see last month's convocation), let us add one point that we made in English in Tokyo on August 28th. Ancestor worship, as a foundation of primitive religion in the Far East, must be understood as the full awareness of filial love. It is not about blood relations since we have not chosen our father or mother; it is through a psycho-somatic shock as absolute as the act of faith made by Abraham when God asked him to sacrifice his son, that we become aware of our sacred filial duty.

On August 30th we went to the cemetery of Aoyama Boshi in Tokyo to pray at the grave of Admiral Yamamoto Shinjiro[280] (died Feb. 20, 1941), former aide-de-camp of the current Mikado. In the presence of his son J. Tadashi Y., we thanked God for having permitted that after 35 years of pleading and petitioning, a humble icon of Mary "stella matutina" for the conversion of Japan, be placed, as the admiral had wished, in the parish Church of St. Antoine des Quinze-Vingt, where six other friends of Japan, now deceased, Paul Claudel, Vl. Ghika,[281] Daniel Fontaine, V. B. Totsuka, Rose Bicknell[282] and Violet Susman had also asked that the icon be placed. In the Catholic cemetery at Tamabuchi we also visited the graves of the two priests Totsuka and F.X. Iwashita, and that of Rose Bicknell; we also went to the 140-bed hospital founded by V. B. Totauka and Violet Susman in Sakuramashi under the sign of the Good Samaritan and the invocation to Fr. de Foucauld. We have received the second edition of the life of Foucauld in Japanese (with the translation of *Our Model*) from Sr. Marie Gabrielle to whom we gave the first edition in 1947 through the Little Sisters of Foucauld in Tokyo and the Little Brothers in Kawasaki (near Yokohama). As with the Badaliya, Foucauld's writings were a source of meditation for the Japanese community of the Good Samaritan in Sakura-

---

[280] Yamamoto Shijiro's friendship with Paul Cludel led to his conversion to Christianity and work with the Bon Samaritain in Tokyo.

[281] Vladimir Ghika (1873–1954) (mistakenly spelled *Ghaka* in the original text) was a Rumanian Orthodox prince who converted to Catholicism in 1902 and was ordained a priest in 1923. A contemplative man devoted to helping the poor and the downtrodden, he was also a theologian, a diplomat and a friend of such prominent intellectual figures as Mauriac, Maritain, Bergson, Jammes and Claudel, among others.

[282] Devoted assistant to Violet Sussman, her poor health led to her death in 1927 shortly after their arrival in Japan.

mashi. A nephew of V. B. Totsuka's, Mr. Taneaki Otabe, is about to publish a biography of his uncle.

50. Convocation - November 7, 1958
21 rue Monsieur, Paris 7

Friday, November 7, 1958 will be our day of *Private Fasting for a serene Peace* between Christians and Muslims, particularly in *North Africa* and in the Middle East. Our monthly Mass will be at 6:30 pm in the chapel of the Dames de Nazareth, 20 rue du Montparnasse.

We shall pray and reflect together about the widening prospects, in spite of everything, that Christian France now has of confirming its North African vocation, especially in Algeria and the Sahara. We know young conscripts who are finding themselves becoming more and more involved in their social mission of aid to the peasants and nomads of the *blad*[283] and want to fulfill it as elder brothers would, fully understanding that the meaning of non-violent "social service" must become the ideal of tomorrow's army, thereby leading our race to settle side by side with the Arab and Berber majority under the sign of sacred hospitality.

Let us pray that each breach of sacred hospitality committed there by one or the other party, be repaired, and reproved.

Because of our great debt to the meditations contained in Charles de Foucauld's *Directory*,[284] we shall pray that the Foucauld exhibit, which is opening for one month at the National Archives on November 28th, help make the hermit of Tamanrasset the arbiter before God of all the problems of Muslim-Christian coexistence that our Franco-African conscience has to face with increasing urgency. As early as 1913, three years before our friend's death, the oldest member of the Badaliya, thanks to a prophetic pamphlet from the saintly Fr. Crozier,[285] had the premonition that Foucauld would become the victim and ransom of Islam: because,

---

[283] *Blad:* means "a small village," and in North Africa, it refers to the interior of the country.

[284] Foucauld's "Directory" written from 1909–1913, was dear to Massignon who assured its first edition in 1928 along with encouraging the writer René Bazin to write the first biography of the future Blessed Charles de Foucauld.

[285] L'Abbé Antoine Crozier (1860–1916), member of a young religious congregation of Prado founded by Father Chevrier, was a spiritual light in the area of Lyon. Foucauld made a special visit to him on his last trip to France.

according to the profound insight of Charles Le Cœur,[286] the explorer of the Tibesti, Foucauld's particular vocation "was to sanctify eternal Islam (because all that was, continues to be for all eternity) by having it bring forth a Saint in Christianity" (*The Rite and the Tool*, 1939, p. 335).

At the close of the "Mediterranean Colloquium" that took place on October 6th–7th, in Florence, three of us went up to Mt. Alverna[287] and Cortona in order that St. Francis, who protected the birth and growth of the Badaliya founded 24 years ago in Damietta, the place of his ordeal,[288] to offer our thanksgiving to God with our ex-voto, placed where he received the stigmata.

Two others went to pray to our Lady of Fatima, who appears more and more as the sign of the reconciliation we so long for; we are trying hard to help Muslims who are ill go to Lourdes for the feast of December 8th; and the election of the new Pope, John XXIII, who knows and loves the East—Orthodox as well as Muslim[289]—brings us the promise that he will be united in spirit with these pilgrims to Lourdes.

During this octave of the Latin Commemoration of the Dead, a feast liturgically and historically connected to the cult of the Seven Sleepers (Thess.1:4–12), let us remember that Asia and Africa keep the memory of the names of their dead ancestors far better than we do (save for a few Trappists, Carmelites and Carthusians). However, from Japan we are bringing back the certainty that a powerful solidarity unites us with the suffering Church, the true "Church of Silence" in Christ Jesus, who opened His Heart to us, by the thrust of a spear, while his spirit was in Hell to free suffering souls. As we have shown in relation to the "City of the Dead"[290]

---

[286] Charles Le Coeur (1903–1944) French orientalist and ethnographer.

[287] L. Massignon, his godson, Jean-Mohammad Abd al-Jalil and Giorgio La Pira.

[288] Damietta, Egypt is where St. Francis visited the Sultan during the 5th Crusade, and as reported by Bonaventure in his biography of the Saint, offering to undergo a "trial by fire" as a witness to the Truth of Christ. Massignon saw this as the willingness of St. Francis to offer himself for the salvation of the Sultan, and thus, Islam. In 1934 Massignon and Mary Kahil made the first vow of Badaliya prayer at a small Franciscan church in Damietta. See Buck *Dialogues with Saints and Mystics: In the Spirit of Louis Massignon*. 2002 KNP London/NY ch.4 and 5.

[289] Msgr. Roncalli was the Nuncio for Greece and Turkey for many years before he was elected Pope.

[290] Massignon is referring to his essay "La Cité des morts au Caire. Qarâfa—Darb al-Ahmar," The City of the Dead," probably published not long before the date of this

in the Qarâfa in Cairo, visiting tombs hastens the coming of the Day of Justice and the explosion of the Resurrection. "Ubicumque fuerit corpus, ibi congregabuntur et aquilae."[291]

51. Convocation - December 5, 1958
21 rue Monsieur, Paris 7

Friday, December 5, 1958 will be our day of *private Fasting for a serene Peace* between Christians and Muslims, particularly in *North Africa* and in the Near East. Our monthly Mass will be at 6:30 pm in the chapel at the Dames de Nazareth, 20 rue du Montparnasse.

Calm is being restored in Lebanon but it is clear that in Iraq and Egypt the Algerian crisis (not to mention the plight of the Palestinian refugees) is thwarting any attempt at reconciliation. As was said by one of us at the Colloquium in Florence, as long as one does not put oneself in the other's place—in the spirit of "Badaliya," of fraternal substitution with the enemy, the world is heading toward a catastrophe, whether it be by justifying counter-torture against terrorist torture or by nuclear tests as an "effort to prevent" war. (A fiendish obsession which only Prayer, Fasting and the Holy Sacrifice of the Mass can exorcise from those unfortunate people, baptized or not, who advocate and intensify these practices of genocide). When will women understand that taking the life of other women's children is not the way to save the life of their own?

On December 5th, the first pilgrimage of Muslims who are ill (8 have already registered) will leave for Lourdes (December 6th–8th) under the supervision of several of our members who learned to help each other at the pilgrimage in Vieux-Marché. Under the sign of the Immaculate Conception, foreseen in the Qur'an (sura 3:36), the *Fatiha* will be said in Lourdes, as it was in Vieux-Marché, with humble trust in the only two Pure beings, Maryam and Issa.[292]

This morning, one of our members, acting in the fraternal "Badaliya" spirit, is having a Mass celebrated in Paris (St. Jacques du Haut Pas at 9:30

---

convocation in vol. LVII of the *Bulletin de l'institut français d'archéologie orientale au Caire.*

[291] *Where there is a body there is a gathering of eagles.* Massignon's interesting vision of "the explosion of the Resurrection."

[292] Mary and Jesus are named Maryam and Issa in the Qur'an.

am) for his Sister's Husband,[293] thereby fulfilling the desire for intercession that she had voiced to him long ago, during her own agony. Her desire is now being passed on to the prayerful souls who are reading this letter of convocation.

We are also being asked to think prayerfully about the idea (coming from Lyon) of having a three day Muslim-Christian retreat in a neutral country (Rome?) in order to obtain the Serene Peace for which Algeria is hungering and thirsting.

It is clear that our country can only be saved if it *Recovers* its word of honor. In this regard, let us ask our country not to espouse the hypocrisy of Soviet bureaucratic "psychology," since it is absurd and degrading to imitate them while denouncing them at the same time. In any case, the spirit of the "Badaliya" forbids us to have anything to do with this monstrous reversal of "brotherly substitution." We were created to share love, not hatred.

52. Convocation - January 2, 1959
21 rue Monsieur, Paris 7

Friday, January 2, 1959 will be our day of *private Fasting for a serene Peace* between Christians and Muslims, particularly in North Africa and in the Near East. Our monthly Mass will be at 6:30 pm in the chapel of the Dames de Nazareth, 20 rue du Montparnasse.

Several of us, members of the Christian Committee for French/Islamic Understanding, are reminding everyone of the appeal the Committee issued again this year for a Christmas truce, and are urgently pleading with all those in authority for the cessation of all violence and for a just peace between Christians and Muslims. They are also reminding us of the solemn Declaration made by this Committee in front of the Paris Mosque on October 12, 1955: "We came here tonight to pay homage to all the victims and to say the *Fatiha* in Arabic for all of them, especially the women and children fallen on both sides. We think that the Government of the French Republic has not yet treated Muslim Algeria as it does Christian Auvergne and Brittany. We want the government to treat Algeria's chil-

---

[293] Pierre Girard (1888–1935), father of three of Massignon's nieces. His wife, Henriette, died April 26, 1936.

dren like our children from now on, her women like our women, her men like our men; as men who are free to choose their destiny."

As Gandhi did in Delhi in 1947, in front of the Muslim women with whom he had fasted for justice, we swear under oath that we shall continue to work at keeping our word and serving the claims of justice. The committee members are asking the other members of the Badaliya to pray that they keep the word they gave right to the end to all those who at this moment, and all over the world, are persecuted for the sake of justice.

Several of us went up from Nancy to Our Lady of Bermont (near Domrémy) to thank God and Joan of Arc (to whom we prayed for the last two years that she intercede) for the liberation of the French Muslim lieutenant Abdelkader Rhamani, who wrote a letter to the President of the Republic begging him, in the name of 51 Algerian officers, to respect, through them, the honor of the Army in Africa, which is indivisible before God and before men. The entire Badaliya will pray that the Muslim and Christian dead from the Army in Africa may obtain for us "the peace of the brave," in fraternal equality.

Let us fast and pray in thanksgiving on January 2nd, especially for the "Muslim-Christian pilgrimage" to Lourdes that took place on December 8th. May this pilgrimage blessed by John XXIII, bear the spiritual fruits that Msgr. Theas wrote to us that he is expecting. The Archbishop of Smyrna wrote to us of his joy, devoid of jealousy, about this pilgrimage made "in common" by Christians and Muslims, something he has not so far been able to make happen in Ephesus (*Panaya Kapulu*). In a statement published in the Lourdes newspapers on December 8th, we stressed the fact that if, for the last four years our Muslim theological adviser has allowed Muslim pilgrims holding candles and reciting the *Fatiha* to participate in the procession before the dolmen-crypt of Vieux-Marché in commemoration of a miracle, a momentary Resurrection effected by God alone, it is because the worship of the Seven Sleepers of Ephesus is not an idolatrous cult into which we would have led these Muslims: a dead man does not come back to life by himself. In the same way, he also accepts that Muslim pilgrims holding candles and reciting the Fatiha should go to the miraculous pool in Lourdes, as long as they are reminded that adoration is offered to God alone, the sole author of observed miracles, and not to the created means He puts to use in some cases.

This is why the faith of those Muslim pilgrims so struck the Christians in Lourdes, reminding them of what we forget all too often: miracles Suspend the normal chain of secondary causes of events and sets them directly in motion, whether it is a question of the veneration of a sacramental, such as the holy water from the Grotto, or even by a cult of extreme devotion, hyperdulia, offered to the "Aqueduct of Grace," as we call the Immaculate Purity of the Praying and Supplicant Virgin. If Our Lady obtains miracles for us, it is through her great humility, her incessant self-annihilation in the hands of her Creator, who, in an ineffable way, becomes her "Father," her "Son" and her "Friend." Through this *Fiat*[294] marked by the Sign of the Cross, He assumes, through Her, a more than perfect creature who has emptied herself of everything, all of our humanity, in order to save it. A love as strong as death shines forth in Her when she begs for a miracle by substituting herself for the miserable entreaties of the imperfect creatures that we are. This compassionate Love strips her of all material goods or spiritual consolation, pierces her Heart like a sword, and mystically likens her to our Savior on the Cross when the miraculous Precious Blood gushes out at the thrust of the spear, the soul torn away from the flesh. It is when her "I" "annihilates itself" (as at the wedding at Cana), that the "It is I" of the Divine Word, yielding to the Blessed Virgin's prayer, takes command and makes the water miraculous.

For their part, the Muslim pilgrims (along with we Christians) at Vieux-Marché as at Lourdes, will eventually understand that if one cannot attribute everything to created causes here below, neither is everything a kind of blind miracle due to the abstract magic of rituals, or the formalizing of purifications; that in miracles God is *Personal* and that the Marian "Fiat" introduces the three powers of the miraculously cured person's soul to the mystery of the supra-essential life of love, the mystery "of Love, the Lover and the Beloved," these Three in the Unity of *God alone*.

One of our members, who was one of the organizers of this pilgrimage but could not accompany it any further than Paris-Austerlitz, either on the way there or on the way back, is asking the Badaliya to pray for

---

[294] Mary's *fiat (Let it be done unto me according to Your will)*, her total acceptance of God's will for her when she is approached by the angel and told she would bear a son. Massignon saw Mary's *fiat* as the witness of how all Christians are called to respond to God.

two Muslim patients (from the Brévannes sanitarium, MM S. A. and E.H.M.), who "substituted" themselves with him in order to pray in Lourdes for his mother, who made the pilgrimage fifty years ago.

In the same spirit, the Little Sisters of Foucauld of the Way of Bastide, who welcomed the Muslim pilgrims in Lourdes, were asked to have a thanksgiving Mass said for Mother Marie Agnès (Sr. Violet Susman) who made the pilgrimage in 1924 and was cured of Pott's disease; this allowed her to go to Japan and found, under the auspices of Foucauld's Directoire, the charitable organization in Sakuramachi which one of us went to visit from Tokyo last September 4th; she prayed for the Badaliya until she died, and we must thank God for and "through" her.

53. Convocation - February 6 1959
21 rue Monsieur, Paris 7

Before the circular letters for the month of February, being sent later, this notification takes place as a reminder for our monthly Mass at the end of our private fast and our meeting which follows.

The Mass will take place as usual in the chapel of the Dames de Nazareth, 20 rue Montparnasse, Friday, February 6th at 6:30 pm. It will be celebrated by a friend of the Badaliya, R. P. Dom Albéric[295] from the Trappists at Bricquebec. M. Professor Massignon should be with us by that time, returning from the Orient and Rome. Meeting after the Mass.

54. Convocation - March 6, 1959
21 rue Monsieur, Paris 7

Friday, March 6, 1959, monthly Mass at 6:30 pm in the chapel of the Dames de Nazareth, 20 rue Montparnasse, followed by a meeting at the close of our day of *private Fasting for a serene Peace* between Christians and Muslims, particularly in North Africa and in the Near East.

In awe of the "manner" in which, both in Corsica and Antsirabe, the King of Morocco, Mohammed V, pursues his work of reconciliation between the Arabs and the French, the Christians and the Muslims, in order to

---

[295] This Trappist took part in the small private group in the "Prayer of Sodom." Massignon liked to go for retreat at this Abbey in Normandy.

build a Community[296] of peace and justice in which no acts of revenge are allowed ("*Die rache ist mein*")—we informed our friend Ahmed Benani, his Chief of Protocol, that our monthly fast on March 6th dedicated in the first place to war-torn Algeria, would be offered in order that God answer the King of Morocco's very noble prayer.

One of us has just returned from Jerusalem, where he again had the "*Fatiha*" said for our friend, Professor Hajj Lounis Mahfoud (ibn Meslûd), on January 28th, in union with his widow who thanked us for our fidelity; it was also said for the protection of the Waqf Abu Madyan at the Al-Aqsa, and for the annual pilgrimage to the Seven Sleepers (Vieux-Marché), several members of which (as we all remember) organized the Muslim-Christian pilgrimage to Our Lady of Lourdes on December 8, 1958; the *Fatiha* was said not only in the Waqf's small Mosque but also inside the Al-Boraq Mosque[297] and in Nabi Yaqîn[298] in the company of the son of Imam Ansari (from the Al-Haram Al Sharif).[299] We visited the chapel of the Seven Sleepers in Rome, 7 via S. Sebastiano, on February 14th with Professor C. Cecchelli, and he reminded His Holiness John XXIII that his predecessor Clement XI, a great friend of the Near East, had restored it in 1710. A charitable Ephesian organization would like to have it "reassigned" in order to make it into its center in Rome. We asked that the liturgical rights of the Melkite Church upon which the Badaliya is dependent, not be infringed upon.

Thanks to our visits to Cairo, Beirut, and Damascus, we were able to observe the vitality of our local groups (we could not visit the Badaliya in Alexandria but we are aware of the zealous fidelity of its leader, Professor Naguib Baladi). A short stay in Rome allowed us to have a private audience with His Holiness John XXIII, during which he had us draft a Note on the meaning of our offering of "Badaliya," which is intimately linked to the relics of Christ's Passion, and the Holy Sacrifice of the Mass—

---

[296] At the end of 1958, President De Gaulle transformed the French Union inherited from the 1947 Constitution (IVth Republic) into a community of more and more autonomous States which led to rapid total independence.

[297] A small Mosque not far from the Al-Aqsa Mosque.

[298] *Nabi Yaqin*: an ancient cemetery on the border of the Hebron desert.

[299] "Noble Sanctuary:" The Arabic name for the Jewish Temple Mount that includes the Dome of the Rock and the Al-Aqsa Mosque constructed on the Mount, or the site, of the ancient destroyed Temple.

said in Arabic—it is also connected, through its foundation in Damietta, with the Franciscan mystery of Mt. Alverna,[300] (a Mass was said on January 15th, at Kenisset el-Arwâm in Damietta, for the 25th anniversary of the foundation of the Badaliya on February 9, 1934.[301] Another anniversary (the 9th), of January 28, 1950,[302] was celebrated in the Church of St. Ann of Jerusalem).

The leader of our Roman group, Msgr. Paul Mulla-Zade, a professor at the Pontifical Institute, son of a Turkish Muslim physician from Crete, had a stroke on February 26th; several of us had seen and consulted with him during the days preceding it. All our groups are praying for this exemplary priest and steadfast friend.

Our diverse groups have asked that our monthly text avoid focusing too much on France's spiritual vocation or on Algeria's wounds and keep in mind the different national customs in relation to the connections that our rule orders us to keep with our friends living in a Muslim environment. These customs vary with the complexities of superiority or inferiority felt on one side or the other. Furthermore, this trip allowed us to conclude that, despite the false news reports that poison the press, whether on the part of oil corporations, the Soviets, racisms (Israeli racism not being the only one in existence) or various sorts of idealisms, (the author of the pamphlet said to be by "Hanna Zakariyâ"[303] has just died in Paris: let us ask God to forgive him)—all eyes are fastened on France and its Prime Minister, who does not seem likely to betray France's promise and is, for this reason, considered by most to be capable of solving the Algerian problem. Let us pray that he does not lose heart as he works on this great undertaking.

Let us examine in what spirit the members of the Badaliya, in whatever country, direct their "substitution" for their Muslim friends in the

---

[300] St. Francis received the gift of the stigmata (the wounds inflicted on Jesus Crucified) on Mt. Alverna in August 1224.

[301] Louis Massignon and Mary Kahil made their original vow of "Badaliya" on February 9, 1934 in a Franciscan church in Damietta, Egypt. See Buck, "Dialogues with Saints and Mystics," p. 147.

[302] Massignon was ordained a Greek Catholic Melkite priest by Bishop Medawar in Cairo on January 28, 1950. See Buck, "Dialogues with Saints and Mystics," p. 152.

[303] A Dominican, Father Gabriel Théry, wrote this pamphlet under the pseudonym, Hanna Zacharias.

milieu where they work and live. As Gandhi reminded us, and as Abbé Pierre[304] was telling us once again in Beirut on his return from India, it is clear that in these times of blind hatred and obdurate scorn for those who are weak, the unwritten Law of sacred Hospitality, of the right of asylum for any helpless foreigner in France, even if he is a *Nordaf* worker,[305] is the eternal inalienable norm of our friendship, and if need be, of our sacrifice: to these friends we owe the highest kind of Christian charity.

Little Sister Magdeleine of Jesus[306] was stressing the same thing with admirable force on February 15th at Tre Fontane, as she was telling us about offers made to her Little Sisters to conduct "surveys" on the work or living environment of the Muslims among whom they are called to bring divine hospitality: how could we, she said, (even with the laudable intention of helping the "organized" and officious charity of some philanthropic groups and associations), betray the trust and the friendship of these humble (supposedly abnormal) people—if, because of this trust, we *made use,* even in the smallest way, of the things that we discovered in our working environment about their family situations, their material suffering and their moral misery.

What is obvious to the Little Sisters, and to social workers (some understood it in a heroic way in Algiers) and priests—is not to violate the *virgin point*[307] in the souls of these unfortunate people whose friends we claim to be. And that is equally true for any member of the Badaliya.

The only way of speaking the truth, as I said in Beirut, is to safeguard the honor of those with whom we work and share a lawfully earned daily bread, (a bread that has not been bought with *pretium stupri*).[308]

Expert technicians know very well that they cannot loyally and honestly serve the foreign country to which they were sent by their own coun-

---

[304] A fervent defender of human rights and especially the right to housing, Abbé Pierre (1912–2007) was one of the most popular French personalities.

[305] Nordaf: An insulting and pejorative, (untranslatable) term for a North African.

[306] Little Sister Magdeleine, Magdeleine Huttin (1898–1989) was the Foundress of the Little Sisters of Jesus, in the spirit of Charles de Foucauld. Their Mother House is at Tre Fontane in Rome.

[307] *Le Point Vierge*, a theme throughout the writings of the Sufi saint al-Hallaj and often used by Louis Massignon in his reflections. (The center of the human soul where the inviolable spirit of God dwells) See Buck, *Dialogues with Saints and Mystics*, p. 185.

[308] Bought with an illicit gain.

try, if they compromise their country's honor by informing against the host country. It is not only the integrity of any homeland that is in question here, it is the very effectiveness of police repression which is the first system to be contaminated and duped by these "informers" from whom the police imagine they can get a minimum of truthfulness by covering up their "corruption."

As Gandhi admirably said, our vocation is to be *True* because divine holiness is true. In order to save our homeland, our family or ourselves, we must stop incriminating others for the sins that we continue to commit; furthermore, we must, in a spirit of brotherliness and heroic non-violence, "assume" the violence of our adversaries so that the violent deeds we commit because of them may be forgiven.

55. Convocation - May 1, 1959
21 rue Monsieur, Paris 7

Friday, May 1, our monthly day of *private Fasting for a serene Peace* between Christians and Muslims, particularly in North Africa and in the Near East.

May our fast bring fraternal assistance to *Pax Christi*[309] and to its National Day for Peace that it has organized for ten days later. May there be peace wherever we ask for it, first of all, throughout the entire French community.

May 1st will be at *St. Séverin* this time, monthly Mass will be celebrated at 7 pm.

Our monthly meeting will occur *before*, and not after Mass, at 6 pm, at St. Séverin, (parish hall, 3 rue des Prêtres St. Séverin) where we are invited to hear our friend, Miss Germaine Tillion, director of studies at the École Pratique des Hautes Etudes at the Sorbonne, speak on *Algeria's social structures*. This is a subject she has studied on the ground, on behalf of the government, for the past 20 years since she began with a monograph on a small mountainous clan in the Aures, the very place where the conflagration of the insurrection began in November 1954, following 4 years of unassisted famine.

Our hearts will burn at the extreme poverty of these humble people whose "upward social mobility" has been our responsibility for the past

---

[309] *Pax Christi* is an international Catholic organization established in 1945.

130 years. It is no longer a small clan, they number at least 837,000 people, *Displaced People* for operational purposes, far from their ancestral villages, far from their plots of land, their springs, their cemeteries, expatriated, and gathered, "regrouped into camps."

Miss G. Tillion[310] will help us meditate on the overwhelming duty to assume, in place of all these "crouillats,"[311] all these humble "life journeys" uprooted from all their roots, firstly their roots in the land; they lack Bread.

This followed by "roots in heaven" because at this moment, through some ill-omened aberration, an unofficial baccalaureate reform project aims to take advantage of this state of physical misery to "rid" these poor people of their traditional ideals by abolishing modern Arabic, this magnificent language of civilization, to replace it with a "North African Arabic dialect" (sic), that has been arbitrarily constructed by means of a patois that would not allow for intellectual thought or for spiritual prayer, and would prepare for the adoption of French and the "French" integration of our Muslim Algerians without their consent. This project, tried first in Tunisia where it has been one of the sources of indignation against us, and one of the causes for the loss of our protectorate, then in Morocco, where it also failed, can only push these poor people, for whom we pray, into wild hatred of the "psychologists" who wish not only to wash their brains, but also their souls, of their belief in the God of Abraham, the God of Hospitality who we ignore in them. All of us who know Arabic and are indebted to this Semitic language, marked by its witness of the God of the Last Judgment invoked in the *Fatiha*, will pray that we be spared of these unworthy measures by France. For the French language to be loved by the Muslim Algerians as a language of common hope, we too must also love their maternal language as a noble language, and one full of promise.

---

[310] Germaine Tillion (1907–2008), French ethnologist who specialized in the study of the people living in the Aurès Mountains in eastern Algeria. During World War II she joined the French Resistance and was deported to Ravensbruck, Hitler's only death camp for women only. Having returned to Algeria after the war, she found the country's economic conditions appalling and in 1955 created Social Centers offering education, health and professional training programs to young Algerian men.

[311] Colonial French insult.

56. Convocation - June 5, 1959
21 rue Monsieur, Paris 7

Friday, June 5, 1959, feast of the Sacred Heart, monthly Mass at 6:30 pm in the chapel of the Dames de Nazareth, 20 rue du Montparnasse, followed by a meeting at the close of our day of *private Fasting for a serene Peace* between Christians and Muslims, particularly in North Africa and in the Near East.

The appeal that our friend, Mademoiselle Germaine Tillion, launched on May 1st on behalf of the 837,000 "regrouped" Algerian Muslims who were displaced on account of operational necessities, was, thanks to Msgr. Rodhain,[312] brought onto the national stage by Cardinal Feltin[313] and Pastor Boegner;[314] may some measure of compassion finally take root in the numb and stony hearts of so many French people.

Our Moroccan friends are asking us to pray for the charitable organization founded in El Kbab by our friend, Fr. Peyriguère,[315] who died on April 26, 1959 in a Casablanca hospital after making himself, like Foucauld, "poor among the most poor." The Badaliya is commending itself to him for protection.

A family of Kabyl friends who became Catholics and kept fraternal bonds with their Muslim brothers, was stricken by the death of M. Amokra Ould Aoudia, a lawyer and counsel for Algerian defendants, who was killed while working in his legal profession; the sacred immunity of justice was violated right in the middle of Paris; we are hurting from this new pain inflicted before God and before men on our Country that is being brought to ruin by those who want to "save" it in this manner. Let us pray, in M. Aoudia's name, for his blinded murderers.

---

[312] Msgr. Jean Rodhain (1900–1977), from the Mission de France, founded Catholic Charities after World War II.

[313] Maurice Cardinal Feltin (1883–1975): Archbishop of Paris from 1949 to 1966.

[314] Marc Boegner (1881–1970): President of the Protestant Federation in France. During World War II he devoted himself to trying to save Jews and political refugees; on numerous occasions during the Algerian war he denounced the cruel policies and practices of the French government. Observer at the Vatican II Council, he was very favorable toward the ecumenical movement.

[315] A follower of Charles de Foucauld, Fr. Albert Peyriguère (1883–1959) lived most of his life among the Berbers in El Kbab in Morocco, ministering to the sick and the very poor and forcefully denouncing injustice wherever he encountered it.

Let us offer our June as well as our July fast to God so that the noble intervention of Mohammed V may bear fruit. Let us also pray that in this land of Morocco where Marxism is spreading, the souls of *Muslim "worker priests"* be found among the religious students of the Qarawiyyîn.[316] They are needed there, too.

57. Convocation - July 3, 1959
21 rue Monsieur, Paris 7

Friday, July 3, 1959, monthly Mass at 6:30 pm in the chapel of the Dames de Nazareth, 20 rue Montparnasse, followed by a meeting at the close of our day of *private Fasting for a serene Peace* between Christians and Muslims, particularly in North Africa and in the Near East.

Counting from June 12, 1953, this will be *our two hundred and seventy-fifth monthly private fast.* If we include the additional fasts: Ramadan, Kippur... we are nearing a figure of 300, that reminds us of the duration of anti-Christian persecutions, of the Catacombs, and the number of years that the Seven Sleepers waited. Counting from 1954, (centenary year of the battle of the Musabbilun of Tichkirt[317] and date of the beginning of the current Algerian tragedy) this will also be our *fifth year* of sorrowful compassion for all the victims, beginning with those who are "occupied," whether "rebels" or not.

It seems to us that this summer will be decisive, and since we may not have any bulletin in August or September, we are asking all our friends to multiply their spiritual efforts and acts of social generosity during these three months in order that the horror of the Algerian tragedy may soon come to an end. Despite a new surge of conscience and humanity among some, the acts of cruelty that the two parties are inflicting upon each other point more and more clearly to malevolent psychoses which cannot be exorcised through simple reasoning, common sense or practical interest, but only through incessant, relentless, wrenching, desper-

---

[316] A great Mosque in Fez where an ancient traditional Moroccan University was established in the middle of the 9th century.

[317] Tichkirt: Allusion to the (temporary) victory won on July 20, 1854 by Lalla Fadhma n'Soumeur (1830–1861)—nicknamed by the French "the Joan of Arc of the Berbers"—with her Mujahidin and Musabbilun (also transliterated in French as moussebiline: freedom fighters) over the powerful army of Maréchal Randon, who was Governor General of Algeria from 1851 to 1858.

ate *prayers*, strict *fasting*, and total self-sacrifice—especially when confronting this underhanded and clandestine war against "the father of lies"—and through our non-violent but public witnessing to the Truth. The following was said about Hallaj, the mystical martyr of Islam: "If there is a kind of love that demands the shedding of blood (that of our comrade in battle), there is another kind of love that demands that we shed our own blood by letting ourselves be wounded by the swords of Love, and this is what supreme Love is."

May all those who are able come next July 25/26 to our Breton Pilgrimage of the Seven Sleepers of Ephesus in *Vieux-Marché* (Côtes du Nord), during which our living Muslim friends will be united with those who died, faithful to our fraternal pact, like Hajj Lounis Mahfoud (died in Setif, June 5, 1957). *We shall say the Fatiha for them.* This year, mention of the Seven Sleepers in the *Song of Roland* will bring us those participants for whom national archeology serves as a meditation on [the idea of] "anticipated resurrection,"[318] (See: Bédier edition, lines 1427/1429; Foerster edition, lines 1278/81). On July 12th several Masses will be said for this Muslim-Christian pilgrimage.

As in 1953, *we shall have a special fast* next August 14th, the last day of the *Siyâm al-'Adhrâ*, the great Marian fast of the Eastern Church (including the Church of Silence). As in 1953, we shall ask Msgr. Joseph Descuffi, Archbishop of Smyrna and Ephesus, and our beloved Archbishop of Peluse, Msgr. P. K. Medawar, to bless it. On that day we shall be in special union with our associates, the nuns of Rabat (and Nazareth) who at this moment are about to become the first Arab-speaking Melkite nuns.

Let us pray for a deceased Daughter of Charity, R. Sr. Sovich, a great friend of our sodality; she was very keen on placing its ex-voto in the Chapel of the Convent in Teheran, and in Damascus, where she died three months ago, not long after founding a "Badaliya." Let us also pray for a living man, Fr. Louis S. Pommet, who offered the Holy Sacrifice for us in Chicoutimi (Canada) on May 27th.

Every Friday, at 7:15 pm, our friends will be united in a spirit of self-offering at the Mass (including litanies) said in Algiers, in the Bab el-Oued

---

[318] In other convocations Massignon refers to the Seven Sleepers as "ces VII Martyrs ressuscités anticipés... ces VII veritables Lazare" ('these seven martyrs anticipating the final 'resurrection'... these seven genuine *Lazarus*').

parish, "for the material and spiritual well-being of the Muslims," in the very spirit, therefore, of our annual vigil of the "Laylat al-Qadr," the "Night of Destiny."

P.S. We received a letter dated June 25th from the American Ephesus Society who are undertaking, with the financial guarantee of the Latin Archbishop of Smyrna, the restauration of the St. John of Ephesus Basilica (blessed by Pope John XXIII). Islamic and Christian unity is at this moment of primary concern to the Americans in order not to lose the Muslims. The Seven Sleepers is the only devotion common to both Muslims and Christians. "It is necessary to get the Seven Sleepers started" a subject practically unknown in the United States. Through a small brochure "rather popular and compelling." Let us pray during the pilgrimage at Vieux-Marché for this realization. Let us remind the Americans who remember La Fayette, that the Chapel of the Seven Sleepers in Vieux-Marché had been the property of the mother of La Fayette and La Fayette bequeathed it to the town (now Plouaret) in 1825.

58. Convocation - August 14, 1959
21 rue Monsieur, Paris 7

Call from the "Friends of Gandhi"
For a day of private fasting on August 14 [1959]

In the current world situation, many people are already resorting, often heroically, to fasting, a discipline whose social efficacy Gandhi was the first to demonstrate.

There are also many who are beginning to see the promise of a truce in such mercy-laden anniversaries as the one taking place next August 15th.

In view of the increasingly tough technology used in international conflict that threateningly hangs over, *sine die*, the war in Algeria, and paralyzes even the best among us in the humble, humane obligation to bear public witness to the Truth, (Gandhi's *Satyagraha*, that, through his life and death, he taught us is our inalienable means of salvation)—the very small French Association of the *Friends of Gandhi* wishes to remind every man and every woman of good will that it would be just and good to meditate in union with one another in a *Private fast for a serene peace on August 14, 1959*, from sunrise to sunset in an effort to extinguish war in the entire world—in which we feel a sense of solidarity as we resort with Faith to this non-violent weapon and rely on the fraternal support of all those who understand us world-wide.

August 14, 1959 at Sunrise

It is Gandhi's own voice that we are consciously passing on today in Paris, having gone to hear its echo at the place of his final pilgrimage at the end of his last fast for peace, where he, a Hindu, fasted with so many fervent Muslim women, in Mehrauli, south of Delhi, on January 27, 1948, at the Qutbuddin Bakhtiyar Mosque. Two of us went to Mehrauli on behalf of the *"Friends of Gandhi"* with this in mind. (Louis Massignon with two Muslim members of parliament, H. Haykal and Matin Daftari on January 6, 1953, and Mrs. Camille Drevet, on January 27, 1957). We are not forgetting that six months [and ten years] earlier, on August 15, 1947, Gandhi's non-violent efforts had achieved India's independence.

This is why first of all we are asking our Muslim friend, Cheikh Niazi bin Dilal Qutbi, caretaker of the Mehrauli Mosque, whose father had welcomed Gandhi there, to have the *Fatiha* said for the intentions of our private fast: August 14th corresponds to the 9th day of the month of *safar*, 1379 of the Hegira.

On that day we shall take our inspiration from other illustrious examples such as the "Day of Fasting and Prayer" (April 29, 1863) instituted by the President of the United States, Abraham Lincoln, during the war provoked by the emancipation of the black slaves—a profoundly biblical fast echoing the Jewish Yom Kippur, that many of us fast with them, for the salvation of the world.

For all of us Christians, from the Latin and Eastern Churches, especially the Silent Church—August 14th marks the close of the "Fast of the Virgin," on the eve of the great feast of her Dormition or Assumption. Members of the Marian pilgrimage will be going up from Smyrna to Ephesus and promised to keep us in their thoughts.

Even our friends from faraway Japan, above all the Shintoists, will remember on August 14th how, on that same day in 1281, at the Grand Shrine of Ise, their people gathered, pleading for their lives, and were saved the next day by the defeat of the Mongol invaders.

May all of our friends in the Middle East and in the Far East who are faithful to this "form of prayer" from India, whether Hindus or Buddhists, spread this call to fast, this silent cry of human compassion where all our souls are at one with theirs.

On behalf of the Friends of Gandhi

LOUIS MASSIGNON

CAMILLE DREVET

59. Convocation - October 2, 1959
21 rue Monsieur, Paris 7

Friday, October 2, 1959, monthly Mass at 6:30 pm in the chapel of the Dames de Nazareth, 20 rue Montparnasse, followed by a meeting at the close of our *54th Day of Fasting for a serene Peace* between Christians and Muslims, particularly in North Africa and in the Near East.

(N.B. 54th: we mistakenly thought our fast of July 3rd was the "275th" because we were thinking of a *weekly* fast, only recommended by the Badaliya over the last five years for certain Ramadans and emergency cases; for example, during last July and August a group of Muslim Algerian friends, adhering to non-violence and exiled in Tunisia, observed a weekly fast despite an oppressive heat; they informed us about it on the feast day of the Assumption).

Our latest appeal [from the "Friends of Gandhi"] sent July 3rd, recommended that we remain steadfast and multiply our efforts to abandon ourselves to God through constant prayer, strict fasting and abundant sacrifices. It insisted on participation in the *Private fast* on *August 14th*, at the close of the great Fast of the Virgin in the Near East, especially in Ephesus, where we were promised the special support of the Marian pilgrimage that went up from Smyrna to Ephesus; it also insisted on our taking part in the *Breton Pardon of the Seven Sleepers of Ephesus*, a Muslim-Christian pilgrimage celebrated for the eighth time in Vieux-Marché (July 25–26).

It gives us great joy to announce that beyond Ephesus, where a good number of our members were present on August 14th, our idea was spread, a little bit everywhere, throughout the world on that day, thanks to an *Appeal* that the board of the *Friends of Gandhi* unanimously agreed to publish: (the text is enclosed on a separate page), it was summarized in *La Croix* (8/7), *L'Homme Nouveau* (8/15), *Le Monde* (7/24, 8/13), *Action Civique Non-Violente* (Nº III). Besides humble participants with no other diploma than their human compassion (fasting, as we have said here in relation to our fast of August 14, 1953, is the true way of attaining the Beatitude of those who "hunger and thirst for Justice" on behalf of the oppressed who are deprived of it), a good number of independent scientific personalities gave us their support. This would have gone straight to Gandhi's heart because, by supporting us, these scientists were subscribing to a mode of thought that transcends the senses. From the head of a scientific mission in Japan we received this message: "The idea that, however far from France we had found ourselves, however isolated we had been as anonymous travelers on a ship crossing the strait of T., nevertheless, you had truly lifted us up by giving us the means to intercede and take action." A European jurist in Denmark, after confessing that he had never completely fasted before, told us of his joy "to have been able to join in the most beautiful human enterprise of our times because it is connected in the noblest way with the salvation of humanity." While visiting an exhibition on Foucauld in Rome on the morning of August 14th, a specialist on India was struck by the resonance of our fast with Foucauld's "*Caritas*" and wrote to us: "A deep intuition tells me that today's fast is being observed by the powerful as well as by the humble, and I have faith in its effects which may not reveal themselves immediately but will someday be perfectly clear to us, I am sure of that." From the Indian Minister "for Scientific Research and Cultural Affairs" who had observed our beginnings in 1953 in Delhi with a rather skeptical eye, came this remark (in his letter of 8/12) that our Gandhian action "for increasing goodwill among men" is becoming effective: "Prayer and Fasting have a great role to play in such endeavors." His remark is closely akin to the conclusion that Jacques Maritain makes about Gandhi, and our fasts, in his "Philosophy of History" (p. 74 in the English text, p. 87 in the Jeunet French translation): this common effort based on fasting and prayer to obtain more just governmental policies in specific cases, or to increase mutual understanding and pacifist cooperation between various groups (Muslims, Jews, Christians)—begins almost imperceptibly. *But its significance for the future is no small matter.*

The Imam of the Mehrauli Mosque (India, 9 kms south of Delhi) Allama Niazi Qutbi, son of the Imam who had welcomed Gandhi on January

27, 1948, cabled us that he "prayed hearty."[319] He had also welcomed two of us in 1953 and 1957. And one month later, through a divine coincidence, September 16th happened to be the day when France, in a very noble statement delivered by its president,[320] committed herself for the first time to treating Muslims in Algeria as our equals, our brothers in the human family; meanwhile, in Mehrauli, September 16th was the first of the three days of the annual *Mawsim*[321] (Sept. 16–18, 1959, that is to say 12th–14th Rabi al-Awwal, 1379 of the Hegira, Mawlid al-Nabi (celebrated in 1948 on January 26–28th, in Gandhi's presence, for the reconciliation of his country with the Muslims).

One of our friends, a Frenchman residing in Pondichery,[322] insisted on having his donation and his greetings delivered personally to the Imam of Mehrauli through official channels on August 14th.

The Mehrauli Mosque has been served since the XIIIth century by non-violent contemplatives belonging to the Afghan Sunni order of the Tshishtiya;[323] as it happens, our fast was observed by a number of Tshishtiya participants from Herat, Kabul and Karachi. Their Brahman Tamul friends from Mr. Pamanabhan's pro-Gandhian group also fasted on the 14th, the same date that some Buddhist friends made a point of "reflecting" on our effort.

A pertinent and bitter French Jewish critic, Rabi,[324] concluded his analysis of the degradation of conscience in France, faced with the Algerian tragedy, (in the July issue of *Esprit*) by stating that there is little chance of salvaging the situation, "*Unless a miracle happens. And everything must be done to achieve this miracle. Everything, even prayer*, but prayer so fervent that it breaks open the heavens."

---

[319] "Prayed hearty:" in English in the original text.

[320] On September 16, 1959, General De Gaulle made this declaration.

[321] "*Mawsim*" literally means season. Massignon is referring here to the seasonal celebration of the birthday of Prophet Muhammad, or *Mawlid al-Nabi*, which is fixed on the 12th day of the month of *Rabi al-Awwal* in the Muslim calendar.

[322] Given that since 1954 there were no residents of France in Pondichéry, perhaps Massignon was confusing the place with his friend, Jean Fillozat (1906–1982), who was the director of the French Institute in Pondichéry.

[323] Sufi brotherhood spread throughout India founded by Khwâdja Mu'in al-din Tshîshti (141–1236).

[324] Wladimir Rabi, a renowned journalist published "Conversations en Algérie" in 1959.

We think that it is to this kind of prayer that St. Ignatius of Antioch devoted one of his Epistles in which he talks about this silent call, this strangled little cry, blurted out by a very pure young girl moved by divine compassion as she faced the atrocious misery in the world. It is this cry that caused the Angel of the Annunciation to appear in Nazareth at the time of Israel's greatest despair.[325]

We also think that it must have been for our salvation that an echo of this cry was heard on August 14th. On the previous day, August 13th, this year 9 Ab in the Jewish calendar, Israel was commemorating the two destructions of the Temple by fasting and reciting the 150 Psalms (at the Wailing Wall before 1948 and now at the Cenacle). We were told how several noble-minded Jews tried to answer the call of the "Friends of Gandhi," by extending their fast for Israel, on August 13th, to August 14th in order to take part in our fast for all of humanity. And this is very important: because from now on, since the world's salvation depends on Israel, Israel must no longer fast for itself alone, but for the entire world.

And this brings us to propose to all of our friends, *in gratitude to Israel*, that we fast with them on October 11th–12th, from *sunset to sunset*. In fact, this is the date this year of Israel's Yom Kippur, its great Day of Atonement, on which some of us have been fasting for several years. This year we would like to fast more intensely and in larger numbers on behalf of the Arab refugees who were driven out of Palestine in 1948; for whom our noble friends from Israel, Martin Buber, Martin Plessner, the journal *Ner*,[326] and the disciples of the admirable R. Judah Magnes, are calling for an official Declaration, similar to the one France made on September 16th for Muslim Algeria.

We still have to report on the Breton Pardon of the Seven Sleepers of Ephesus at Vieux-Marché. Just as the Christian procession was coming out of the chapel in order to reach the square where the Fire of Joy in Charity was going to be lit, the parish Rector himself invited the Muslim pilgrims who were coming out of the crypt of the Seven Sleepers to join the procession with their banner embroidered with the evangelical

---

[325] Massignon suggests that when the Angel appeared to the Virgin Mary it was in response to her own impassioned prayer.

[326] An Israeli journal that formed a Committee for a free Algeria with the approval of Ben Gurion, indirectly preparing for the exile to Israel by the Jews of this country.

part of the *Ave Maria* (the one recognized by Islam) written in Arabic characters. This banner (carried in Lourdes on December 8th by the head of the Muslim delegation, Mr. Makhlufi Touati) was also carried the next morning to the spring of VII veins, that we know is exactly symmetrical with the spring of seven veins at the Seven Sleepers of Guidjel (near Setif) where our friend Hadj Lounis Mahfoud had twinned the Muslim pilgrimage with the Breton pardon in Vieux-Marché (where there is now a plaque dedicated to his memory in the crypt).

The reputation of this pardon is growing in the U.S.A. where the *American Ephesus Society* is preparing brochures founding a movement of Muslim-Christian reconciliation based on the cult, common to both traditions, of the Seven Sleepers. The famous convert, Thomas Merton,[327] from the Trappist monastery of Our Lady of Gethsemani in Kentucky, told us how much he was praying with us. Support from the contemplative Orders is decisive. It is only since we got the Trappist monasteries throughout the world to pray for the "resurrection" of Foucauld's works after his death, that his works have started to resurface little by little. But the question here is not so much of undeserved oblivion as it is of hatreds that we must overcome, "Exorcise," a word dear to us, that the Leader of France used on September 16th against the two terrorisms currently confronting each other not only in Algeria, but elsewhere in the world, to the particular detriment of underdeveloped and helpless nations.

Of the two terrorisms, Marxism is the most visible. But the other one is the more perverse because it claims that communism should be fought with the most forbidden weapons. It seduces the "Party of Order" by offering it a means of technological power in order to physically and psychologically coerce and "tear underdeveloped nations away from communist propaganda." It is of that idea that we must dare to disabuse the naïve righteous members of the Moral Rearmament and the *Blue Army*, who believe that gifts from impenitent public sinners are poison-free, and that "anticommunist" violence is a genuine seal of spiritual authenticity. [One cannot] fuse, as does Arnold Toynbee[328] in his Litanies of the Saints of syncretism, Isis with Mary, and Mithra with St. Michael, or incorporate into the "One Front of Spiritualism" the most discredited

---

[327] Thomas Merton (1915–1968), had a great admiration for Louis Massignon.
[328] Arnold Toynbee (1889–1975), world renowned British historian.

and degraded social debris of Buddhism, such as the administrative lamas of Tibet or the pensioned bonzes of Laos, under the pretext that all well "organized" churches featuring an "acceptable orthodoxy," a "respectable" hierarchy and duly honored bank accounts, have to be accepted just as they are.

Since communism derives its entire strength from the putrid decomposition of these demeaning spiritual organisms in which rules replace "morals" and training techniques replace "mysticism," the seeds of authentic spiritual life will remain like a cyst until everything explodes.

It is not with the powerful well-paid prelates who exploit spiritual values that the pure and holy Church must ally herself for her mission of ecumenical unity, but with the hearts broken from misery in the "churches of silence" and "concentration camps," that are not the exclusive property of the USSR: Helas! Some can be found in France.

As it pursues its conquest of the visible skies, all-powerful technology will further and further inflate the despair of atheism, that is more and more unable to escape the horrendous prison of the expanding Nebulae. Only primitive minds such as those subservient to the USSR, could find solace in the extraordinary impact of Lunik-II on the moon. For those capable of reflection, mankind will never be able to live in "the eternal silence of these infinite spaces," it can only imagine them; human life was not organized on their scale. And while our space is being subjected to this inhuman hypertension, our Time on earth is shrinking and becoming condensed; everything is taking place like a spiral shrinking of the ray of our Einsteinian Time Curve, our hearts could not escape lethal tachycardia except by tending, in a movement of universal compassion, towards a sole virgin point of *Fiat Lux*, of *Marian Fiat*,[329] the very point at which the universe conceived by Lemaître[330] suddenly appears, the Omega point of Teilhard de Chardin.[331]

---

[329] A striking similitude of the words of Scripture inaugurating the Hebrew Scripture and the Christian Scripture.

[330] Canon Georges Henri Le Maître (1894–1964), a Belgian Astrophysicist and Mathematician who wrote numerous studies on general relativity and the expansion of the universe.

[331] The Jesuit Priest, Pierre Tielhard de Chardin (1881–1955) was a theologian and paleontologist notable for *The Human Phenomenon* (*Le Phénoméne humain*). His

60. Convocation - November 6, 1959
21 rue Monsieur, Paris 7

Friday, November 6, 1959, monthly Mass at 6:30 pm in the chapel of the Dames de Nazareth, 20 rue du Montparnasse, followed by a meeting at the close of our *55th Day of fasting for a serene Peace* between Christians and Muslims, particularly in North Africa and in the Middle East.

Resolutely committed to focusing our meditation, our prayers of compassion, and our spiritual efforts on the North African (and Near Eastern) problem, that we have been addressing by means of non-violence and demands for civic advocating of the truth since 1953—we cannot possibly refuse to use the same proven and effective means in other areas of interreligious contact where members of the Badaliya are being called upon to participate.

Thus we received a request from Canada to pray and take action by helping to establish a French-speaking Catholic Institute of Islamic Studies opposite the McGill Protestant Institute in Montreal. The publication, with imprimatur, by the Commissariat of the Holy Land in Ottawa of a book written by one of our members, Fr. Giulio Basetti-Sani, OFM, entitled *Muhammad and St. Francis of Assisi*,[332] that focuses on the highest vocation of the Franciscan Order by linking the *ordalie*[333] at Damietta

---

spiritual reflections envisioned all of creation moving toward a convergence into the "Cosmic Christ."

[332] First published in French in 1959 and then in English in 1976 and 1980. Fr. Basetti-Sani was a student and close friend of Louis Massignon.

[333] "Ordalie" alludes to the encounter that took place in Damietta in 1219 between St, Francis and the Sultan of Egypt, Malik al-Kamil, a nephew of Saladin. According to the early biography by Bonaventure, in his wish to convince the Sultan of the truth of Christianity, Francis challenged him to a trial by fire whereby Francis would agree to walk through a blazing fire and remain unharmed, as did Shadrach, Meshach, and Abednego in the Book of Daniel 3:1–97. The Sultan is said to have politely refused. The scene is represented in the fresco cycle by Giotto on the life of St. Francis in the San Francesco Church in Assisi. The earlier chroniclers of the Saint's encounter do not mention this particular challenge but the intended message that Basetti-Sani explores is that Francis was treated with respect by the Sultan, a friendship was established and Francis' approach through dialogue and peaceful means was a model ignored by the crusading armies. There is a saying of the Prophet Muhammad recorded in Islam that tells of a challenge to a group of

with the stigmatization on Mt. Alverna,[334] is at the origin of a movement of spiritual friendship among the French Canadians and the Eastern Christians. The latter are enduring Muslim reactions to the colonial excesses in Algeria without resentment. They want to return "good for evil," even and especially, when faced with missionary apologetics or dreadful "doctors" who try to "vilify" this Muslim theology that was so instrumental in the development of scholastic Dogmatics in the Latin Middle Ages, and when faced with those who forget their duty of brotherly friendship toward those other children of Abraham, despite the moving exhortations by the French Head of State.

There is also *Japan*. We already mentioned the small Japanese Catholic group that, as early as 1923, had helped us defend Foucauld's methods, as well as the spirit that was to lead to the creation of the Badaliya in 1934. This group had founded the first Catholic hospital in Sakuramachi (Koganei, Tokyo) and staffed it with Japanese nuns of St. John (of Ephesus). When we visited them in 1958, we recognized the spirit of the Badaliya in them, and now the Archbishop of Tokyo, Msgr. Doi, and the Bishop of Yokohama, Msgr. Arai, are encouraging us through their letter and special blessing to organize a supporting committee for the hospital.

As for the *Seven Sleepers of Ephesus*, and our plan to found a Badaliya in Rome, a Cardinal of the Holy Roman Church has just blessed our organization and agreed to give it his support.[335]

We have already spoken of the confusion into which "the desecration of the Heavens" by the Soviet rockets plunges simple souls. We must meditate more deeply on this intense desire for liberation and elevation towards the truth by the underdeveloped masses in Africa and Asia, whose gaze is being turned by the USSR toward the interplanetary exploration of the Skies now emptied of the traditional images that all religions had previously projected onto them. The Einsteinian space curve has not yet managed to persuade the masses that the straight line

---

Christians that they refuse to take. According to Basetti-Sani, St. Francis visit to the Sultan was a reparation for those earlier Christians inability to trust their faith.

[334] Basetti-Sani envisioned that the stigmata of St. Francis was received as a sign of "substitutionary prayer," *Badaliya*. St. Francis was offering himself for the salvation of the soul of this one Muslim friend, the Sultan.

[335] Massignon is probably speaking of Cardinal Montini who later became Pope Paul VI in 1963 and was an active member of the Badaliya in Rome.

of our imagination actually completes a circle. Yet, there should be a way to get them accustomed to the idea that our mental perspective, that goes back to Ptolemy, has undergone a "Copernican reversal," and that, not unlike Chesterton's[336] "topsy-turvydom," visible space is "turned upside down," like a glove put on inside out; the interplanetary explorer, by the force of ascending straight up into space, (that the impact on the moon has proven), suddenly finds himself "turning over," and descending upside down toward the targeted star. People who have been at the front remember the sharp crack of the bullet which suddenly pivots on its own axis and yet does not deviate from its initial rectilinear trajectory. The same goes for the upward thrust of our prayer that goes toward this Father who is in the Heavens, even if their limit should recede indefinitely with the passionate flight of the Nebulae. Once there, our thought can only come back down towards the Omega Point, the center of the Universe.

It is by prostrating ourselves, as did the seven sleepers, on our small corner of earth, that we come closer to God, to Heaven, to the most sacred reconciliation there is. "Prostrate yourself and come closer" ("*usjud wa'qtarib,*" Qur'an, 96:19).

Trying to fight the godless apologetics of Soviet rockets by recalling the more and more radiant apparitions of Mary, bestowed upon mankind like so many forerunners of the apocalyptic Apparition of the Judge whose hands are pierced by the scales of his Justice—is not enough. During their commemorations, these apparitions "rise again" only in the hearts of those whose Faith is close to that of the seers who were once their unique witnesses. Furthermore, these apparitions do not show up in the Creed where the Parousia stands alone.

Yet we are moved by these apparitions because they correspond to a desire for a miraculous liberation from a prison for technological robots. It is this desire that the USSR exploits among the Afro-Asian populations now weary of the economic propaganda of the ex-colonialist Powers, who wish to perpetuate, by synchronizing with it, the traditional religious imagery founded on the obsolete physics dating from Aris-

---

[336] The Anglican writer Gilbert Keith Chesterton (1874–1936), converted to Catholicism in 1922.

totle and Ptolemy. But does God need our lies to strengthen what is falling apart?

Contemplative life provides a glimpse of how this upward thrust of religious devotion toward Heaven can be rectified. Hallaj would say: "when man succeeds in disciplining his body through a strict observance of the law, and surrenders for good to a life of asceticism, he rises to the Plane of "Those who have come close to God." He then finds himself slowly *Going down* the steps he had previously climbed until he receives in his heart the visitation of a Guest, God's Spirit, of whom Jesus, son of Mary, was born. So, let us not fear those who want to force us to look into the depths of the empty Heavens, for the Signs that we shall discover there will come down into our hearts, like intelligible omens of the Final Consummation of the world. The Kingdom of God is within us already, like an inviolable promise, come down from above.

N.B. Useful details on the experience of fasting can be found in Fr. Regamey's *Fasting Rediscovered* published by Editions du Cerf; mention is made, among other things, of our participation.

61. Convocation - December 4, 1959
21 rue Monsieur, Paris 7

Friday, December 4, 1959, monthly Mass at 6:30 pm in the chapel of the Dames de Nazareth, 20 rue du Montparnasse at the close of our 56th day of *private Fasting for a serene Peace*, between Christians and Muslims, particularly in North Africa, and the Near East.

"The practice of discreet and silent fasting as a weapon in the spiritual battle against the evil powers that incite us to murder and violence" is the weapon of contemplative virtues, concludes Fr. Régamey, OFP,[337] calling attention to our humble and patient effort, started over six years ago, at the end of his book, *Rediscovering Fasting.*

We must pursue this effort, *sine die*, at all costs, right to the end, until our spiritual and temporal leaders manage to eradicate from our soil the methods of inquisition that use both physical and moral torture on the Adversary, and forbid our countrymen to "return" the iniquities we so rightly blame him for committing. May our humble prayer, burn-

---

[337] Father Pie Régamy (1900–1996), Dominican theologian had just written this book with Camille Drevet, J. Md. Abd al-Jalil and Lanza del Vastro.

ing like a candle in the darkness, rise each day to exorcise these insane technological methods, used by both sides, that are causing the digging of
mass graves at increasingly deeper dimensions (best left undisclosed).

Considering the situation we are in, the right to speak no longer
belongs to the diplomats whose "No" hides under a "Yes" that only means
"Maybe." The same goes for the theologians of Canon Law who continue
to teach that any pledge made to an "infidel" is null and void, which is
literally exact but spiritually blasphemous, because it is a violation of
the Holy Name that must not be invoked in vain, especially among the
sons *of Abraham*. And [it is blasphemous] even among the pagans, such
as St. Paul's Athenians to whom he conceded the existence of an "unknown
God," not, I imagine, solely out of "tactical respect." Was there any room
for "tactical respect" in the heart of the Apostle who wanted to die as an
"anathema" for his enemy brothers?

Let us meditate on the example of St. Louis, *the prophetic witness of
the vocation of Eternal France before Islam*, both in Damietta, in Egypt, and
in Carthage, in Africa. This meditation is more current than ever. Often
maligned, the crusade of 1270 has been seen as "doomed to failure"
because of miscalculations over military and economic interests. Nobody,
except Michelet,[338] (and even he did not really do so), deigned to pay
attention to the revealing words (the holiest of holy words committing all
of us baptized French men and women, whether we bear his blessed
name or not), that St. Louis said in St. Denis on October 9, 1269 to the
ambassadors of Mustansir, the Hafsid ruler of Tunis, proclaimed Commander of the Faithful in Mecca in 1258, following the sack of Baghdad.
They had just attended the baptism of an adult Jew (a baptism on which
we had rather not dwell given the atrocious cruelty of the Christians who
periodically would tear children away from their Jewish mothers, for the
sake of a baptism, considered as an apostasy [by the Jews], so that the
mothers preferred to have the rabbis strangle their children according to
the rite of the *Aqeda*, "the binding of Isaac" on his pyre). With a divine
naiveté St. Louis said to the ambassadors: "Tell your master that I so
desire the salvation of his soul that I would like to spend the rest of my life

---

[338] The historian, Jules Michelet (1798–1874) told this story in his *Histoire de France*,
volume III.

in the prisons of the Saracens and never see the light of day again, if, at this price, I could make your king and his people Christian like this man."

St. Louis had come to know the prisons of the Saracens in 1249, at the time of the crusade at Damietta, during his internment at the Dar Ibn Luqman of Mansourah (commemorated in Egypt two years ago by a postage stamp); 20 years later, he *desired* those prisons (as much as St. Francis had desired the *ordalie*, also in Damietta, in 1219, thus prefiguring the true vocation of the Franciscans: to be burned, stigmatized for the love of one single Muslim soul).

In 1269, these words of divine madness uttered by St. Louis were not "understood," but exploited by an amazing apologist, Ramon Marti, author of the *Pugio Fidei* used by Pascal in the *Pensées*. He headed the Studium of the Dominicans founded in 1243 in Tunis where, with equal distrust on either side, Muslim theologians and Christian theologians were seeking, on the basis of a philosophical propaedeutic,[339] to establish a scholastic theology both correct and common to the three Abrahamic monotheisms—an *intellectual reconciliation*—with the help of Jewish translators equally expert in Arabic and in Latin.

Facing the Dominicans in Tunis, a group of "legitimate" spokesmen had surfaced "logicians," refugees from Murcia, disciples of the mystical philosopher Ibn Sab'in. According to R. Brunschwig's[340] hypothesis, the Crusade was recommended to St. Louis by Ramon Marti; he thought that it could deviate from its route to the Holy Land to make a peaceful stop in Tunis for a Muslim-Christian meeting more elaborate than the one St. Francis of Assisi had attempted in 1219 with Fakhr Farisi for the salvation of the soul of Malik Kamil. But the pirates of the Christian bank, with the Templars at their head, and the professionals of armed aggression, managed to break the truce immediately after St. Louis died, in the utter destitution of his supreme sacrifice; and the Dominican Studium had to move back to Murcia in 1271.

It is only in 1536 that the Kingdom of France, threatened with death by the German-Spanish block, was able to pledge its word to the Turk-

---

[339] *Propaedeutic*: Providing basic philosophical instruction.

[340] Robert Brunschwig (1901–1990), historian and orientalist, Professor at the Sorbonne and co-creator of the well-known revue, *Studia Islamica* in 1953.

ish Commander of the Faithful, and keep it for over two centuries, by signing the "Capitulations"[341] without consulting the Canon lawyers.

Let us close with three pieces of news about Japan, Kairouan and Orléans. On November 23rd, Msgr. Rupp, Bishop of the Foreigners in Paris, celebrated a Mass in the St. Antoine des Quinze-Vingt church, in front of the icon offered by Admiral Yamamoto Shinjiro for the first Japanese Catholic hospital founded in 1938 in *Sakuramachi* ("sakura" means "branch of the cherry tree in bloom") by Rev. Fr. Dr. Totsuka, and two other friends of the *Badaliya* and of Charles de Foucauld. In Orleans, the *"street of the Seven Sleepers"* was shown to us by Mr. Emile Campion, a pilgrim to Vieux-Marché and a friend of Huysmans;[342] it adjoins the former St. Pierre le Puellier church (where Joan of Arc's mother was buried in 1458) and the *"street of the Africans"* where, during the Crusades, Muslim prisoners captured in Egypt and Syria would be herded together ("during summer nights, they amazed the inhabitants of Orléans with their tumblers' songs and dances," says M. Lepage in *Les Rues d'Orléans*, 1901—these were more likely the *dhikr*[343] of the Sufis). Let us add that, this year, the town wanted to "regroup" its Algerian Muslim workers in St. Pierre le Puellier but the Christian neighbors, refusing to have anything to do with them, had them herded out of town. Let us pray for both sides.

In Kairouan, the progressive "decolonization" brought on the expropriation of the Malcor hermitage where our friend Fr. Charles Henrion[344] had been living for 30 years with five men and women religious in Ain

---

[341] A kind of commercial treaty signed by Suleiman the Magnificent and King Francis I allowing the establishment of the French in Turkey and fixing the jurisdiction to be exercised over them and guaranteeing them individual and religious liberty. This system disappeared after World War I.

[342] Joris Karl Huysmans (1848–1907), well-known French writer. See Buck, "Dialogues with Saints and Mystics: In the Spirit of Louis Massignon." Chapter I.

[343] *Dhikr* means *remembrance*, invocation or glorification of God, and is one of the Sufis' primary practices. The Sufis *make dhikr* by repeating God's name in various forms, Qur'anic verses and religious poetry, and try to achieve, with the help of music and dance, uninterrupted communion with God and spiritual ecstasy.

[344] Charles Henrion (1887–1969) was converted in 1911 under the influence of Paul Claudel and Maritain and ordained a Priest in 1925 along with Emile Malcor. The two Priests founded the Fraternity of Aïn Blartha in Tunisia in the spirit of Charles de Foucauld. Some women, attracted by the same ideal, settled nearby. At the time of this letter the President of Tunisia, Bourguiba, decided to expel them from

Blartha (Sidi Saad). Let us pray that those expelled thank God for this ordeal, as did the monks of Grandmont celebrated by Foucauld in his *Directoire*; let us pray above all that the graves of their dead, especially that of Mercedes de Gournay, who died while tending Muslim children during an epidemic, may not be the object of a "preventive" exhumation as was Foucauld's grave in Tamanrasset, in violation of his will and out of distrust for the Muslims.

P.S. In the XVth [arrondissement], on November 23rd, two of us participated [in solidarity with] the funeral held in N.Y. of a Christian Orthodox artist—the *poor Man* who, with magnificent generosity, had made us the *fraternal gift of his Fast* in 1953, at the beginning of our activity; in the poor church, by the light of the candles we held in our hands, we saw, above the faithful, the icon of the Pokrov of Bogomateri,[345] the effigy of the National Protector of all the Russians, the One who spreads the Veil of Tears, the One who our little Badaliya has taken as its Patroness. We also prayed that our friend Giorgio La Pira, who so courageously brought a little *Italian* Madonna to Moscow, may understand that the Church of Silence will only find salvation through the *Russian* Mercy of the Madonna, by her vow, of the One who suffers in her heart, who cries in her heart; it is She, as Pius XII had foreseen in 1942, who will save us all.

Tunisia saying that there was no place for foreigners who were not contributing to the development of the country.

[345] *Bogomateri* means mother of God in Church Slavonic.

Annual letter #XIII

begun in Damiette, Egypt on December 19, 1959
(completed in Paris on March 26, 1960, Hallaj's birthday)

1. General Moral Report for the Year 1959

T his year has been marked by a climate of severe tension spread throughout the world including the Islamic-Christian conflict that has caused us to suffer in North Africa and in the Near-East. This conflict is basically due to only one particular case of this tension. This tension originates from a duel between two concepts of global economic exploitation, the Soviet and the Western. One is atheistic, and wants to base achieving a higher standard of living on an "international" egalitarian system for workers. The other, which calls itself religious, admits, despite this claim, to national discrimination and racial preferences, which then drives more and more foreign laborers towards communism, disappointed with the ineffectiveness of religions, and the conclusions of their administrations in dealing with the physical "capacity to strike," and the power wielded by money.

It is thus from everywhere and daily, due to the progress in communications and information, that human suffering stirs our sorrowful and persistent prayer as "substitutes," for these masses of laborers uprooted and carried along by movements that fan economic speculations, while displacing them to labor camps.

However, from everywhere among these "displaced persons" we also hear isolated cries of compassion rising up from pained and sorrowful souls who will join the exiled and the outcast, live among them in friendship as willing inmates and witnesses to a superhuman promise of escape, to the beyond, offering pacifying temporary relief, while waiting..

We, of the Badaliya want to join those generous and noble souls who have come from every denomination and social background, evoking, without knowing it, a particular Image of the scorned Just One (already encountered by Plato, *Polit.2,362*), whose blessed Name we know, and that too many of our foreign conquerors have caused to be cursed by their victims. Let us know how to pray and fast with them. On August 14, 1959, the "Badaliya" thus associated itself with the true disciples of Gandhi. (See below, *Fasting*).

The main "zones of suffering" that political Machiavellianism allows to remain, are made up of these gigantic prisons surrounded by electrified barbed wire that are called "concentration camps." The invention of nuclear weapons has rendered impossible the notion of a war of liberation undertaken from *Outside* the perimeter. In the Soviet world, in particular, it is in confinement, through the liturgical meditation dear to the Church of Silence, that we will lay the ground for the possibility of *exchanges between visitors of prisons*, between Soviets and Westerners, which is being prepared with admirable patience by the *International Committee of the Red Cross*.

Alas, the Europeans also have these accursed camps here in Algeria. And even in mainland France. We remember that, already three years ago, Little Sister Magdeleine of Jesus obtained permission from the Interior Minister for the religious sisters of Foucauld to be temporarily interned, as "voluntary prisoners," in order to "improve" the mental environment of the detainees in the centrally located house prisons. Faced with the scandal of these metropolitan housing camps (Larzac, Thol, etc...) J. Pyronnet heroically formed teams of men praying and fasting to be able to be incarcerated in these North African camps. Let us pray that God makes us worthy to imitate divine charity in this way, in complete Gandhian non-violence.

In 1959 a number of us visited the Western "zone of pain" known as the Palestinian "Refugees," excluded from the international definition of "refugee," which applies to the "Volksdeutscher"[346] and to the Israelis, and who are "hostages" of the Western politics of the oil companies, who are playing see-saw with Israelis and Arabs. The UNWRA[347] spends an enor-

---

[346] "Volksdeutscher:" a Nazi term for ethnic Germans living outside of Germany.

[347] United Nations Relief and Works Agency providing relief for Palestinians.

mous amount to improve the "under-nourishment" of these one million people (9 kilos of bread per month per person), but its "paternalistic benevolence" only results in pushing these hostages towards communism. The second Western "zone of pain," alongside the camps of repression in Algeria that the C.I.C.R.[348] has been able to visit (incompletely) since March 22, 1956, are the "camps for the re-located" comprising one million innocent people "displaced for strategic reasons." For more than a year, despite laudable efforts (especially by Catholic Charities), undernourishment remains worse than in Palestine, infant mortality is more than abnormal, and the "psychological" efforts deployed to teach them "to love France" by doing away with Arabic and Qur'anic schools can only result in the same resentment felt in Palestine towards the "benefactors," especially in the case of the young. *"Sicut sagittae in manu Potentis, ita filii excussorum"* (Ps. 127:4).[349]

Around these two "zones of pain" along the Islamic-Christian border, exchanges of cultural retaliation are intensifying. Despite opposition from the French Ministry of Education, and of the Ministry of Justice, too many Algerian military divisions are pursuing supplanting the Arabic language with French, and Islam with nothing, (by an atheism, in fact, bowing to force). As a result, in the UAR (Egypt and Syria), they are countering this with measures against minority Christian schools, seeking to inculcate Islamic superiority by taking advantage of quarrels causing division among Christians. (N. Luka, a Copt of American Protestant background, has written a pamphlet against the Christian mysteries and sacraments that the UAR government distributed in the Christian schools where these many painful incidents, sometimes under persecution, awakened pure Christian faith, and sympathy from Muslim friends.)

A third "zone of pain," only attracting the attention of a minute number of Muslims for the moment, is forming in South Africa, beyond the Belgian Congo which is attaining independence without too much conflict. Through a kind of resonance causing all of Africa to vibrate, the Dutch settlers, using a Christian deviation that reaches only extremist Algerian settlers, want to bring about complete racial segregation of the Bantu workers drawn from the North to the mines, (or "sold" by the Portu-

---

[348] International Committee of the Red Cross.
[349] Psalm 127:4, "Like arrows in the hand of a warrior are the sons of one's youth."

guese State in accordance with the inhumane Mozambique Convention of 1906).

In Dakar, lapsed Catholics, who are not however lacking in authority, have chosen the moment when Black States are gaining independence to attack Islam, thus risking "ruining" the efforts of a newly forming pocket of Christians in the South of Chad. In Paris, the hardening of the average Frenchman towards the North African workers continues, but the majority of students in the UNEF [National Union of Students] want Peace in order to continue their studies, instead of receiving the imprint of a "morale of war" whose insufficiencies Father Beirnaert has shown, (in "Etudes"). The unavenged death in Paris, of Mr. Amokrane Ould Daoudïa, who was from a respected Christian Kabyl family, is testimony to an indefensible mindset (would that he had remained a communist). In the United States, the Trappist, Reverend Thomas Merton, at the Monastery of Our Lady of Gethsemane in Kentucky, supports us in prayer, and the American Ephesus Society in Lima, Ohio combines its efforts for the basilica of St. John of Ephesus to our efforts for the VII Sleepers. Our representative in Rome, Msgr. Paul Mulla Zadé, died on March 3rd, struck down at the beginning of his Mass. One of his friends is replacing him. A note on the "Badaliya" and the priesthood was delivered to the Holy Father in a private audience on February 16th.

II. Our Life of Substitution in 1959

As previously, we are classifying under their five Muslim headings the community and fraternal insertion of our religious actions into the painful context outlined above:

A. Profession of Faith or Testimony

The profound unification of our lives by holding fast to a suffering Christ comes from a subtle and deep love that does not need to reveal itself through verbal pronouncements in these times of hypocrisy and "clear conscience" in which we live. We do not hand over the Sacred Name of The One we love to the impure. And if we participate in the sacraments and take part in devotions, rosaries and litanies, our vocation is not (see below *Prayer*) to display our meditations in external ways, especially not in order to "attract Muslim friends." It is in the silence of certain kinds of social work with them that the presentation of the truth, that they must find in themselves, is formed in us, for them.

It was, however, necessary that we be attacked by name in a "fatwa" from Al-Azhar (See its Majalla, Oct. 1959). In the study group from Dar es-Salam in Cairo, a)[350] where the "Badaliya" only includes friends, [we were accused of being] a type of missionary endeavor disguised as scientific orientalism of higher learning. Sheik Bahy knows, however, that according to its organizational rule (# 4), the "Badaliya" does not in any way aim for an "external conversion" of its non-Christian friends. It asks them to deepen, through an "internal conversion," in line with the God of Abraham, their present denominational position (See the autobiography of Ghazali) by adopting a reflective and self-abnegating b)[351] way of life capable of engendering in them that Face "that Mary formed in herself of Jesus," in the very depths of their Muslim hearts; that Face that will come to mold their own through a "baptism of desire."

In respect to baptism, we are also being attacked by some of our Christian brothers that are calling us "Qur'anisers," and who would like us to forge ahead and administer sacramental baptism to our friends. The expulsion of the "renegade" Moriscos[352] and the negative results of the Inquisition allow us to reply by referring to Phillip's example, when he baptized Queen Candace's eunuch on that road to Berseda where we so often meditated. It was after the eunuch *understood* the passage in Isaiah on the sacrifice of the Lamb, that Phillip was able to baptize him in the sign of the sacrificial Cross. As long as the adult does not desire to be

---

[350] a) In regard to this the "Mardis de Dar es-Salam" (meeting annually since 1951) published some articles about their orientation; on Gandhi, Ephesus, Fatima, the Qarâfa, and Isé. An important book in Dutch by Hans van Bielefeld, "De islam als Nd-Christelijke religie," underlined that a more objective movement towards the comprehension of Islam is taking shape among Roman Catholics. In France this movement was the subject of a monograph appearing in "Catholic International Information," (Paris, October 1959) from Giulio Basetti-Sani's "Mohammed et S. Francis" (Commissariat de Terre Sainte, Ottawa, 1959) to the work by Miss D. Masson on the Bible and the Qur'an.

[351] b) According to the thought of many Muslim Mystics since Tirmidhi (studied at this moment by Dr. Osman Yahia) and Hallaj, up to Ibn Arabi and his Moroccan disciples in the XVII century, (mentioned by Kattani, fihris, 2, 191, etc.)

[352] Moriscos were Spanish "moors," Muslims who converted to Christianity after the reconquest of Andalusia, Spain by the Christians in 1492.

clothed in the Blood of Christ and the Fire of the Spirit (the Eastern Church does not separate Confirmation from Baptism), it is wise to postpone sacramental baptism. Actually, we think that the rush by some of the "baptizers" is at the root of the animistic reaction that is forming in the now independent Black Africa. And we cannot forget that the "Badaliya" began in Damietta, where St. Francis offered himself to the Baptismal Fire of the Spirit for the Sultan and where he received the promise of Baptism by Blood in his stigmatization.

B. Prayer

It is said that prayer is a *lifting up* of the soul towards God. It is, mostly, an attempt at escaping sin, an expatriation, a path out of the stranglehold of anxiety where the soul feels its intimate vocation strangled by its communal destiny, to which it must consent by the offering of a total sacrifice, exhaled towards heaven.

All the naive imagery of Christian devotion rising up to God has been shaken this year by the incredible success of the two Russian rockets, one grazing the moon, the other photographing the face of the moon that is completely invisible to the Earth. The more discreet and less cluttered Muslim imagery of prayer has also been damaged in that ultimate created remnant that divine Transcendence allows in Islam: the *jihat al-'uûw*: the *side of the Above*, where the Throne of God exists, as it does for Israel. Averroes himself believed in this "perpendicular absolute," through which, according to Ozanam, the mathematician goes to God.

But there is no infinite straight line imaginable today, and in the present state of our theories of physical mathematics, the most rectilinear "rising of prayer" has to undergo the Einsteinian curve. It can only follow, according to its circular, centripetal movement, a simultaneously ascending and descending spiral, inscribed on a cone, in order to reach the summit of this cone "where the duration is eclipsed," by the supreme, Essential (and Final) Point, which is but an Instant. The space of our perceptions is "upside down," in a "topsy-turvy" state, said Chesterton, since by the force of lifting oneself towards a star, one is propelled towards it head down. The mental perspective of our prayer undergoes a "Copernican reversal;" its highest ecstasy is prostration. The "heavenly" apparitions which seem to fly over our earthly prison, these "Marian assumptions," corresponding to the descent of the Judge on the Last Day, "land" spiritually in the center of our hearts, allowing the Savior to emerge. (Teilhard de Chardin's "Omega Point").

C. Almsgiving

"Jesus served the poor humbly," Pascal said. c)[353] It is what Charles de Foucauld practiced, and what was so forcefully taught by Father René Voillaume to the Little Brothers. The idea that Islam will be impressed by the material lavishness of our apostles is absurd. We must not, at any cost, enter the disdainful system of the sportula[354] (like the cigarettes distributed by the high level civil servant from the tips of his fingers as he "honors" the sick with his visit at the Muslim hospital). The silent presence, deprived of friendship, denies the two idolatries of our times denounced by Jacques Maritain: "the fecundity of money, and the finality of usefulness;" in which charitable Christians believe more than Muslims, alas!

D. Fasting

We have remained faithful to our days of monthly private fasting for a serene Peace between Christians and Muslims. Arriving at 56 days from 45 and even adding supplementary fasts, we are far from the symbolic number of 300 that we are hoping for. But, on August 14th, thanks to the "Friends of Gandhi" we touched a critical juncture in the Algerian drama as an unhoped for number of associates from all denominations joined us, from Los Angeles to the strait of Tsugaru (Japan), from Mehrauli (where the Tshishtiya joined) to New York (Jewish friends), to Kairouan (non-violent Algerian refugees), to Karachi and Bombay. At the end of the year, we followed the burial of a Russian artist who, in 1953, had given us as alms the deeply moving offering of a voluntary day of fasting (among so

---

[353] c) In Japan, the very miserable support lent by several of us to the hospital of the Japanese Sisters of S. John in Sakuramachi, was encouraged twice by the Archbishop of Tokyo, and now Cardinal Doi.

The social promotion of the East African and South African Bantus was humbly recommended by us to the prayers and sacrifices of the Martyrium in Namugongo (Uganda: Box 2055, Kampala), visited by us in 1955, near to the source of the Nile (a plaque of the "Badaliya" was put up there as an ex-voto).

[354] Sportula: a kind of private dole customarily distributed by patrons to their clients in ancient Rome.

many involuntary ones); Our Lady of Pokrov, our patron, was waiting for her at the end of the chapel, among her candles.

In order to understand Fasting, let us go back to Dostoyevsky's[355] meditation on Christ's fast of forty days on the mountain and his three temptations; on bread that must be earned by work; on the miracle that must be earned by suffering; on the glory that is not acquired by making a pact with brutal Force.

E. Pilgrimage

Pilgrimage is "crossing the ford" in order to join our predecessors in the beyond, those explorers of the Road to Salvation, in order to meditate on their desire in certain chosen places. Here are ours in 1959:

Jerusalem (with Bethlehem, Hebron, Mambre, Beni Naïm); for many; *Damietta* where our friend Giorgio La Pira was eager to arrive on January 6, 1960 coming directly from Mt. Alverna, in the Franciscan spirit of the "Badaliya." As for Damiette in France (near Gif), it does not yet have its chapel dedicated to St. Louis. Reflecting on a statement by St. Louis (to the Tunisian ambassadors at St. Denis, on the feast of St. Abraham, October 9, 1269) on *his desire to die in a Saracen prison,* as long as their Emir (Caliph at that time) and his people convert, (experienced at the time of his crusade to *Damietta*), we have better understood the "Franciscan" character of the last crusade where St. Louis was to die six months later in Carthage.

Our Lady of Bermont, (near Domremy): where we are to pray with *Joan of Arc* for wounded Algeria.

Beaulieu-les-Fontaines (near Lassigny); St. Joan of Arc's first prison, where the Canadian Sisters of Joan of Arc (founded on Christmas 1914 in Worcester, Massachusetts; now at Bergerville near Sillery, Quebec) had a house.

Our Lady of Fatima: where we hope the crypt of the Byzantine church currently being built will be dedicated to Our Lady of Pokrov, patron saint of all the Russian Churches.

Our Lady of the Asylum Seekers, venerated in Valencia, Spain by St. Vincent Ferrier; visited by us in 1954 for the unfortunate one who was

---

[355] In The Brothers Karamazov.

the object of the first prayer of the "Badaliya," and who died there (at the Mislata prison) where we commended his soul to the 1955 French pilgrimage. This year we are invoking NS [Nostra Seynora] in the same way for one of the first members of Father de Foucauld's group, a Catalan cleric, an "asylum seeker," since she is the patron saint of Catalonia, and since 1413, of her procession on Good Friday in Perpignon.

Seven Sleepers of Ephesus: In Vieux-Marché; in Sefron; in Rotthof; in Orleans (adjacent to the tomb of Joan of Arc's Mother).

62. Convocation - February 5, 1960
21 rue Monsieur, Paris 7

Friday, February 5, 1960, monthly Mass at 6:30 pm in the chapel of the Dames de Nazareth, 20 rue Montparnasse, followed by a meeting at the close of our 58th day of *private Fasting for a serene Peace* between Christians and Muslims, particularly in North Africa and in the Near East.

The six weeks just spent with our groups (Cairo, Alexandria, Beirut) and their subsidiaries still in the process of formation (Damascus, Jerusalem)—with return via Rome—helped us understand the suffering that they have to endure along with minority Christians of every Rite, especially in Egypt and Syria; in reaction to the physical and moral pressure of our "Christian" culture upon North African Islam, the RAU[356] school books exalt the historical value of Islam (on February 8–9th, in Damietta, Mansoura and Fareskour, they will celebrate the captivity of St. Louis whose salvific significance was recalled in our last "convocation"); the books also praise the artistic splendor of the Qur'an (with arguments à la Chateaubriand), thus preparing the future RAU boy and girl scouts for an Islamist mentality favorable to a "Qawmiya"[357] unification (a word, as we know, with ambivalent, fascist and Marxist connotations).

Let us pray that they [the minority Christians] know how to endure their plight with heroic patience and remain a hundred per cent loyal to the RAU in order that the State recognize the true traditional Arab

---

[356] Acronym of République Arabe Unie—in English: United Arab Republic, a political merger of Southern Egypt and Northern Syria that lasted from 1958 to 1961. Cairo was the capital and Gamal Abdal Nasser, the President.

[357] Qawmiya: Arab word meaning "belonging to a group or a clan." It usually refers to Arab nationalism.

Christianity that has always been there, and that took such an active part in the struggle for "Qawmiya" independence in Syria, and that cannot be reduced to the natural religion devoid of mysteries expounded by a modernist Copt named Nazmiluqâ in a brochure, 65,000 copies of which were distributed (then partly taken back) in the schools of the RAU. Moreover, Muslim Syrians are so different from each other that the Emir Mostafa Chehabi and Professor Mubarak, from the Faculty of Canon Law in Damascus, testified to the part assigned to Arab Christians in the future of the RAU.

This reaction [of hostility to Arab Christians] that sprang from the Algerian tragedy and was accelerated by the Suez crisis (November 5, 1956) could be alleviated if a Jewish-Arab appeasement happened in Palestine. The problem of the refugees in Jordan, (they live in permanent structures but they only get nine kilos of food per person, per month) is that they will not be out of the hands of the United States before 1961, which is quite worrisome.

For the sake of the internationalization of the Holy Sites under the sign of Abraham, we paid a visit on January 20, 1960 to the Tlemcenian Waqf of Abu Madyan at the Al-Aqsa; once again the Fatiha was said by the muezzin for our dear friend Hajj Lounis Mahfoud; because of Abraham, we also visited Hebron, Nabî Yaqîn and Mambre.

The former mayor of Florence, our friend Giorgio La Pira, who plans to hold another Colloquium in Florence, gave us great pleasure by making *the pilgrimage to Damietta (January 7, 1960), by starting from Mt. Alverna*, like a true Franciscan, according to the spirit of the Badaliya, he told us. For his Peace movement under the sign of Abraham, a Melkite Mass was said in the Church of Our Lady of Peace (Dar es-Salam).

Groups of Muslim intellectuals, notably in Cairo, joined us in our Gandhian fast on January 29th (revived from the one held on August 14th last year) for world Peace (and Peace in Algeria, which is again being torn apart).

The "Foucauld-Peyriguère" notebook came out in Dar es-Salam (published by Vrim). We are more than ever certain that the heroic weapon of non-violence will finally win and that human thought (which was capable of "splitting" the atom) will pierce the spiritual Heavens through the pure prayer of the meek, the persecuted and the outcasts.

63. Convocation - March 4, 1960
21 rue Monsieur, Paris 7

Friday, March 4, 1960, monthly Mass at 6:30 pm in the chapel of the Dames de Nazareth, 20 rue du Montparnasse, followed by a meeting at the close of our 59th day of *private Fasting for a serene Peace* between Christians and Muslims, particularly in North Africa and the Near East.

On March 3rd, we shall especially remember our venerable friend, Msgr. Paul Mulla-Zadé, who suffered a stroke a year ago while saying Mass in Rome on February 22nd, and died on March 3rd. In his place, Msgr. A. Glorieux is willing to take charge of the Badaliya in Rome; and we shall be more united with him in prayer on that day.

Cardinal Marella, who came to St. Antoine des Quinze-Vingt Church on the 26th to pray to the icon "Stella Matutina" placed there for [the conversion of] Japan, told us of a new connection linking us to the Mother Superior of the hospital in Sakuramachi; she was raised Christian Orthodox and remains very attached to the Byzantine liturgy, the one celebrated by the Badaliya.

On February 18th, Fr. Moubarac went and prayed for us at the tomb of Hallaj in Baghdad.

The Muslim Ramadan of 1379 [AH] begins on February 28th; let us take to heart our participation in spirit in all the acts of reconciliation and reparation that will be asked of them during this month of fasting. The Night of Destiny (27th day of Ramadan) falls on March 25th; that night we shall gather for Mass (it will be confirmed by a special notice), and remember our friend Hajj Lounis from Sétif and his union with us on that night in 1957, before he died.

Notice promised as reminder for March 25, 1960 Mass
64. Convocation
21 rue Monsieur, Paris 7

As in past years, we shall meet in the crypt of the St. Sulpice Church for the Mass of the "Night of Destiny" on Friday, March 25, 1960 at 8:30 pm (the entrance to the crypt of the Rosary is on rue Palatine, under the south tower: recitation of the rosary followed by Mass).

It so happens that this year the Christian celebration of the mystery of the Annunciation in Nazareth falls on the same day as Islam's vigil for the Night of Destiny, on the 27th day of its 1379 Ramadan fast.

This is the Night "when the Holy Spirit comes down with the Angels," to the earth, to bring Peace (Qur'an, Sura 97): "by the permission of the Lord."

Under the virginal, Marian veil of prayer, on this blessed Night, let us huddle together with all the oppressed on the earth.

65. Convocation - April 1, 1960
21 rue Monsieur, Paris 7

Friday, April 1, 1960, monthly Mass at 6:30 pm in the chapel of the Dames de Nazareth, 20 rue du Montparnasse, followed by a meeting at the close of our 60th day of *private Fasting for a serene Peace* between Christians and Muslims, particularly in North Africa and the Near East.

Numerous friends joined by Muslims prayed fervently at our vigil on the "Night of Destiny," March 25th, at 8:30 pm in the Crypt of the Rosary in St. Sulpice Church; the coinciding of our "Annunciation" (*Bishara*) with their "Laylat al-Qadr" is rather rare. Over the 1300 years, it was recorded in 688, 753, and 981 of our era, with the last three coincidences having taken place in 1502, 1731 and 1797.

Two new "Badaliya," dedicated to a life of silence, contemplation and brotherly compassion were just born in Mali and in Normandy. May they be able to practice this "recapitulation" of sacred memories, of friends from past generations for whom we must "substitute" ourselves in order to bring their desires and wishes to completion, not only in France and in Islamic lands, but wherever the Consoling Spirit draws them. We cannot say enough about how much these "calls from outside" (coming from such venerated friends as J.K. Huysmans, Daniel Fontaine, Charles de Foucauld, Jules Monchanin, Vincent Totsuka, Violet Susman, Vladimir Ghika) strengthened our sense of our vocation of "Badaliya" toward the living, those whose anxious waiting fills our heart with anguish and desire.

There would not be any atheist left among them if, as Gandhi used to say, we realized that every man who thinks wants only to "think the truth," and that therefore, our quest is at one with his, since God is True. It is simply futile that they try to wall off the Church with her "right-thinking members," casting the impious, along with the communists and other atheists, into the Outer Darkness—woe to the souls considered "untouchable" by our "apostles" who are invited not "to get their feet wet" at a time when fate throws all of us headlong into the waters of the Abyss, with or without a diving suit equipped with indulgences. "Whoever wishes to save his soul, will lose it."

This is why we are telling all those who are now saying about the Muslims what they said about the communists, namely that with people who do not keep their word only brute force will do: any isolated and distraught man is a man to whom we should speak in order to save him, even if, as has been historically proven, he is one of those Muslims to whom we failed to keep our word far more times over the years than he failed us. (We stand to gain if the list of promises we failed to keep to Algerian Islam were not extended indefinitely). In this regard we can only commend the non-violent Gandhians who, at the risk of being put in jail, go to pray and fast at the door of the camps in France where they herd the Nordaf,[358] without trial, and sometimes even after acquittal.

Let us also pray, especially on Good Friday (during our fast) for the Sheikh al Islam of Morocco, our friend Ben Larbi Alaoui, who resigned from the Crown Council because of the judicial scandals around the "conspiracy," that lumped together "heterogeneous" defendants for "reasons of state." We shall also pray for the "Mediterranean Colloquium" scheduled for October 4th in Florence by Giogio La Pira, a Franciscan pilgrim to Damietta.

66. Convocation - May 6, 1960
21 rue Monsieur, Paris 7

Friday, May 6, 1960, monthly Mass at 6:30 pm in the Chapel of the Dames de Nazareth, 20 rue du Montparnasse, followed by a meeting at the close of our 61st day of *private Fasting for a serene Peace* between Christians and Muslims, particularly in North Africa and in the Middle East.

Now the Algerian conflict has been going on for over five years while Black Africa, which is on the road to independence, begins its promotion among other nations, even in Kenya where England realized the ineffectiveness of the awful "segregation" imposed upon the Kikuyus "sus-

---

[358] Nordaf: An insulting and pejorative term for a North African.

pected" of sympathy for the "Mau-Mau rebels" of Kenyatta. Yet this is the moment that the Dutch colonists of South Africa (3 million of them) have chosen to toughen "apartheid," the policy of absolute segregation that pens in the majority of 10 million South African Blacks, keeping them outside of our social life, our schools and even our catechisms, treating them like "the sons of Cham destined for slavery" because of their father's sin. Note that most of these Blacks are Bantus, "sold" into hard labor as miners each year to the Mines in Transvaal under the Anglo-Lusitanian convention, known as the Mozambique convention, that was signed by Portugal, a State professing to be Catholic under the sign of Our Lady of Fatima. In a frightening kind-of "musicality" of "consonance" between North and South, the merciless toughening of the Dutch colonists on the Cape arouses an echo in the harshness of Latin colonialism in Algeria and in the newspapers in their pay. It would take very little for them to bring the already repressive system in the concentration-type camps and Algerian living conditions in line with the absurd norms of the South African "labor camps." As we offer up our fast on May 6th, we must ask God to save our "dear and old country" from imitating the South African apartheid.

The principle of camps for internment does not make sense unless it comes from such invaders as the Nazi occupiers of France from 1940–1944. The expansion of camps in Algeria drives their already miserable inmates to despair and makes them join the FLN[359] or even the Communist Party; no psychological action can make them our friends given the physiological and moral misery into which we plunge them, even with the best of intentions in the world.

As for setting up "preventive" internment camps in France, as on the Larzac plateau, in Thol and in Vincennes, no god-fearing Priest, Minister or Rabbi can possibly approve of it. Several of us went to have ourselves arrested in front of the camp designated for house arrests in Vincennes on April 30th, in a perfect demonstration of "non-violence;" no French citizen can accept that people should be torn away from their families and their jobs without trial, or even worse, after acquittal, in the

---

[359] FLN: Front de Libération National, an organization of Muslim Algerian nationalists who fought for independence from France from 1954 through the cease-fire (Accords d'Evian) of March 1962. It later became the sole Algerian party and is now one among many Algerian parties.

name of "special powers," and left in conditions that revolt our conscience, whether Christian or not. Haven't the Bishops told us that it is forbidden to seek the good of the country through "intrinsically evil means"? It seems to us that they expect each of us to understand that and act accordingly—through non-violent civic demonstration, to which the Badaliya can only bring its prayers, fasts and sacrifices out of the depths of its powerlessness and poverty. Substituting itself for the victims, it understands the position of non-violent actions and, as long as the internment camps in France remain in operation, will ask to be locked up there with them, out of compassion for those who suffer as well as for those who make them suffer; suffer in Christ.

67. Convocation - June 3, 1960
21 rue Monsieur, Paris 7

Friday June 3, 1960, monthly Mass at 6:30 pm in the Chapelle des Dames de Nazareth, 20 rue du Montparnasse, at the close of our 62nd day *of private Fasting for a serene Peace* between Christians and Muslims, particularly in North Africa and in the Near East.

The failure of the conference at the "summit" of the Big Four[360] had immediate repercussions on regions already torn by racial hatred, reviving enmities in the very places where we are concentrating all our efforts and all our offerings to God so that a little friendship and compassion may be rekindled among adversaries. Whether dealing with South Africa's policy of apartheid or the detention camps, much patience will be needed, and heroic non-violence, so that the powerful of this world cease to resort to physical violence, and to cunning slogans, that are an even worse "rape of consciences."

In our letter No. X, we quoted Pascal (Prov. XII),[361] "It is a strange and tedious war, when violence attempts to vanquish truth. All efforts of violence cannot weaken truth, and only serve to give it renewed vigor.

---

[360] A meeting held on May 14–15th in Paris with de Gualle, Eisenhower, Macmillan and Krutshev intending to relieve the East/ West tensions.

[361] The *Lettres provinciales* (Provincial letters), also known as the Provincials, are a series of eighteen letters written from 1656 to 1657 by French philosopher and theologian Blaise Pascal under the pseudonym Louis de Montalte in the midst of the controversy between the Jansenists and the Jesuits.

All the lights of truth can do nothing to stop violence, and only serve to irritate it all the more." This rather pessimistic observation needs to be re-sketched: of course, if those that believe they hold the truth force it on their "enemies" like a flaming rocket, they will not persuade them. Quite a number of fundamentalist orthodox do this at the expense of fraternal charity. The truth of non-violence is naked and disarmed on the Cross, after having been clothed in the robe of madness by Herod. Truth is the Spouse of compassionate and suffering souls, who are ready to follow the Master, allowing themselves to be dragged along "in the dirty water of the gutter," like the willing and silent "suspects" of May 28 at the traffic circle of the Champs Elysées.[362] Let us try to humble ourselves as much as possible in order to touch hardened hearts in our implacable claim on the truth.

In the firmament of human history, the stars point to the way of non-violence, surrounding Jesus Christ, from Antigone to Socrates to Gandhi. Louis Corman ("Le vrai visage de Jeanne d'Arc [The true face of Joan of Arc]," 1951) has admirably portrayed her pure compassion: "I carried my own standard when I was charging at my adversaries so as to avoid killing anyone. I have never killed a person...I have never shed any blood." In opposition to the "violent" among Catholics on the left, and the "activists" who pray that Foucauld's canonization (after Joan's) may "canonize violence," we think that Joan, by accepting the Bishop's death sentence, shows us the heroic way of reconciling obedience with our *conscience* that forbids us from consenting to Evil ("potius mori quam foedari"); with respect for the law of common *honor*, they cannot force us to serve it by committing Evil, without sinning. Despite what Louis Aragon[363] stated (after Napoleon, in a famous passage in Caulaincourt's "Mémoires"), there is a way to save the group's *honor* without violating the virginity of a single *conscience*. Truth, moreover, is one for the consciences of a human group that is founded on, and lives, fraternal equality in Justice: "Our innermost consciences are one single Virgin, said Hallaj, that only a suggestion from the Holy Spirit penetrates."

---

[362] Massignon participated in this sit-in and was arrested with others and released the following day.

[363] The poet, Louis Aragon (1897–1982) greatly admired Massignon despite his communist sympathies.

68. Convocation - July 1, 1960
21 rue Monsieur, Paris 7

Friday, July 1, 1960, monthly Mass at 6:30 pm in the chapel of the Dames de Nazareth, 20 rue du Montparnasse, at the close of our 63rd day of *private Fasting for a serene Peace* between Christians and Muslims, particularly in North Africa and in the Middle East.

There will be no meeting on Friday, August 5th or on Friday, September 2nd, but on those two days we shall fast as usual and a Mass will be said in the morning for all our intentions in the Church. We wish to remind all of you that the Muslim and Christian pilgrimage to the Seven Sleepers of Ephesus will take place this year on July 23–24th in their chapel in Vieux-Marché (Côtes du Nord); during the pilgrimage we shall pray that next year we may be able to go to the cemetery of the Seven Sleepers in Sétif to give thanks where our friend, Professor Hajj Lounis Mahfoud, had joined us in spirit on Algerian soil during our Breton pilgrimage *for a serene peace*. We shall try our best to have many of our friends from all denominations take part in the *fast* on the August 14th vigil of the Assumption, like last year, when the Archbishop of Smyrna and Ephesus commended our little sodality and the "Friends of Gandhi" to the participants on his Marian pilgrimage to "Meryem Ana" (Turkish name for Panaya), for Peace in the world.

The arrival of an Algerian Muslim passenger at Orly on June 25th with the intention of an eventual negotiation for Peace, strengthens us in our commitment to fasting, prayer and sacrifice—the basis of nonviolence as a means to exorcising evil passions, racism and fanaticism, on both sides.[364]

After 39 years, the sealing a month ago of our coat of arms (a Heart pierced by a Spear) on the altar in the chapel at the same prison where the first desperate brother for whom the Badaliya was founded in Damietta, killed himself (in Mislata de Valencia in Spain),[365] should confirm us in our vocation.

---

[364] The first meeting of the GPRA, Provisional Algerian Government, at Melun that ended in failure.

[365] An allusion to Luis de Cuadra, Massignon's Spanish friend who threw himself out of a window of the Valencia prison on June 12, 1921. His suicide had a lifelong effect on Massignon.

It is in the same spirit that we carried our "substitution" to the point of participating on April 30th (in Vincennes) and on May 28th (on the Champs Elysées) in the self-offering of the non-violent demonstrators who got themselves arrested in order to release the North African suspects who were illegally incarcerated in concentration camps without trial (which is a sacrilege, *Harâm*).[366]

Needless to say, we refuse to let this pure offering be turned into a strategy of extreme political protest or be used by complete pacifism on behalf of a general strike of our civic duties. Gandhi, like Socrates, showed that publically bearing witness to the truth, the *satyagraha* of the non-violent, must keep us "imprisoned by love" in the heart of our City that we must not abandon, even if we should be condemned, especially when it is in a state of sin.

Truth cannot triumph over violence except through the gift of oneself; bearing the suffering caused by others without ever causing them to suffer, even from the slightest moral pressure founded on the "superiority" of our Faith. Will the Christian physician who cured a Muslim demand that his patient tip him by converting to Christianity? Truth remains forever nailed to the Cross, disarmed and naked, repudiating all violence and especially the "soft paternalistic pressure for the good" that moral theology justly reproves in excessively authoritarian parents and religious superiors, and considers sufficient cause for the annulment of a marriage or an ordination.

In its humble role, the Badaliya is absolutely poor. We have been thinking about this for a long time, from the Feast of the Ascension to the Sacred Heart and for the duration of Pentecost, and not without serious inner doubts or anxiety over the future of our organization.

As you all know, the Badaliya refrains from asking for any kind of subsidy, such as subscriptions, dues or donations for Masses, and it receives as it gives, for the love of God, without any administrative specifications, and like the Curé d'Ars, it relies directly on divine providence; in *tawakkul mutlaq*: in total abandon. Let us never forget this.

Thanks to our friend Jean Scelles, (from the Christian Committee for French-Islamic Understanding, who intervened on behalf of our 1954 fast in Rome) we are able to quote the following excerpts from his "Bio-

---

[366] Literally: prohibited by the faith.

graphical note on Cheikh Tayeb el-Okbi," one of our best "associates in prayer and fasting" in Islam:

Tayeb el-Okbi died at the age of 73 on May 21, 1960 in St. Eugène (near Algiers, 39 rue Salvandry). Born in the Aurès mountains (from the Bou-Abderraham tribe), he was educated in Mecca; during the first world war he was sent to jail as an Arab nationalist by the Turks (Smyrna, Thrace); released, he went back to Mecca where King Hussein[367] entrusted the weekly newspaper *Umm al-Qura* to his care; he also became the tutor of Prince Abdallah, the future King of Jordan. Disappointed by the evolution of the situation in Hedjaz, he went back to Algeria. With Ben Badis and Lamin Lamoudi he created the Association of the Algerian Ulama[368] for the reformation of Islam. While Ben Badis was intensifying his political opposition, el-Okbi withdrew to Biskra for five years then came back to Algiers where he was well known and highly regarded as a theologian and a poet, and devoted himself entirely to religion. In 1931 he was made the religious preacher for the Circle for Progress (9, Place du Gouvernement) at the request of the leading families of Algiers, who he soon forced to welcome the crowd of humble people, small shop-keepers, workers and converted pimps, into the Circle. By inviting students as well, he disturbed the Office of Indigenous Affairs, which raised the "assembly" against him and in 1937 led to his being falsely accused of having taken part in the assassination of the Mufti Ben Kahoul. After a two-year-long trial he was finally rescued by courageous French friends. From then on he withdrew more deeply into a life of contemplation, especially after the war years (1940–1945) during which he had put all his energies into helping the needy (soup kitchens, night shelters run by

---

[367] Sharif Hussein bin Ali (1853–1931). Emir of Mecca and King of the Arabs, he was the last of the Hashemite Sharifians that ruled over Mecca, Medina and the Hijaz in unbroken succession from 1201 to 1925. Sharif Hussein is best known for launching the Great Arab Revolt in June 1916 against the Ottoman army.

[368] The Ulama were religious scholars, who promoted a purification of Islam in Algeria and a return to the Qur'an and the Sunnah, or tradition of the Prophet. The reformers favored the adoption of modern methods of inquiry and rejected the superstitions and folk practices of the countryside, actions that brought them into confrontation with the marabouts (respected local spiritual leaders). The reformers published their own periodicals and books, and established free modern Islamic schools that stressed Arabic language and culture as an alternative to the schools for Muslims operated for many years by the French.

the Kheiria Society), meanwhile adopting an increasingly ascetic mode of life for himself (eating only two or three dates for supper).

For his work on religious reform he took his inspiration from Ibn Taymiya, the great XIVth century reformer. Although he was an opponent of the marabouts, he did not reject all forms of mystical life, like so many secular reformers. He was in favor of the gradual emancipation of women. He wanted a Higher Islamic Committee to be created in Algeria. He accepted multi-religious coexistence; with the Jews (he had condemned the 1934 pogrom in Constantine and founded the Union of Monotheist Believers (then called "Abrahamic"), but blamed the Zionist State for its anti-Arabism and its ensuing influence on the French press. [Massignon] Our oldest member who, as early as 1949, was entrusted with a mission of aid to the Arab Refugees from Palestine, joined forces with al-Okbi (and the Qadi Ben Houra) in order to be able to visit the Refugees in the name of Algerian Islam and to defend the Tlemcenian Waqf of Abu Madyan at the door of the Al-Aqsa Mosque in Jerusalem (from 1952 on).

In the field of education, el-Okbi worked on improving the teaching of Arabic, adding the teaching of French to it for the sake of a certain kind of bilingualism that the administrators failed to understand.

With regard to Christians, without hesitation el-Okbi considered them as "Muslims" as long as they "abandon themselves to the will of the Lord," "Muslimûn." He conceded that they believed in a kind of divine Trinitarian "trilogy," in the style of Ibn Arabi, and insisted on the "ternary"[369] imprinted upon every man. He professed that Jesus would be the Judge at the Last Judgment, "Malik Yawm al-Dîn;" he had a deep veneration for Lalla Meryem[370] and had named his three next-to-last children: Yusuf, Aissa, Maryam [Joseph, Jesus, Mary]. On our last visit in 1955 we found him in his bedroom. He did not leave it for the whole duration of the Algerian conflict, that we could say, caused his death.

---

[369] Ternary, a mathematical "triple."

[370] Literally Lady Mary or Saint Mary (the Virgin Mary): Saints in Islam (in the majority, male) bear ordinary personal names preceded by the reverential term of address *Sidi* (master, sir, elder brother), or *Lalla* (madam, lady, miss, grandmother; elder sister).

69. Convocation - October 7, 1960
21 rue Monsieur, Paris 7

Friday, October 7, 1960, monthly Mass at 6:30 pm in the chapel of the Dames de Nazareth, 20 rue du Montparnasse, followed by a meeting at the close of our 68th day of *private Fasting for a serene Peace* between Christians and Muslims, particularly in North Africa and in the Middle East.

October 1st marks the feast of Our Lady of the Pokrov (the Byzantine patron of the Badaliya), the One who wept over Constantinople, as well as the feast of our Lady of la Salette who wept over the Latin Church, and finally Yom Kippur, Israel 's great fast. On the 7th let us be sure to take it to heart and join in the fast of Kippur.

The oldest member of the Badaliya[371] started drafting the annual letter (# XIV) to our little association on August 15th in the clinic of the Academy of Science in the USSR; taking pity on the misery his attacks of neuritis were causing him during the sessions of the XXVth International Conference of Orientalists in Moscow, where he was sent as the French delegate, his colleagues had him hospitalized almost by force for sixteen days, from the 12th to the 27th of August, lavishing him with their care so as to help him get "stronger." He spent sixteen days of contemplation under the veil of Our Lady of the Pokrov, (once so venerated in Moscow where there were two churches dedicated to her), in union with the Church of Silence (at present there is a silent detente over religious practice in the USSR). Fifteen days before, bent over a cane, he was able to take part in the Muslim-Christian pilgrimage of the Seven Sleepers in Vieux-Marché (July 24th), which was very fervent; for the first time, the Bishop had sent one of his general vicars, Fr. Gloaguen (de Paulle), along with a personal gift. There was wide coverage in the press and there were moving letters. By a strange coincidence, it was the archeologist George Wagner, author of an essay on the portal of the Seven Sleepers at the Grigorievsk Cathedral of Youriev-Polotsk, just published in "Soviet Archeology," who alerted the Soviet Academy of Science to the physical condition of Professor L. Massignon in order to bring about his "first class" hospitalization in the clinic.

---

[371] Massignon often refers to himself as "the oldest member of the Badaliya."

Obviously these trifling details are of no comfort to us in light of the increasing aggravation of the Algerian crisis, the folly of the supporters of the rebellion (that neither Socrates nor Gandhi would have allowed—the righteous man dies stricken by the laws of his City) and the just as crazy madness of those who maintain that our conscience (Christian or not) can participate in torture without being violated by the Devil, and can indefinitely lie "out of patriotism."

We just received direct oral news unexpectedly from a small Muslim group called the "pilgrims of the VII Sleepers" dedicated to Muslim-Christian peace founded by one of our colleagues from Sétif; he was killed in 1957, three of his brothers were "eliminated" without trial, and their mother died of grief; the survivors persevere in their non-violent stance, they fast our fasts and continue to spread their sacred ideal even though caught between two abject forms of terrorism.

The fast on August 14, 1960, made in conjunction with the Friends of Gandhi in memory of the fast in 1959, was observed by many people (except by the old comrade now writing to you, who on that day, "was fasting from being unable to fast" in his Moscow clinic).

Letter # XIV will contain information on "cases of real compassion" (the true foundations of the Badaliya), adding to our annual letter # X; we would have liked to talk about the subject at the Xth Conference on the history of religions in Marburg in Sept.1960 (the Conference was first told of the existence of the Badaliya in 1958, in Tokyo) by examining how, according to Husserl, Ricoeur, Sartre and Waelens, one "becomes one's pain."

70. Convocation - November 4, 1960
21 rue Monsieur, Paris 7

Friday, November 4, 1960, monthly Mass at 6:30 pm in the chapel of the Dames de Nazareth, 20 rue du Montparnasse, followed by a meeting at the close of our 69th day of *private Fasting for a serene Peace* between Christians and Muslims, particularly in North Africa and in the Middle East.

These two regions of suffering for which we are praying, are becoming the tributaries for new bloody conflicts arising in Cuba, the ex-Belgian Congo and South Africa, painfully resonating with those in Algeria. And where immense China, exasperated at being denied entry into the UN, is preparing to intervene, thus inciting the USA to impose upon us an internationalization, asked for by the last friends we have in Black Africa. The French settlers in Algeria find themselves at the very center of the world duel, and the scales have not yet fallen from their eyes. Let us pray for them.

Let us also pray that Zionist Israel, the Near Eastern equivalent of the French settlers in Algeria, cure itself of its anti-Arab colonialism and become clearly Asian. For several years we have been inviting our friends to understand that Peace in Algeria depends on a prior Judeo-Arab reconciliation in Abraham. We prayed at length on *Yom Kippur* (Sept. 30–Oct. 1st) for this goal (and for the intentions of our medical friends, who, following the example of our academic colleagues in Moscow, had us admitted the day before, for 24 hours, to a state hospital for urgent surgery, that actually took place on October 4th—the feast of St. Francis—in a private clinic much better equipped for post-surgery convalescence). As long as Zionist Israel does not help bring about a Franco-Arab reconciliation in Algeria, there will be no possibility for Peace or even for a Truce.

The same goes for the threat of civil war in France (in 1958, Israeli planes had been offered to the May 13th movement).[372] When shall we be able to *love our enemies*, as our Rule teaches us, and as the Declaration of the Cardinals and Archbishops of France reminds us? Nor should we forget Msgr. Ancel's letter on true non-violence: the Righteous Man does not abandon his City, he dies there, if necessary, stricken by its laws; See: Socrates, Gandhi, and above all, Christ.

P.S.: November 4th is the anniversary of a compassionate Breton woman, Catherine Daniélou, who died in 1667; she prayed for a Bishop of Leon devoted to the Seven Sleepers.

71. Convocation - December 2, 1960
21 rue Monsieur, Paris 7

Friday December 2, 1960, monthly Mass at 6:30 pm in the chapel of the Dames de Nazareth, 20 rue Montparnasse, at the close of our 70th day of *private Fasting for a serene Peace* between Christians and Muslims, particularly in North Africa and in the Near East.

---

[372] On May 13, 1958 an army junta led by General Raoul Salan seized power in Algiers.

Here we are in the 70ᵗʰ month of our humble efforts (only thirty more consecutive fasts before we reach the one-hundredth), the month when the most noble French men, ranging from the Head of State to the Priests of the Mission de France,[373] will make a supreme attempt to exorcise the violent and murderous spirit that for over six years has sacrificed half a million Muslims to death and caused two million "suspects" to be incarcerated with the intention of "protecting them from communism and making them love France, the France of Joan of Arc" (alas).

More than ever convinced, thanks in part to Gandhi, of the effectiveness of humble and non-violent means to making Peace triumph, we shall mention in our letter number XIV that the works of Christian mercy encompass the Five Pillars of Muslim community life: prayer, fasting, almsgiving, pilgrimages and the *profession of faith as testimony*. By joining in those together with them, we shall have solved the problem.

Our letter number XIV will also show how, as a special sign of witnessing, the action of substitution by the Badaliya has become universal, expanding beyond the zone of Muslim-Christian suffering, to substitution as Testimony for the dead, by visiting cemeteries and prisons while reflecting on Resurrection and Liberation, throughout the world.

Today, the oldest member of the Badaliya, whose present ordeal reduces him to fasting "in spirit" on this 70ᵗʰ fast, will restrain himself to a brief outline of what our mediation should be as Witnesses in the zones of Muslim-Christian suffering.

In two essays, "The City of the Dead in Cairo" and "The Rawda of Medina,"[374] he explained the profound call that has drawn him, a Christian, to the Muslim cemeteries for fifty years, following countless women and children who come every Friday, his witnessing reviving the Faith of the dead in the Resurrection in Justice (touching their tombs, Testifying in their place). In Medina, in particular, the three tombs in Prophet Muhammad's burial chamber are, from right to left, those of Muhammad,

---

[373] A society of worker priests founded just after World War II by the Archbishop of Paris, Cardinal Suhard. Banned by Rome in 1954, it was reinstated at the end of Vatican II, in 1965.

[374] Rawda: A space in Prophet Muhammad's burial chamber described by the Prophet as a small stretch of heaven on earth beside his pulpit. Both these articles were originally published in the *Bulletin de l'Institute français de d'archéologie oriental* in 1958.

Abu Bakr and Umar; to the right there is a fourth spot left empty to this day, which is reserved for *Jesus son of Mary* whose Second Coming, as a Sign of the Resurrection and of the Last Judgment that Omar, on his return from Jerusalem, believed to be imminent. It is still awaited there, and the miniatures, "Dalail," by Jazuli,[375] this manual for all the pilgrims to Medina, focus their meditation on a great Lamp above the four spaces, the *Qandil al-Muwajaha*,[376] copied from the Holy Sepulchre, *lucem sanctam quam olim Abrahae promisisti et semini ejus;*[377] the Messianic Promise, of Resurrection.

Here too, as with the ordeal involving the Christians of Najran,[378] Islam postpones our reconciliation till the second coming of Christ.

But it is for us, who long for Justice for the oppressed, for us "other Christs," to be the precursors, the forerunners of this Day of Glory, by visiting the prisons and cemeteries of the Muslims with the spiritual desire to merge with them completely so that we may rise from the dead together, as brothers; this is what Lyautey had wanted in Chella, and Foucauld in Tamanrasset (I refused to attend his exhumation in 1928 which I perceived as a profanation of his legacy; his body will have to be brought back there, as the officers in the Sahara requested).

(N.B. In the same spirit, we implore Foucauld's followers in Tunisia not to exhume the body of their Sister Mercédès de Gournay from Aïn Blartha (Sidi Saad) for fear of a "desecration").[379]

---

[375] Imam Muhammad ibn Sulayman al-Jazuli›s, *Dalail al-Khayrat*, is a set of prayers that Muslims recite in order to ask God for blessings upon the Prophet and upon themselves.

[376] *Qandil al-Muwajaha*: literally the "lamp of confrontation" that spreads it's light on all believers.

[377] "Sacred light that of old you promised to Abraham and his descendants."

[378] According to sayings of the Prophet and Muslim tradition, known as the *hadith*, it is narrated that during the 9th–10th year in the Muslim calendar, an Arab Christian envoy from Najran (currently in northern Yemen and partly in Saudi Arabia) came to Muhammad to argue which of the two parties erred in its doctrine concerning Jesus. After likening Jesus' miraculous birth to Adam's creation, Muhammad called them to Mubahala (Cursing), where each party should ask God to curse the lying party. The Christian envoy, the traditions add, declined to take part in Mubahala and chose instead to pay tribute in return for protection for their property and religion.

[379] Exhumed from his tomb and from Tamanrasset, Foucauld's remains were buried in a simple monument in El Goléa (the gateway to the Hoggar), a safer place than southern Algeria at the time.

This demand for a fraternal Profession of Faith, an Act through which we share in Christ's divinity that is called the Resurrection, must direct our holy impatience toward all those places where this symbolic Crypt of the Seven Sleepers of Ephesus is honored, and especially toward its threshold where the body of the Magdalen rested for so long;[380] she is the first one to bequeath to us the direct certainty of this Victory of Love over Death. She is crying it out to us.

Let us pray that one day—why not next summer—our Breton pilgrimage to the Seven Sleepers of Ephesus may be twinned with an Algerian pilgrimage, also Muslim-Christian, to the Seven Sleepers of Guidjel, near Sétif, in the place where our friend Hajj Lounis Mahfoud (and his family, who remain faithful to him) professed, in union with us, his Faith in the Resurrection for Justice.

---

[380] There is a tradition that St. Mary Magdalen accompanied St. John and the Virgin to Ephesus, and that she was originally buried at the entrance to «the Grotto of the Seven Sleepers» in Ephesus. According to Massignon, she was moved by the crusaders in the 10th century to Constantinople and perhaps later in 1279 to Ste. Baume, a cave shrine dedicated to her in Provence, France.

Annual Letter # XIV

Started in Moscow August 13–14, 1960
Completed in Paris January 6, 1960.

S uddenly immobilized on August 12th by an attack of neuritis during the XXV International Congress of Orientalists and hospitalized by my colleagues at the Clinic for the Russian Academy of Sciences (completely covered by the Association's Social Services) at the initiative of an archeologist[381] who is a disciple of Ignace Kratchkovski (with whom I had published the *Diwân* [collected works] of Hallâj). Kratchkovski is the author of a study of the entrance door depicting the VII Sleepers at the Youriev-Polski Cathedral. I found myself staying at 50 Lenin Street protected by the collective prayer of the old Donskoî Monastery. I stayed there from August 12th to August 27th, my soul in splendid solitude in the middle of this immense country under the Veil of Our Lady of the Pokrov, our Patron Saint. [She is] the Patron Saint of Moscow, who venerated her before 1918 at the Cathedral of Saint Basil (E. Kremlin), then more to the East in Pokrowskaîa (Baumann Quarter), and finally at the Pokrowski Monastery (SE: Rogojski), near to Andriêwski, (where André Roublev painted the Trinity of the Angels of Mamre). *Gospodi, pomiloui.* (These icons are now in the Trétiakov Museum). I had to give up my flight to Tashkent (the tomb of the Hallajian, AB. Qaffâl) and to Samarkand (the tomb of the Hallajian, Faris), but at the Clinic I received a visit by an Azerbaijani scholar from Baku, Ibn Bâkûyé, a devotee and the first biographer of Hallâj. It was a reminder of an old unfinished obligation.[382]

At the Clinic my reflections were concentrated on a recapitulation of the events in the "life" of our small Badaliya, especially since 1947 when it was taken on by the Eastern Church on the day of Epiphany. Now, four-

---

[381] George Wagner, an archeologist presenting at the conference.
[382] Massignon is referring to the second edition of his thesis on Hâllaj.

teen years later the founders, (obstinately praying, suffering, offering and hoping *for one single soul*, [Luis de Cuadra], a sinner that thirteen years of despair caused to pass from Christianity to Islam, then to suicide), have found in the depths of their painful "substitution" (that seemed in vain) for this soul-friend, a strange resurgence of the grace for which we begged. [It is] surging up again for a *multitude of other souls* mysteriously linked to that one in despair, and also [linked] to the promise of salvation, that beyond death, like during his life, we pledged, on the Cross, to that soul there.

And it is thus that year after year, beyond the Egyptian milieu where we had suddenly recognized in this one soul our "Fellow Man," the ravished Face of Christ, [we went on] to other encounters with the same grace that made us recognize our "fellow man" in other age-old sufferings. At first at the common borders of Islam and Christianity in the Mediterranean, and then beyond to the ends of the earth. The absolute compassion of the Good Samaritan removed us from a detour on the road to Jericho, and thus [led us] to the ecumenical consideration of all humanity in space and time.

Let us therefore quickly look again at the XIII annual letters to the Badaliya for a quick "transhistoric" recapitulation. We will underline in passing the lasting consequences that [this recapitulation] permitted us to envision for the Badaliya, as a means of relief for the apparent squandering of our efforts.

Part I

Letter # I ([written] at the end of 1947) "explains" our 1939 Rule. Our goal is to fulfill the secular vocation that Arab Christians, as a minority, are called to in relation to their Muslim brothers in order to make them rediscover, at the price of offering our lives, that "Light that illuminates every person who comes into this world." That is what they [the Muslims] call the *Fitra*, that brings healing to the broken hearted, liberation to captives, and ultimate justice to the oppressed. [Theirs is] an age-old [Arab Christian] vocation that has been unfulfilled since the ordeal, the *Mubahala*, at Medina where Muhammad asked them (in vain) to bear witness, and [also] unfulfilled since the ordeal at Damietta where Saint Francis offered himself (in vain) in front of Fakhr Farisi for one lone soul, that of Malik Kâmil (a).[383] The traditional Muslim imagination presents the [Fitra] in human form as "Jesus, son of Mary" who is able to be conceived through compassion in the virgin point of the purified heart (b).[384] Through an exquisite interversion, the measure of our fraternally compassionate intercession becomes the confirmation of our predestination to love. We recognize the Face of the Suffering Christ in them at the catalytic moment when they internally conceived Him, united together by this universal human Passion by which the penitent Mary Magdalene died (c).[385] The unique role of Damietta for the Badaliya, affirmed since 1947, and year after year reflected on by our pilgrims, was confirmed on January 5, 1960 at the pilgrimage by our friend Giorgio La Pira, initiator of the movement for Islamic-Christian reconciliation, who arrived in Damietta directly from Mt. Alverna (where Saint Francis, through his stigmatisation, fulfilled so many souls by his offering at Damietta for one single soul). [Thus] affirming Damietta and Mt. Alverna as the two bases for his Franciscan movement which is [now] in full flight (c bis).[386]

Our letters #II-III-IV (1948–1949–1950), extended our action to works of mercy by visiting the *Arab Refugees,* both Muslims and Christians confined in the Holy Land where we guided the episcopal French Mission in 1949. We are visiting them every year. But this is a temporary situation that must end in 1963.

---

[383] (a) Leaving for Tunisia, Saint Louis also spoke of his desire to return to the Sarassin prison (at Damietta, for the salvation of one single soul, that of Mustansir: October 9, 1269).

[384] (b)The Qur'an names "Jesus, son of Mary" and at the same time, Divine Word (*kalima* Qur'an 3:40 [See Qur'an 3:45 and 3:49]) and Spirit of God (rûh: ibid. 4:169 [See Qur'an 3:55 and 4:159]). It seems to indicate that it is he who will pronounce the Word that will judge at the Last Judgment (ibid. 3:55), after having emitted the breath that will resurrect. It is from inside their heart, as the catalyst, that we hope that the Muslims will retrieve our Only Savior; we neither mean to diminish their trust in a scholastic theology very close to our own for an anarchic mysticism (fatwa by Ch. M. al-Bahyy against our friendship for Hallaj, ap. *Majallat al-Azhar*, rajab 1372– March 1953, p. 893–93) nor to develop with the Catholic missionaries in Cairo a program of "colonization" of intellectual Muslims (our friends at Dar es-Salam, ibid. ap. *Majallat al-Azhar*, jum. 1st 1379–Nov. 1959, pp. 396–397).

[385] (c) From the sermon by Eckhart on "Love is strong, like death," for July 22nd [the feast of Mary Magdalene].

[386] (c bis) See Guilio Basetti-Sani, *"Muhammad et Saint Francois"* Com. Holy Land Ottawa, 1959.

In 1951, our letter #V described the unexpected developments in our effort in two ways: the public defense of the Muslim Workers in Paris, who were being mistreated in every way, by gathering in silence in front of the Paris Mosque, and the pilgrimage to the incomparable *Marian Center of the Theotokos in Ephesus.* Beside the Hazreti Meryem Ana (venerated by the Turks in Panaya), we "found" the ancient center of the contemplative Church and of its three witnesses, Mary, John, and Mary Magdalene, "at the threshold of the *Crypte of the Seven Sleepers* in Ephesus (the most ancient Synoptic text for July 22nd).[387]

Our public defense of the Muslim workers in Paris since 1929, sustained by the participation of several of us in evening courses for them is shown by our presence on July 21, 1954 at the funerals of those who were "killed" on the 14th, and by our sermon on October 12, 1955 in front of the Mosque to gain respect for their honor as men. [These two actions] drove us to organize an annual pilgrimage in common with them to the Seven Sleepers Chapel in Vieux Marché (Côtes du Nord) beginning in 1954. Meanwhile, in pursuing the study of the Muslim devotion to the Seven Sleepers in Islam (Sura 18:8–25 in the Qur'an, so dear to Hallaj), with our Muslim friend, Hâjj Lounis Mahfoud, who was killed on June 5, 1957, we joined the pilgrimage of Vieux Marché to the one in Guidjel in Sétif. With the support of the Latin Bishop of Smyrna and Ephesus our work in Eastern Turkey since 1951 has gained permanent spiritual support. A third project in 1951 for the creation of internationally secure zones in case of conflict, remains on hold in Geneva (d).[388]

In Letter # VI from New York at the end of 1952, [we wrote how] meditating on the *Fasting of Abraham Lincoln* in Washington, for the Blacks, made us discover the spiritual weapon of *Fasting*, so unrecognized in Europe. January 6, 1953 we meditated for the Muslims in Delhi in *Mehrauli*, [the place of] *Gandhi's last pilgrimage.* (I understood that private Fasting is fully part of the Badaliya). Our fasts, first for Morocco and

---

[387] See photos of the House of Meryem Ana and the ruins of the church dedicated to Mary Magdalen once built over the cave of the Seven Sleepers in Ephesus via www.dcbuck.com.

[388] (d) See our "Le respect de la personne humaine en Islam et la priorité du droite d'asile sur le devoir de juste guerre," ["Respect for the Human person in Islam and the priority of the right of asylum as an obligation of just war"] (Appeared in the Revue 'Intern de la Croix Rouge,' Geneva, June 1952, pp. 448–468).

its exiled Sovereign, [Muhammad V] then for Algeria, have affiliated us with thousands of believers, both Muslims and Christians of all denominations. Our monthly fasts number 71.

The same year, we rediscovered (after so many Requiem Masses said at *Saint Basil of Madawaska* for him) here in Madawaska and in Maine, traces of the poor offering made by a dying youth offering himself for the oppressed French in Acadia in 1935.[389] We have revived this ember and for its 25th anniversary a "Badaliya" was founded in Montreal in 1960.

The same year, the correspondence of the Intercession of the Tears of Mary in La Salette and the vision of Saint André Sâlûs in Blachernae, made us reflect on the importance of the Russian devotion to Our Lady of the Pokrov [Veil]. [We] visited in 1951 and recommended her to the Bishop of Leiria for the dedication of the crypt of the Byzantine church, Our Lady of Fatima. We took her for our Patron Saint.

Again in 1952, in the name of the Word of honor given by France we aided in the diplomatic defense of the *Waqf of Abu Madyan* founded by the Andalusian refugees from Tlemcen at the Wall of Lamentation on the threshold of the Al-Aqsa Mosque. This place is very holy. It guards the entrance to the Al-Aqsa where a chapel on the left is designated for the devotions of Muslims for Mary. (The place of the Presentation of Our Lord). It also contains the *Wall of the Lamentations* of Israel where the Jewish people mourn the destroyed Temple on the 9th of Âb by reciting the whole Psalter there. We have noted that if the Bible is the body of the Messiah the Psalter is the Heart, and that this place is predestined for the reconciliation of Jews and Arabs, without which the *Serene Peace that we desire between Christianity and Islam remains inaccessible.* Our pilgrims visit it every year, reciting the *Fatiha* for our friend Lounis Mahfoud. And the Waqf Abu Madyan remains, with the pilgrimage to the Seven Sleepers in Sétif, the two axes of our prayers for our Muslim friends.

Letter # VII (1953) describes the expansion of our Fasting for Morocco, (visited August 14, 1955) united to Ephesus and blessed by the Pope, and the announcement of the creation of our *Foucauldian arab Coat of*

---

[389] Massignon's son Yves died of tuberculosis on October 29, 1935. He had been conducting a study of the French in Acadia, Canada before his illness and death.

Arms, since then placed in a dozen churches (e)[390] throughout the world. December 11, 1953, Mass was celebrated at Béni Nãim facing Sodom (in the spirit of the celebrated prayer of Abraham, Genesis XVIII) by the Superior of Saint Anne in Jerusalem and explicitly associating [the prayer] with the black Martyrs of Namugongo (visited January 1, 1955) in Uganda, these pure witnesses to the male chastity betrayed by our unfortunate friend [Luis de Cuadra] who committed suicide in Valencia.

Letter # VIII (1954) refers to the visit to the *Mislata* prison in Valencia 33 years after the suicide in 1921. It was only in April of 1960 that our coat of arms (a pierced heart on a plaque) was able to be embedded in the altar of the prison chapel. In 1954 we had asked for this of the Franciscan, Msgr. de Masamagrell, who had blessed our offering in 1934 for this despairing [friend]. [The plaque} was embedded in 1960 by caring friends of an Arabized Spanish man, A.H.M., who comes to celebrate Mass there as an action of grace for him and for us (letter December 16, 1960). It is clear that the Badaliya in Cairo must periodically imitate this friend by rediscovering, through the Mass in this Spanish prison, the most ancient and profound source of our hope in the hereafter. Letter # VIII also mentioned the visit made to Mohammed V exiled in *Madagascar*, thanks to the delegation of one of us to the Committee for the amnesty of those politically condemned overseas, [who are] working towards liberation from the labor camps, then for the return home of the Madagascan members of parliament [who have been] imprisoned for 13 years (from March 20, 1956 to June 3, 1960). The letter also mentions our farewell to Mrs. Flora Ravoahangy (September 20, 1960). In 1954 three of us examined a Chapel in a place called "Damiette" the creation of which depends on *Gif S. Yvette* with the clergy. After six years the project, that would have given us a place of recollection at the gateway to Paris, remains on hold (1960).

Letter #IX (1955) mentions the creation of the Latin *Sodality of the Foucauld Directory* with the personal participation of several of us at the

---

[390] (e) Tehran and Damascus (Sisters of Charity), Baghdad (Carmelites) Jerusalem (Saint Anne), Beirut (Little Sisters of Foucauld), Ephesus (Panaya), Cairo (Dar es Salaam), Damietta (Franciscans), Namugongo (Martyrium), Tamanrasset (Borj), Beni Abbès (Entrance to the Chapel), Rabat ("Badaliya"), Vieux Marché (VII Sleeper Martyred Saints), Aix-en-Provence ("Badaliya"), Tananarive (Carmelites), Benedictines of Toumliline, Saint Anne in Madawaska.

Foucauld Association in Béni Abbès, and the project to fuse the Eastern Badaliya with this Latin Sodality (cabled to Zamalek in Oran November 17, 1955). But the Melkite Archbishop, who is its patron, can only consider such a fusion when there is an ecumenical easing of tension (f).[391]

We will go back to examine letter # X subsequently in the second part.

Letter #XI (1957) indicates the organization of our evening in sympathy with the 27th day of Ramadan, the *"Night of Destiny."* Suggested by Charles de Foucauld, this is perhaps the most timid and the most secret fraternal step taken by the Badaliya. It still continues in two or three churches: March 25, 1969 at Saint Sulpice, unexpectedly before a Muslim of notable status. The scandalous incarceration in Rabat of Abdulwahid ibn Abdallah, a sheikh accused of having used an exclusively French saint *by invoking Joan of Arc for the liberation of his country*, has made us measure the abyss of racist stupidity "monopolizing" this Compassionate person ordained to the universal. And several of us [went] to "pray" with Joan of Arc at Our Lady of Bermont in Beaulieux les Fontaines, for Algeria, torn apart like France was in her time. It must continue (g).[392]

Letter # XII (written in Isé, Japan) told of the rediscovery, (in the charitable work of the *Japanese hospital at Sakuramachi*, (h)[393] with the branch of a cherry tree flowering), of the tombs of the "Good Samaritans of the Heart of Jesus," Admiral Yamamoto Shinjiro, Dr. V. Totsuka, and Sr. Rose Hermielle Bicknell, whose prayer sustained our very first efforts of Badaliya in Paris. I ask our brothers and sisters to remember this hospital as an act of grace. It is through the prayer of their co-director, Sr. Violet Susman, that a sign of grace was obtained for the Badaliya in Cairo of which I was a direct witness[394] (Christmas 1949).

Letter # XIII (1959) made mention of the personal support that some members of the Badaliya gave to non-violent civil action. They voluntarily made themselves subject to arrest the following year in

---

[391] (f) See a note added to the 3rd edition of the "Directory" by Foucauld, 1961.

[392] (g) See "The Prayer of Our Lady of Bermont for Algeria" August 17, 1956 and "Commonweal" magazine NY August 9, 1957, by Mrs. Fremantle.

[393] (h) See notice appearing in Rythmes du Monde, Bruges, February 8, 1960, pp. 123–125, and "Stella Matutina" duplicated (1959).

[394] Alludes to Massignon's ordination to the Priesthood in Cairo on January 28, 1950 in the Greek-Melkite Rite a few weeks after the death of S. Violet Susman.

front of the Vincennes camp and at the traffic circle on the Champs Elysées (April 30 and May 28, 1960). These members simply wished to
demonstrate their sympathy for the North Africans held without judgment in the camps, as well as their Gandhian wish to suffer with them.
[This was] not to follow them in insubordinate acts or in desertion, like
the Boisgontier, Jack Muir[395] affair, where these generous but extravagant minds engaged themselves. Socrates did not desert Athens, but
died there struck down by the Laws of the City. Also Jesus, as well as
Gandhi who took no action of secession at the time of Noakhali in 1947.
On another side, we have criticized the two *Superstitions* that falsify so
many "missionary" works such as the *Fecundity of money* and the *use of
profit*. They lead to economic "associations" with strangers with whom
they refuse all spiritual solidarity, confining themselves to "suppose"
(?) that God makes them "carry our sin." Like the (*leschabet-goy*), the
Christian worker to whom the Jewish factory owner "rents out" his factory for the 24 hours of the Sabbath so that he [the Christian] "carries
his sin" [for him] against the Lord's day of rest. This is the most atrocious caricature of the Badaliya.

Part II

Let us now examine our statements on reflection and action formulated
in our letter # X (1956).

1) The Case for Transference of Physical
and Moral Pain through Substitution

We are taking part in an experimental finding that is accessible to everyone. We are not at all proposing to make it into a philosophical theory.
For many psychologists substitution remains only an idea, and the psychosomatic shock that we have suggested to them is purely a mental
representation. For Sartre, the sensation of suffering is the result of the
reaction of the exterior world against the blossoming of our projects.
Thus, "I exist my pain," that is to say, "a particular way to exist in my

---

[395] Young conscientious objectors who lobbied for a civil service role rather than
military in Algeria and were instead imprisoned.

inauthenticity." De Waelhens[396] thinks that pain is only a limited, passing phenomena, it is the projects "that make me exist' (sic).

The mystical experience affirms that the shock of compassion takes place in the body at the point where the soul engages itself in it, in the heart, engraves in us the invincible certainty that compassion cures, *ipso facto*, the pain in us that caused such despairing confidence of a sinner in his evil, by predicting the cure that our irrevocable solidarity will bring to the sinner (i).[397] The one who ceases to be compassionate in order to "save himself" has not truly "discovered the Other." The one who has truly felt the shock remains nailed to the Other. It is the last short stay of Saint Julien the Hospitaler under the mask of the disease of sin. The sinner clings to us so that we drown with him, and if he is a believer he believes that God is the author of his evil. He claims, like Satan in the *Tawâsîn*,[398] to abandon himself to God by loving his sin. It seems nearly certain to me that this Other is under this mask of soiled humanity as the Poor, the Lord Himself, the True creator. Under the mask of a tempter, in whom, we must find, through a profound probing, the virgin point where the Lord resides. [He is] attracting us to an absolute, heroic and promethean Desire to save, in this degraded specimen, all the murderers of the laws of society and nature. [It is] a call beyond the Law that kills, to a superhuman Justice. (It is by no means consoling to me to read that in 1681, the prudent hierarchy once again commanded Christian doctors to stop treating the sick who refused the sacraments. Alas!)

It seems that evil only inflicts the sinner so that he turn to a doctor. And Thamar seducing Juda inoculated him with infection in order to force him to act justly [Gn. 38:1–26]. Let us confess discreetly that the psychosomatic shock of absolute compassion affects every man. It is a substantially real grace that, *without our feeling it*, must emanate from Christ "in agony until the end of the world," "factus peccatum" (without having sinned; not like us). It is a call that only an attentive spiritual direction can confirm and guide, to a singular vocation to follow the steps of the Only Savior in order to "complete that which is lacking in the Passion of Christ in ourselves." [Col.1:24].

---

[396] Alphonse de Waelhens (1911–1981), a Belgian philosopher.

[397] (i) Abstract, intellectual evidence, almost transcendental.

[398] One of the principle works by al-Hallaj on Satan.

2) The Extension of "Substitution" in Time and Space: The Two Cities

The principle obstacle to this extension is the paternalistic mania to enclose the privileged elect in the City outside of all contact and from all contagion from evil. And, as much as possible, to restrict relations with the City of the elect to the commercial benefits [found there], not only perishable but also corrupt. [This] excludes all solidarity in spiritual sympathy with our associates "outside the law," claiming that our unhealthy contract doesn't soil us since only our partner "caries our sin." That is what the Jewish bankers appeared to accept "to carry" in the Middle Ages for the Islamic State, and (alas!), for the Church in 1312. The Law forbid loans with interest only to their brothers. (Deut. XV: 6).

One finds the same impure mix of good and bad in the creation of the "mounts of piety" by the Franciscan *lawists*,[399] or in the astonishing masquerade in the Orders charged with the redemption of captives in Barbary [North Africa] where they chastised certain captives in our cities [in public], who were too poor to ransom themselves, in order to collect funds from the curious onlookers for their next trip as "redeemers."

Without violence, our small Badaliya witnesses to its horror toward these "interest-bearing" caricatures of divine compassion.

3) How the Badaliya Is Born in the Soul

Describing one night of meditation in Isé, Japan, in 1958, we have shown how, in the primitive world of the Civilization of Rice, a Marian dawn rose up indicating how the mirror of the pure and humble heart is able to conceive the clear light of the "fiat" (j).[400]

4) The Humble and Axial Role of "Substitution" in the Preparation for World Unity

The compassionate person only cures those who are sick at the price of his own health. Jesus resurrects Lazarus and then Mary Magdalene anoints

---

[399] Pejorative term referring to the capitalistic system of the English economist John Law (18th century).

[400] (j) See "France-Asia," Tokyo #164 (1960), pp. 14:19–2, in English. "Mardis de Dar-es-Salam," Cairo, 1959, pp. 25–32.

him [Jesus] for burial because the miracle of life provoked his killers into killing him. The Badaliya, like the Greek Catholic Rite to which it belongs, cannot survive without uniting itself to the resurrection of its double (here it is the Orthodox Church).

5) Truth and Violence

Violence is immediate, whereas Truth is a gradual persuasion. In Badaliya the truth is not "found" through accepting the transference of pain, but through working in common to re-educate, to set things right and to endow them with integrity so that together we earn "lawful" bread in the Honor of comrades. This bread nourishes us with a communal word of truth that [makes] us "explicit and transparent to one another" (k).[401]

Part III

Moral report for the year 1960:

Some local Badaliya groups have been added to the one in Paris [including] Aix, Cairo, Alexandria, Beirut, Rome (temporarily inactive), Casa (inactive), Jerusalem and Dakar. We have prayed for those who have died, the first [being] Msgr. Hughes and Reverend Father Christophe de Bonneville, then Antoine de Chaponay, Marie Popovitch, Reverend Father Paul Soueïd and Msgr. Paul Mullazadé. This year we have lost Sheikh Tayeb el-Okbi and Mrs. Millie, mother of our friend, Scelles-Millie, who lit the candle from our pilgrimage to the Seven Sleepers in Vieux Marché before her mother in her agony.

Let us label our actions of "substitution" according to the Muslim social classification of Five Basic [Pillars]:

A. Testimony

As witnesses of our faith in the Resurrection, ([which] in Islam is linked to the Last Coming of Jesus), our visits to the Qarâfa cemetery in Cairo

---

[401] (k) "The rule of a renounced life heroically lived makes Jesus, son of Mary (Spirit and Word) conceived and born in the depth of the heart who thus believes in the sanctified soul." This is the opinion of several Muslims (Tirmidhi, Hallaj) and since Ibn Arabi, followed by certain congregations. (For example, in Morocco to the XVIII century by Isa Tha'âlibî, M. Saghîr ibn 'Ar. Fâsî and his disciples, Ifrânî and M. Dar'î Tamgrutî).

ended this year on January 5, 1960 with a visit made by four members of the Badaliya with Mr. Hasan Qâsim (the only survivor of the two authors of the annotated edition of the *tuhfa* of *Sakhâwî*) and Mr. Muhammad Burhûma. From there to Saint Okba, in Dhulnûn all the way to Nabîha Wafaîa and Ibn al-Fârid while thinking especially of Fakhr Farisi, the negotiator for Saint Francis in Damietta (l).[402] At the same hour our friend, Giorgio La Pira prayed to Saint Francis for reconciliation. We were able to visit the VII Sleepers in Damascus, and at their pilgrimage in Vieux Marché and at the Waqf Abu Madyan, (visited January 2, 1960 after Hebron, Beni Naîm and the Holy Sepulchre and Bethlehem) [we were] thinking of our friend H. Lounis Mahfoud. After two letters, one of the members of his group in Sétif was able to tell us directly of their fidelity to [our] prayer, fasting and pilgrimage for a serene peace in Algeria.

The vigil for the Night of Destiny was celebrated at Saint Sulpice March 25, 1960.

A committee to support the Japanese hospital in Sakuramachi was dedicated to Saint Anthony from the XV/XX February 28, 1960.

The Ambassador to France, Stan. Ostrorog, went to meditate for us in Mehrauli. He told me that he would go back again, when he suddenly died in Paris.

B. Prayer

They are praying for us in several Islamic cities in Arabic, Turkish, Persian, and Hindi. Our coat of arms (the pierced Heart) was embedded in the altar in the Mislata chapel in Valencia at the end of April 1960. According to a letter from our friend, A.H.M., on December 16th a Mass was celebrated there for two healings in December 1960. A member of the Badaliya in Paris celebrated a Mass at Gethsemani for the Badaliya. In Moscow we prayed to Our Lady of the Pokrov in August 1960.

C. Fasting

Those who were able persevered in our monthly Fast. Those who were not able fasted spiritually, notably August 14th with the Friends of Gan-

---

[402] (l) On the Hallajian, Fakh Farisi, and the *ziyârât* in Qarâfa see our "City of the Dead in Cairo" in BIFAO, Cairo t. LVII (1958), pp. 25–79 with illustrations, and our "Rawda of Medina" in BIFAO t. LIX (1960), pp. 241–272 with illustrations.

dhi and on Yom Kippur on September 30th. We fasted at the end of March with qadi Benlaôi Alawi in Fés in order that his advice of non-violence be heard by his Monarch.

D. Alms

Several [of us] were arrested two times with the non-violent [demonstrators] for the suppression of the camps for North African suspects, April 30th and May 5th, without adhering to the other activities of this group of generous, but extravagant Gandhians. The Madacascans freed in 1956 were flown back to their country on June 3rd.

E. Pilgrimage

Pilgrimage to Vieux Marché and to Our Lady of Bermont. The restoration of the Roman chapel of the VII Sleepers is under consideration. (The pilgrimage to the VII Sleepers in Rome was September 14, 1960 and in Sefrou October 28, 1960). The Ephesus Society in Lima, Ohio published "Saint John" in Zuzic where there is a study of Mary Magdalen and the VII Sleepers.

(pp. 73–84). On May 1st a Mass was permitted in Namugongo at the martyium for the promotion of the Bantus among the nations. Cardinal Rugambwa thanked us. Also for putting a relic of Karoli Lwanga on the dias at a meeting for Justice in South Africa in regard to the Bantus, in memory of Gandhi and his non-violent actions in this country.

Bibliography

Notice of publications with mention of the Badaliya
- "The soul of the people," Paris, 1955, # 321: French translation of the English duplicated lecture notes of a talk at the Continuing Committee for Muslim-Christian Cooperation session in Alexandria, Egypt, February 9, 1955.
- Mrs. Anne Fremantle, in "The Commonweal," New York, August 9, 1957.
- W.L. Hawryluk, "'Christianskij Golos' on Our Lady of Pokrov, patroness of the Badaliya," appearing in *Ukrainian*, Munich, July 13, 1957.
- "The religious significance of Gandhi's last pilgrimage," Note 1, p. 23 in *Les mardis de Dar El-Salam*, Cairo, 1956, analysis in Polish appeared in the magazine *ZNAK*, Cracow, November, 1959.
- G. Jäschke, *Die Welt des Islams*, 1959, p. 149.

- G. Basetti-Sani, *Mohammed et Saint Francois*, Ottawa, Canada, 1959, p. 269, note 37, pp. 269–280.
- P. Dalmais, "Dialogue islamo-chrétian," # 6, *Parole et Mission*, p. 433. V. Monteil, report by Pierre Rondot, "Islam and Muslims today," in *Abstracta Islamica*, series XIII, pp. 21–22.
- Arabic translation of the 1939–1947 Rule, by Father Jean-Mohammed Abd al-Jalil, h.c. (for the members).
- "Sodalité du Directoire" (Foucauld), article appeared in the bulletin, "JÉSUS CARITAS" of the Foucauld Association, 1956. Reprinted as an appendix in the 3rd edition of the *Directoire*, by Foucauld, Paris, 1961.

72. Convocation - January 6, 1961
21 rue Monsieur, Paris 7

Friday, January 6, 1961, Feast of the Epiphany: monthly Mass at 6:30 pm in the chapel of the Dames de Nazareth, 20 rue Montparnasse—our 71st *private Fast for a serene Peace* between Christians and Muslims, particularly in North Africa and in the Middle East, has been moved up to January 5th, the vigil of the feast.

Our 70th fast coincided with the review of the Algerian situation by the Head of State; his call for a humane, equitable understanding between the two communities pierced the abscess: the riots of December 11th and 12th broke out, showing to the French extremists that the days of racist attacks on North African Arabs are gone, and to the Muslim extremists that "revenge" is a thing of the past. However, both sides still have to be made to accept the prospect of building and living a new future together. It is only in honoring each other and sharing their "lawful bread" with their fellow workers that they will find the word of truth that liberates.

Our friends from the Christian committee for French-Islamic Understanding published the following text (featured at the top of a column in the 18–19th of December 1960 issue of *Le Monde* before the vigil in Notre Dame that Mohammed V had joined in spirit):

- The committee "once again expresses its sorrow over the continuing hostilities in Algeria and reverently bows before all those who died in the recent riots.
- stresses that we are not dealing with a war between Christians and Muslims but with a tragedy linked to evolution in the world.

- declares that pre-election confrontations between processions of demonstrators carrying simplistic slogans cannot replace the necessity of dialogues that seek out legal procedures capable of ensuring the future of Algeria, as well as the rights of the diverse segments of its population, in a spirit of mutual respect and hospitality.
- In order to shorten the Algerian conflict, the committee implores all leaders and politicians to take an official stand in favor of a *first truce* that would start on Christmas day and would renounce all violence for eight days."

(N.B. This call was broadcast twice in Arabic over the Radio).

"A tragedy linked to evolution in the world:" yes, to decolonization, and therefore to the end of the usurious exploitation of the colonized. As for the search for a new economy, the Western world has not yet found one that would challenge the murderous Marxist critique that links the theory of the salaried mercenary with that of a "reward in paradise," (whereas God must be loved for Himself without the need for a tip. He is the "great reward promised to Abraham").

This is why, with regard to Algeria, the prayer we offer as "substitutes" for Muslim victims of usurious methods contrary to religious morality, must go back through past generations to the origins of usury, which was not due to mere profane iniquity but to the perverse simony[403] practiced by religious States. The Muslim State, which was founded on the canonical prohibition of usury and on the enduring principle that Jews and Christians should not be forced to convert, had the idea of making usurious (forbidden) profits for itself by associating with bankers as arbitrators (mostly Jewish) who were destined to "bear its sin" (by giving it discounts). This is a sin of hypocritical simony that denies spiritual solidarity, a sin that Jewish casuists,[404] in their pride as God's favorites, appeared to accept before the God of Abraham. These bankers funded Muslim colonialism in the High Middle Ages, then organized Christian colonialism (through slave trade). At the council of Vienna in 1312, Christianity accepted that the Jewish race "bears its sin" by practicing usury.

---

[403] Simony: The practice of buying or selling places of honor in the church.

[404] Casuists: One who advocates moral doctrine through clever but false reasoning (Websters Dictionary).

So much so, that now both Christian and Jewish capitalists are in agreement about continuing to exploit the Muslims,—as well as other underdeveloped nations in need of "their paternal support,"—an untenable position in the face of Marxist propaganda.

Therefore, as substitutes, we must first of all pray for a prompt liberation of underdeveloped nations from the economic slavery created by usury. However, since Muslims are Semites, circumcised men who are not only beings of flesh and blood but believers who received, through a covenant, God's promise of immortality, enslaving them today makes us as *sacrilegious* as the anti-Jewish Crusaders in the Middle Ages, and later the followers of Hitler. The strange psychosis of terror that has taken hold of the activists in Algeria for the last fifteen days is like the inhumane surprise of an incredulous executioner having to face the resurrection of the victims he thought he had buried (or incinerated) for good. The God of Abraham is not the God of the dead, but of the living.

How can this psychosis of terror be exorcised? According to the rule of our "Badaliya," we, along with all the contemplatives and co-sufferers[405] in the monasteries, must pray more fervently than ever, (in order to save our living brothers), for their victims, "their" dead. For over fifty years now my prayer in Abrahamic Muslim and Jewish cemeteries, (in Cairo, in Istanbul, in the valley of Josaphat where Muslim pogroms desecrated Jewish tombs, just as Christian pogroms desecrated Muslim tombs in Andalusia and Macedonia), attaching my suspended witness to the God of Abraham, to that of all victims of hatred, has proven to be the surest way of appealing to divine Mercy during a tragedy such as ours.

The Muslim dead in Andalusia, the *Moriscos*,[406] were horribly treated in the Middle Ages, stigmatized by our forced baptisms and sacraments, their bodies and consciences sacrilegiously constrained, and finally expelled to the Maghreb because they were "not susceptible to conversion" (sic). (In the *Asiatic Journal* of 1927, Cantineau published a terrifying letter from the Mufti of Oran, secretly sent to the persecuted Moriscos, explaining

---

[405] Massignon's word "compatient," here translated as 'co-sufferer,' does not appear in the dictionary and is much stronger than the word "compatissant" (compassionate) and refers to the "substitutionary prayer" of Badaliya.

[406] This is the name given to those Muslims, whose ancestors lived in Spain in Andalusia for 800 years, who were forcibly converted to Christianity in 1492 and expelled in 1609.

to them how to *expiate* the sacrilege that the sacraments we imposed upon them, under threat of *auto-dafés*,[407] made them commit).

The Jewish dead of Andalusia, the *Marranos*, were similarly "converted" and horribly tortured by us in their bodies and consciences, scattered throughout Europe, then trapped by Hitler's atrocious genocide. Once finding refuge in the Holy Land, they should have negotiated their re-implantation with their Arab brothers, as Gandhi was advising them, instead of raging madly against their former companions in persecution under the Christian inquisition. In Algeria as well as in the Near East the two communities are being spurred on by European and Western oil companies whose policy is to divide in order to rule.

We have often mentioned that Jerusalem is the holy city for both communities, especially the Temple area, and that the Holy Place par excellence for Israel in Jerusalem, more than Mount Moria, is the *Wailing Wall*, the "Wall of those from the Maghreb." For more than a thousand years it is the place where pilgrims have been mourning their dead and their destroyed temple on the 9th of Ab, the anniversary of the two times that Jerusalem was overtaken (587BC; 70CE), by reciting the 150 Psalms, the most solemn prayer of humanity. (If the Bible is the Body of the Messiah, the Psalter is the heart). Now, it is in this place, delegated to all her dead, that Israel meets representatives of the Muslim dead from Andalusia, (or used to meet, for, since 1948 Great Britain has been allowing Jordan, in a retaliatory move, to bar access to the Wall on the 9th of Ab). The descendants of these Andalusians originally came from Tlemcen (Algeria) and founded the Waqf Abu Madyan in the XIVth century along the Wall of the Temple, around the entrance for the "Maghrebins" of the Al-Aqsa Mosque, forming an enclave in the place where Israel comes to shed the holy tears that earned her the right to return to the Holy Land. Through Algeria, it is France whose consul has the responsibility for this Waqf, which our friend Hajj Lounis Mahfoud, who was killed on 6/5/1957, was entrusted to inspect along with one of our members.[408] For the first time since 1957, the latter will not be able to inspect the Waqf in January, or recite the Our Father and the *Fatiha* for Hajj Lounis; he begs all

---

[407] *Auto-dafés*: The threat of burning in Hell.

[408] Massignon is referring to himself.

his readers to replace him in spirit in the fulfilment of this sacred obligation.

Because it is there, in the Al-Aqsa that the reconciliation between Jews and Arabs can and must take place, in front of the Wailing Wall, *Hayt al-Mabâkât*, so that peace can prevail between Christians and Jews in North Africa and in the Near East. Indeed, while the Jewish psalmody rises toward this Wall, inside the Mosque (former church of the Presentation of Our Lady), in the left nave, covered with Qur'anic verses about Mary, the Muslim women of Jerusalem come to humbly invoke the Mother and the Child (whose "cradle" is exhibited in a nearby grotto). We think that these two prayers, mutilated and shattered by centuries of persecutions will finally bring about the reconciliation between Jews and Arabs in the Holy Land, which is the key for a serene peace in Algeria.

By January 6th, the Arab PanAfrican conference will have begun in Casablanca (on the 3rd) on the two contentious themes, " the Congo" and "Algeria." Let us pray that the tears of the dead be stronger than the cries for vengeance. French speakers will be invited by African Muslims to an Islamic-Christian colloquium that is timidly being organized in Abidjan (Black Africa) for February. May we find consolation in this sign of renewed hope.

73. Convocation - February 3, 1961
21 rue Monsieur, Paris 7

Friday, February 3, 1961, on the day after Candlemas, monthly Mass at 6:30 pm in the chapel of the Dames de Nazareth, 20 rue Montparnasse at the close of our day of *private Fasting for a serene Peace* between Christians and Muslims, particularly in *North Africa* and in the *Near East*.

We may soon have to add, and in *South Africa*. Our call on January 6th for a truce "repudiating all violence" was well worth the effort, bringing us moving letters confessing that this was indeed the solution, but that the waning decolonization still carries too much foul, unappeased hatred on both sides. Why? Because, the sadism of torturers attests to it. Our secularized societies find themselves face to face with the sin of *sacrilege*, the abuse of sacred Hospitality, whether on the bodies of young men, or on souls subjected to the slavery of inquisitions. A double sacrilege, because when they torture the sons of Abraham, circumcised men, whether they are Jews or Muslims, they violate the pact of Abraham with God.

It is therefore not solely toward suffering humans that we turn our "compassion of substitution" with its fasts, prayers and sacrifices, it is toward the bloodied Body of Christ martyred in His Poor Ones. Focusing our contemplation on the Holy Places common to the opposing factions among the descendants of Abraham—there are two that for months and years we have been recommending to our friends:

1. The Tlemcenian Muslim Waqf of Abu Madyan in Jerusalem, that is made up of both the Wailing Wall, where Israel used to recite and should continue to be able to recite the 150 psalms—this scriptural Heart of the Messiah—and the threshold of the Al-Aqsa, where the presentation of Mary took place. We asked our friends in Jerusalem, in the absence of our delegate this year, that the Fatiha be said there, especially for H. Lounis, before Ramadan 1380 (beginning on February 9th: the Night of Destiny will fall on March 8th).

2. The Crypt of the Seven Sleepers of Ephesus, with the tomb of Mary Magdalen guarding its mysterious threshold of awaited resurrections, a sign of hope for Islam as well as Christianity. "Studia Missionalia" at the Gregorian University in Rome is publishing a description of ours about the Seven Sleepers with illustrations. We hope to hasten the resumption of worship in their chapel at 7 Via Porta San Sebastiano in Rome (as we did in 1955 in Rutthof), and also the resumption of the Muslim and Christian pilgrimage to the Ahl al-Kahf of Guidjel (Sétif), twinned in 1956 with Vieux-Marché.

3. We said above "and in *South Africa*." Islam wants to move up from the Sudan to the Congo, and beyond to the Bantus through East Africa. Its democratic tendencies constitute an attack on the feudal conservatism unfortunately supported in Ethiopia, Uganda and Rwanda by Christian colonists (the Afrikaners consider the "sons of Cham" doomed to slavery). The Christians have one last chance, which is the one that a saint, Msgr. Livinhac prepared for them in Nalukolongo by catechizing the chaste young martyrs who were burned at the stake on June 3, 1886 in Namugongo. Through providential design, the White Fathers from Algeria went all the way there to urge these young men to a sublime heroism, too neglected by the Muslim "military" morality and its occasional sadism toward slaves. Let us pray that the martyrs of Namugongo be wise guides,

not only of national emancipation for the Bantus, but also of the ideal of heroic chastity for tomorrow's youth throughout the world. Heroic chastity (Gandhi's *brahmacharia*) and fasting as a bodily discipline, are the two bases for the planetary holiness of the future, for which we so many times said, and made others say, the "prayer of Abraham," in order to find "ten just men" who would redeem Sodom from the sin of wanting to "abuse the Angels."[409]

74. Convocation - March 3, 1961
21 rue Monsieur, Paris 7

Friday, March 3, 1961, monthly Mass at 6:30 pm in the chapel of the Dames de Nazareth, 20 rue Montparnasse at the close of our day of *private Fasting for a serene Peace* between Christians and Muslims—this is the 74th fast—particularly in North Africa, in the Near East, and in South Africa.

During this time of Lent, we urge you to join your sacrifices to those of the Muslims who are observing their Ramadan. Friends of ours circulated our call for *solidarity between our Lent and their Ramadan*, so that the long-awaited negotiations may be prepared in an atmosphere of mutual respect and avoidance of vindictive violence.

Next March 14th, several churches will host the vigil of the *Night of Destiny* (Laylat al-Qadr, 27 Ramadan) during which, as in preceding years, we shall implore God to grant the desires for peace expressed that night by the Muslims. In Paris (in the crypt of St. Sulpice Church: gathering starts at 7 pm; silent prayer; intermittent recitation of the rosary starting at 7:30 pm; Mass at 8 pm).

Enclosed with this convocation are two appendices:

1. - to the latest annual letter, #XIV (1960): the text of the prayer said for the Badaliya while hospitalized in the Clinic at the Academy of Sciences in Russia last August; prayed under the sign of Our Lady of Pokrov; this text was given to us years ago at the front in Macedonia on 7/27/1916 by Pappa Dimitri, pastor of the (Uniat) Greco-Slavonic par-

---

[409] Gn. 18–16–33 as well as many references to this story in the Qur'an. See Massignon's "The Three Prayers of Abraham" in Mason H. *Testimonies and Reflections* 1989. U. of Notre Dame Press, Notre Dame IN, p. 3 or Massignon L. *Les trois prière d'Abraham* 1997. Les Editions Du Cerf, Paris, for the full text in French.

ish of Kukush (Kilkish, diocese of Salonica): *Otche Nashe*[410] and *Bogoro-ditse Devo.*[411] We are asking our friends from Our Lady of Fatima to say this prayer with us for ecumenical reconciliation. This is the immemorial Eastern Ave Maria through which all graces are obtained.

2. - annexed to our next annual letter #XV: the text of the Sunday prayer of the Latin Church and the Ave Maria, translated into *Swahili*, the future national language of the Bantus throughout Africa, from Uganda to South Africa. This is directly connected to our presentation of the plaque of the Badaliya to the shrine dedicated to the martyrs of Namu-gongo (January 31, 1955) for the promotion of the Bantus among civilized nations; we received much encouragement from Cardinal Rugambua, first Bantu Cardinal of Tanganyika.

[Our prayer of Badaliya remains] under the sign of the blessing granted to us early on by Msgr. L. Livinhac, reverently remembered, who catechized the martyrs of Uganda, and after Fr. de Foucauld's death, was the only Bishop to help us to keep his work alive. (See the third edition of his "Directoire" just published by Le Seuil, pp. 156–158). We owe this text to Fr. J. Soul, a Spiritan[412] (December 24, 1943); and we are recommending this new effort of "Badaliya" to our venerated friend, Rev. Fr. Jean Delmer, from the White Fathers, who was in Tanganyika near Kirando, right in the middle of Swahili territory when we last heard. Over 30 years ago, he founded a journal about missionary aid in Algeria (*Khouan de Sidna Aissa*[413]), that placed their actions, reported in *Arabic*, on the level of the only true martyrs' crusade on Islamic soil, that of offering themselves, even to death, for the love of souls as did St. Francis and Foucauld. Fr. Delmer had even adopted the list of invocations—suggested in my

---

[410] "Our Father" in the liturgical language known as Slavonic used by several Eastern Churches.

[411] "Mother of God, Virgin" in the Slavonic Church. It is the beginning of the major Marian prayer of the Eastern Church: "Rejoice Mary, Mother of God, Virgin, full of grace, the Lord is with Thee: blessed art Thou among women and blessed is the Fruit of Thy womb, for thou hast borne the Savior of our souls. Meet it is, in truth, to glorify thee, O Birth-giver of God, ever blessed, and all undefiled, the Mother of our God. More honorable than the Cherubim, and beyond compare more glorious than the Seraphim, thou who without stain didst bear God the word, true Birth-giver of God, we magnify Thee."

[412] Congregation of the Holy Spirit founded in service of the French colonies.

[413] "The Brothers of Our Lord Jesus."

"Pro Hallagio[414]—to all our martyrs "killed there by the swords of love;" a list that was then incomprehensible to most, but indispensable to the Badaliya, and that we intend to include in our letter #XV. His journal later became "On Islamic Soil," run by Fr. Jules Declercq (currently the pastor of St. Croix, in the Kasbah of Algiers), then later by Fr. Emile Janot. We are recommending our Swahili initiative to both of them, which we entrusted to the heavenly intercession of Msgr. Léon Livinhac, second general superior of the White Fathers, who wrote his "Duc in altum"[415] on March 19, 1909 to Foucauld.

PS. Following the announcement of the death of Mohammed V, we are asking the members of the Badaliya to join the Clarisse of Rabat [Sisters of Poor Clare] in spirit in order that the new King may take his inspiration from his father's spiritual leadership.

75. Convocation - April 14, 1961
21 rue Monsieur, Paris 7

Friday, April 14, 1961, monthly Mass at 6:30 pm in the Chapel of the Dames de Nazareth, 20 rue Montparnasse.

Since Good Friday falls on March 31st, our day of *private Fasting for a serene Peace* between Christians and Muslims (the 75th), will be moved back from April 14th to March 31st, so that we may be united more deeply with the whole Church and her Soledad,[416] as we pray for this Peace in North Africa (and for the negotiations in progress),[417] in the Near East and in Bantu Africa.

Without any publicity the Mass on the Vigil of the "Night of Destiny" brought together more than 100 participants in Paris and an even larger number of friends farther away, both Christian (often in high places) and Muslim (Tunis, Rabat, Algiers). We shall pray before God especially

---

[414] "About Hallaj," the Sufi martyr crucified in Baghdad in 922, the subject of Massignon's magnum opus. In his devotion for al-Hallaj he composed a series of invocations under this Latin title, *Pro Hallagio* in 1922.

[415] "Va plus au large" or "Go even further," a warm and encouraging letter.

[416] Spanish for "solitude," also one of the Spanish designations of the Virgin Mary: Our Lady of Solitude.

[417] Negotiations at Évian were delayed following a coup by the Generals Salan, Challe Zeller and Jouhaud (April 21) provoked by the press conference of General de Gaulle (April 11) implying the succession of Algeria.

for one of them, who just died in a car accident, our friend the vicar general Guiot de Cambrai who prayed this summer for the Badaliya in Jerusalem.

May the intentions of our fast on March 31st, Good Friday, be truly and fraternally ecumenical, dedicated through substitution to the most abandoned of men, to the most "underdeveloped," to those who are oppressed by a loveless technology, in order to hand to them the Marian cup of the milk of human kindness.

76. Convocation - May 5, 1961
21 rue Monsieur, Paris 7

Friday, May 5, 1961, monthly Mass at 6:30 pm in the chapel of the Dames de Nazareth, 20 rue Montparnasse at the close of our 76th day of *private Fasting for a serene Peace* between Christians and Muslims, particularly in North Africa, in the Near East, and in Bantu Africa.

As proved by the events of April 22–25th,[418] this serene peace can be obtained only through a double pre-requisite—the restoration of a fraternal, mutual respect of Christians for one another, and of the Muslims for one another. These are the preliminary conditions for a sincere social understanding between Christianity and Islam.

Not only between their living, but between their dead. Our fervent visits to the tombs of our Muslim brothers in the cemeteries in their own countries (as we know, it was not until after the Crimean War, that a Muslim cemetery was created in Paris and now in Bobigny), should not make us forget the desecrations committed by our Middle Ages (in Andalusia) and by our modern age (in Macedonia where the sight of such desecrations filled me with sadness). We must ask God that we may not be struck in turn by their talion.[419] Perhaps it will be through the control of a "secular state" with multi-denominational cemeteries on Islamic soil that peace will be reached, if they stubbornly refuse to restore respect for tombs by believing sons of Abraham, which depends on the sacred Right of Asylum that was so atrociously violated by the racist incineration camps.

---

[418] Collapse of the coup in Alger.
[419] Talion: the law of an "eye for an eye, a tooth for a tooth."

In this regard, the "return of the ashes" of Maréchal Lyautey from Rabat to the Invalides[420] is symbolic. Lyautey, who was the first great Frenchman since Francis I and Bonaparte to have a Muslim policy, had entertained the desire to be buried right next to the Muslim cemetery of Chellah, near to his Muslim friends, with the hope (discussed by Borély in Lyautey's Tomb) of being raised and judged next to them on the Last Day. From the beginning this intention was not understood by either side. The epitaph was changed, and the tomb became a kind of annex to the Residence of the protectorate, constituting an irreverent appropriation of the soil where he had requested hospitality.

We must pray that the burial of Foucauld contrary to his will in El Golea, in the Sahara, may not give rise to a similar misunderstanding, and, above all, to something against the wishes of his heart that was so attentive to the sensibilities of the Tuaregs, his friends, who buried him in Tamanrasset in a clumsy way.

Let us repeat once again how urgent it is to restore respect for human dignity through an internationally "effective" definition of the right of asylum for the helpless, the children, the elderly, the women, the wounded (and the dead) (see the *International Review of the Red Cross,* Geneva, June 1952). This right is the basis for a reconciliation with Islam.

In the Qur'an, hospitality granted to "the guest of God," that is to say to any traveler in need (*ibn as-sabil*),[421] is defined as a way of practicing the canonical duty of Giving Alms (*Sadaqa*:[422] sura 2, 172, 211; 9, 6 and 60 [see Qur'an, Sura 2:177].) Under the roots AWA, JWR, DYF,[423] the Qur'an gives 26 examples of the heroic practice of "divine" hospitality (for this is about the given word, infinitely noble and generous), from the Prophets (Abraham and Lot; Mary at Rabwé; the orphan Muhammad; the Seven Sleepers in the Cave). These examples have served as models for innumerable selfless acts of hospitality in history (even before 1954 Professor Kirèche-Djedou was calling attention to the general practice of hos-

---

[420] Famous Tomb in Paris. Against Lyautey's wishes the celebration at Les Invalides took place May 10, 1961.

[421] *Ibn es-Sabil*: "son of the road."

[422] *Sadaqa*: Charity

[423] Arabic words are formed through a system of basic root letters. AWA: to give refuge, JWR: a neighbor, DYF: to offer hospitality

pitality in the Algerian Hodna[424] toward any passer-by, who was always given a place of honor under the tent). This is *l'ikrâm al-dayf, l' iqrâ, al'dakhâla, l'ijâra*.[425]

This hospitality must not be short-lived, it must endure. To this end we must accept to live communally, as equals. I tried to explain this in the last Foucauld Association bulletin (*Jesus-Caritas*, # 122, pp. 101–104) under the title "The honor of fellow workers and the word of truth."[426]

Our prayer in Swahili, annexed to our "convocation" last March 3rd reached the man who inspired it, our friend Fr. Jean Delmer (in Muyaga, through Ruhigi in Urundi), who answered that he was joining us in spirit with all his heart.

A friend from Nancy went up to Our Lady of Bermont near Domrémy to pray for Algeria.

Our friend, the Sheikh Niyazi Qutbi, caretaker of the Mehrauli Mosque (near Delhi) where Gandhi came to pray a few days before his death, will pray for the intentions of the Badaliya and of the Friends of Gandhi in May 1961, on 24 *dhulqa'da* 1380 (anniversary of Hallaj) and on 9 Dhu al-Hijjah, the day of *Arafât*, the most solemn day of the Pilgrimage, the *Hajj*. On that day may our thoughts as Christians join this figurative Sacrifice that represents the Sacrifice of Abraham, the Father of all Believers. After the next 24 hours or so, these two days will fall on May 12th and 26th.

77. Convocation - June 2, 1961
21 rue Monsieur, Paris 7

Friday, June 2, 1961, monthly Mass at 6:30 pm in the chapel of the Dames de Nazareth, 20 rue Montparnasse at the close of our 77th day of *private Fasting for a serene Peace* between Christians and Muslims, particularly in North Africa, in the Near East, and in Bantu Africa.

The seventh year of the Algerian crisis and the seventh year of the humble effort of the "Badaliya" to make Christian France aware of her grave responsibilities toward Muslim persons and souls, causes us to

---

[424] Hodna: Basin wedged between two mountain ranges in the North East of Algeria.

[425] Honor the guest, offer hospitality, to be introduced as a guest, and to protect one's neighbor.

[426] Found in French in *Parole Donnée*, pp. 292–295 and *Écrits Mémorable*, vol. I, pp. 32–35.

meditate on our knees before the Evian[427] confrontation that places France as an international target at the center of the duel between capitalism and communism.

Conscious of how few and seemingly weak we are, we can, and we must increase our supernatural faith in the "arma Christi," in our participation in the poor, yet effective means that Jesus used all his life to save men from the perverse seduction of the powers of blood and money that are supposedly "at the service" of order and truth.

It is not true that the history of the world is forged by racial hatred, or by the bestial torture that fallen and skeptical spiritual leaders, favorable to inquisitorial methods, put at the service of degenerate Statesmen, or even propose to Churches, so as to bring about the Unity of the human species.

Those of us who were involved in the social history of the last decades in France as well as overseas, know that the history of the world is directed, illuminated, through the worst crises, the worst "birth pangs," by pure professions of faith, by the heroic non-violence of witnesses whose apparent defeat, draped in the imperial purple of martyrdom, already plants the seeds of the kingdom of God in the center of every soul of good will.

Let us not listen to the wretched souls who want to erase the names of the "defeated ones" from our history books, and who claim that Roland in Roncevaux and Joan in Rouen would teach us an unhealthy submission to slavery. It is not out of weakness that Joan said: "I did not kill anybody"—it is thanks to her non-violent sacrifice, in spite of everything, that today's France remains united with the Passion of Christ through her many poor and scorned souls.

Therefore let us continue to turn to fasting, to truly gracious almsgiving, to solitary and fervent pilgrimages (Beaulieu, Domrémy and Bermont, Rouen for Joan), to "heart wrenching" prayers, and to testify to the God of Abraham.

Let us pray, as "Badaliya" with all the Muslims who are oppressed like us by the violence. We did so on the day of the Qurban (May 24th in Mahrauli in India, May 25th in Algiers), meditating on the sorrow of so many parents who lost their Sons to the war. Let us pray for the "residents in

---

[427] May 18, 1961 the negotiations at Evian began, then were interrupted by nationalist demonstrations.

reunification camps" who are beginning to be "liberated;" let us pray for those "interned in concentration camps" who are beginning to be "released." Not too late for a reconciliation, let us hope. After saying so many times that the Muslims cannot keep their word (sic), and after violating their hospitality, it is very necessary that we trust their word and return to the hospitality ignored by colonialism.

After reading our article in the *Foucauld* bulletin (# 122, pp. 101–104) entitled "the honor of fellow workers and the word of truth," a son and grandson of French settlers in Algeria wrote us these lines: "(Muslim) hospitality is indeed a fundamental notion, even on the political level, and I hope that it will work in favor of the French in Algeria... I talked about this with Muslim friends. Their faces lit up, and one of them told me: 'If the French in Algeria understand this, that would be just wonderful'!" In the words of St. John of the Cross, perhaps this notion will be, "O happy chance! The secret, disguised ladder, by which we shall enter the house at rest."[428] The time has come when each French person in Algeria will have to face the necessity of choosing between France and Algeria. Perhaps at that point we shall have to "leave, if need be, our people, for them."

It is at that point that the "Badaliya" will be completely united with them, in the "arma Christi."

We are not talking about deserting Christianity for Islam, unfinished Islam (as a friend of ours was recently asked to do by his brothers—which united him with Christ even more), or about deserting the Western side for the other one. This is about embarking with them on a common social enterprise where we act as catalysts (rather than through osmosis) in deepening their present human and religious loyalty. Let us hope that our face of friendship substituted for them in their moments of fatigue, will make us become theirs: through compassion, the transference of suffering, and, let us boldly add, of Hope.

78. Convocation - July 7, 1961
21 rue Monsieur, Paris 7

Friday, July 7, 1961, monthly mass at 6:30 pm in the chapel of the Dames de Nazareth, 20 rue Montparnasse at the close of our 78th day *of private*

---

[428] From the first stanza of *The Dark Night of the Soul*.

Fasting for a serene Peace between Christians and Muslims, particularly in North Africa, in the Near East, and in Bantu Africa.

Several of us, informed by the "Friends of Gandhi" about their private fast on June 24th for the same intention, and with the participation of our Muslim friends from Pakistan and India, especially in Mahrauli, moved their 78th day of fasting back to last June 24th.

Our monthly Mass will be said on July 7th for our dear friend Rev. Fr. Jean-Mohamed Abd al-Jalil, OFM, who will be celebrating the anniversary of his ordination to the priesthood on that day. He went to Damietta to pray for us and was the soul of the novena of prayers organized at Mt. Alverna by the Franciscans and Hallagian friends of the Prophet from May 31st to June 8th, 1932 for the 1300th solar anniversary of the Prophet's death. This novena had not been preceded by any special commemoration of the *mawlid*[429] in the hegira year 1300 (January 21 1883): (See Bulletin de l'Institut Français d'Archéologie Orientale du Caire, Fr. d'Archéol, vol. LIX (1960), p. 264, Note 2: about the "Rawda"[430] of Medina).

It is to Rev. Fr. J. M. Abd al-Jalil that we owe the Arab translation of the "commitment" of the Badaliya (mimeographed in our green brochure), and he knows of our fraternal participation in all his desires for this world of Islam for which we are substituting ourselves with him, even to his hopes for Justice, founded on faith in Christ's eschatological Return.

July 22–23rd, 1961, is the 8th pilgrimage of our members with their Muslim friends to Vieux-Marché (near Plouaret, Côtes du Nord). Despite our wishes, it still will not be publically twinned with the symmetrical Algerian Muslim pilgrimage to the cemetery of the Seven Sleepers of Guidjel, but we were directly assured that our friends there will be closely united with us in spirit since they continue to share in our monthly fasts.

The pilgrimage this year falls on the exact day of the feast of Mary Magdalen whose reclusive cell, where she died in Ephesus, marks the threshold of the crypt where the Seven Sleepers were immured alive for Justice (according to witnesses in the VIth and VIIth centuries, and according to Gregory of Tours). The sign of the mystery of the Magdalen, the

---

[429] Birthday of the Prophet.

[430] A space in the Prophet Muhammad's burial chamber described by the Prophet as a small stretch of heaven on earth.

blessing on this First of all Hermits, falls on pilgrims visiting these Seven Ephesian martyrs.

Letter # XIV of the Association of the Friends of Ephesus (Paris) which is coming out this month, contains details about this connection between the Magdalen and the Seven Saints of Vieux-Marché, and a monograph published by the Gregorian University in Rome (ap. "Studia Missionalia") will be available this year for the pilgrims at Vieux-Marché.

Our Auresian friend Hajj 'Ali Hidoussi, *métoualli* [watchman] for the Tlemcen Waqf of Abu Madyan in the Al-Aqsa of Jerusalem (its need for protection was officially registered last November 10th in Israel, and is extending for 75 blocks)[431] died in Jerusalem on February 18, 1961, leaving a widow Mme. Nymet H. and five children. Let us pray for this devoted friend and his family.

As in previous years, no "convocation" will be sent in August or September (because of vacation), but as in previous years, the members of the little "Badaliya" are invited to fast (and attend Mass) on the first Fridays of these two months, August 4th and September 1st. With great fervor, for these will be the 79th and 80th fasts offered in order that a solution to the Algerian crisis may be found that will not provoke an international catastrophe. Such as the one exasperated Ibero-Lusitanian racists are working to bring about, along with Irgun [Israeli] extremists and, above all, Afrikaners who will not at any price accept the social promotion of the Bantus for whom we are requesting the most insistent prayers under the sign of the blessed martyrs of Namugongo (Uganda), Blessed Karoli Lwanga and his companions, burnt alive in 1886.

79. Convocation - September 1, 1961
21 rue Monsieur, Paris 7

Friday, September 1, 1961, Masses will be said for the Badaliya and its 80th monthly fast for a serene Peace between Christianity and Islam especially in North Africa, the Near East and Bantu Africa.

Our friend, the Imam Niazi Qutbi, from the Mosque in Mahrauli (near Delhi where Gandhi prayed for Peace with the Imam's father Hilal Qutbi, five days before he was killed) had asked us through the "Friends of

---

[431] After the Arab-Israeli war of 1967, the area was levelled to the ground, the North African quarter demolished and its inhabitants forced to leave after a warning of only two to three hours.

Gandhi," our associates in our fasts for peace, to pray with him for peace on August 26–28, 1961 (12–14 rabi'1, 1381 of the hegira, by one day or so). As this *sacred* call did not reach all of us in time, we ask the members of the Badaliya who did not fast on September 1st to be united in prayer with Mahrauli for our usual intentions, with particular fervor and, if possible, through fasting, on *Thursday, September 7th*, the vigil of the Nativity of Our Lady so dear to the Melkite Church (the Byzantine year starts on September 1st). (Those who have fasted on September 1st will meditate and pray with us).

The whole of North Africa, rallying to the neutralist block by the Bandung Afro-Asiatic Third Force, in effect brings us face to face with the vocation that His Eminence the Cardinal of Montreal had advised us to follow (1). Situated half-way between Western capitalism and Russian-Chinese communism, "Asia and Africa" are knocking on the doors of Christian hearts with vehemence. They are asking us to pray with them for Justice, especially the Muslims. [These include] the Moroccan Caïd, Ben Larbi Alaoui (with Sultan Mohammed V) as early as 1953, the Indian, Imam Niazi Qutbi, the same year, the Algerian professor Hajj Lounis Mahfoud (died in 1957) as early as 1954, with his brothers and friends, who continue to pray, and finally even this year at the pilgrimage of the Seven Sleepers of the Stiffel[432] (Vieux-Marché), professor Amadou Hampaté Ba, from Bamako, cultural adviser in Mali.

Our prayer must also be linked with that of the Turkish Muslims who come more and more often to pray at Ephesus under the mantle of the Assumption of Mary with almost all the Byzantine Churches, united or not, under this veil of Our Lady, whose feast is our patron feast: in this year of ecumenism.

(1) See his letter of November 26, 1956 (appended to our annual letter # X). [See Convocation #29].

80. Convocation - October 6, 1961
21 rue Monsieur, Paris 7

Friday, October 6, 1961, monthly Mass at 6:30 pm in the chapel of the Dames de Nazareth, 20 rue Montparnasse at the close of our 81st day of

---

[432] Breton name of the site of the Chapel of the Seven Sleepers and the fountain (stiffel) fed by a spring with seven veins nearby.

private Fasting for a serene Peace between Christianity and Islam, particularly in North Africa, the Near East, and Bantu Africa.

Several of us, upon the request of the Magnes group (from the Ihud, which is struggling for a fraternal reconciliation between Israel and the Arabs), moved this 81st day of private fasting back to September 20/21st (Kippur).

It is absolutely necessary that this reconciliation take place one day. One can even sense that without this preliminary reconciliation, there will not be any reconciliation between the Roman Catholic settlers, who are exasperated by the FLN's assassination attempts, and the Algerian Muslim majority.

We have always prayed that the States in the Bandung pact, whose Muslim majority has just expressed its agreement with the Gandhian President Nehru at the Belgrade Conference, be recognized as equals among nations. We think that a time will soon come, in accordance with Nehru's and Gandhi's wish, when Israel will have to come home to Mother Asia, a neutral party between the two blocks. And, in order to survive among the Muslim countries of the Near East, it will have to give up building its economy (especially with regard to oil) on its outdated role as a colonial bridgehead and collaborate with the Afro-Asians on the economic emancipation of underdeveloped countries. Only then will the Jewish segment of the Algerian population in its turn consider a future coexistence with Islam in Africa, (where economic agreements concluded between Israel and French-speaking Black states with a Muslim population will quickly put pressure on Israel to seek reconciliation with the Muslims).

It is most difficult for the Roman Catholic settlers in Algeria who find support in the European racism of the Belgians in Katanga, the Portuguese in Angola and Mozambique, and above all the Afrikaners and Rhodesians, (and those for whom we have prayed during the last seven years), to conceive of a future in which they would live in fraternal harmony with the Muslim majority because they refuse to subject their dignity as Christians and Europeans to a religious and racial supremacy. Yesterday's oppressed Arabs would have the tendency to want to become oppressive tomorrow. (One realizes this with regard to the most Arabized of Eastern Christians, the Coptic minority in Egypt, who cannot emigrate, and do not want to be humiliated).

Our "Badaliya" rule however permits us to glimpse a small light at the end of the tunnel where economic necessity is willy nilly pulling together the most extremist of Algerians, Muslim and Christian. For the last seven years we have been "substituting ourselves" for the Muslims in order to "understand" the validity of their claims "from within." Without ceasing to do this, we must also "substitute ourselves" for the Algerian Christians (and Jews) in order to "understand" their present exasperations "from within."

In our letter X we noted Pascal's profound words on "the strange and long war" of violence against truth. "All the efforts of violence cannot weaken truth and only serve to raise it higher. All the lights of truth are powerless to stop violence and serve only to excite it even more" (Provinciale XII).

We did not hesitate to demonstrate publically, in courts and even on the street, silently and nonviolently, against the impunity of many illegal actions, of many crimes committed against the Muslims. In this demented, "possessed" period of ours, I have had to recognize, with Pascal, that bearing witness to the truth, even in non-violence, only irritated all the more our blind opponents, and even made them worse (as for the victims, they would judge us as lukewarm). Now we certainly do not want to trigger reprisals that would induce the victims to take revenge—but rather to convert their persecutors, who are also our brothers.

Why this apparent failure of non-violence in the service of testimony to the truth (and to the whole truth, which is absolutely essential)? Gandhi explained it by saying that a brutal testimony in favor of the truth, under its non-violent physical appearance, conceals the recourse to spiritual violence, to a weapon more threatening than the worst of material weapons. The weapon of Truth is understood as our privilege and as a monopoly, and through it we force the opponent to humiliate himself as a liar, while in his most indefensible acts of physical violence there is a dim consciousness of a truth that is his that will not submit to our Truth so long as we fail to understand his. The temptation of martyrdom, this danger of pride in noble souls, reveals under its physical non-violence, a spiritual violence that wants to wound the sinner's soul by crushing its sin.

What should we do at a time when the threat of a civil war (and perhaps a religious one as well, when one thinks of the blind hatred of certain missionaries, assiduous readers of the writings of the wretched H.

Z.[433] against the "Mahometan" imposture allied with communism [sic]), is becoming clearer and clearer in Algeria as well as in France?

[We should] be more gentle and humble when we have to defend the Truth (is there anything more defenseless and sweetly persuasive than a live crucifix)?; and not defend the Truth as our personal property, but accept to be struck down for Its sake, and even to be *struck down by It*, as It is understood by our dissident, exasperated brothers: for we want to die as an anathema for our brothers who are lost. And we do not want our country to be torn apart by civil war.

Recourse to justice in the courts in order to resolve such a deep conflict with our brothers (on both sides) is outmoded. In the communal life envisioned by Charles de Foucauld we find the following lines: "While hating evil, they will love men. They will be universal friends in order to be *universal saviors*. They will avoid trials, 'will not debate in the courts,' will relinquish their rights rather than engage in disputes, and 'will accept abuse.'(Directoire article 212, p. 65 of the 3rd edition, 1961).

There is no other way for Truth to overcome violence.

Our Breton pardon and Muslim-Christian pilgrimage (2000 pilgrims) to the chapel of the Seven Sleepers of Ephesus at Vieux-Marché, on July 22–23, 1961, coincided with the crisis in Bizerte.[434] The prayerful atmosphere was serious and fervent. At the same time that the secular *Gwerz*[435] was being sung on the way to the fire of joy, our friend Amadou Hampa-

---

[433] Condemning works of Hanna Zacharias.

[434] In 1954, the French Government decided to stop deploying military forces in Tunisia which was under protectorate since 1883. The country became independent in 1957, and Habib Bourguiba became president of the Tunisian Republic. In spite of those events, France still had military forces based at Bizerte. In 1961, Bourguiba asked France to evacuate the base. Following French rejection of Bourguiba's request, Tunisian troops began a siege of the base on July 19, 1961. In the next two days French forces broke the blockade and surrounded the entire city, taking a toll of 1,300 Tunisian lives.

[435] *Gwerz*: The Breton canticle, the story of the chapel and it's nearby spring of seven veins. Massignon recognized the filiation between the Pardon of the Seven Saints in Brittany and the cult of the Seven Sleepers of Ephesus in the similarity between verses 6–31 of the *gwerz*, traditionally sung in ancient Breton during the Pardon and verses 9–26 of Sura 18 in the Qur'an. For the full text in English of both the Qur'an, Sura 18 and the Breton gwerz. See Buck, 2002. "Dialogues with Saints and Mystics: In the Spirit of Louis Massignon" KNP London, New York. ch. 8.

té Ba from the Dakar Institute, and now a cultural adviser in Bamako, recited the *Fatiha*, and later *Sura 18* in front of the holy spring. His warmly presented short talk was broadcast by SORAFOM in the 12 French-speaking countries in Black Africa, bringing our greetings to our missionaries there. (1)

Let us not forget October 1st, our patron feast. Our Lady of the Pokrov (Veil), is the patron of Moscow (where we appealed to her last August from the clinic at the Academy of Sciences), "the One who weeps" in the East at the Blachernae, as in the West at La Salette.

(1) In his "*Sayyidnâ 'Isa Ruh Allâh,*"[436] published in Oran in 1958, a Sheikh of the Allawiya[437] of Mostaganom, *Abdallah Reda*, singles out this text, as a premonition of coming events, from Origen's commentary on the 4th Gospel: "Like the sleepers in the Cave, Jesus will wake up in the world in the same state as when he left it; and the sleepers, those who also withdraw into the Cave and trust God to handle their affairs for the best, will be brought together again in one single group to accompany Jesus (to the Last Judgment)" (p. 65).

81. Convocation - November 3, 1961
21 rue Monsieur, Paris 7

Friday, November 3, 1961, monthly Mass at 6:30 pm in the chapel of the Dames de Nazareth, 20 rue Montparnasse, at the close of our 82nd day of *private Fasting for a serene Peace*, particularly in North Africa, the Near East and in Bantu Africa, between Christians and Muslims.

The fanatic hatred now growing under the perverse provocations by two extremisms, on both racist and religious grounds, must prompt us to work harder than ever at restoring fraternal and mutual respect of Christians among themselves and of Muslims among themselves, by becoming a humble *footbridge*, a "Marian aqueduct" between the two camps.

---

[436] "Our Lord Jesus, Spirit of Allah/God." It is under this title that Jesus is celebrated as a "'Master of spirituality" in some *hadith* (sayings) of the Prophet in Islam. See Tarif Khalidi, *The Muslim Jesus: Sayings and Stories in Islamic Literature.* Harvard U. Press 2001.

[437] The Tarîqa or SUFI Brotherhood, Allawiya, was founded in 1918 in Mostaganem near Oran, Algeria by Sheik Ahmed al-'Alawi (1869–1934). Open to modernity and to other spiritualities there are many disciples in Algeria, Morocco and in France.

The Holy Father granted any non-Christian having particular devotion to the Blessed Virgin Mary, permission to come and pray in her sanctuary of Hazreti Meryem Ana, in Ephesus, and it is the custom at Our Lady of Africa, in Algiers, to open the doors during the benediction of the Blessed Sacrament so that the Muslim and Christian crowd gathered together at the doorstep may receive the same grace.

Our vocation, in our smallness, makes us a rich soil consecrated as a meeting place for believers, for universal fraternization, and this is the reason why from the start the Jesuit, Fr. Christophe de Bonneville, of blessed memory, recommended that we say the *Fatiha* dedicated to the Judge, the "King of Judgment Day."

It is for this reason that we fast for our Muslim friends during their fast, from sunrise to sunset (a survival, by the way, for them of the fast of Israel and the early Christians, as we told the Holy Father in our filial address on September 4, 1953, following our private fast that He had blessed on August 14, 1953, (see His letter of August 19th, SS[438] # 305732); an address that was "handed personally to its August Addressee" (see his letter of October 14, 1953, SS # 310772, forwarded, like the preceding one, through the agency of our delegate in Rome, the late Msgr. Paul Mullazadé).

It is for this reason that in the most solemn fast of our Muslim brothers, we keep vigil with them during their Night of Reconciliation on the 27th: the Night of Destiny, with the celebration of the Holy Sacrifice offered for their reconciliation with God, through us. (Their Laylat al-Qadr being a survival of the original Christmas (originally Epiphany).

At a time when the Muslim reaction, against the unfortunate collusion of too many Christian colonies with cultural and economic colonialism, is creating very painful situations in Egypt (let us pray for the Badaliya there) and in Tunisia,—we absolutely should not brandish the truth like a club, but offer it, defenseless on the Cross, naked on the Cross. It is insane to excommunicate the Abrahamic monotheism of the Muslims in the name of a static affirmation of the dogma of the Trinity. The Trinity is not an arithmetic tri-theism but the divine deepening of the mysterious and transcendental Unity, the Pure Act in the inner life, uniting the Beloved with the Lover in Love, like the three powers of the

---

[438] S(ub)S(cripsi): Latin for the papal signature.

soul—memory reduced to hope, intelligence reduced to faith, will reduced to Desire for God—that are but One in the depth of our soul.

It is in the same spirit that we should not be satisfied with the quest for a skeptical compromise with Islam of the same kind that we are trying to negotiate with Israel, whereby we imagine that the suitable formula for a Judeo-Christian reconciliation is to erase the insult to Mary's purity from the Talmud and to skip the words "His Blood be on us" in the Gospel. For the Synagogue of Nazareth was legally right to cross the blessed name of Jesus off its "Megilloth" in which it (fictitiously) said "son of Joseph;" and we must show Israel that the scandal of Esther who was handed over to the Stranger, the scandal of Thamar's incestuousness, of Rahab, of Ruth, end up in the Messiah's genealogy along with the founder of God's Temple, Solomon, who was the "son of the adulterous woman," Bethsheba. Likewise for "His blood be on us and our children," which is a legal consequence of the Sacrifice of Isaac and of the Scapegoat.

What is unfortunate about the reconciliation between Christianity and Islam is that, as with Israel, we are seeking to found it on a compromise, a "deal" in the most mercantile sense of the word, a commercial promise with interest, the very thing that Leviticus forbids (XXV: 36–37: Do not exact interest from your countryman... You are to lend him neither money at interest nor food at a profit"). Since the Council of Vienna, there has been a mutual pledge between Christians and Jews about the exploitation of the soil, whereby Israel means to "have us bear the sin of usury," while we also imagine that Israel is bearing this sin for us. These two sins, in opposite directions, cancel each other out as in a year-end bank statement; but it is the God of Justice alone who is being made bankrupt by his children.

And now, the negotiators on both sides, Muslims and Christians, are desperately trying to found their peacemaking on a mutual pledge. This is impossible since there is no subservient third party whom they could both subject to colonial exploitation. Also today, one often hears in the country that failed to keep its word toward Mokrani,[439] Ben Bella,[440] etc...

---

[439] Mokrani, a Kabyle Berber Sheik who headed a mass revolt against the French in 1871. The French responded by confiscating all the fertile land in Kabylia, reducing the Berbers to penury.

[440] Ben Bella: A soldier in the French army during WWII, Ahmed Muhammad Ben Bella (1916–) was among the leaders of the Front de Libération Nationale (FLN),

that *Muslims do not keep their word*, that there is no way of making them keep their word, that it is the same thing with Communists, etc... Leaving aside the problem of the Communists' trustworthiness, which is the "puzzle" now facing the new UN Secretary General, a Buddhist, we wish to point out that with Islam, it is not in *respect for the bank deposit* (as with Israel, to whom the Catholic clientele has been giving preference since the medieval "Pope's Jew") but in *respect for the person of the Guest* that one's word of honor should be founded, and even if one has killed the Guest, in respect for his dead body. *We need a truce of God to bury the dead.*

This was known to the old Jewish women of Tunisia who at the end of anti-Semitic riots, went out, at the risk of their lives, to sponge up the pools of Jewish blood spilled over the streets in order to save it from being tarnished. For blood is the sign of the soul who prayed to God and believed in the Word of God in his Book: it has been made sacred.

In their godless fury, the extremists from both camps in France have forgotten this ultimate step. It is no longer only in Algeria but also in France that the dead bodies of warring parties disappear, incinerated or drowned—we saw this happen these last few days to our great shame. And two members of the Badaliya have had to pay to save the body of a Kabyle Christian from dissection (without being able to dare rescue any Muslim body). They may say "let the dead bury the dead;" my answer is that giving the dead a decent burial, thanks to a truce, is the last pre-requisite we have left in order to escape the approaching blood bath, and that the Badaliya must pray for this Truce first of all.

82. Convocation - December 1, 1961
21 rue Monsieur, Paris 7

Friday, December 1, 1961, monthly Mass at 6:30 pm in the chapel of the Dames de Nazareth, 20 rue Montparnasse at the close of our 83rd day of *private Fasting for a serene Peace*, particularly in North Africa, the Near East and Bantu Africa, between Christians and Muslims.

The intention of our Fast is now becoming the main focus of intention for all souls of good will, throughout the world, who are concerned with the salvation of a world increasingly possessed by racial passions,

---

the first prime minister of independent Algeria 1962–1963, and its first president 1963–1965.

corrupting greed, violence, and murder to the point of a desire for collective suicide by means of nuclear machines meant to sustain life, not destroy it.

Therefore we do not hesitate to propose to those of our members who will feel so inclined, to move our *Private fast* back eight days to Friday November 24th in order to have it coincide with the fast that the "Friends of Gandhi" scheduled for that day just about everywhere in the world. It includes a minute of silence at exactly 3 pm, which may sound familiar to a Christian soul meditating on "*Eloi, Eloi, lama sabachthani?*"[441] We fast out of respect for human dignity, for the North African workers in Paris who were so horribly ill-treated during their recent non-violent demonstration;[442] and defiled even in their burial during which the Name of the God of Abraham could not even be invoked. The Name of our God, after all, of the One who is, not only the God of the dead, but of the living,—[we shall fast] in communion with all the victims of violence.

December 1st is the anniversary of the death of Charles de Foucauld, our friend. On that day we shall pray especially for Reverend Mother Marie Charles de Jésus (born Capart),[443] foundress of the first Foucauldian contemplative monastery at the Mazes (near to Montpellier), who died on November 9th in Brussels, after many years of suffering inflicted by self-righteous people. This is how God treats his friends, during their lives, at least; for after their death, He makes the truth shine forth and returns justice to them. We shall pray that this may be done with gentleness, but also in total truthfulness.

Of course it is understood that within the Holy Church we must, in a spirit of universal brotherhood, apply the rule, mentioned in last month's convocation, enjoining us not to brandish the truth like a club, but to offer

---

[441] "My God, my God, why have you forsaken me?" One of the Last Seven Words of Christ from the Cross reported in the NT: Mark 15:34

[442] A nonviolent demonstration on October 17th by the FLN was brutally put down by the French police under the Prefect Maurice Papon leaving 200 dead and many wounded.

[443] Alida Capart (1885–1961) was the first to envision a foundation of women following the rule of Blessed Charles de Foucauld. In 1933 she founded the Little Sisters of the Sacred Heart in Mazes, near to Montpellier. Constrained by a canonical decision she retired to Belgium and was not reinstated until 1953.

it, defenseless, naked, on the Cross. So that, for the sake of this pure, very misunderstood vocation, (like the exile of a certain

Moroccan King), our little Badaliya, which was born to share, not hatred, but love, may help those who did not know love, discover it: "Videbunt in Quem transfixerunt."[444]

---

[444] "They shall look on him whom they have pierced." Jn. 19:37.

Annual Letter #XV

Begun and completed in Paris
Christmas 1961–Easter 1962

F ounded in 1934, the Badaliya had its initial brochure (with statutes, since 1940, and "imprimatur," since January 6, 1947) explained in *Letter I* at the end of 1947, under the headings: 1) the call and the place; 2) the goal; 3) the means which becomes the end; 4) substitution realized 5) simplicity of attitude; 6) to prove to Him that we love Him, by dying.

This analysis has been taken up more methodically in *Letter #X* (Christmas 1956), in seven paragraphs: 1) Cases of transference (of pain); 2) extending the "Badaliya" in time and space: the two Cities; 3) how the "Badaliya" originates in the soul; the Suffering Virgin, patroness of the Badaliya: Our Lady of the Veil; 4) the humble and central role of "substitution" in the preparation for world unity; 5) Truth and violence; 6) Statistics: the small number and the masses; 7) At the limit (follows a moral report on the preceding year.)

In letter XIV (1960–1961), the first thirteen letters were summarized, including a repetition of the first five paragraphs of letter #X and the final moral report listing our actions of substitution in relation to the five Muslim social *Usûl*, [pillars] or social Foundations, Testimony [Profession of Faith], Prayer, Fasting, Almsgiving, and Pilgrimage, thus showing how we hope to have them find for themselves, deep in their hearts, through catalysis, our Unique Savior, Jesus son of Mary, whom their tradition holds as an unfinished imprint of his face (paragraph 9 of our fundamental text).

Here we will follow the same classification of the five pillars for the moral report of our activities in 1961–1962:

A. Testimony

Here we are talking essentially about bearing a testimony of *Faith in the Last Judgment*, for it is at this point that there appears in Islam a certain presence of Jesus who is very closely associated, by Islam as well as Christianity, with this Day of Judgment (*Yawm al-Din*). This Muslim faith, which is so strongly oriented both toward the past and to the "holy light already promised to Abraham long ago," makes "catechumens" of our Muslim brothers, just as the Hope in the Messiah makes "catechumens" out of our Jewish brothers *with whom* (and not only for whom) we ought to pray, because the fullness of the Third theological virtue, Charity, has been given to us.

Let us add, in "ennobling" the celebrated medieval parable of the "Three Rings,"[445] that the three Semitic languages conveying these three Virtues, Hebrew for Judaism, Aramaic for Christianity and Arabic for Islam, have, as Semitic languages, a "capacity to inspire." We have said elsewhere (*French Encyclopedia*, vol. XX (1959, "the world in formation," p. 20–38-9), *Carmelite Studies* (1949 "technique and contemplation," pp. 44–45),[446] and (in the Second Prayer of Abraham, 1935 p. 37)[447] how a trilateral Semitic root is mysteriously found "transformed" as it passes from Aramaic to Arabic; (*r h m*, to love, becomes "to have pity;" *s b r*, to think, becomes "to endure;" *f r q*, to redeem, becomes "to separate"). It is as though the flower of Abrahamic revelation sown in Israel, blossomed with Christ in Aramaic, found itself "consumed" in Arabic with the burning winds of Judgment. Not without an imprint of the promise made to Abraham upheld in the Arabic, as Dhorme has shown (in *Mél*, by L. Massignon, Damascus, vol.2), and only in the literal Arabic recitation of the Qur'an, (in the *I'I'rab*), the functional trivocalization of the final vowels, (*a, i, ou*), the foundation of the primitive Semitic grammar since *Hammourabi's Accadian* and Abraham's time, (and Ishmael: Gen. 17, 20; 21, 13), is "Abraham's heritage" [found] in the enunciation, or the intona-

---

[445] "The Three Rings," tales of Boccace in the *Décameron*, repeated in *Nathan Le Sage*.

[446] The article by Louis Massignon, "La syntax intérieure des langues sémitique et le mode de recueillement qu'elles inspirent" can be found in *Écrits mémorables,* vol. II, Éditions Robert Laffont, S.A. Paris 2009, pp. 236–246.

[447] "L'Hègire d'Ismaël" in *Les Trois Prières d'Abraham*. Paris Ed. du Cerf, 1997, p, 59–122.

tion of the prayer; since the consonant is only the skeleton of the trilateral roots, whereas the vocalization brings it the blood of life, the Spirit.

We have thus prayed with them and for them, in Arabic, at Hebron and Beni Naïm, in Jerusalem (Waqf Abu Madyan), in Bethlehem, and in the Arabic liturgy of our Eastern Rite.

B. Prayer

Our Arabic coat of arms (the pierced Heart), placed in numerous Christian prayer sites, in Europe, Asia, Africa and America has been the springboard for our prayers of substitution, and the witness at Masses generating graces; notably in Mislata in Valencia.

In addition to the Arabic version of our basic text (attached to Letter #1), we offer our members who are especially drawn to praying for countries with Slavonic and Bantou liturgies, the Our Father and the Hail Mary in Slavic: (Otché naché, Bogoroditsé Dévo) and in Swahili (a).[448]

C. Fasting

(Blessed by Rome: letters of August 19, 1953 #55, #305732, October 14, 1953 #55, #310772)

This year we have renewed the Fast of Jonas (of Nineva), *Siyam Nînuwî*, from the medieval Eastern churches (three days starting on Monday, three weeks before Lent; see Biruni, *Tafhîm*, 177).[449] In addition to our monthly private fasts, a number of us have joined the friends of Gandhi fast at (Mehrauli), and on Kippur (in memory of our friend R. Judah Magnes, who wanted a reconciliation between Arabs and Jews living together in one State, equally.) And we have joyfully greeted the expansion of this method of fasting used by the non-violent movement for Justice into the four continents. We have especially prayed for God's blessing for our

---

[448] (a) Those who have not received these prayers sent with the convocation letter of March 3, 1961 may request it from us.

[449] Abu'l-Rayhân al-Biruni (973–1048), from an Iranian family, was one of the great medieval Islamic scholars. He was an outstanding astronomer, mathematician, physicist, physician, geographer, geologist and historian. He was a contemporary of the famous physician Ibn Sina (Avicenna) and is known to have corresponded with him. Al-Biruni's book *Al-Tafhim-li-Awail Sina'at al-Tanjim* summarizes work on mathematics and Astronomy.

friends during Ramadan, on the evening of the Night of Destiny, where one finds the imprint of the ancient Epiphany of the Arab Christians of the Hauran.[450]

D. Almsgiving

Fundamentally, almsgiving is the giving of one's self, that is to say, *hospitality*, which is a synthesis of the works of mercy. The practice of hospitality, essential in "Abrahamic" Islam, is also essential to the Badaliya, because this movement asks us to take in the Poorest of the Poor, the Exile par excellence, God, who we welcome, hidden, "substituted" in the most defenseless of our foreign guests; here, in France, the North African Muslim workers. One of us has magnificently practiced supreme hospitality, that hospitality of Tobiah and Chariton,[451] towards a North African Arab victim of violence, by procuring a decent burial place for him. Moreover, we have tried (unsuccessfully) to bring about a "truce for the dead." Let us recall, with St. Benedict, the mysticism of hospitality; that the Virgin extended hospitality to the Holy Spirit on the day of the Annunciation, touching ever so lightly, as did Abraham at Mamre (Gen. XVIII, 2–9), the very basis of the mystery of the Trinity whereby God is at once, the Guest, the Host, and the Hearth. "God loves the foreigner, the ger (tr. in Greek "prosélytos," which is weak; better would be "ephistios" Deut. 10:18–19). As the rule of St. Benedict reminds us in his chapter 53, hospitality is the basis for the Last Judgment (Mt.25:35), where the Judge will say to the Elect "*Hospes fui, et suscepisti Me;*"[452] and this rule prescribes in the first place to pray with the Guest.

E. Pilgrimage

First, our visits to the graves of our deceased friends, testifying with the Muslims to their Faith in the Resurrection, in the spirit of Messianic Hope and Life-giving Love. Those who were unable to renew their prayerful

---

[450] There is evidence of a Christian presence in this area of southern Syria from the third century.

[451] OT: (Tobit 1:17–20) Tobiah vowed to bury those without a tomb which inspired the establishment of the medieval Chaiton brotherhood.

[452] (Mt.25:35) "I was a stranger and you welcomed me."

visits this year to the cemeteries in Cairo, Istanbul, Damascus, Beirut and Jerusalem have done so in spirit.

This is also a pilgrimage in commemoration of our deceased members; to those that died first, Archbishop Hughes, Father Christopher de Bonneville, Father Monchanin, Father Paul Soueïd, Msgr. Paul Mullazadé, Antoine de Chaponay, Marie Popovitch, and Mrs. Millie. In 1961–1962 we add the names of Reverend Mother Marie Charles of Jesus (Brussels), Monsignor G. Guiot (in Cambrai), Little Sister Yva of Jesus (Cairo), and Mrs C. Thibeaudeau (Montreal). We entrust our anxieties and torments to the intercession of these dear souls.

And we recommend to the prayers of our members the souls of our Muslim friends and collaborators who have died, from Sheikh Tayeb el-Okbi and Hajj Lounis Mahfoud (including his brothers) and Guellil, to Ali Hidoussi and Mr. Mohand Aberkane, who have joined us in our prayers, pilgrimages and fasts for reconciliation.

This year our main visits to special sites (in preparation for ecumenism) have included Ephesus, Vieux Marché (in Brittany, the Sunday following the feast of the Magdelen), and Rome, three sites for the Seven Sleepers. Princess Pallavicini has had their chapel repaired at 7 via Porta S. Sebastiano and in the 1961 *Studia Missionalia* of the Gregorian University in Rome, the Abbot Y. Moubarac has published a systematic "compendium" of the articles that have appeared in the *Revue des Études Islamiques* from 1954 to 1961 (in which the relationship of the Clouds of Magellan with the Arab ships in the Indian Ocean dedicated to the Seven Sleepers has been examined.)[453] A number of us have made the pilgrimage to Our Lady of Bermont, so dear to Joan of Arc who we invoked for peace in Algeria.

Bibliography: We can add to the titles cited in letter XIV: António de Cértima, *O primeiro dia do homem fora do paraíso*, Lisbon, 1961, Atica, pp. 126–127.

83. Convocation - January 5, 1962
21 rue Monsieur, Paris 7

Friday, January 5, 1962, monthly Mass at 6:30 pm in the chapel of the Dames de Nazareth, 20 rue Montparnasse at the close of our 84th day *of*

---

[453] Louis Massignon noted in *Les Nuages de Magellan* that the Arab pilots in the Indian Ocean invoked the aid of the Seven Sleepers for their safety.

private Fasting for a serene Peace, particularly in Bantu Africa, between Christians and Muslims.

The Christmas truce, recommended every year in Algeria by our friends from the France-Islam Friendship committee and publicized by the AFP,[454] was mentioned only in *Le Monde* and *Le Parisien Libéré* this year. There is no doubt that the growing hatred between the two international powers gives rise to two adverse factions in every third world country. This is getting clearer and clearer in "decolonized" Africa, especially in the former Belgian Congo. European neo-colonialism is trying to take control of the aid programs to underdeveloped countries by favoring the "tough" ones, from the Afrikaans in South Africa, to Katanga as well as Algeria and Israel; this can only drive the Third World towards communism. That Christianity should be tempted to join forces with this neo-colonialism in order to preserve the goods "acquired" under the colonial regime would be "natural;" however, the great movement of compassion for underdeveloped nations, which is the honor of its missiology, goes against this temptation. And we must pray first and foremost that Christians resist it at all costs, staying there when the soldiers and the colonial banks are gone, having tried, as was seen in Goa, to take the relics of the Saints with them instead of leaving them to those among whom they wanted to die. This claim by India for these relics is quite remarkable, as Cardinal Léger was telling us in a letter five years ago: "Asia and Africa are at our doors; will the Church open them? *They will enter in spite of us.*"

We cannot discourage their covetousness, often savage, like that of the Barbarians in fifth century "Romania." If necessary, we must give them our possessions and our lives. This is what may well happen in Egypt for example, where the first members of the Badaliya are suffering, in expiation for the faults of others. Our prayer goes to them first, and also to the Copts who have no outside recourse even though they are natives of that country.

As for the situation in Algeria, where after eight years of interracial fighting, an actual civil war is arising between Europeans—it is, as we have often said, the outcome of a sheer "possession" by the demons of hatred, from which we can only deliver our human brothers by means of the clas-

---

[454] Agence France-Presse, one of the three largest news agencies in the world.

sic "weapons," prayer, fasting, sacrifice, alms and the heroic recourse to God alone.

The annual letter XV, which will probably be distributed with the next convocation, will help us relive our latest experiences. Remember, Foucauld wrote to us to go frequently over the *double* history (within yourselves), of the graces received from God, and of our infidelities. Merry Christmas.

84. Convocation - February 2, 1962
21 rue Monsieur, Paris 7

Friday, February 2, 1962, monthly Mass at 6:30 pm in the chapel of the Dames de Nazareth, 20 rue Montparnasse at the close of our 85th day of *private Fasting for a serene Peace*, particularly in North Africa, the Near East and Bantu Africa, between Christians and Muslims.

That Christians and Muslims should pray *together* for this peace so ardently desired, and awaited for so long, is becoming more and more clear. Any attempt at an agreement on economic and cultural grounds without religious sincerity between Christians and Jews on one hand, and Muslims on the other, can only scare the Third World and drive it towards Communism. Besides, it is not only in Algeria that underprivileged Muslims are driven towards communism by the violent practices of the international colonial consortium, but also in France where the presence of half a million Algerian Muslim workers should be respected, for this is the true guarantee that the safety and dignity of the million [French] compatriots we have in Algeria will be maintained. They should be respected not only in their working life but also in their funerals, as we pointed out during the painful events on October 17th in Paris; hospitality toward foreign guests extends to their burial rites including prayers according to their faith.

The divine root of the spirit of the Badaliya in the practice of Hospitality towards this Poor man, this expatriate par excellence, is God, who hides in the guise of the most miserable of our foreign guests, that is to say the North-African Muslim workers. Allusion was made in our recent convocations to the gesture one of us made as a "substitute," having recognized one of our students from the evening classes for North Africans at the Morgue. He felt obligated to make sure that the victim would receive a decent burial. He felt encouraged to do so by the fact that this Muslim had recently become a Christian, but since he was still Muslim in the Official Public Records, our friend had to follow the victim's body (after a detour for a hurried final absolution)[455] all the way to the Muslim cemetery in a corner of Thiais.[456] And, at root, what our friend had "recognized" in this body, was not only a baptized man, it was Christ, our Victim, with the features of a North-African, our Brother.

A wretched monk, who, out of patriotism, thought it permissible to abuse Arab hospitality by acting as an intelligence agent, dared to give a "sociological" definition of hospitality as "the invention of a neutral territory accepted by all, making life as a traveler possible" (sic). Whereas Semitic hospitality, of which Arab hospitality is the last remnant in these racist times, is the mask of the Expatriate that God puts on to take us to our true Homeland. The Virgin gave hospitality to the Holy Spirit on the day of the Annunciation. This mystery touches the very heart of the mystery of the Trinity in which God is at the same time the Guest, the Host and the Hearth. It says in Deuteronomy (X: 18–19): "God loves the alien, giving him food and clothing. So you too must love the alien, the *gèr*, (the Greek word "proselytos" is weak; "ephestios" would be better) for you were once aliens (gèrim) yourselves in the land of Egypt." Hospitality is at the root of the Last Judgment (Matthew XXV: 35), when the Judge will say to the Chosen: "I was hungry, thirsty..., I was a stranger and you invited me in, I was naked and you clothed me... sick... in prison..."—the rule of St. Benedict echoes these words in chapter 53: "omnes supervenientes hospites tanquam Christus suscipiantur, quia Ipse dicturus est" "Hospes fui, et suscepisti Me;"[457] and it prescribes praying with the guest first. For any gesture of hospitality that is not salvific is worthless, any act of substitution that is not "healing" and liberating is only an illusion, any word of welcome that is not a "resurrection" for the alien is only literature.

---

[455] The special prayers for forgiveness over the deceased before being laid in the grave.

[456] The "cimetière musulman" Massignon is referring to is not an independent cemetery but an area or "carré" designated for Muslims within the large cemetery of Thiais, a suburb south of Paris. There are about 70 of these "carrés" throughout France.

[457] "All the guests that come to present themselves will be welcomed as being Christ because He himself said to us, 'I was a stranger and you welcomed me.'"

85. Convocation - March 2, 1962
21 rue Monsieur, Paris 7

Friday, March 2, 1962 we shall have our 86th day of *private Fasting for a serene Peace*, particularly in North Africa, the Near East and Bantu Africa, between Christians and Muslims.

Our monthly Mass will be transferred from March 2nd to March 4th at 7:30 pm; it will not be celebrated at the Dames de Nazareth but in the crypt of the Church of St. Sulpice.

For the following reasons:

1. The Muslim Ramadan having begun on February 6th, the 27th day of Ramadan falls on March 4th, and, as in previous years, we shall willingly join in the prayer of our Muslim friends in Algeria who will be keeping vigil with us during this *Night of Destiny*, Laylat al-Qadr, our living friends, and dead friends, such as Hajj Lounis Mahfoud and Mohand Aberkane, our associates in the pilgrimage of the Seven Sleepers of Ephesus, who gave their lives for this serene Peace that may be about to dawn.

2. The three-day fast of the Ninevites, *Sawm Nînawî*, that begins on the Monday three weeks prior to Lent, was celebrated by the Eastern Church a thousand years ago (See Biruni, *Tafhîm*, 177), and according to the Julian calendar, falls on dates corresponding to February 27th to March 1st in ours. This fast will help us to meditate on our union with the Muslim's Ramadan in the very theocentric spirit of the early Christians during Lent; the spirit of the prayer of absolute abandon by the Prophet of Nineveh, Jonas, (*Dhûlnûn Yûnus* for the Arabs), swallowed up by the sea monster, a symbol of Sheol.[458] This prayer from the Bible [Jonas 3:1–10], repeated in the Qur'an (10:23), is considered by the Muslims to be the very prayer of the Seven Sleepers buried alive in the Cave. It is the irresistible prayer that snatches them, along with Lazarus, from the cave of death, since Jesus himself said that the three days that Jonas spent in the belly of the whale were the very Sign of His descent into Hell, and of His Resurrection, the guarantee of our own. Hallaj recited it during his last trial.

---

[458] Sheol is a Hebrew word meaning place of the dead.

3. We shall offer our private fast for the Latin Lent that begins on March 7th, and for the Eastern Lent that begins for our separated brothers on March 22nd.

In this solemn hour for France, Africa and the entire world, we insist on the extraordinary value of Fasting—the Threshold to the Passion and Death redeeming any soul who wants to fast with the Lord for Forty Days in the Desert. It is not only a question of a fast for the stomach or the tongue, but a fast from all sweetness and consolation in prayer. It is hard, but nonetheless essential, to be determined to renounce ourselves entirely if we want to obtain Serene Peace for others; this Peace for which we are going to observe our 86th humble day of fasting. The essence of the Fast is in ceasing to count on the possession of any spiritual good, even of Sovereign Good. They say that this is what the descent into Hell means, but it is precisely this sacrifice to humility that Satan, in his jealous desire for divine perfection, refused to make: this crucifying sacrifice that liberates souls by setting fire to the Hell of jealousy and hatred in order to make cool air and Peace reign.

The entrance to the St. Sulpice crypt that is being put at our disposal, is located underneath the south tower, south side. This convocation will be required at the entrance.

P.S. Now, after the death of our friend and associate, M. Mohand Aberkane in Algiers on February 5th, who was faithful to our common weapons of non-violence, prayer, fasting and the pilgrimage to the VII Sleepers, we learn of the "peaceful" death, in Cairo on Saturday, February 24th, of our dear *Sister Yva de Jesus* (Provincial of the Little Sisters of Foucauld in the Middle East). One of the first to embrace the Badaliya in 1936, she meditated on it and lived it as a daughter of suffering and of desire, vowed to compassion and passing through all the stages of this work of substitution for Islam, from Damietta (the offerings of Saint Francis and Saint Louis) to Baghdad (to the tomb of Hallaj), and in passing through Ephesus (Saint John, Mary Magdalene and the VII Sleepers) with her General Superior, to whom we declare our feelings of fraternal pain. Let us not forget Sr. Yva's mission in Iran, notably in Mechhed where she witnessed to our prayer. We cabled our co-foundress [Mary Kahil] in Cairo of our sharing in her mourning.[459]

---

[459] Yva Kemeid was a cousin of Mary Kahil.

86. Convocation - April 6, 1962
21 rue Monsieur, Paris 7

Friday, April 6, 1962, monthly Mass at 6:30 pm in the chapel of the Dames de Nazareth, 20 rue Montparnasse.

The day of *Private Fasting for a serene Peace* between Christians and Muslims, particularly in North Africa, the Near East and Bantu Africa,— our 87th day has been postponed until Good Friday, next April 22nd.

Now that promises, based on a bond of sacred hospitality between the children of Abraham, have been kept at last and are beginning to bear fruit,[460] we must more humbly than ever prostrate ourselves before God in our fasts, meditations and prayers. Thus a number of Muslim friends joined us in our minute of silence for peace, on Friday March 16th at 3 pm; recalling Gandhi's visit for peace in Mahrauli in 1948 with the son of the Imam who had welcomed Gandhi there on that day.

Hospitality is fraternal, takes place among equals, and does not tolerate arbitrarily privileged priorities. Arabs, Kabyles and Muslims have not forgotten this virtue, and we should not forget it either, whatever it costs us.

The annual Mass commemorating the founding of the Badaliya in Damietta was celebrated last March 23rd in the Church, Kenisset al-Arwâm.

Let us pray for the next pilgrimage of the Seven Sleepers of Ephesus at Vieux-Marché. In a meeting about Ephesus (to which John XXIII alluded with a view to October 11th, the first day of the Council he is preparing), the Archbishop of Smyrna, Msgr. Joseph Descuffi who came especially from the Near East, recalled the importance of Christians and Muslims praying together to the Seven Sleepers of Ephesus (and to Mary Magdalen) for the reconciliation to which we have devoted ourselves.

87. Convocation - May 4, 1962
21 rue Monsieur, Paris 7

Friday, May 4, 1962, monthly Mass at 6:30 pm in the chapel of the Dames de Nazareth, 20 rue Montparnasse at the close of our 88th day of *private*

---

[460] Massignon is alluding to the Evian Conference in March 1962 during which a cease-fire was finally arranged between the French government and representatives of the FLN.

Fasting for a serene Peace between Christians and Muslims, particularly in North Africa, the Near East and Bantu Africa.

The death of Msgr. G. Guiot from Cambrai, of Little Sister Yva of Jesus in Cairo, and now the death of our friend Mme C. Thibaudeau in Montreal on April 3rd, makes us turn toward these dear interceding souls, so that the prayers, the acts of abstinence, the supplications of our poor little Badaliya sodality may be heard: so that, at last, a pledge before God, the God of Abraham, Isaac and Jacob, may be sealed, that will reconcile Muslims and Christians in total faithfulness. They are now in the next world, beyond our reach, with our first dead—Archbishop Hughes, Fr. Christophe de Bonneville, Fr. Paul Soueïd, Msgr. Paul Mullazadé, Antoine de Chaponay, Marie Popovitch. All together, we implore them to ask God to have mercy on this torn world. May their works of mercy obtain this ardently desired Peace.

We must not tire of repeating what we said here on February 2nd: the divine root of the spirit of the "Badaliya" is in the practice of hospitality toward the Poorest of the Poor, the Alien par excellence, God, who hides under the guise of the most defenseless of our foreign guests, and is the One who will tell us on Judgment Day, "Hospes fui et suscepistit Me" (Matthew XXV: 35). Let us welcome this guest, with respect, with fraternal devotion, in blessed equality from this side as well as from the other side of the "Mare Nostrum."[461]

88. Convocation - June 1, 1962
21 rue Monsieur, Paris 7

Friday, June 1, 1962, monthly Mass in the chapel of the Dames de Nazareth, 20 rue Montparnasse; *contrary to general practice it will be celebrated at 7 pm* instead of 6:30 pm. At the close of our 89th day of *private Fasting for a serene Peace* between Christians and Muslims, particularly in North Africa, the Near East and Bantu Africa.

Let us not tire of repeating that Christians, Jews and Muslims must pray *together*, for the coming of this Peace, so ardently desired and so long awaited. Any attempt at an agreement on economic or even cultural grounds not rooted in the sincerity of their hearts and united in *their*

---

[461] "The Mediterranean" over which a million Europeans were fleeing from Algeria.

Faith in the God of Abraham, the Father of all the Faithful, can only scare the Third World and drive it into the camp of the Professional Atheists.

We prayed on the feast of the Sacrifice that was asked of Abraham last May 14th (*Qurban*). We shall also fervently pray next June 13–15, on the occasion of the *Ashura*,[462] a feast of Judeo-Christian origin in Islam, before praying with Charles de Foucauld from the bottom of our hearts on June 29th, feast day of the Sacred Heart pierced by the soldier's spear.[463]

N.B. There is a possibility of a spiritual retreat in Assisi from Monday, September 3rd to Friday, September 7th. The retreat is being proposed to members and correspondents of the Badaliya who wish to interiorize the spiritual attitude of the sodality and examine their conduct toward the world for which they have chosen to offer themselves as "substitutes" in the brotherhood of Abraham and the spirit of St. Francis.

For information, please write to the Badaliya office in charge of the organization of this retreat: 4 rue des prêtres Saint Séverin, Paris V.

89. Convocation - July 6, 1962
21 rue Monsieur, Paris 7

Friday, July 6, 1962, 89th day of *private Fasting for a serene Peace* between Christians and Muslims, particularly in North Africa, the Near East and Bantu Africa.

There will be no Mass in the chapel of the Dames de Nazareth.

In the present solemn circumstances,[464] we are asking all of you to join, at least in spirit, if not in the flesh, in the prayers of the pilgrims at the IXth pilgrimage of Muslim-Christian reconciliation to the Seven Sleepers of Ephesus at Vieux-Marché (Plouaret station, Côtes du Nord) next July 21–22nd.

---

[462] *Ashura* is celebrated on the tenth day of the Muslim month of Muharram when Shii Muslims commemorate the martyrdom of Imam Husayn, grandson of the Prophet, at Karbala. Massignon interprets this day of fast as a Day of Atonement originating in the Judeo-Christian tradition.

[463] Charles de Foucauld had a great devotion to the Sacred Heart of Jesus, the emblem that he sewed on the front of his tunic and the name that he gave his Union Sodalité of praying Christians, both lay and religious.

[464] After 132 years of French colonial presence, Algeria became an independent Arab State on July 1, 1962.

90. Convocation - October 5, 1962
21 rue Monsieur, Paris 7

Friday, October 5, 1962, monthly Mass at 6:30 pm in the chapel of the Dames de Nazareth, 20 rue du Montparnasse at the close of our 92nd day of *private Fasting for a serene Peace* between Christians and Muslims, particularly in North Africa, the Near East and Bantu Africa.

With regard to the Near East: relying on the secular vocation of France and the Franciscans for the defense of the multi-national character of the Holy Sites, our prayer must continue to help preserve the Abu Madyan Waqf, which was founded by an Algerian from Tlemcen, and should therefore be transferred to the new Algerian State.

With regard to North Africa: we must implore divine mercy so that the Church may institute, and encourage more and more, an Eastern Rite liturgy in Arabic throughout the region, thereby introducing, as in Black Africa, something better than the Latin Rite, by establishing an African implantation of the Catholic Church.

With regard to Black Africa and more particularly Bantu Africa: a bishop from Cameroon acknowledged that veneration of the Seven Sleepers of Ephesus (the Muslim Ahl al-Kahf) provides a solid spiritual bond for Muslim-Christian friendship. At the pilgrimage of these Ephesian martyrs this summer in Vieux-Marché (Côtes du Nord), this was the ninth, the Muslim delegate sent by two deputies in the Comoro Islands, M. Mohamed Taki, president of the Students from Comoro Islands in France (there are about forty of them) recited in public, in a tone of humble and fervent faith, in front of the spring with seven veins, verses 8–25 from the 18th Sura of the Qur'an, an expression of total abandon to God by the seven brothers buried alive for justice. He added that each Friday, in every Mosque, these verses are recited at the beginning of the public service in order to affirm the faith of the congregation in a future resurrection with these VII Martyrs "resurrected" ahead of time. (N.B. These VII genuine Lazaruses are "guarded" by the sister of Lazarus of Bethany, Mary Magdalen, whose tomb is located at the entrance to their Ephesian cave).

Thus M. Mohamed Taki reminded us of the eschatological importance of the Seven Sleepers for the Muslim faith in a final resurrection with them, thus with Christ and through Christ, as it was for Lazarus.

M. Fernand Benoît in an article in "Provence Historique," (University of Aix, June 1962, pp. 233–235) thinks that the relics of the Seven Sleepers were brought along with those of Mary Magdalen to the crypt of St. Lazarus (St. Victor de Marseille) and to the Cave in Ste Baume.[465] As for the Comoro islands, each house, each rice-paddy, each *dhow*[466] is dedicated to the Seven Sleepers. The four *qadis*[467] in the Comoros have approved this dedication by *fatwa*.

Their *shafiite*[468] ritual is based on *Nawawi*[469] and *Shafi'i* himself. Let us add that our prayers in Swahili eminently apply to the Comoro Islanders whose dialect is getting more and more "swahilized," and that the last two pilots in the Indian Ocean to use Magellan's Clouds as their Southern Polar Star were Comoro Islanders (devoted to the Seven Sleepers), MM. Ahmed Cheik, pilot of the dhow "Sancta Maria" (in Moroni) and Souhali M'Dahoma, pilot of the *dhow* "The Pearl of the Comoros" (*Mutsamudes*).

Let us finally pray for an end to the anti-Christian hatred professed by the new worker's party known as the "Black Muslims," which has

---

[465] Along with the tradition that the Magdalen died in Ephesus and was buried at the entrance to «the Grotto of the Seven Sleepers» there is another one according to which the Virgin Mary, Mary Magdalen, Martha and their Egyptian servant, Sarah, along with Lazarus and other companions, escaped persecution by setting out to sea in a boat with neither sails nor oars, arriving miraculously in Provence. The place now known as Les-Stes-Maries-de-la-Mer (The Saint Marys from the Sea) houses a carving of the boat with the two Marys in it. The Magdalen holds a chalice that some say is the Holy Grail and others that it contains the precious ointment with which she anointed the feet of Christ. The relics of the servant Sarah lie in the crypt of the church in Les Saints Marie. She became the patron saint of the gypsies who gather for an annual festival on May 24–25. Mary Magdalen is said to have preached the Gospel in Gaul, then retired to a cave in La Sainte-Baume (meaning *balm* in the ancient High French used by church scholars). La Sainte-Baume is a spectacular 700 meters high mountain side where she spent the last years of her life as a hermit.

[466] *Dhow*: A sailing ship.

[467] *Qadi*: A judge who administers Shariah law.

[468] *Shâfi'ite* is one of the four schools of *Fiqh* or Islamic jurisprudence in Sunni Islam, founded by Imam Shafi'i (767–820). It gives equal weight to the traditions (hadith) and the Qur'an, emphasizing the consensus of the Islamic community as the most important secondary source of law.

[469] *Sharaf al-Nawawi* (1233–1277), one of the best known legal jurists and scholars of this school and widely acknowledged as the intellectual heir to Imam Shafi'i.

been organized in the United States against its Christian employers, mostly in Chicago.[470]

91. Final Convocation
21 rue Monsieur, Paris 7
(Massignon died October 31, 1962)

As the first Friday is on the day of the Dead (All Soul's Day), monthly Mass will be on November 9 at 6:30 pm in the Chapel of the Dames de Nazareth, 20 rue du Montparnasse, at the close of our 93rd day of *private Fasting for a serene Peace* between Christians and Muslims, particularly in North Africa, the Near East and Bantu Africa.

Our Patriarch, Maximos IV has invited us by letter to offer our prayers during this fast, along with the sacrifices of those who are suffering and can only participate spiritually, for all the intentions of the Ecumenical Council that began on October 11, where several of us are participating; that the Council may fraternally preserve the traditional venerable, liturgical and canonical rituals of the Eastern Church, to which the Latin Church must associate itself, while considering the modern demands of the International Apostolate, especially in Arab and Black Africa.

We are saddened to have lost, on September 22, the mother of our very dear member, Father Xavier Eïd,[471] rector of Cairo's Dar es-Salam. We have also lost a friend in our search for spiritual contact with Muslim mysticism, in Father Carme Bruno Froissart.[472] Numerous members would have wished us, in previous convocations, to have rejoiced in the serene Peace achieved in Algeria since 1962. We are still very concerned, not so much because of the lack of understanding on the part of the Christians that have left and regret the failure of an outdated "colonial" Latinization, but for the liberal illusions of French teachers and executives that very generously return to Algeria to continue the task of education-

---

[470] The Black Muslim movement was founded by the charismatic leader, Malcolm X who was later assassinated at the age of 40 in 1965.

[471] Father Xavier Eid was a very close friend of Mary Kahil and served as the Pastor for the Greek-Melkite Church in Cairo. Our Lady of Peace, for 50 years. Massignon and Mary founded their interfaith center, Mardi de Dar es-Salam, in this parish.

[472] Father Froissart, Marie de Jesus in religious life (1892–1962) managed the revue *Nouvelle études carmelitaine, mystique et missionaire*, from 1931 until his death. Massignon published many articles in this spiritual and intellectual journal.

al and social formation for which they will receive a standard of living much superior to that of the Muslim population whose advancement they are there to ensure. They risk, in short order, colliding with the same jealousy that was encountered by the three hundred primary teachers that our dear Taha Hussein[473] sent to Egypt with a supplementary stipend that was agreed to by France and that placed them above the standard of living of their Muslim colleagues, hence a total failure.

In this period of general austerity into which the Muslim population of Algeria will enter, it is clear that, like the Brothers and Sisters of Foucauld, generous French people that come to their aid should share their standard of living. This, however, is obviously unthinkable for the technocrats who would prefer perhaps to reduce their number while increasing the recruitment of directors of education, those who train Muslim teachers.

---

[473] Taha Hussein (1889–1973) a well-known Egyptian writer who was sent to Cairo as Minister of National Education for the French government from 1950–1952.

The Badaliya Today

L ouis Massignon envisioned the Badaliya prayer movement as a call to a vocation meant for those Christians living as a minority in Muslim countries. It was a means of encouraging them to see their vocation as "Eastern Christians" as a witnessing to the love of Christ for all of humanity by loving their Muslim neighbors as Christ loves them. The outcome of this prayer of Badaliya, of offering oneself to God in "substitution" for another, is being willing to stand with them in their poverty, despair at injustice, persecution and exile and even to suffer in their place. To suffer and die in the place of a Muslim sinner out of love for Christ included praying for the souls of those who had died, that they achieve the fulfillment of their total submission to God through the compassionate prayers of Christians who desire to put themselves in their place. The Badaliya prayer was therefore a prayer for all those who await salvation.[474]

In order to think the way another thinks and to live according to that person's culture one must first learn their language. Therefore Arabic was the language of the Badaliya since it was the language already used in the liturgy of the Eastern Christian Churches. Although the Badaliya prayer was adopted by many people around the world who did not speak Arabic or were not living in Arabic speaking countries, Massignon encouraged those who had an aptitude for it to learn to pray in Arabic.

Massignon was concerned about what would happen to the Badaliya groups after his death, and even as early as the 1950's there were already fewer members in Cairo. On September 7, 1962, shortly before his death, Massignon wrote to Mary Kahil questioning the future of the Badaliya. When he died on October 31, 1962, the Badaliya prayer group

---

[474] Harpigny, Guy. 1981. *Islam et Christianisme selon Louis Massignon.* Louvain, La Neuve, p. 117.

in Paris disbanded, although Fr. Youakim Moubarac,[475] a longtime faithful collaborator in editing the *Revue des Etudes Islamiques*, and heir, in some ways, to Massignon's cultural and spiritual vision, tried to secure the Badaliya's hitherto orphaned life. In the "Massignon archives" there are four Convocations written by Fr. Moubarac that go back to 1964 and 1965. Prayers and Masses were offered on the anniversaries of Massignon's death and his conversion experience on May 3, 1908. Moubarac later published 3 volumes called *Opera Minora* of Massignon's articles and minor works. In 2010 a selection of writings from *Opera Minora* were published again in 2 volumes called, Louis Massignon: *Écrits mémorable*. Although the movement seemed to disappear in Cairo with Mary Kahil's death in 1979, at the Greek Melkite Church, Sainte Marie de la Paix, the Interfaith group, *Les Frère Sincère* (The Sincere Brothers), that Mary Kahil established during WW II, continued to meet for many more years. Both Louis Massignon and Mary Kahil continue to be remembered there today.

Many have seen the prescient vision of Louis Massignon and Mary Kahil in the Vatican II document, *Vatican II: Church relations with non-Christian religions (Nostra Aetate)* # 3,[476] as well as the *Dogmatic Constitution on the Church (Lumen Gentium)* # 16 that reads in part: "But the plan of salvation also includes those who acknowledge the Creator. In the first place among these, there are the Muslims, who, professing to hold the

---

[475] Fr. Youakim Moubarac (1924–1995), a disciple whose profound kinship with Massignon bound them together in their scientific research on Islam and solidarity with the Muslim community in North Africa.

[476] The Documents of Vatican II. *Nostra Aetate:* "Upon the Muslims too, the Church looks with esteem. They adore one God, living and enduring, merciful and all-powerful, Maker of heaven and earth, and speaker to men. They strive to submit wholeheartedly even to His inscrutable decrees, just as did Abraham, with whom the Islamic faith is pleased to associate itself. Though they do not acknowledge Jesus as God, they revere Him as a Prophet. They also honor Mary, His virgin mother; at times they call on her too with devotion. In addition they await the Day of Judgment when God will give each man his due after raising him up. Consequently, they prize the moral life, and give worship to God especially through prayer, almsgiving and fasting.

Although in the course of the centuries many quarrels and hostilities have arisen between Christians and Muslims, this most sacred Synod urges all to forget the past and to strive sincerely for mutual understanding. On behalf of all mankind, let them make common cause of safeguarding and fostering social justice, moral values, peace and freedom."

faith of Abraham, along with us adore the one and merciful God, who on the last day, will judge mankind." We are reminded that Massignon was a friend of Cardinal Montini, Pope Paul VI, who in 1965 completed the initiative of the Second Vatican Council begun by his predecessor Pope John XXIII in 1962.

There are also both religious and lay Christian communities dedicated to living in Muslim countries throughout the world in the spirit of Massignon's mentor, Charles de Foucauld and in the spirit of the Badaliya. A most poignant example is the Trappist community established in Tibhirine, Algeria under their prior Christian de Chergé who was abducted and executed along with six monks of his community in Algeria in 1996. They achieved that ultimate wish concealed in the Badaliya spirit that Massignon so often voiced as his, "desire to die as a martyr on Islam's soil." Many books have been written documenting the life of this dedicated community and the recent film, *Des Hommes et des Dieux,* "Of God and Men," is a powerful testimony to the spirit of the Badaliya that they so fervently embraced.

Following the spirituality of Blessed Charles de Foucauld, The Little Sisters of Jesus, founded in 1939 by Little Sister Magdeleine of Jesus, are dedicated to the discovery of the "other," to the imitation of Jesus, and to Love all human beings as brothers and sisters. They have communities in Africa, North America, Europe and Oceania and seek to live and serve in the midst of the poorest Muslim populations. One of the communities of the Little Brothers of Jesus, founded by Fr. René Voillaume in the early 1930's, established their foundation in Tamanrasset, Algeria where Foucauld lived with the Muslim Berber Touareg people until his death in 1916. There are Secular Fraternities in 51 countries with 6000 members praying in the spirit of Charles de Foucauld. The original *Union Sodalité* made up of lay people, priests and religious established by Brother Charles in 1909, and for whom he intended his original *Directoire,* had 46 members when he died, including himself and Louis Massignon. It continues to thrive as a part of the Secular Fraternities under the care of Father Jean-François Six in Paris and now has 1000 individual members worldwide.

In 1982 a Jesuit priest discovered an ancient monastery in the desert in Syria, abandoned before 1831 by the last monk to live there. The beautiful 11th century frescoes were disintegrating on the crumbling walls, yet it attracted Father Paolo Dall'Oglio to imagine restoring this Christian presence in the midst of Islam. Today Deir Mar Musa is a community of Christians who are living the Badaliya prayer of their mentor Louis Massignon. The Syriaque Church in Nebek, the closest city, is attached to the Syriaque Catholic Rite, the Semitic dialect closest to the ancient Aramaic that Jesus spoke. Deir Mar Musa is about 15 kilometers into the desert from there. The community is dedicated to Muslim and Christian relations. They use Arabic in their daily office of prayers and the sacraments, and chant their morning psalms and hymns in ancient Syriaque. They receive visitors from all over the world and encourage their Muslim and Christian neighbors to come as well. In 2012, after 30 years, due to the civil war that has engulfed the country, Fr. Dall'Oglio was evicted from Syria. He then travelled throughout Europe raising awareness of the situation facing the Syrian people. In an effort at effecting reconciliation between rebel factions, and out of the depth of his vow to live with and for his beloved Muslim and Christian Syrian friends, Fr. Paolo returned to Northern Syria in July 2013. There has been no definitive word since. The community continues to survive with the hope for the peace and reconciliation at the heart of their own vows to Badaliya that inspired their founder.

The shared Muslim and Christian pilgrimage celebrated at the Chapel of the Seven Saints in the tiny hamlet of Vieux-Marché in Brittany, France that Massignon mentions so often in these letters continues every year to this day. The Muslim and Christian shared emphasis was added on to the annual traditional village pilgrimage in Vieux-Marché beginning in 1954. Massignon invited Muslim friends and transported his "students" from Paris to attend the celebration every year until his death in 1962. Today, the Qur'anic verses from Sura 18 continue to be read at the Spring with seven veins by local Imams.

The spirit of Saint Francis guided the Badaliya prayer movement from its inception. Since the time of their founder in the 13th century a branch of the Franciscans, designated by the pope, have dedicated their lives as Custodians of the Holy Sites in the Holy Land. Their presence in the midst of all three Abrahamic traditions invites them to the *Badaliya* prayer both as Disciples of Christ and in imitation of their founder's own discipleship before the Sultan of Egypt at Damietta, Egypt.

In December 2002 a small group gathered in Boston, Massachusetts to revive the Badaliya prayer movement in the United States and to discern how to live the Badaliya prayer in countries where Christians are the majority. Massignon's letters to the Badaliya members makes it very clear that the vocation, or call to Badaliya prayer, became more and more universal for Massignon himself the more deeply he immersed himself in it. If it is first and foremost a call to offer our lives out of our love for Christ, then it demands that our love extend to all human beings, to love them as Christ loves them. Massignon saw the Badaliya in every victim of injustice, every refugee and every falsely held prisoner and ultimately in those perceived as one's "enemies." Many conflicts in the world today are extensions of the same conflicts that he addressed with compassion and prayer in his letters and social actions. The problems created by the overwhelming volume of refugees as a result of world-wide conflicts continue to await solutions while those countries closest to the conflicts struggle to provide hospitality. Moreover, human mobility is changing the rules of hospitality for every country as a result of increasing globalization. The misunderstandings and prejudices on the side of Christians as well as Muslims demands that both communities make an effort, through the non-violence so dear to Louis Massignon, towards the mutual understanding and reconciliation called for by the prayer of Badaliya for a serene peace everywhere. The Badaliya reminds Christians in the "Western" world that our "Eastern" brothers and sisters are still living as a minority in the midst of Islam throughout the Middle East, and in the midst of Islam and Judaism in the State of Israel. The prayer of *Badaliya* calls us to pray with, and for, all three Abrahamic faith traditions for Massignon's "serene peace with justice."

In 2012 the Badaliya USA celebrated its 10th anniversary. Today there are more than 100 members praying in spirit with the Badaliya each month in different parts of the country along with several members in other countries, including England, France, Germany and India. A monthly convocation is sent via e-mail to suggest the themes for the prayer with quotes from Massignon, Blessed Charles de Foucauld, Gandhi and many other sources of inspiration. Following Massignon's original Statutes we are guided in our prayer to include a period of silent adoration, adding to it a commitment to learning more and more about the faith of our Muslim and Jewish brothers and sisters in Abraham. Many are also committed to fast and pray for Peace in the world every First Friday of the month in solidarity with the *Union Sodalité de Charles de Foucauld* centered in Paris, France. The Badaliya prayer movement continues to add members and encourage interfaith exploration and engagement. In a commitment to non-violent peaceful resolution to conflict through "crossing over" to the other and witnessing to the love of Christ for all of humanity, we pray to successfully build bridges between faiths and further mutual respect and world peace.

In 2013, following in the spirit of Mary Kahil's "Sincere Brothers" interfaith prayer gatherings, the Badaliya USA has joined with the Peace Islands Institute, a Muslim initiative by followers of the Turkish Muslim theologian and spiritual guide, Fethullah Gülen. The Gülen movement promotes education, interfaith and intercultural dialogue worldwide. It is clear from the final Badaliya letters that Massignon had come to the realization that peace and reconciliation would only come when Muslims, Jews, and Christians prayed for it together. Massignon's transformation through the Badaliya prayer led him to the action necessary to conquer the forces of hatred and division active in the world then, as now.

Books in English by Louis Massignon

Massignon, L. 1983. *The Passion of al-Hallaj: Mystic and Martyr.* 3 vols. Translated by H. Mason. Princeton, NJ: Princeton University Press.

_____1989. *Testimonies and Reflections: Essays of Louis Massignon.* Selected and introduced by H. Mason. Notre Dame, IN.: University of Notre Dame Press.

_____1994. *Hallaj: Mystic and Martyr.* Translated, edited, and abridged by H. Mason. Princeton, NJ: Princeton University Press.

_____ 1994. *Essays on the Origins of the Technical Language of Islamic Mysticism.* Translated by Benjamin Clark. Notre Dame, IN.: University of Notre Dame Press.

Books in English about Louis Massignon:

Basetti-Sani, Giulio O.F.M. 1974. Trans. A.H. Cutler *Louis Massignon: Christian Ecumenist.* Chicago, IL: Franciscan Herald Press.

Buck, D.C. 2002. *Dialogues with Saints and Mystics: In the Spirit of Louis Massignon.* London, New York: Khaniqahi Nimatullahi Publications. (See: www.dcbuck.com)

Gude, M.L.1996. *Louis Massignon; The Crucible of Compassion.* Indiana: University of Notre Dame Press.

Mason, H. 1988. *Memoir of a Friend.* Indiana: University of Notre Dame Press.

Articles about Louis Massignon, the Badaliya Prayer and a Muslim-Christian Pilgrimage

Buck, D.C., "The Badaliya prays for and with Muslims," in *National Catholic Reporter*, December 17, 2004.

Buck, D.C., "A Model of Hope: Louis Massignon's Badaliya," in *SUFI*, Autumn 2003, Khaniqahi Nimatullahi, London. (See: www.dcbuck.com)

Buck, D.C., "A Shared Muslim-Christian Pilgrimage," in *SUFI*, Spring, 2005, Khaniqahi Nimatullahi, London.

Buck, D.C., "Louis Massignon (1883–1962) A Tribute to a Pioneer in Interfaith Relations," in *The Fountain*, November-December 2012. The Light, Inc. Clifton, NJ.

Ex-Voto of the Badaliya

Described by Louis Massignon

"A plaque was designed and created in September 1953, thirty-three years after our vow to fast monthly, (during the exile of the Sultan of Morocco), the inscription in Latin, "Jesus-Caritas" was translated into Arabic, "YASU' IBN-MARYAM HUWA'L-HUBB," (Jesus, son of Mary, is Love), and the heart was pierced.

At the top of the Cross, the sword of compassion burns and seals the Heart of Mary; the angelic reverberation of the Thrust of the Lance of the soldier, felt through the wounds of mystical substitution.

It was offered as an ex-voto as often in its Latin form as in its Arabic form in several chapels in the Middle East: Tehran, Baghdad, Damascus, Jerusalem, Beirut, and Ephesus; In Africa: Cairo, Damietta, Namugongo, Tamanrasset, Beni-Abbes, Rabat; and in Europe: Vieux-Marché, Aix-en-Provence."

The Emblem of Charles de Foucauld

A Plaque in metal made of copper on a brass foundation was designed in 1920–1921 at the request of Louis Massignon by the sculptor, Pierre Roche, (Ferdinand Massignon, Louis Massignon's father). It was based on the monogram from the letters of Charles de Foucauld with the words "Jesus Caritas," (Jesus is Love) on his drawing of the Sacred Heart mounted on a Cross.